King
without a Crown

ALBERT
Prince Consort of England
1819-1861

Daphne Bennett

J. B. Lippincott Company
Philadelphia and New York

Genealogical table compiled by
Jeffrey Finestone

U.S. Library of Congress Cataloging in Publication Data

Bennett, Daphne.
King without a crown.

Bibliography: p.
Includes index.
1. Albert, Consort of Queen Victoria, 1819-1861.
2. Great Britain—Princes and princesses—Biography.
3. Great Britain—History—Victoria, 1837-1901.
I. Title.
DA559.A1B38 1977 941.081'092'4 [B] 77-22108
ISBN-0-397-01143-1

To David

Contents

PART FOUR: FULFILMENT 1851–1861

List of Illustrations

All illustrations are reproduced by gracious permission of Her Majesty Queen Elizabeth II, with the exception of Nos 8, 24, 25, and 26 which are reproduced by permission of the National Portrait Gallery, London.

Preface

———

IT WAS with the greatest reluctance that I accepted the invitation to write about the Prince Consort. What could there possibly be in a man I regarded as a dreary and unromantic German to make it worthwhile devoting years of research to him?

For I was at odds with him already. I could not forgive him for sacrificing his daughter Vicky's happiness to the dream of German unity which obsessed him, even though he too suffered deeply from the separation which clouded her life and lived in daily anxiety from the moment she left England (still only seventeen) as the wife of the future king of Prussia. It would be impossible, I thought, to achieve that rapport between biographer and subject which is so essential.

How wrong I was!

The spell of Albert's personality began to weave itself round me as soon as I saw his native Coburg. Here I found the clue to the sympathy which had been missing. I started to see things as he had seen them, and gradually the impossible rapport grew up between us. Apart from obvious details and the Iron Curtain which surrounds Coburg on three sides and cuts it off from Gotha, neither the little town nor the Thuringian countryside has changed very much since Albert and his brother Ernest used to ride the few miles from the Rosenau (the hunting-lodge Albert called 'the paradise of our childhood') to the Ehrenburg palace which forms one side of the Schlossplatz, the heart of the town and still the citizens' favourite meeting-place. The duke and his family did not cut themselves off from their people, but were part of the life that flowed round them in the streets. The great wooden doors of their palace were open night and day to their subjects, every one of whom was given a holiday when the two boys were confirmed in the Hall of the Giants, the ducal throne-room. This too is little changed. It is curiously intimate in spite of its splendour – so indeed is the whole of the Ehrenburg – and at once it seemed absurd that fashionable Londoners like Lord Torrington and Lord Alfred Paget should have spoken derisively of it when they came to escort Albert to London for his wedding and sneered at him for being only a petty German princeling. Coburg in the 1820s and 1830s was, in fact, far less parochial than the other small German states; its ducal family had connexions all over Europe, and in this above all Albert was a true Coburger.

The Veste, the fortress which was the family's original home, provided other clues. Against the background of the dark Thuringian hills it towers on its rock above the valley of the little river Itz even beyond its confluence with the upper Main, and dominates the landscape for miles around. But it seems a symbol of refuge and protection rather than of menace. Coburg was still a feudal duchy in Albert's time, and the patriarchal traditions of the dukes had a profound effect in shaping his own highly responsible attitude towards those less fortunate than himself and in stimulating the reforming zeal which astonished English society because it seemed out of place in a man so close to the throne. Luther had lived in the Veste for six months when Albert's ancestors sheltered him from his enemies in 1530, and he had preached in the castle chapel where Albert later worshipped and spoke the words of Luther's Bible. What more convincing an origin could there be for the strong conscience which was the mainspring of Albert's life?

But this was not all. The artistic taste from which England benefited so greatly was evidently also awakened in the Veste, where the young Albert was surrounded by some of the best paintings of the two Cranachs – born only twenty miles away – though it was also fostered by the collections in his Gotha grandfather's palaces and museums. Unlike Queen Victoria, Albert was surrounded from birth by rare and beautiful objects, and unlike her he had the run of several well-stocked libraries, so that he was accustomed to the world of books and the internationalism of learning from his earliest days.

Even the Rosenau, though only a hunting-lodge, was filled with books. The little yellow Schloss, so rural to this day that only bird-song disturbs its peace, held an enchantment for Albert that seemed exaggerated until I saw it myself. Its charm is too elusive to describe in words. The house itself is not particularly beautiful, but it has the same startling effect as an unusual jewel in a perfect setting. The fountain is dry now, the garden overgrown and neglected; but the woods and hills where Albert loved to roam are as they always were, and so is the feeling that time stands still here and that nothing else in the world is of any significance.

With my mind thus prepared by the surroundings in which Albert grew up, I began work on the archives, and at once found my excitement mounting still more. Albert's true personality started to emerge from the pages of his own and Stockmar's letters. It was quite different from that of the stiff and solemn German I had been led to expect. Instead, a warm and sympathetic human being gradually took shape before my eyes, a man glowing with life and vitality. It was these qualities, the letters made me realise, which had provided the impetus for the devoted service he gave to England, where wider fields of influence lay open to him, enabling him to develop a greater range of abilities than he could ever have shown at home. His upbringing fitted him for his later task, and the two halves of his tragically short life made a single perfect whole.

My book has been written in the light of these discoveries, and in it I have tried to describe him as he really was and to set his remarkable career in its true perspective.

Many people have given me generous help in my work; indeed, I have been overwhelmed with kindness by everyone I have approached. Most important of all has been the patience and unswerving support of my publisher, David Burnett; it was his idea that I should write this book, and he has been a tower of strength from the beginning. Next, my most grateful thanks are due to Friedrich Freiherr Stockmar von Wangenheim for permission to use papers belonging to his great-grandfather. Dr Klaus Freiherr von Andrian-Werburg, archivist at the Ehrenburg, gave his time unstintingly and made my visit to Coburg immensely fruitful. I also owe much to Mr Trevor Kay, Sub-Librarian of Trinity College, Cambridge, and to his assistant Mrs Pat Bradford, who guided me through the papers in their care. I offer my warm thanks to Dr Elizabeth Leedham-Green, Assistant Keeper of the Cambridge University archives, for much help with the Romilly papers; to Mr Thomas Wragg, Keeper of the Chatsworth archives, for showing me the Paxton papers; to Mr Mark Baker, archivist at Wellington College; and to the staffs of the manuscript departments of the British Library and the Victoria and Albert Museum. Dr Ronald

Hyam has, as usual, taken endless pains to advise me about books, and Dr Edward Ford kindly interpreted the symptoms of Albert's illnesses for me : I thank them both warmly. My thanks are also due to the late Sir James Butler, Dr David Newsome, Mr Alan Palmer, Mrs Felicity Butcher, Mrs Weide Clarke, Mr Julian Roberts, Mrs Marjorie Millman, Miss Julia Nash and Mrs Wendy Parmée for their help in various ways, and to Mrs Joanna Sanders for typing my manuscript.

DAPHNE BENNETT
Cambridge, March 1977

Prologue

PRINCE Albert of Saxe-Coburg and Gotha, who married Queen Victoria in 1840, has usually been described as cold, formal and prosaic, given to an excess of virtue after the manner of his age – in short, as a rather dull and uninteresting character. Strangely enough, this misleading and incomplete picture of her husband derives mainly from Queen Victoria, who not only commissioned and directed Sir Theodore Martin's biography, but even wrote a good deal of it herself. In truth, however, Prince Albert's personality was warm and kindly; he possessed a lively and at times over-sensitive imagination, and there was a streak of romanticism in him which he owed to his mother and to the legends of their native Thuringia of which he was so fond. But whereas his mother ruined her life by her romanticism, the careful reflection and scholarly caution with which Albert approached the problems of politics made him for ten years the dominant figure in England and the most powerful man in Europe.

The Families of Queen Victoria

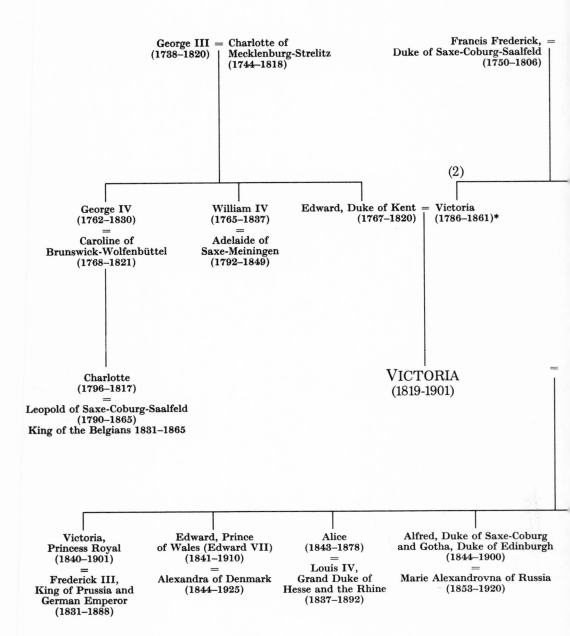

George III = Charlotte of
(1738–1820) | Mecklenburg-Strelitz
(1744–1818)

Francis Frederick, =
Duke of Saxe-Coburg-Saalfeld
(1750–1806)

(2)

George IV
(1762–1830)
=
Caroline of
Brunswick-Wolfenbüttel
(1768–1821)

William IV
(1765–1837)
=
Adelaide of
Saxe-Meiningen
(1792–1849)

Edward, Duke of Kent = Victoria
(1767–1820) | (1786–1861)*

Charlotte
(1796–1817)
=
Leopold of Saxe-Coburg-Saalfeld
(1790–1865)
King of the Belgians 1831–1865

VICTORIA
(1819-1901)

=

Victoria,
Princess Royal
(1840–1901)
=
Frederick III,
King of Prussia and
German Emperor
(1831–1888)

Edward, Prince
of Wales (Edward VII)
(1841–1910)
=
Alexandra of Denmark
(1844–1925)

Alice
(1843–1878)
=
Louis IV,
Grand Duke of
Hesse and the Rhine
(1837–1892)

Alfred, Duke of Saxe-Coburg
and Gotha, Duke of Edinburgh
(1844–1900)
=
Marie Alexandrovna of Russia
(1853–1920)

Genealogical table compiled by
Jeffrey Finestone

and Prince Albert

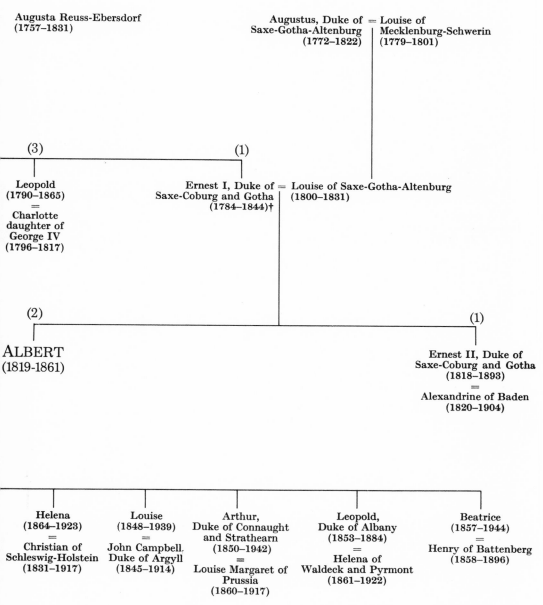

Augusta Reuss-Ebersdorf
(1757–1831)

Augustus, Duke of = Louise of
Saxe-Gotha-Altenburg | Mecklenburg-Schwerin
(1772–1822) | (1779–1801)

(3)

(1)

Leopold
(1790–1865)
=
Charlotte
daughter of
George IV
(1796–1817)

Ernest I, Duke of = Louise of Saxe-Gotha-Altenburg
Saxe-Coburg and Gotha | (1800–1831)
(1784–1844)†

(2)

(1)

ALBERT
(1819-1861)

Ernest II, Duke of
Saxe-Coburg and Gotha
(1818–1893)
=
Alexandrine of Baden
(1820–1904)

| Helena
(1864–1923)
=
Christian of
Schleswig-Holstein
(1831–1917) | Louise
(1848–1939)
=
John Campbell.
Duke of Argyll
(1845–1914) | Arthur,
Duke of Connaught
and Strathearn
(1850–1942)
=
Louise Margaret of
Prussia
(1860–1917) | Leopold,
Duke of Albany
(1853–1884)
=
Helena of
Waldeck and Pyrmont
(1861–1922) | Beatrice
(1857–1944)
=
Henry of Battenberg
(1858–1896) |

* widow of Emich Karl, Prince of Leiningen
† Duke Ernest succeeded his father as
Duke of Saxe-Coburg-Saalfeld in 1806,
but on a rearrangement of the family
territories in 1826 surrendered Saalfeld
to another branch of the House of
Saxony and acquired Gotha instead.
His style thereafter was Duke of
Saxe-Coburg and Gotha.

Part One
Destiny 1806-1840

1

'This paradise of
our childhood'

AT dawn on the freezing cold morning of 9 December 1806 the people
of the small duchy of Coburg were awakened by the mournful
tolling of the passing bell, a sign that their duke was dead. The
news was unexpected and potentially calamitous. Less than a week
before he had ridden through the streets, begging them not to waste
their lives in resisting Napoleon's troops and assuring them that he
would do everything in his power to shield them from what they
dreaded most – the horrors of foreign occupation. Now suddenly
he was gone and their protection with him. The duke had died in
his bed without a struggle, from a cold which had turned to pneumonia overnight, although his people knew that the real cause was
heartbreak at the state of the land over which he had ruled for only
six years. His reign had been overshadowed by the French threat
that hung over Germany for the whole of that time, but Coburg had
been fortunate in escaping invasion until after Napoleon's victories
at Jena and Austerlitz smashed Prussia and Austria in 1805 and 1806.

Like his predecessors and most of the other German princes,
duke Francis Frederick had served as a soldier before taking over
the government of his tiny principality and the management of the
family estates; but eighteenth-century military traditions had not
been enough to make good the weakness caused by the fragmenta-
tion of the Holy Roman Empire into three hundred states (many of
them no larger than Coburg), and successive European coalitions
had collapsed before the revolutionary fervour of the French and
the military genius of Napoleon.

The gentle and unassuming Francis Frederick had always been a
reluctant soldier; he had preferred to devote himself to the kindly

3

government of his almost entirely peasant subjects and was rewarded by their loyalty and devotion. His upbringing had been very grand; his mother Sophia Antoinette, a princess of Brunswick-Wolfenbüttel, lived in great splendour, though married to one of the least wealthy of the German princes, and (according to her grandson Leopold) was not suited to be the wife of a poor man. She had no idea how to manage on little money and the family was soon reduced to nothing since she insisted on behaving 'as if Coburg were a great empire'.* Her easy-going husband had left everything in her hands, and her extravagance meant that her son inherited a mountain of debts when he succeeded to the dukedom in 1800. But for Napoleon, Francis Frederick's good management would have overcome this handicap and might have fulfilled his ambition to hand over a solvent state to his heirs. His sudden death not only put an end to these hopes, but gave Napoleon an excuse to march into Coburg. 'Where is the new duke?' he demanded and, when told that Ernest and his fifteen-year-old brother Leopold had been in Berlin for over a year, promptly appointed a military governor, who began at once to rule Coburg through secret police. In the absence of her son, duke Francis Frederick's widow Augusta did her utmost to protect his people and to keep up their spirits by the example of her courage, although virtually a prisoner in her own castle. Before the unusually severe winter was over, she was reduced to burning the furniture for fuel to prevent her family from dying of cold, watching, as she did so, French soldiers cutting down for their own use the avenue of trees in which her husband, a keen amateur botanist, had taken particular pride. Then, frustrated by months of apparently pointless suffering, she gave the French police the slip and escaped to Berlin in the hope of meeting Napoleon and persuading him to withdraw the occupying forces and reinstate her son. In August 1807 the treaty of Tilsit made it possible for Ernest to return home.

Augusta's children and grandchildren exercised a quite astonishing influence on the destinies of England and Europe in the nineteenth century; the two generations included two kings, an empress, the consorts of two reigning queens, one of whom was Queen Victoria, and Queen Victoria herself. It was Augusta's blood which revitalised the failing Coburg stock by transmitting her own strength of character and intellectual power to her descendants, particularly her grandson Albert, thus making the reigning house of a small and

* Sources for this and subsequent quotations are given in the Reference Notes at the end of the Bibliography.

hitherto unimportant duchy into the centre of a vast and influential network. The first signs of this appeared in the two youngest of her seven surviving children, Victoire and Leopold. Of the rest, Antoinette and Julie made unhappy marriages, the elder to the duke of Württemberg and the younger to the Grand Duke Constantine of Russia, and soon separated from their husbands. The children of Augusta's daughter Sophie and Count Mensdorff-Pouilly became the life-long friends of Prince Albert and his brother Ernest. When her second son Ferdinand married the Roman Catholic Hungarian heiress, Antoinette Kohary, Augusta was unjustly accused of betraying her Lutheran faith and letting greed outweigh conviction; in fact it was the romance itself which had moved her.

Leopold, her youngest child, born in 1790, was endowed with brains, good looks and a twofold ambition: to advance his own career – for the youngest son of an impoverished duke this was a necessity – and to restore his father's duchy to its pre-Napoleonic standing. As his extraordinary career took shape the latter became transmuted into dynasticism on a European scale and left the petty politics of Coburg far behind. Distinguished service with the Russian army earned Leopold rapid promotion, although his pockets were always empty. He made his mark through tact and mental agility as one of the Imperial representatives at the victory celebrations in London in 1814 and was a member of the Russian delegation to the Congress of Vienna. In London an old acquaintance, the duchess of Oldenburg, sister of the Czar and his own relation by marriage, threw open her doors to him and introduced him to Princess Charlotte of Wales, heiress-presumptive to the English throne. At the time Charlotte, a lively self-willed eighteen-year-old, was in disgrace for passionately refusing to marry the man her father had chosen for her, the unattractive prince of Orange. Although she now imagined herself in love with the dissipated prince of Prussia, Leopold was too handsome and too persistent to be ignored. The courtship was carried on in the face of fierce opposition from the Prince Regent, but in May 1816 they were married at Carlton House in London, the last wedding of an heir to the English throne ever to take place in a private house. The Prince Regent's snubs gave Leopold the chance to remove Charlotte from London and the atmosphere of immorality that clung round her father. The Regent retaliated by spitefully putting it about that Leopold was effeminate, wore platform soles (the truth being simply that he was the taller) and a feather boa (in reality the fur scarf which all aristocratic Russians wore to keep out the cold) and would soon proclaim himself King of England, and made great play with the nick-name he had jeeringly bestowed on his

5

son-in-law, 'le marquis peu-à-peu' – quite forgetting how inept it was to describe the man who had carried off the biggest prize in Europe as cautious and slow-moving.

The marriage was popular in England; the obvious happiness of the young couple endeared them to everyone; there was general satisfaction that Charlotte had chosen to marry a man about whom there was not a breath of scandal (which was more than could be said for her father or her rejected suitor), and the Commons voted him an annuity of £50,000 without one dissentient voice. The clubs relished the report that Leopold had got the better of the Prince Regent, and all London welcomed the romance, for Charlotte was popular and Leopold had fought in the great 'Battle of the Nations' against Napoleon at Leipzig. But England's hopes and Leopold's happiness were extinguished together when Charlotte died giving birth to a still-born son in November 1817.

Leopold's chance to play a leading part in the politics of England was gone, although he continued to live intermittently at Claremont (the house which had been bought for them outside London near Esher) until he became King of the Belgians fourteen years later. Instead of moving steadily towards the centre of affairs he had to stand aside, a critical observer of George IV's reign; instead of becoming the consort of the Queen of England, by the time George IV died in 1830 he was considering (and rejecting) the offer of the controversial Greek throne. But Leopold, like his nephew after him, was made for kingship and when Belgium broke loose from Holland he accepted the throne that Louis Philippe of France had wanted for one of his own sons. In July 1831, Leopold left Claremont for Brussels and the crown of Belgium.

Augusta's youngest and last remaining daughter, Victoire, had been married off at seventeen to Prince Emich Karl of Leiningen, her mother's brother-in-law, who was a widower twenty-three years older than herself. The reason for so apparently odd an arrangement seems to have been Augusta's fear, during a sudden illness, that she might die and leave her daughter without a protector. The marriage was not unhappy; if there could be no love, there was mutual respect. Twelve years later, in 1814, Emich Karl died, leaving the twenty-nine-year-old Victoire as Regent of the remote little state of Leiningen in the Black Forest, until their young son should come of age. From this lonely and isolated situation she was rescued by the peculiarities of George III's family. After Charlotte's death there was no direct heir to the English throne, since George IV refused to have anything to do with his wife Caroline. Of his six brothers, only two were legally married, and

none of them had legitimate offspring, although they were plenti-
fully supplied with bastards. One of the brothers, Edward duke of
Kent, had carried notes secretly from Charlotte to Leopold at the
time when the Prince Regent was doing his best to prevent the
marriage; in return, when the duke set out on a continental tour
soon after Waterloo, Charlotte gave him an introduction to Leopold's newly-widowed sister Victoire. Charlotte's intention can only
be guessed at, but with match-making in the wind, it is not unlikely
that she hoped that the two might like each other. Edward could
not forget the attractive widow, but he did not press his suit until
1817, when Parliament demanded that in return for their annuities
one of the royal dukes should provide a heir to the throne. At first
Victoire was reluctant to surrender her independence, but eventually
gave in. They were married in the Hall of Giants in the Ehrenburg
palace in Coburg in May 1818, and the 'little Mayflower' who was to
become Queen Victoria was born just a year later.

The eldest of Augusta's sons, duke Ernest, was the last to marry.
Handsome and dissolute, he preferred to flit from one mistress to
another rather than settle down with a wife, until it became clear
that, unless he produced a son, Protestant Coburg would eventually
pass to the Roman Catholic heirs of his brother Ferdinand and
Antoinette Kohary. Although a rake, Ernest looked about him for
an innocent young girl; his eye fell on the dazzlingly pretty sixteen-
year-old Luise, the charming and intelligent daughter of Duke
Augustus of Saxe-Coburg-Altenburg. For her part Luise was overwhelmed by the Byronic curls and flashing blue eyes of the romantic-
looking man who rode into the courtyard of the castle at Gotha one
spring day in 1817 to ask for her hand, so that it was not difficult to
imagine herself in love.

There was already a great deal of talk in Gotha about duke Ernest
and his affairs, particularly about his relations with an actress,
Mademoiselle Panam, known in Parisian theatrical circles as 'la
belle Grecque', by whom he was supposed to have had a child.
Duke Augustus must have been aware of his prospective son-in-
law's reputation, but he seems to have regarded it as acceptable in
a nobleman and to have supposed that, having sown his wild oats,
Ernest would now settle down. All the accounts of Albert's mother
show her to have been an enchanting young girl. Sensitive and
affectionate, at an early age she showed signs of a lively intelligence,
reciting her father's poetry with feeling at four years old and at six
taking an interest in his scientific instruments and collection of
coins. Her one great passion was music, and she poured all the

yearnings of a wildly romantic nature into her piano-playing. She was highly emotional; there is a story that during her confirmation she suddenly realised that she was kneeling over the vault where her mother (whom she had never known) lay buried, and instantly burst into wild sobs. Her childhood was happy in a simple way; when she was not reading poetry or playing the piano, she would dream innocent fantasies of the future, many of them mixed up with the folklore of her native Thuringia, which she loved deeply and never wished to leave.

On 31 July 1817 Ernest and Luise were married in Gotha with great pomp and all was set for them to live happily ever after, for Luise had no doubt that it was a marriage made in heaven. 'My duke' as she called Ernest, was a kind and attentive husband for a year or two, amused by the charm and vivacity of this sparkling girl, and since Gotha was considerably larger and richer than Coburg, Luise's substantial dowry made it possible for them to entertain lavishly. The whole country smiled at the rake's reform, but Ernest had settled down only in the sense that his gay life was led at home rather than in Berlin or Paris. Their first child – christened Ernst Augustus Karl Johann Leopold Alexander Eduard (Luise was nothing if not tactful) was born on 21 June 1818 at the Ehrenburg Palace in Coburg. The noises of the busy town all around her accentuated acute post-natal depression and determined her to break with tradition next time and go for her second confinement to the Rosenau, duke Ernest's hunting lodge four miles outside the town. There, to the soothing sound of water splashing into a fountain in the little courtyard, Albert was born on 26 August 1819. There, two months later, Pastor Genzler baptised him Albrecht Franz August Karl Emanuel with water from the river Itze in a silver bowl which was used every day in the house: the simple surroundings of his christening were to be symbolic of his whole life. There, too, in this 'paradise of our childhood', the boy cut his first tooth, took his first steps alone and spoke his first words. Ernst and Albrecht, how well the names went together! Luise played with her sons as if they were three children together. There was no doubt which of them was her favourite, and she asked no more than that he should grow up to look exactly like his handsome Papa. Her wish was granted, if the paintings in the palace at Coburg are to be trusted.*

* This close resemblance was forgotten later, when rumours began that Albert was illegitimate, the offspring of a liaison between Luise and the Jewish Court Chamberlain baron von Meyern. Their source is unknown, but may have been a chance remark of Melbourne's, who told the Queen in 1838 that he did not care for the marriage of first cousins. Later, he was supposed to have become reconciled to the match only after Leopold and Stockmar had let him into the 'secret' that Victoria and Albert were not

Two years after Albert's birth, duke Ernest began to neglect his wife and to return to his former ways. What time he could spare from hunting, he spent with new mistresses. Lonely and humiliated, Luise consoled herself with harmless flirtations, but soon fell seriously in love with a young army officer. Because she was so open and honest she made little effort at concealment. When Ernest discovered what was going on, with consummate cruelty he seized the chance to rid himself of the wife he was tired of, picked a quarrel and stormed out of the house. The same evening he sent her a curt note demanding a separation. Too proud to try to hold a reluctant husband, Luise left Coburg in September 1824; abandoning the children she loved so passionately was the most painful thing of all. Although he had taken from her the two beings she loved best in the world, Luise never uttered a word of recrimination against her husband. Ernest divorced her in 1827; seven months later she married her lover Alexander von Hanstein and died in Paris of cancer only four years afterwards.

Albert never saw his mother again, but he never forgot her. Secure in her affections, he had been the happiest of children until now; his mother's sudden disappearance was traumatic and left a mark which lasted all his life. As a child, he did not convey by a single word what the loss meant to him, but the journal which he began to keep at the age of seven shows an astonishing tendency towards introspection and self-analysis, which no doubt reflects the insecurity he experienced after her disappearance. He became quiet and subdued, subject to unreasonable fits of weeping – there are many entries in his journal such as 'I cried at my lesson today', 'I cried because I could not find a word', or 'after dinner we went to Ketschendorf. On the way I cried'. Perhaps because he was so docile and obedient in the circle of the family (a warning finger and a severe frown were enough correction when he was naughty), no one guessed the depth of his feelings or how much he had been hurt. He had seen his parents quarrelling and knew that, in some way he could not understand, his mother's disappearance was his father's fault. At first he was certain that she would soon come back; when she did not, he began to hate his father with the singlemindedness

---

cousins after all. The story was always highly unlikely, for all these men were far too conscious of the dignity of monarchy to allow the Queen of England to marry a bastard, but it was repeated at intervals until conclusively disproved 40 years ago. The strongest evidence comes from Albert himself. He was almost obsessional in his abhorrence of sexual licence, but always spoke of his mother with great tenderness, pressed Stockmar for an account of her last illness and later, after his father's death, had her body transferred to the new mausoleum which he and Ernest had built in the Hofgarten at Coburg.

characteristic of children. Because he was intelligent he knew that this was wrong, and because he could not stifle the feeling of hatred he began to develop a sense of guilt which was itself a burden. The frequent occasions when he turned suddenly pale, fell asleep at meals and fainted away without reason may well have been physical signs of the strong emotions which he was suppressing.

Another unusual feature of his early years was an extraordinary and unnatural fascination with death. Every childish illness made him think that he was dying and all through his life the annual birthday letters to his brother revert to the theme that the passing years bring the grave nearer. The idea of death bit deep into his childish mind, and if we are to take his own words literally his wretchedness at this time even made him wish for his own death. 'Papa always said he could not bear to think of his childhood, he had been so unhappy and miserable,' wrote his daughter Vicky, 'and had many a time wished himself out of this world.'

Strange as this is, it would be an over-simplification to put it down to what has sometimes been called the 'Coburg melancholy'. It was far more than this. All the evidence (the journal, the tears, the unnatural docility, his own unhappy memories and finally the advice Stockmar gave King Leopold in 1835 to get Albert away from his home background) points to a stressful and unhappy childhood which might easily have soured him for ever. That it did not is partly due to the tutor Florschütz who created a peaceful and regular schoolroom life for the two boys, and to Albert's own strength of character. But he developed a habit of hiding his real feelings and took refuge in fantasies to make the tensions of the real world more bearable: 'Children find a way to cure themselves', he wrote to Stockmar some years later, no doubt drawing on his own experience at this time. In these fantasies the bullying duke Ernest was replaced by a much more agreeable Papa. Seeking, after the insensitive fashion of his time, to 'make men of them', duke Ernest drove his children much too hard. One winter, when Albert was only ten, he forced them to ride over the mountains to Gotha; they arrived cold and exhausted, but were too frightened to complain.

Their lives would have been harsh and loveless but for their two remarkable grandmothers (one of them, Augustus of Saxe-Coburg-Altenburg's second wife Caroline, was in fact no blood relation at all), who acted as shields against duke Ernest's bullying, and the boys were devoted to them. On the day their mother rode out of the Rosenau for ever they were both ill with whooping-cough, so within a few hours the two grandmothers moved in and took charge. They had a great influence on Albert's life. Augusta, the elder of the two, had the stronger will; Luise's stepmother, Caroline, was the more progressive; thus they complemented each other in a remarkable way. Although Augusta was prematurely aged and crippled with arthritis (Victoria and Albert remembered her walking with a stick, one hand on her bent back), she was a woman of commanding presence. She was a staunch liberal, and it was from her that Albert began to learn the rudiments of constitutionalism and how it was possible to be deeply religious without becoming a bigot : for instance, her Lutheran faith did not prevent her from having brisk and commonsense views on Catholic emancipation – it was wrong not to grant it.

Duchess Caroline of Saxe-Coburg-Altenburg was as clever and energetic as Augusta but her interests tended more towards music and literature; it was she who gave Albert his taste for romantic novels and his love for the theatre. When the boys stayed with her, there was no nonsense about not keeping them up late if there was something worth seeing in the playhouse in Gotha. Although childless herself, she understood a child's mind very well, and it was she who had the imagination to give them small plots of ground to make into their own gardens and who one Christmas bought them a miniature cart drawn by a goat that was a source of endless delight. With her easygoing nature, she never forced Albert to meet strangers or to do anything that made him nervous and shy.

Not long after Luise had gone away, Prince Leopold's friend and secretary, Baron Christian Friedrich Stockmar, came riding into the courtyard of the Rosenau on what he later called an errand of mercy. Prince Leopold had no faith in his brother's ability to bring up his children properly, so had sent Stockmar to find out what was being done for their welfare.

Stockmar was suited by nature to be the confidant of royalty. He was born (in 1787) and educated until eighteen in provincial Coburg, but his medical training at Würzburg, Erlangen and Jena, and his service as an army doctor during the Napoleonic wars, had already begun to broaden his outlook and excite his interest in politics before Leopold (who made his acquaintance during the 1814–15 campaign) offered him appointment as personal physician in 1816 and as private secretary after Charlotte's death the following year. Thus Stockmar's connexion with England was already forged before Albert's birth, and it was in England that he had first deepened his understanding of the courts he was to serve with disinterested vigour for the next forty years. His tact and his silent activity alike recommended him; government ministers as well as crowned heads found his advice invaluable and his usefulness as a go-between beyond praise. Describing his position at Victoria's court as 'a very peculiar one', Lord Liverpool wrote in 1841 that Stockmar might be called 'a species of second parent to the Queen and Prince' whose only object was their welfare and only ambition to be of service to them.

Leopold sent Stockmar to Coburg because he felt he owed it to Luise, of whom he had been very fond (she had been the one person who was able to comfort him after Charlotte's death), to take some of the responsibility for the upbringing and education of her two sons. The results of Stockmar's scrutiny (written down ten years later, with the benefit of hindsight, but presented in outline at the time) brought about a vital change in their training by removing them from feminine care. Both boys were intelligent, his report said, but Albert more so than Ernest. Albert was the more sensitive, also the more secretive, but only in small things; in the larger things of life, he was the more open. Albert showed qualities of leadership which Ernest did not. At play Albert was every bit as tough as Ernest and the other boys with whom they mixed; since these were village children, the remark has some meaning. Unseen by the boys, Stockmar had watched them at a game of 'soldiers' and had noticed that both showed imagination in planning manoeuvres and energy in carrying them out. Albert never hung back, nor did he cry even when badly hurt, but was always in the forefront where the play was roughest. With all the ferocity of a passionate nature, Albert was never slow in challenging Ernest to a fight. The behaviour of the younger brother in the rough-and-tumble of gang-warfare in which the boys engaged, was, however, strangely at variance with his docility and subdued manner at home. This was inexplicable and Stockmar was struck by it. It was, he said, 'very marked'. Yet at home there were criticisms. Of the two Albert cried more easily and about trivial things, or even for nothing at all; in certain moods he could be 'frightened of a mouse'. Stockmar took a grave view of this propensity to tears, but after watching carefully, he thought that he knew the answer: too much feminine coddling. The result of the report was drastic. Out went Müller, the nurse, and in came Florschütz, the tutor. The grandmothers were frantic. Since the boys were subject to attacks of croup, wrote Duchess Caroline, they ought still to sleep with Müller, 'for a woman accustomed, as Müller has been for so many years, to be with children, naturally sleeps much less soundly than a man who is not used to being with little children'. But as it turned out, Prince Leopold's confidence in Stockmar was not misplaced; the change was for the better.

12

The children soon discovered that Florschütz's stern exterior hid a heart of gold. He came of good Coburg middle-class stock and although only twenty-five had already been for some time tutor to the two youngest sons of duke Ernest's eldest sister, Alexander and Arthur Mensdorff. Many of duke Ernest's old-fashioned friends deplored the choice of a man of known liberal principles as the boys' tutor (later on, some of them even blamed Florschütz for letting them attend lectures in philosophy at Bonn, on the ground that such studies might lead to anarchy!). Mathematics and Latin formed the basis of Florschütz's teaching (he knew no Greek, and Albert never learned it), together with wide reading of modern literature in German, French and English. Florschütz spoke English well, so that Albert was familiar with it from the age of four; as it turned out, nothing could have been a better preparation for his future. Florschütz's influence on Albert was profound. He was a born teacher who gave Albert a love of learning for its own sake, and there is no doubt that Albert's passionate interest in science was a direct result of having physics and chemistry presented to him in an interesting way as a boy. These subjects did not form part of the curriculum of German schools, so it was extraordinary that Florschütz was able to teach the boys to a standard high enough for Albert to converse intelligently in later years with scientists like Faraday. Both boys had a talent for natural history, which Florschütz encouraged by arranging for regular instruction by a professor of mineralogy from Frankfurt.* Above all, Florschütz taught them to go to the root of everything, to accept nothing at second hand, to use their eyes and to look about them for beauty in nature, art, literature and humanity, and he was the first source of Albert's high ideals and strong sense of purpose.

Like his uncle Leopold before him, Albert found his greatest relaxation in music. Into music he poured his joys and his sorrows; it was not only a solace, but an escape. One day Florschütz was so alarmed by the withdrawn look on his face as he played that he spoke sharply to him to bring him back to reality. He must have had a great natural talent, for his father refused to 'waste money' on music lessons save, grudgingly, a few from the local church organist, who developed in him a passion for the organ which remained with him throughout his life.

The frequent visits of the two elder Mensdorff cousins to the Rosenau made no difference to their regime; Florschütz liked

---

* This was the origin of the classified collection of rock specimens which they made as boys and later established formally as the Ernst-Albrecht Museum. It is now housed in the Naturwissentschaftliches Museum in the Hofgarten.

nothing better than to teach all four boys together. Competition, he believed, was good for them all, and since Alexander and Arthur were quick and clever, Ernest and Albert had to be on their mettle not to be outshone. Besides the Mensdorffs, there were plenty of other boys of their own age about, for they were always allowed to play with the local children – in Coburg there was none of that segregation of classes which so astonished Albert when he came to England. It was Albert, not Ernest, who was the leader in their games in the woods, in the attics of the Ehrenburg palace or in the hall of the Rosenau, and any of these might ring out with the sound of sudden fierce dispute. For Albert liked to win, and he set about doing so with all the ingenuity he could muster, bending his brother and their friends relentlessly to his will as often as he could. He showed no sign of that selfless submission and sweet reasonableness that had such a place in Queen Victoria's imagination. Albert always won on the frequent occasions when the two brothers came to blows, but although their temperaments were totally dissimilar they were as devoted to each other as identical twins. It was quite usual to see them making off together, the best of friends and laughing at a shared joke, directly after one of their sudden bitter quarrels. At intervals between the rough-and-tumble of their games, Albert felt the need for periods of solitude and quiet, and at quite an early age would wander alone into the hills or ride off on his own for several hours at a stretch. This was all part of his paradoxical nature, which demanded the regeneration that only solitude can give after a bout of activity.

During the cholera epidemic of 1831 the four Kohary children and their parents fled for refuge to the Rosenau, for the Coburg area was one of the few which remained free from the infection. Duke Ernest decided not to risk the journey, but to stay in Italy with his mistress, so there was nothing to stop the six of them from enjoying themselves. Victoire Kohary was the only girl among them; she was beautiful and even-tempered, and Florschütz regarded her as a civilising influence. Queen Victoria professed to believe that she herself and Albert were destined for each other from the cradle. Albert once told her, she says, that he remembered his nurse prophesying, when he was only three, that he would one day marry the Queen of England. But even if Müller really used these words, she is not likely to have meant Victoria, for Queen Adelaide was still young enough to have more children; it was not until nearly ten years later that Victoria's succession became probable. During the interval the two grandmothers may sometimes have talked sentimentally about Albert being 'the pendant to his pretty cousin',

but Prince Leopold – who had far more to do with Albert's upbringing than his own father – always had his eye on Victoire Kohary,
heiress through her mother to a vast fortune, as the most suitable
wife for Albert. That she was a Roman Catholic was no impediment
in his eyes; a Lutheran himself, he had married a daughter of Louis
Philippe as his second wife and ruled over Roman Catholic Belgium
without it troubling his conscience in the slightest, and he saw no
reason why Albert should not feel the same. It was not until the
mid-1830s that, after consulting Stockmar, he changed his mind
and Victoire had to give way to Victoria as the greater catch.

2

'To sacrifice mere pleasure
to real usefulness'

King Leopold and Stockmar took the final decision to drop Victoire Kohary as Albert's future bride in the autumn of 1835, and they did it with the ruthlessness of which both were capable when their minds were made up. Albert was to achieve everything of which Leopold had been so cruelly cheated, but he could not do this without preparation. Leaving nothing to chance, and with complete faith in their ability to make Albert fit to marry a queen regnant, they proceeded with merciless precision step by step towards their goal.

The trust and understanding between the man who was now King of the Belgians and the doctor from Coburg, dating back to their service together during the Napoleonic wars, and cemented when Leopold begged Stockmar to stay by his side when he was shattered by Charlotte's sudden death, was so complete that Leopold could send Stockmar off on a mission with absolute confidence, certain that he would carry the business through as he would have done himself. Without this unique relationship the moulding of Albert's personality could not possibly have been accomplished. They were in a fortunate position for fulfilling their purpose: Stockmar had been in England for the whole of the time Leopold had lived there during and after his marriage, they shared a love for the country and had kept in touch with prominent English statesmen. Even more important, Leopold had maintained a regular correspondence with his niece Victoria after he had left England, and she adored the handsome uncle whom she looked on almost as a father; he had enormous influence with her and could inspire her sense of duty. As a result, he was in the extraordinary position of being a father-figure to both the young people between whom he was now trying to bring about a union, and had a tremendous power over their destinies.

Glowing letters about Albert's progress came regularly from Florschütz to Stockmar, who forwarded them to the Palace of Laeken. They were a little too glowing for Stockmar's taste, and he mentally accused Florschütz of exaggerating. The boy was certainly clever and good-looking and had a pleasing nature; Stockmar had found him remarkably well read, but with blind spots, which meant that he was developing in too one-sided a way. He was attracted towards philosophy and loved novels and light literature, but showed no interest in current affairs – yet he would be swept off his feet in England unless well-grounded in politics, so this considerable gap would have to be filled. Besides, he lacked polish, was not confident enough and was handicapped by his shyness, which was especially marked with strangers. A visit to Coburg by King Leopold in the spring of 1836 confirmed most of Stockmar's observations and amplified them. Albert was handsome already, and was certain to become even handsomer when he filled out. With his long legs, well-defined waist, pink-and-white complexion and light-brown hair curling loosely about his ears, women were sure to find him attractive. Leopold thought his nephew's shyness charming, and shrewdly guessed that it did not emanate from lack of confidence. In short, Albert was the kind of youth that any woman would be glad to have as a husband.

Not long after his return to Brussels, Leopold's good opinion of Albert was confirmed in a letter from Stockmar which said that he found Albert 'a handsome youth who, for his age, is tolerably developed, with pleasant and striking features; and who, if nothing interferes with his progress, will probably in a few years be a well-built man with a pleasant, simple, and yet distinguished bearing. Externally, therefore, he has everything attractive to women, and possesses every quality they find pleasing at all times, and in all countries. It may also be considered as a fortunate circumstance that he has already a certain English look about him.' Many people had praised his character, but Stockmar did not think he yet knew him well enough to venture an opinion of his own, and went on: 'He is said to be prudent, cautious, and already very well informed. All this, however, is not enough. He must not only have great capacity but true ambition, and a great strength of will. To pursue so difficult a political career a whole life through requires more than energy and inclination – it demands also that earnest frame of mind which is ready of its own accord to sacrifice mere pleasure to real usefulness. If simply to fill one of the most influential positions in

Europe does not satisfy him, how often will he feel tempted to regret what he has undertaken. If he does not, right from the start, regard it as a serious and responsible task, upon the thorough fulfilment of which his honour and happiness depend, he is not likely to succeed.'

Stockmar and Leopold both knew Albert and his background so well, and both realised so fully the immensity of the burden they were proposing to lay upon his shoulders, that they were inclined to see shortcomings in him where none – save those inseparable from his youth and inexperience – really existed; moreover, they were writing for each other's eyes alone. Stockmar's words must be read in this light; they can scarcely have conveyed such a chilling impression to Leopold as they do to us. But it is none the less true that Stockmar often blundered badly in his handling of Albert because he was always inclined to see weaknesses in him where there were none and to blind himself to real virtues; consequently he sometimes drove when he should have restrained, discouraged when encouragement was needed, and weakened Albert's confidence instead of bolstering it. The source of this blindness was his mistaken belief that Albert had inherited the shortcomings of his mother, whose follies, he thought, had brought about her own ruin. A passage from a letter he is said to have written in 1839 after their Italian trip* makes this point forcibly:

'The Prince bears a striking resemblance to his late mother and is in many respects cast in her mould. He has the same quick and acute mind, the same fineness of intellect, the same desire to appear good-natured and amiable to others and the same talent for doing so, the same love of *espiegleries* and of seeing the funny side of men and things, the same habit of not sticking to anything for long. . . . Full of the best intentions and the noblest designs, he often fails to carry them out.'

Most of this is very wide of the mark indeed; Albert's quick and sensitive intelligence came from his mother, but he resembled her in almost nothing else.

The two men agreed that their plans must be kept secret from duke Ernest, at least for the present. The duke was so indiscreet that if they told him the whole continent would know in a week, and this would kill their hopes stone dead. Leopold had been horrified

* See p. 25, below. In his edition of his father's papers, Stockmar's son calls it 'a fragment' and places it in May 1839. By content and context it seems to belong rather to the 1836 report, and an editorial mistake may have been made over an evidently undated sheet of writing. Whatever the date at which they were written, however, the words represent an opinion which Stockmar often expressed and which he stubbornly adhered to throughout his life.

18

to learn that duke Ernest had carried the boys off to Berlin directly after their confirmation on Palm Sunday 1835, but he was too late to prevent it. The trip was their reward for good conduct, Ernest wrote in high glee from the wicked city. For one mad moment Leopold contemplated sending Stockmar to Berlin to bring them back (or Albert at least); they might be contaminated by mixing in a society which was counted the most lax in Europe. Leopold's mind would have been easier if he could have seen for himself what was happening there. With great good sense, the sixteen-year-old Albert soon dropped out of his father's and brother's daily round of pleasure and stayed alone in his room in the Hotel d'Angleterre reading or, if the weather was good, explored the city. The military atmosphere that pervaded it astonished him as much as it did his daughter Vicky twenty-two years later; it was one huge camp, filled with dissipated army officers grown fat on good living and with nothing better to do than wait for war. He found no joy in the place and longed to return home, meanwhile philosophically accepting his loneliness in a strange and uncongenial town.

The Berlin trip brought home to King Leopold and Stockmar the urgent necessity of rescuing Albert from his father's clutches and for pressing on with the rest of their plans. The situation in England had changed dramatically of late; it was now certain that Princess Victoria would become Queen. The biggest prize in Europe must not be allowed to fall into the wrong hands, and there were plenty of these to give them cause for concern. Stockmar had heard from Melbourne that the duke of Cambridge was taking it for granted that his son George would become Victoria's husband, and that there were others in the running; the Prince of Orange, duke Ernst of Württemberg, Prince Adalbert of Prussia and (more serious) the Czarevitch Alexander, heir to Nicholas I. Most disconcerting of all was the discovery that duke Ernest was proposing his elder son as a candidate. They told each other that one look at the brothers together would soon put a stop to that nonsense – a piece of stupid over-confidence which might have jeopardised their plans, for Ernest's dark liveliness held a great fascination for some women.

With all speed King Leopold arranged for his sister, the duchess of Kent, to invite the two boys to Kensington for Victoria's seventeenth birthday in May. It was sooner than he would have liked (Albert needed a bit more polishing first, he thought). But another pair of attractive Coburg brothers (Ferdinand – or Fernando, as Victoria playfully called him – and Augustus Kohary) had just been staying with 'Aunt Kent'; and although one of them was already betrothed

19

to the widowed Queen of Portugal and the other was no beauty, yet Leopold had hard work to reassure himself that they were merely an 'aperitif'. He was taking no chances, and to England Albert must go.

The arrangements were made so swiftly that before he knew where he was Albert was sailing down the Rhine towards Rotterdam with his father and Ernest, sitting on deck in the spring sunshine studying his English grammar – he had no intention of looking a fool in front of his cousin. Half-way across the Channel the weather broke and Albert, who was already suffering from travel nerves, was dreadfully sea-sick. This may explain why he did not care for Victoria at all when he first saw her.

After the statuesque beauty of Victoire Kohary, this short, plump girl with the protruding blue eyes and receding chin did not appeal to him. On the first evening she was in such good spirits that she laughed too frequently and too loudly and made Albert's headache so unbearable that he was glad to submit to his aunt's fussing and go to bed early with a steaming cup of camomile tea. Next day he liked Victoria a little better, but the late hours and constant amusements (all indoors) not only bored him but prevented his stomach from recovering completely. The simple, almost spartan Coburg life had not prepared him for a round of balls, receptions and levées. His country origins showed in his looks – he became pale and his eyes were soon red from lack of sleep. More than once he wondered whether the holiday was worth all the trouble of getting to London. And there had been plenty of trouble. King William had been so angry when the visit was proposed that he did his utmost to stop them from landing, shouting that he had already chosen Prince Alexander of Orange to be Victoria's husband and wanted no Coburg upstart in his country. Persuaded by Melbourne to change his mind William had allowed the boys to attend a levée and had been quite won over by Albert's good looks and pleasant ways. At Victoria's birthday ball Albert was introduced to two of his rivals, Prince William of Brunswick and the Prince of Orange. They made no impression on him at all, but they noticed his pale face and woebegone expression, and made great sport behind his back. Fate played into their hands, for Albert felt suddenly faint while dancing with Victoria and had to leave the floor in a hurry; he stayed 'a prisoner in my room' for twenty-four hours, a prey as much to humiliating thoughts as to the after-effects of sea-sickness. From then on, nothing seemed to go right; he was bored, and longed to go home. Only on the last morning did his mood change. He was playing the piano before breakfast when Victoria came in and stood beside him. He looked up and was astonished and touched to see that there were tears in her eyes. For the first time he felt that there might be more to her than he had yet discovered.

They went next to Paris. A few days there ought to have made up for the shortcomings of London, but instead of letting the city stimulate his appetite for culture Albert allowed small things to spoil his enjoyment. He could not sleep properly because, like his mother, he was so sensitive to noise; the narrow streets gave him claustrophobia, and he was ashamed of his father's open flirtations. Far worse, duke Ernest had let slip a confidential remark of the duchess of Kent to the effect that Leopold was anxious for him to marry Victoria 'some time in the future'. The thought chilled him – endless years of wearisome late nights and boredom like that from which he had just escaped! Moreover, it was only a few weeks since the hours he had spent in the libraries of Coburg had led him to plan the life of a writer for himself.*

There followed a two-month stay in Brussels, where tactful Uncle Leopold had arranged just the kind of atmosphere that he knew his exacting nephew enjoyed. He had rented a small but pretty little house in a quiet cul-de-sac in the centre of the town for the trio, and at the sight of this haven Albert's confidence in his uncle increased, as Leopold had intended that it should. Regular life, and peace and quiet for work, suited him down to the ground. He was not a prig, only very young and as yet not interested in much besides intellectual things. The wily king pandered to all his nephew's little foibles, arranging the sort of outings which he knew would appeal to him in order to prevent him from spending too much time in the study. In August he took the boys and their tutor to the army camp at Beverloo, where they watched a mock battle. When one side got into difficulties from which it could not extricate itself, Albert greatly admired the skill with which Leopold directed the retreat, for he was going through a phase of hero-worshipping his uncle. The manoeuvres, and the flat plain on which they were conducted, later gave him the idea for Aldershot.†

The time passed so pleasantly that duke Ernest's demand that they return for Christmas came as a shock. White-faced and tight-lipped, Albert rushed to the palace, his father's letter in his pocket. They did not want to go back to Coburg for the holidays, he moaned,

* Disgust at the poor quality of a French translation of Goethe's *Faust* which he had come across also made him realise how bad most translations from German were, and determined him to make better versions himself. It made his hair stand on end, he wrote, to see the profound genius of German literature made to appear ridiculous.

† See pp. 238, 256 and 282 for Albert's realisation that the army needed a training area and for his part in acquiring land for the purpose at Chobham and Aldershot.

'it would mean falling behind in our studies'. It was all the king could do not to smile at this proof of his success in widening his nephew's horizons. Too wise to show it, however, he advised Albert to write a 'reasoned and calm letter' to his father. 'We should be glad to accept your invitation to go to Coburg,' Albert wrote, 'but if we are to benefit from our stay here, I am afraid that we must deny ourselves the pleasure.' Duke Ernest agreed, and Albert gave the credit to his own persuasiveness. In fact, it was a letter from Leopold that had done the trick. There was nothing for it but to let his brother into the secret – just as the duchess of Kent had said, he was preparing Albert for an important position which would raise the House of Coburg in the world.

To capitalise on his first success, and to forestall further inter-ference from his brother, Leopold at once set about arranging the next stage in the boys' education. They must go to a university. Stockmar recommended Bonn which, although newly-founded, had already gained a high reputation by attracting men of international fame; it was not lax like Berlin nor vulgar like Munich and Heidel-berg, and above all it was within easy reach of Brussels.

Wisely, king Leopold insisted that the boys enrolled as ordinary students and not (as they were entitled to do) as noblemen who could come and go at will and attend lectures as they pleased. It was his intention that Albert at least should learn a good deal. Besides, he had a certain right to decide these things for the boys, since he was paying half the fees, duke Ernest having declared that he could not afford them.

Bonn suited Albert to perfection; he was utterly happy, attending lectures and seminars held by men like Professors Quetelet, Bethmann-Hollweg, Perthes, Schlegel and Fichte. Fichte had a profound influence on Albert, and taught him that 'through work and effort shall come salvation'. So far as the lighter side of life went, amateur theatricals and fencing seem to have occupied most of the time Albert did not spend at his studies. His imitations of the pro-fessors' mannerisms were wildly applauded, and he won the first prize in a fencing competition for which there were nearly thirty entrants.

One hot June afternoon in 1837, Albert and his friend Prince William of Löwenstein returned from a long tramp beside the Rhine to Godesberg and back with Albert's greyhound Eos, to learn that William IV was dead and that his cousin Victoria was Queen of England. Urged on by Leopold, Albert sent her a polite little letter of congratulation; he dismissed her reply as 'condescending', noticing that she wrote rather as Queen than as one cousin to another, and he was glad to put her at the back of his mind now that she was the ruler of so powerful a country. For her part, Victoria was soon enjoying her new position so much that all thoughts of marriage – particularly to Albert – began to recede. When, a little prematurely, Stockmar had mentioned Albert to her, she promptly came out with the startling remark that she did not think him sufficiently experienced and grown up for her to be able to judge whether he was likely to be a fit husband for the Queen of England.

In one way, Queen Victoria's frivolous behaviour brought matters out into the open. King Leopold made up his mind to take Albert into his confidence and to talk to him frankly and honestly of a possible marriage with Victoria. Albert might co-operate, he told Stockmar, if the case were presented to him in a proper light and all the difficulties carefully explained, so that he did not feel that he was being coerced. If he reacted well, and they were able to go ahead, then two things would have to be combined: there must be a well-planned programme of further education, suited to his future career in England, and Albert must win Victoria's affection before he asked her to marry him – for Leopold knew well enough that pressure alone would not work with his niece, and that there must be love as well. The talk took place at Laeken in March 1838, and Leopold reported on it to Stockmar. 'He looks at the question from a most elevated and honourable point of view; he considers that troubles are inseparable from all human positions and that, there-fore, if one must be subjected to plagues and annoyances, it had better be for some great and worthy object rather than for trivial and paltry ends.' Leopold's words leave a lot unexplained, for they give no hint of Albert's true feelings. The philosophical generalisa-tions of the letter tell us nothing of the very human emotions of dis-may, even distress, which must have overwhelmed Albert. All that can be said is that he certainly did not reject the idea of marrying Victoria out of hand and that therefore it cannot have been totally abhorrent to him.

Soon after this, another important decision was taken: the brothers were to be separated. Tactfully, King Leopold explained to Albert that it would be for the good of both if Ernest were to go to Dresden for military training, he on a tour of Italy with Stockmar. Victoria's accession made a separation inevitable. Ernest was a chip off the old block – at eighteen he was already having indiscriminate affairs with servant girls – and Albert might become contaminated if left too long in his company. Besides, Albert still needed more social polish; he must acquire the airy sophistication that the Queen seemed to favour in young men. Stockmar had noticed that, young though he was, Prince William of Brunswick had it and so had a dashing Russian Grand Duke; these two were enjoying a huge success at Buckingham Palace at that moment but Albert scorned to notice them.

There was another matter, too; Stockmar had put it into Leopold's head that 'Albert did not depend enough on himself.' If by this Stockmar meant that Albert was not self-reliant, he was completely wrong. In 1835, when only sixteen, he had shown initiative and common sense by filling the hours he was left alone in Berlin usefully and without complaint. In London, in 1836, he had gone about by himself, exploring the unfamiliar streets and looking for second-hand bookshops. At Bonn he branched out on his own, finding new friends and investigating new interests like buying pictures. During the summer vacation of 1837 he organised a highly successful short tour of northern Italy and Switzerland for Ernest, Florschütz and himself. There had been one hopeful sign during this tour, and Leopold noted it with satisfaction; on a visit to Ferney, he had managed to secure a scrap of Voltaire's handwriting and had promptly sent it off to Victoria.

Anguish at leaving Bonn was lost in the still greater anguish of parting from Ernest. 'I cannot bear the thought of that moment,' he wrote to William of Löwenstein; and to his grandmother 'I must now give up the custom of saying "we" . . . "we" expresses the harmony between different souls.' To Florschütz he became quite dramatic – he could not suffer more if Ernest died, and he was choked with tears as 'bereft of everything that makes life worthwhile', he watched his brother's carriage out of sight. But there was one more parting to tear Albert to pieces – Florschütz was not to go with him to Italy. During the time in Coburg between the Swiss tour and the last few weeks at Bonn, he had fallen in love with the daughter of Pastor Genzler and was going to marry her. Albert was shocked to find he bitterly resented the fact that he and Ernest were no longer all in all to 'Herr Rath'.

Grumbling, duke Ernest accompanied his son to Munich on the first stage of his journey, but it was a relief to Albert to exchange his father's bad temper for the hypochondria of Stockmar, who was now to be his guide and companion. The rest of the journey to Florence was one long nightmare. What demon possessed Leopold and Stockmar not to put it off until the spring? Perhaps the fear of rivals urged them not to lose a single day in transforming Albert into the kind of man Victoria could accept, but it was bad luck that the winter of 1838/9 was one of unparalleled severity. The only lodgings they could find in Verona were damp and dirty, but sitting on chairs and wrapped in Stockmar's rugs, they came to no harm. On the road to Florence the carriage stuck in a snowdrift; they had to wait several hours to be dug out, and could then only proceed at a walking pace in twelve degrees of frost. By the time they reached Florence on Christmas Eve, Albert was in pain from an abscess in a tooth; he was in bed for five days, and Stockmar too kept to his room 'as a precaution'. Albert told Ernest that he had not expected Stockmar to come out of all this alive!

A first experience of Italy is bound to have a tremendous effect on a sensitive nature brought up north of the Alps, but it was to leave a particularly deep impresson on Albert. He was always responsive to artistic stimuli, but had not yet received them in much number or variety – he was surrounded by Cranachs in the Festung at Coburg, for instance, but knew so little of Italian painting and sculpture that the Donatellos in Florence were 'far more beautiful than I had ever imagined', and he astonished the philistine Ernest by writing that in the Sistine Chapel he 'stood silent, just letting its splendours sweep over me in waves of ecstasy'. Italy awoke interests in Albert which Ernest could never completely share and revealed the first signs of divergence between the brothers. Ernest had a good eye for a bargain, in pictures as in other things, but only Albert would have enriched the royal collection at Windsor by spending a large part of his slender income on Italian primitives, which captured his imagination in 1839, years before they were widely appreciated. Thus Leopold's and Stockmar's instinct was proved right. Albert may or may not have lacked sophistication at the end of 1838, as they thought, but by sending him to Italy at an impressionable age they were opening his eyes to cultural interests which he had so far had little opportunity to pursue but which they correctly judged he would find exciting. At the same time they were widening his horizons and weaning him away from the narrow German intellectualism which appealed to him so strongly that in a moment of revulsion from pleasure a few months later he could fleetingly dedicate his life exclusively to learning.

But Albert did not spend all his time in churches and art-galleries. In that exclusive society, the appearance of such an interesting visitor could not go unnoticed. Invitations flooded in, to balls, dinners, the theatre, the opera and late supper parties that often went on until dawn. Albert's way of life changed abruptly, but he took it all in his stride. He no longer complained of boredom or fatigue, although he had never had so little sleep, and told Ernest that he felt 'like a fish *in* water'. He met more pretty girls than ever before, and his reaction to them (one in particular attracted him, although

25

he never names her) shows how little foundation there was for Queen Victoria's belief that he took no interest in women before he met her. Stockmar thought the same ('He will always have more success with men than with women'), but he was often indisposed and confined to his room during the Italian tour, and so did not always see what was going on. Everything became an even greater pleasure for Albert when he was joined by Francis Seymour, a young army officer whom Leopold attached to the party to help Albert understand the English better, and in Seymour's company he soon began to miss Ernest hardly at all. As a relief from sightseeing, the two of them had great fun singing and playing the piano together, although the only instrument they could hire in Florence was so old and out of tune that the keys kept sticking and Albert learned more Italian from the piano-tuner than from anyone else.

After Florence, Rome was at first sight a disappointment. 'But for some beautiful palaces,' he wrote to his father the night they arrived, 'it might just as well be any town in Germany'. But next day the sun shone and he was captivated, although Florence still held first place in his heart. At Easter, he knelt with the crowd thronging the Piazza San Pietro. Rumours of an important marriage having reached the Vatican, Stockmar had no difficulty in arranging an audience with the pope. Remembering with pride his family's services to the Lutheran cause, Albert refused to be daunted, and in his best Italian boldly though respectfully contradicted the Holy Father when the conversation turned on classical art: it was the Egyptians, he said, not the Etruscans, whom the Greeks had taken as their model. But he thought the pope 'very kind and civil'.

At the end of the tour, Stockmar sent another report to Leopold; it seems to have mixed praise and criticism in equal measure, but only a part of it has survived.* Stockmar's opinion at this time was that while on the one hand Albert's judgement was 'on many subjects mature beyond his years', on the other he had so far shown not the slightest interest in politics and could not be induced to read a newspaper even when the most momentous events were afoot. That Albert took an intelligent interest in many other things did not perhaps make up for this shortcoming in Stockmar's eyes, and it is in any case clear that Albert had still a long way to go before he would be fit for the high position Stockmar and Leopold planned for him. But Stockmar cannot have failed to notice that the lighter side of Albert's nature had made him enjoy the balls and receptions to which they had been invited (though Albert's letters to Ernest show

* This is the 'fragment' referred to in the footnote to p. 18.

that he made little secret of his disapproval), and he was no doubt well aware that the young Victoria also had a passion for such things. Albert's own accounts of their doings show him more carefree than formerly, more given to laughter and more at ease in society, and Stockmar must have observed this. Again, since he benefited from it he presumably approved the resourcefulness which Albert had shown in the small emergencies of travel – they had been uncomfortably lodged when they arrived in Florence, for instance, but Albert quickly found better accommodation in the palace of the Marquis Cerini.

Whatever Stockmar thought, Albert had matured during the Italian tour, and as they started home he began to realize it himself. He had lost 'that awful self-consciousness that used to plague me so', and told Leopold that he had never been so happy and relaxed as with Stockmar and Francis Seymour. But when Ernest, jealous because he sensed that he had not been missed, accused him of having his head turned 'by so much adulation', he indignantly repudiated the charge: 'you seem to think that changing one's character is like changing one's gloves'.

Albert found duke Ernest was in a particularly trying mood when he returned home, and the contrast with the gaiety of Italy soon began to make him miserable. Unknown to his son, Ernest had been to London that summer to press Albert's cause with his sister the duchess of Kent and several ministers, but he had found England in such a turmoil that he had come back wanting to call the whole thing off. It was a blessing, he said brazenly, that nothing was settled and that Albert could withdraw honourably: 'the virago queen might as well marry George of Cambridge, since no one else will have her'. He depressed Albert beyond measure as he mercilessly repeated the stories he had picked up – bitter conflict between mother and daughter, the throne rocking and Victoria thinking of abdication – but so far from turning Albert against marriage with Victoria this awoke all his chivalrous instincts so strongly that for a moment he thought of dashing over to England to protect her. Fortunately, caution held him back.

Almost at once, duke Ernest dragged him off to Karlsbad, where there was so little to do that he was soon 'almost dying of boredom', he wailed to Ernest, adding 'yesterday I nearly hanged myself in desperation when I heard that the reward for all my sufferings is to be a stay at Reinhardsbrunn'. It was hard to believe that only a short time ago he had been so happy in Italy. His father did not leave him alone for a single moment, but nagged him continually, so that his only recourse was to make his mind a blank; but then 'when a man is sunk in idleness, it is difficult to get out of it', he complained to his sympathetic grandmother, and to Prince William of Löwenstein, 'when I say the word "university" and remember all the good resolutions which I made there, I am quite ashamed of my present life'. Puritanical by nature, and made more so by circumstances, he now began to doubt the value even of artistic pleasure and the happiness it brings. Had the Italian trip been worth while, if all it had done was to make him discontented, or was he now paying the price for his frivolity in Italy? His miserable mood made him see flaws that had not struck him before – Italy, he now said, was 'in many respects far behind what one had expected; in the climate, in the scenery, in the study of the arts, one feels most disagreeably disappointed'. Yet at the time he had clearly enjoyed the Italian tour immensely, as his letters at the time testify: 'Art treasures are an unremitting source of pleasure to me', 'I am quite intoxicated with delight when I come out of one of the galleries', and 'the masked balls in the main opera house are great fun; in every box there is supper at 2 o'clock, and I am invited to several'. 'I have spent some thoroughly pleasant and enjoyable hours here in Florence'. The excuse for his preposterous reversal was the nervous strain imposed by his father's bullying, although he accepted it with outward calm, even apparent indifference.

His twentieth birthday was a disaster. He had planned to spend it at the Rosenau, but his father – ruthless as ever – insisted that they go to Gotha. Albert's obedience only increased the tension between them: duke Ernest scolded and Albert sulked, while Ernest, who could have eased things by mediating between them as he had so often done in the past, was far away.

The release for which Albert prayed came in the shape of an invitation from Victoria, so peremptory and so hedged round with conditions that it was in effect a command. She required him and Ernest each to bring only one member of his household (but not Stockmar) and to reach London by 28 September. The imperious tone grated on Albert, and quite changed his previous feelings that she was a defenceless girl in need of protection; his reaction was instantly hostile, for he could be equally strong-willed: 'let her wait', he told Ernest; a trip to London could not be arranged overnight, the king of Saxony was coming to Coburg on 30 September and his visit could not be put off because something better had come up. And when Leopold suggested that it was hardly a good idea to keep the Queen of England waiting, Albert coolly replied 'We really have no option, and we shall not be able to leave before the fourth [of

October].' As far back as the middle of July, Victoria had imposed another and still more important condition before she could consider marriage, requiring Leopold to inform duke Ernest that even if she liked Albert 'I can make no final promise this year, for at the very earliest any such event could not take place for two or three years'. When Leopold at last steeled himself to pass on this message, Albert's reaction was blunt: before he agreed to set foot on English soil, Victoria must know that he had made up his mind not to wait for as long as that; if they liked each other, it must be marriage within a reasonable time or not at all. After what Victoria had said, this clearly meant that at the moment he did not expect – or perhaps even want – to marry her. About the beginning of September 1839, then, all Leopold's carefully-laid plans seemed suddenly to be going astray; the puppets would no longer dance when he pulled the strings, but were taking command of their own destinies.

But although he was so soon to change his mind about Victoria again, Albert's reaction to her rebuff turned out to have been extremely wise. Not only did it show maturity and resolution, but it also made certain his future dominance (in the best sense) over his wife. Moreover it was a decision that he had come to without advice from anyone, and again makes nonsense of Stockmar's criticism that he vacillated and could not make up his mind on important issues. It was exactly the right treatment for Queen Victoria, who later, when enjoying the 'safe haven of a happy marriage', bitterly regretted that she had caused her husband one moment's pain by this suggestion. 'The only excuse that the Queen can make for herself is in the fact that the sudden change from the secluded life at Kensington to the independence of her life as Queen Regnant at the age of 18, put all ideas of marriage out of her mind.'

One morning in early October 1839, two carriages swung out of the Rosenau en route for Brussels, where Albert and Ernest were to break their journey with King Leopold. As the Rosenau disappeared from sight, Albert was buoyed up by a presentiment that cheered him greatly – he would soon be back again, free as air. Since he felt sure of this, he had no regrets at leaving, for he knew that he would return in time to enjoy a long winter at home (duke Ernest had hinted that he was off to Italy alone), with his books, his dogs and the brisk walks that so invigorated him and revitalised his mind for the scholarship which he believed was his true bent.

For he was not really interested in either England or Victoria. He showed complete indifference when Leopold tried to explain away the scandalous stories his father had been telling about the English court. Marriage itself had grown distasteful, its very finality frightened him; it would be the end of Coburg, of the Rosenau, of the youth which unconsciously he wanted to prolong ('The childish time of youth has gone never to return', he had written regretfully to Ernest after the Italian trip), although much of it had not brought him happiness. But up to now he had at least known where he stood; the unknown was always to make him apprehensive. The further childhood receded, the more the pleasures outweighed the misery – Albert only remembered what he wished to remember. This was a part of him that Queen Victoria never understood and cannot be blamed for not understanding. In December 1839 Ernest wrote her a letter that ought to have opened her eyes a little: 'from our earliest years we have been surrounded by difficult circumstances of which we were perfectly conscious and, perhaps more than most people, we have been accustomed to see men in the most opposite positions that human life can offer. Albert never knew what it was to hesitate. Guided by his own clear sense he always walked calmly and steadily on the right path.'

An adept at handling truculent nieces and reluctant nephews, Leopold was the soul of tact while the little party was at Laeken. He sensed that Albert was distracted and not in the mood to receive confidences or take advice, and noticed with dismay that something had happened to make him think that 'the burden' was too heavy. That night Albert remarked in the course of conversation that if a man were to tie himself to a 'position' he would be in danger of losing that elasticity of mind which he 'so much admired in certain eminent men whom it was his ambition to emulate'. Leopold was himself partly to blame for this despondent mood, for instead of telling all, he had made the mistake of divulging only the bad – the young Queen's tactlessness, unkindness and partisanship, her moods and her tantrums – and in doing so had set Albert's nerves on edge and created the unfortunate impression that Albert (who hated to disagree with those he loved and suffered agonies of remorse after a battle with his father or Ernest) would have to cope with a difficult woman who was also a queen. In consequence, he now had to face the fact that the marriage might not take place. Almost in despair, he dashed off a hasty note to Victoria, hinting at her suitor's dark mood.

Much has been written of the sudden devastating effect on Queen Victoria of her second meeting with Albert, who, despite his travel-weariness and sober clothes, looked wonderfully handsome – taller and thinner than in 1836 (his puppy fat had not pleased her then), with bluer eyes and broader shoulders. These assets had always been plain to Leopold, but he could do nothing now except put his trust in Providence and Albert's good looks.

But what did Albert expect to find? He hardly knew. A monster certainly, who had been growing more repellent with every mile that brought her nearer. Gloom at the prospect of facing her, and fears that he might not be able to handle the situation, seized him as his carriage approached Windsor. In a daze he mounted the castle steps – then looked up and beheld a vision. Looking down at him with huge blue eyes, soft brown hair and half-open lips showing small, even teeth, stood a tiny, fragile figure, far smaller and more feminine than he remembered. In an instant his feelings underwent a complete and violent reversal. This was not the monster he had imagined, but the defenceless girl his chivalry had once made him want to protect from the foes his father had described. He quickened his pace, taking the last few steps at a run; seizing her hand in his, he knew instinctively that everything was going to be all right.

Albert and Ernest had to dine alone in their room because, their luggage not having arrived, they had no evening clothes. The respite was welcome, for it gave Albert a chance to recover his composure and try to assimilate the consequences of his new emotions. After dinner, they joined the Queen and her guests in the drawing room; if Albert was silent, it was not from boredom.

Next morning the two brothers went together to the Queen's room to deliver letters from their German relations. The time passed in a flash as they chatted about nothing in particular. To his surprise Albert found his cousin easy to talk to, and that evening, partnering her in five quadrilles, he suddenly found himself enjoying with her the kind of perfect rapport which only exists between old friends. There were more signs that Victoria enjoyed his company the following day. When the party set out for the afternoon gallop she beckoned him to ride on her left side while Lord Melbourne took his accustomed place on her right; it gave him great satisfaction to notice that it was to him that Victoria turned more often. On Sunday, he was invited to ride to church in the Queen's carriage; on the way back she made room for him on the seat next to her, as though it was the most natural thing in the world. Animatedly they discussed music, and this gave Albert the chance to show off a little; he had had it in mind for some time, he said, to compose a chorale for the organ. Dinner that night was a family affair, and although he did not sit next to Victoria she led him to her sofa afterwards to explain the book of Italian drawings which he had brought her. Afterwards Albert taught everybody a new version of the fashionable card game, German Tactics, and they finished up with a hilarious

31

round of Fox and Geese. The noise woke Albert's greyhound, Eos, who yawned as though to say it was time for bed, which amused them all very much.

A shoot had been arranged for Monday. Albert wore red leather top-boots which, he explained to the admiring Queen, were an innovation of the Coburg hunt and very much disapproved of by duke Ernest, but he seemed quite unaware of the sensation his elegant appearance caused. Anxious to know what others thought of this paragon, the Queen asked Melbourne whether his sister, Lady Cowper, thought him handsome, and was delighted with the answer 'she thinks him very good looking'. 'He has no idea', the Queen replied. Albert's prowess as a shot astonished everyone. No doubt because of his unusual get-up, they had taken it for granted that he was a dandy – yet he easily excelled them all, as he did out hunting next day, 'riding like an old hand', as Lord Melbourne's nephew put it in some surprise. Perhaps he would not have shot with so steady an aim if he had guessed that at that very moment Victoria was discussing her marriage to him with Melbourne, even going into details such as the date of the ceremony – all before a word of love or of marriage had passed between them. But his feelings were already in a turmoil ('feelings', the Queen liked to say, 'are important') – one moment he was full of hope, the next sunk in despair – yet he could not help thinking it a good sign that Victoria seemed to single him out for special attention. In order to give her some idea of how he felt, one evening he brought the conversation round to England; he was full of curiosity about her country, he said; customs, habits, climate, everything was of interest to him. The Queen answered as well as she could, 'giving England as good a recommendation as truth allowed'. He told her that since coming to England he had not slept well, to which the Queen significantly replied that she had not slept well lately either.

'That fateful morning', 15 October, was bright and sunny, and as soon as breakfast was over the two boys went hunting. They returned in high spirits, laughing and talking and making a great noise. Albert was changing when a note was brought to him – the Queen wished to see him as soon as he was ready. For the first time, Ernest was not included in the invitation and Albert wondered if this meant something. Victoria was waiting for him in the Blue Room, pale and agitated, though trying very hard to keep her self-control. Albert was trembling too, so that he could not help her to come to the point, but self-consciously talked of other things. Then, all in a rush, the Queen said in a low voice 'that it would make me too happy, if he would consent to what I wished [to marry me]'. Before she could finish Albert seized her hands and showered kisses on them, then, the tension broken, they were in each other's arms, kissing again and again, while he poured out in German all the tenderness that he seemed to have only for her. Victoria murmured something about being unworthy, and Albert said he 'longed to spend his life with her'.

For the moment the engagement was to be a secret. Ernest was to be told, of course, and so was 'dearest Daisy' (her former governess and present confidante, baroness Lehzen), but on one point Victoria was emphatic – not Mama, for she could not be trusted to be discreet. Albert begged to be allowed to tell Stockmar; incredulous that Victoria should really love him, he longed, he said, to make it seem more real 'by pouring it all out to this old friend'. But when the pen was in his hand, he felt so bemused that, after briefly describing the scene in the Blue Room, all he could think of to say were two lines from Schiller's *Lied von der Flocke*;

> Das Auge sieht den Himmel offen,
> Es schwimmt das Herz in Seligkeit.*

Posterity has been led to believe that Albert was sentimental only on the surface, and cold underneath. The truth was very different; he was as passionate a man as his father and brother, but the Puritan in him made him believe that once a man had made his choice, he should never look elsewhere. His shy nature was able to respond to Victoria's exuberant love, so that from the first he was the dominant partner, a state of affairs that was essential (in view of the Queen's position) to their future happiness.

Suddenly there was nothing to do but live happily ever after. Even Ernest, whom he had always put first in everything, dropped naturally back into second place; it was Victoria who suggested that they should tell him at once. Perhaps the only redeeming feature of the reprobate Ernest was his genuine love for his brother, and he showed it when he now emotionally told Victoria how perfect Albert was, and when he soon wrote to her from Coburg 'Albert is my second self, and my heart is one with his. Independently of his being my brother, I love and esteem him more than any one on earth.' It was lucky for the engaged pair that next day Ernest went down with jaundice and they could be alone. What a delight it was to go over the 'anxious past' together, now that all had come right in the end. Accustomed from childhood to keep his emotions under control, Albert marvelled that he was able to pour out his love so

---

* 'The eye beholds the heavens open wide,
  The heart is bathed in blissfulness.'

easily and talk to his beloved so unself-consciously – with no one else except Ernest had he ever done so. The next two weeks were of course idyllic – 'the radiant parts of my life'. 'I cannot even yet clearly picture to myself,' he wrote to Victoria soon after his return home, 'that I am to be indeed so happy as to be always near you, always your protector.'

On 1 November the brothers returned to Coburg, Albert as an engaged man – 'which alters his view of life altogether' Ernest complained to his grandmother. On the way, Albert had the 'great, great pleasure' of finding Victoria's first love-letter waiting for him at Bonn, and he read it with deep emotion. Albert's own letters to Victoria are just as full of passion as hers to him; unable to dissemble, he wrote exactly as he felt, full of love and adoration. In this condition the Rosenau gave him a sense of unreality; everything was the same, yet he was different. Victoria's miniature on his bedside table looked singularly out of place in the masculine setting, yet 'I can hardly take my eyes off it.' Coburg was very puzzled that an engagement had not been announced, but no one dared ask what had happened. Only his grandmother, duchess Caroline, was let into the secret. Was he really in love? the old lady asked tremulously. Yes, she could see he was; he radiated happiness. Instead of the serious reading of former days, he composed 'The song of the orange blossoms' and sent it to Buckingham Palace with a letter full of humour and fun. He was so faithful to her that he refused to join in the Regatta Galop at a ball because he had last danced it with Victoria at Windsor. 'Those happy hours, will, I hope, soon return,' he wrote that night, 'I kiss you a thousand times, may Heaven bless you.'

Mundane affairs soon caught up with them. King Leopold was put out that nothing had been settled about Albert's rank, and suggested a peerage to get rid of the 'foreignship' of his name (he had refused the title of duke of Kendal for himself on his own marriage to Princess Charlotte but regretted it afterwards.) With brutal frankness, the Queen explained that the country would not tolerate a foreigner interfering in the political life of England; 'Now, though I know you never would, still, if you were a peer they would all say the Prince meant to play a political part.' Besides, the rank was not high enough, and she secretly cherished the hope that she would soon be able to follow the example of Donna Maria of Portugal with Cousin Ferdinand and make him 'King Consort'.

Before Albert had properly digested this disconcerting information, Victoria asked him to find out precisely the part his family had played in promoting the Lutheran religion so that she might refute the suggestion that he was a Roman Catholic. The words 'a Protestant Prince' had been omitted from the declaration of her intention to marry which she had read at a Privy Council meeting on 23 November, because Melbourne and the Cabinet foolishly (and against the advice of Wellington and King Leopold) thought it unwise to state the obvious; naturally enough, the omission raised the very doubts they had hoped to set at rest. Only insular narrow-mindedness can explain why these doubts were so widespread; it was singularly tactless – but it ought also to have been quite unnecessary – for Palmerston to inquire of Stockmar whether Albert 'belonged to any special Protestant sect that will prevent him from taking the Sacrament with the Queen', and Stockmar had derived immense satisfaction from knocking such ignorance on the head: 'there is no essential difference between the communion services of the Protestant German and the English Churches, except that perhaps the German is the more reverent.'

Melbourne bungled the question of Albert's precedence by springing it upon Parliament without warning. Queen Anne's husband, George of Denmark, had been given precedence immediately after the princes of the blood royal; but since there were none of these, he automatically came next after the queen. This seemed to give Queen Victoria's uncles rights which, with Tory backing, they were determined to defend to the death. Things would no doubt have been much easier if Melbourne had listened to the diarist Greville, whose researches revealed that the Queen could allow her Consort precedence everywhere except in Parliament and in Council. Albert's future seemed to be in the hands of people who were casual and dilatory (on this occasion anyhow) like Melbourne, old and obstinate like Wellington* or young and inexperienced like the Queen. To confuse matters still more, Melbourne lumped the precedence question together with Albert's naturalisation, although they were entirely separate issues and much better kept apart. He was 'so anxious' to get the naturalisation bill passed (in the circumstances 'anxious' seems a curious way to put it – as if there could be any doubt) that, if it were necessary to prevent opposition, he would withdraw the precedence clause – not altogether, he told a suspicious Lord Brougham (who had instantly asked his reasons) but only for

---

* Greville's curiosity had sent him to Wellington:
  G.   What are you going to do about the precedence?
  W.   Oh, give him the same which George of Denmark had, place him next after the archbishop of Canterbury.
  G.   That will by no means satisfy her.
  W.   Satisfy her? What does that signify?

the moment. As soon as the naturalisation bill had passed the Lords, the Queen wrote in triumph to Albert, who accepted the good news coolly, for it irritated him that her ministers discussed his affairs as though he had no feelings. Victoria at once sensed his anger and longed to do something to propitiate him. Could she make him King Consort by act of Parliament? she asked Melbourne. 'For God's sake, Ma'am,' was the reply, 'let's have no more of that. If you get the English people into the way of making kings, you will get them into the way of un-making them.'

The bickering about his grant humiliated Albert still further. Leopold had given him to understand that his own grant had been passed without question, and that the same would happen now. Albert was unused to the ways of an English Parliament, and was in any case too inclined to be sensitive and to take things personally, especially where money was concerned. A furore arose in the Commons over Lord John Russell's motion for an annual allowance of £50,000, which was contested with as much bitterness as the introduction of income tax in peace-time a few years later. Pocket money at the rate of £50,000 a year was 'quite monstrous', Greville shouted. Why could he not be given the same (£21,000) as the royal dukes? In any case nothing should be given without conditions.* Weakly and without proper information, Lord John admitted that the expense of Albert's household could not exceed £7,000, so he supposed that sum as large as £50,000 was unnecessary. This was the only occasion when a comparison with George of Denmark (who had received £50,000 at a time when the cost of living was less) would have been useful to Albert, but only a timid back-bencher mentioned him and he was shouted down. In the end, Sir Robert Peel's proposal of £30,000 free of conditions was accepted. Pride kept Albert silent, but he did allow himself to say rather pathetically to Stockmar that as the Queen's husband his position would anyhow be more dependent than that of any other married man, and this made it worse. 'Shame, shame', cried King Leopold, but the Tories had the answer to that – let him pay his nephew the difference. It was a horrible experience for a sensitive young man of twenty to have himself discussed in the national press in this way, and it made him wonder whether Victoria was right when she assured him that the marriage was popular. He noted grimly that the Tories had voted to a man against a larger allowance.

The nerves of the lovers were becoming strained; a sharp tone is discernible in their letters at this time, and even small matters were

---

* Albert would have to reside for 6 months of every year in England and give up the allowance if he married a Catholic as his second wife.

blown up out of all proportion. The Queen had a smattering of heraldry, and seized a chance to show off her knowledge, unaware that Albert was expert in the subject. 'As a German prince you have no right to quarter the English arms,' she wrote confidently, 'but the Sovereign has the right to allow it by Royal Command. This was done for Uncle Leopold and I will do it again for you. But it can only be done by Royal Command.' Albert made short work of 'Royal Command': 'I would not have it otherwise than as you say, but it is my right to quarter the English arms with mine, since I have been created before marriage an English prince by act of Parliament and as such may quarter my arms with those of Saxony, as Uncle Leopold did. Have the kindness to have the matter further enquired into.' This was a bad beginning, but worse was to come. The Queen was even more high-handed about his household, and chose it without consulting him. (Someone had put it into her head that Albert might want to fill his household with Germans; there is however, not the slightest evidence of any such intention.) When he protested, she replied that she knew best and her haughty tone was still more annoying when she appointed a household for him along exclusively party lines, filling it with Whigs and putting at the head of it George Anson, who was at that very moment Private Secretary to the Whig Prime Minister, Melbourne. Albert began to sense that not only was she trying to influence his political views but that she had not realised the tricky constitutional issue behind an apparently unimportant question of domestic staff. He had no cause to love Tories (they had just cut down his income), but he was firmly of the opinion that the Crown must be neutral and the royal household therefore non-political. What he did not fully appreciate – he had far too little experience of England to do so – was the relative novelty of his first principle and the virtual impossibility of fulfilling the second. Melbourne inclined to think that the Queen should give way for the sake of peace, since all foreigners distrusted English liberals anyway, but she refused to yield, and confirmed Anson's appointment. Anson was in fact an excellent choice; he never attempted to influence Albert's political opinions and the two men soon became firm friends.

But so short and summary an account does less than justice to the delicacy and complexity of the dilemma over Albert's household which confronted the Queen and her ministers during the winter of 1839/40, or to the slender but vital differences between the rival points of view represented by Melbourne's experience and Albert's idealism. On 29 December 1839 Melbourne replied to an earlier letter from Albert which had drawn attention to the embarrassment which a wrong choice of household staff would entail and proposed to avoid it by choosing political neutrals. Too few neutrals exist, Melbourne replied (though he seems to hanker after more of them), and though he rightly warned Albert not to be mistaken for the leader of the Tories he failed to realise that his own suggestion that the household should have 'a decided leaning to the opinions of the present government' risked the opposite danger. 'The means of preventing embarrassment are in my opinion very short, very easy and very simple,' he wrote.

'The main and principal object is to avoid the reality, the appearance and the suspicion of anything like division of opinion between Your Serene Highness and Her Majesty. Public differences in the Royal Family are always *pro tanto* a weakening and diminution of the authority of the Crown. How much more must this be the case if any discrepancy should exist or be thought to exist between Your Serene Highness and Her Majesty. Your Serene Highness says truly that it will be demanded of you that "you should carefully abstain from party politics". It will be certainly prudent that Your Serene Highness should be considered as sanctioning and countenancing the policy pursued by the active Government of the Queen, however that Government may be constituted. I earnestly counsel Your Serene Highness to take your stand from the beginning upon this principle and never to depart from it. Your Highness will not suspect me of giving this advice because I am at present the Minister. I should urge the same if those who may be considered as my political opponents were at this moment in possession of the chief offices of state. I should apply the principle, which in my opinion ought to be the general guide of Your Serene Highness's whole conduct, to the formation of your household establishment. To compose your Household of persons who are neither themselves nor by their relations connected with political parties is impossible. So many neutral persons fit for the purpose do not exist and would form a strange assemblage if they could be found. Your Serene Highness's household should in my opinion be constituted of persons of rank and character, as many of them as possible members of neither House of Parliament in order to avoid them being pressed to change upon change of administration. But still with a decided leaning to the opinions of the present government, otherwise the conclusion will at once inevitably prevail that Your Serene Highness is adverse to Her Majesty's ministers and you will find yourself, in spite of yourself, taken up by the party in opposition and elevated to the part of leader of the Tories.'

He concluded with the advice that the appointments should be made before Albert came to England, so that they should not seem to be of his own choice but as having been recommended to him.* ˙

Albert's reply was high-principled and analytically clear – too clear to fit the confused realities of English politics, and he quite missed Melbourne's point about there being too few neutrals available. 'There are only two ways to settle the question,' he wrote to Melbourne from Gotha on 13 January 1840,

> '*either* the establishment is formed according to my views and wishes, and I then have a mixed household of Whigs and Tories, who remain with me during every administration in order to prove to the nation that I will belong to no party. As I form it, it stands or falls with me. – *Or* the establishment is formed according to the views and wishes of the ministry. In this case the household will be composed of persons wearing the ministerial colours in order to prove to the nation that I will always support the government of the Queen for the time being. This household then cannot be a permanent one, it stands and falls with the ministry who are responsible for it. A combination of both these systems as your Lordship argues is in my opinion impossible.'

Albert sent a copy of this letter to Victoria (she had already told him that 'nothing could be better' than Melbourne's suggestions), enclosing it with a far blunter one to her in which he mercilessly exposed the Prime Minister's inconsistencies. 'It contains no clear ideas and is self-contradictory,' he assured her; he could not at one and the same time take no active part in politics and countenance the government's activity, 'for "countenancing" is "activity" '; and if his staff were to have a 'leaning' to the government side but not change when the government fell, they would have to turn themselves from Whigs into Tories in an instant. It was all more than he could bear. He had written himself 'nearly blind' trying to make her understand, but would not try again: 'I declare calmly that I will not take Mr Anson nor anybody now.' The final blow came shortly before the wedding; without explanation or apology, and in spite of his protests, Victoria summarily appointed Anson and – evidently lacking the courage to tell him herself – let the news reach Albert in a curt note from Lehzen which contained more than a touch of insolence.†

* CAS 29 December 1839. Cf *Letters* I, i, 208 and Fulford, 48–9. Fulford, who evidently had not seen this letter, erroneously supposes it to have advised Albert to remain a Whig even when the Ministry changed: Melbourne was trying to maintain a much more delicate balance than that.

† Secondary to principles and personalities, but still of great moment to Albert, was finance. Parliament had cut his allowance severely, on Lord John Russell's unwarranted assurance that his household need cost no more than £7,000 a year, but the Queen was appointing a staff as large as that which more than a century ago had cost George of Denmark most of his far larger income. Albert knew that the first instalment of his allowance would not be paid until Easter, and in an attempt to

Some of his edginess was no doubt only the result of nerves, now that he stood right on the brink of the unknown (the wedding had been fixed for 10 February), some the consequence of loneliness and nostalgia for the Thuringian countryside amidst which he was living for the last time. The farewells as he left were overwhelming. He was invested with the Garter (brought over by Lord Torrington*) at a ceremony in the Ehrenburg Palace on 23 January and then had to shake hands with the entire population of Coburg before getting into his carriage. He almost broke down as the Mensdorffs and other friends, who had been galloping alongside, gave a final good-bye salute at the 'Last Shilling' Inn. When he reached London on 8 February he found that Victoria had been in no better shape than he, and confessed to bad temper brought on by pre-wedding nerves. But when, after a moment of shyness and hesitation, they embraced on the steps of Buckingham Palace, all tensions disappeared. She was delighted with his presents – four beautiful fans and a sapphire and diamond brooch – and the only jarring note to remind him of recent disagreements was the discovery that there were only two Tory names on the list of wedding-guests.

The next two days brought the usual crop of trivial incidents. Albert had to act quickly to prevent friction between mother and daughter, when Victoria was roughly brushing aside the duchess of Kent's superstitious objections to bride and bridegroom staying under the same roof before the wedding, by gently reminding his aunt that it had always been customary for the husbands-to-be of Coburg princesses to stay at Schloss Ehrenburg. To his relief, he found that Victoria had foreseen the ordeal to his shyness which a drive in public to the Chapel Royal at St James's on Sunday would cause, and had arranged for morning and evening prayer to be said privately at Buckingham Palace. After dinner that night they read over the marriage service together, using the prayer books which the duchess of Kent had just given them (Albert had noticed with surprise that Victoria had accepted hers very off-handedly only a moment after rhapsodising at length over a 'dear little ring' from the baroness Lehzen, her former governess, though without being able to realise the ominous significance of the contrast). But this was all they had by way of rehearsal for the tremendous ceremonial that

balance his budget vainly pleaded that some of the appointments be postponed for a few months and that he be allowed to have 'only enough gentlemen for appearance's sake'.

* Torrington, a friend of Lehzen and an early gossip-columnist, wrote under the title of 'your Windsor special', and was probably the source of many of the unkind and untrue stories about Albert in the early 1840s.

would take place next day – and that only because he suggested it – despite Melbourne's warning that the last public marriage of a reigning monarch (that of George III in 1761) had been 'the greatest confusion' for lack of foresight, and undignified from start to finish: 'we must make this different', he said but did nothing to ensure it.

Monday started badly, with a downpour of rain so heavy that it woke Albert, but the sun was shining weakly through the clouds by the time he stepped into his carriage at midday for the short drive to the Chapel Royal. The route was lined with cheering crowds, for the last three royal marriages (those of the Prince Regent in 1795, Princess Charlotte in 1816 and the duke of Clarence – later King William IV – to Princess Adelaide in 1818) had been celebrated privately and at night, so that the announcement that Victoria's would take place by day had been greeted with enthusiasm. In the Chapel Royal the lack of rehearsal began to make itself felt at once. No one had told Albert whether he was to sit or stand as he waited for the bride, or whether he should bow to the archbishop or ignore him, and Queen Adelaide only made him more nervous than ever when she kept on pointing out passages in the prayer book and instructing him in the order of procedure in a loud stage-whisper. Only the sombre figure of baron Stockmar, whose pew he could see out of the corner of his eye, helped him to keep his composure. Then everything seemed to happen in a rush. A flourish of trumpets heralded the entry of Victoria, leaning on the arm of the duke of Sussex (who, putting prudence before decorum, was wearing a black skull-cap as usual), a vision of loveliness in white satin and Honiton lace, Albert's sapphire brooch at her throat, her veil thrown back in the manner of royal brides. But the dignity of the procession was marred by the awkward gait of the bridesmaids. No one had bothered to find out whether twelve tall girls could carry so short a train, and they had unexpectedly found themselves forced to take mincing little steps to avoid falling over each other's feet. A plain lot, one of the wedding-guests thought them, their plainness only relieved by the groom's presents – Coburg eagle brooches of turquoise.

Albert made the responses in low tones, but the Queen, though pale, showed no trace of nervousness. The signing of the register brought a general slackening of tension at last, yet even here nothing had been properly thought out. The duke of Norfolk insisted that, as Earl Marshal, he had to sign first, but became so flustered that he lost his spectacles and kept everyone waiting while he searched his pockets for them. Afterwards Albert saw that the duchess of Kent was being left to hover alone on the fringe of the group (he had already noticed with indignation that in the chapel she had not been

41

given the precedence due to the bride's mother) so he bent down and kissed her warmly, hoping in some measure to make up for the Queen's neglect.

Those who had not been invited (among them Charles Greville, the diarist) consoled themselves by denigrating everything about the celebrations, saying that nothing would have induced them to attend 'a mere Whig party' like the wedding-breakfast or to stand in the rain and cheer as the newly-married couple set off for their honeymoon at Windsor in 'very poor and shabby style'.

Part Two
Frustration 1840-1842

3

'Only the husband,
not the master'

ALBERT returned from his honeymoon more in love than ever. Those two close days together had revealed a hundred endearing things about his wife which he had not noticed before. Her zest for life and her sense of fun amazed him, and her extrovert nature was already working wonders with his shyness and bolstering his self-confidence. However great the sacrifice, to be the one chosen to lighten Victoria's burdens and to smooth the path for her was worth a lifetime of toil and trouble, for he was far too realistic not to expect those 'thorns' to which he had referred lightly in a letter giving the news of his engagement to his friend Prince William of Löwenstein. There had been only one jarring note. Without consulting him, Victoria had arranged an impromptu dance on their last day, sending to London for her old partners, Lord Torrington and Lord Alfred Paget, young men of a kind Albert despised. Resentful that she could so soon forget that she had called their love 'a beautiful dream' which was to continue for ever, he was silent and ungracious to her guests, behaviour which sparked off a number of malicious and unflattering stories which it took him years to live down. He had yet to learn that to withdraw into his shell was not the way to deal with the high-spirited, volatile woman who was now his wife.

Long before they reached Buckingham Palace, he was consumed with apprehension. His youthful humiliations still rankled and the very thought that he might cut a poor figure in front of Victoria brought on an attack of shyness and nerves. Victoria, on the other hand, was returning from her honeymoon without having gained the slightest insight into her husband's complex nature. Unaware of the depths which it was impossible for him to reveal in so short a

45

time, she did not think that her marriage could present any problems. Did not love conquer all? Albert, she knew, was as much under its spell as she, so there could be nothing to fear. King Leopold and Stockmar had not opened her eyes; there had been no revelations, no warnings of her husband's bouts of depression, of his self-doubt, of his need for solitude and open spaces. They had not said a word about his dangerous habit of hiding his feelings; they had not lacked opportunities, but they had only used them to praise Albert's virtues, every one of which the Queen had seen for herself.

London was very gay that season and all the best fun centred round Buckingham Palace. There was never a dull moment for the buoyant Queen as she showed off her new husband : she had captured the handsomest man in Europe, who was madly in love with her and she wanted the world to witness her happiness. It never occurred to her that Albert might feel differently. He danced so well that she took it for granted that he enjoyed it all as much as she did. Galloping round the ballroom floor, Victoria light as thistledown in his arms, did indeed give him pleasure but he detested having to do it always in the company of strangers and night after night to the exclusion of everything else. And he hated being on show – the very thought was enough to make him self-conscious. All he asked was to share his inexpressible love with his wife alone, only thus could they become 'one heart, one mind'. He could see (as Victoria did not) how indifferent the palace dances really were. They were still the 'poor affairs' Greville had found them in 1838, badly arranged, overcrowded, with a band that never kept time, and lacking in dignity. There was no proper place for the Queen to receive her guests, no organised presentations, nowhere to sit and watch the dancing, for Lehzen filled the only place where this could be done in comfort – the gallery – with the families of the lower members of the household. To humour him, however, the Queen allowed Albert to organise a grand ball in May, with three of London's best orchestras, plenty of space for dancing and a throne for the Queen to receive her guests.

The late nights were hard to bear, for late nights meant late mornings. They had fallen into the habit of eating 10 o'clock breakfast, and this upset Albert's stomach and left him with a feeling of lassitude that he could not shake off all day. So nothing got done. He ought to have known what to expect; one night during the honeymoon he had described to Victoria the beauties of the sunrise over the Thuringian hills and in reply she had spoken of watching dawn break behind St Paul's – but of course after a night on the dance-floor. Unworthily he complained to his grandmother; 'lack of sleep', he wrote, 'is making me weary; it is difficult to bear'. Albert's inability to stand late nights has been taken for a sign that at twenty he was serious beyond his years and that marriage to this heavy, humourless young German destroyed the Queen's natural ebullience. The truth is that Albert enjoyed fun and gaiety just as much as the Queen, but of rather a different kind. He was clever at planning novelties and arranging charming little ceremonies that delighted and amused her, and gradually taught her to find enjoyment in things she had never noticed before. Her journal is a monument to his ingenuity; she thought each surprise more delightful than the last and received them all with excited pleasure.

In those first few months of readjustment Albert suffered from not having his wife to himself for more than short periods in the day. After breakfast together, followed by a short walk in the grounds, they separated – the Queen to attend to state business, Albert to find employment as best he could. Lonely and jealous that others had the right to be with Victoria though he had not, and even rather jealous of his brother Ernest (who was staying in the palace for the first three months of their married life – a curious idea of King Leopold's) he was hard put to it to find enough to do. Nothing tried his temper more than the free and easy comings and goings of the Queen's former governess, the Hanoverian-born baroness Lehzen, now glorified with the title of Lady Companion. After luncheon, Albert might be enjoying his wife's full attention for a change – perhaps teaching her a new song or playing softly – when the baroness would glide in and whisk her away to attend to some mysterious 'state business', leaving him kicking his heels and nearly choking with anger. At these times the piano was his solace; it was only Ernest who guessed at the turbulent feelings that he hid so expertly.

How different these two cousins, now husband and wife, were from each other! At this period they were as dissimilar as Victoria and Ernest were alike in the relentless pursuit of pleasure and their self-centred determination to have their own way. Many people who saw them together thought that Ernest with his dark Satanic features and his gay and confident air was a better match for the lively young Queen than the shy youth who, for all his good looks, seemed a very dull dog by comparison. It was England's good fortune that, mixed with the Queen's Hanoverian blood, there was a good dose of commonsense inherited from her Coburg forebears. Her romantic nature was affronted by Ernest's roving eye, and Stockmar had not been slow to drop hints about his familiarities with her young and pretty maids of honour. Besides, as she told her uncle

Leopold, she found Albert far handsomer. But was this enough? Lord Melbourne reassured her – it was as good a way of choosing as any. She had picked up a favourite expression of King Leopold's, 'marriage is a lottery' – but applied it to every marriage but her own. Hers had been made in heaven, a heaven that consisted of two good angels, her uncle and his confidential friend baron Stockmar.

While still at Windsor, Albert had been overjoyed to hear the Queen talking of placing their desks side by side so that they could work together. To help Victoria in everything was now the sole object of his life, and it therefore came as a shock to discover that work meant watching, sullen and resentful, while she struggled alone with papers that she barely understood and which he could have dispatched with speed; all he had to do was to blot them when she handed them over with the air of one conferring a favour. It was a sign of the Queen's immaturity, but Albert already suspected that Lehzen's baneful influence lay behind it. She had persuaded the Queen that love and politics did not mix, that the one drove out the other. Angrily, Albert complained to Ernest 'What does this woman know of love'?

It was not so much that he wished to meddle in English politics or that he felt himself better equipped to understand them (although there was a little of that in it too), but that to be ignored and made to feel inferior hurt his pride as a husband and affronted his dignity as a man. It showed all too clearly that Victoria did not trust him: her boxes were shut as tightly as her lips. He was necessarily at a disadvantage because he was living in his wife's home (an unnatural situation that the Queen understood with her head but not with her heart), but King Leopold and Stockmar must take some of the blame for his unhappiness. They had made no attempt to discuss his duties after marriage, but without any warrant whatever had taken it for granted that the Queen would make him her unofficial Private Secretary and had allowed him to believe that she would do so; he must become a 'walking dictionary' for the Queen to dip into. Yet now he found that he was expected only to pursue a life of pleasure and idleness which bored him to distraction. How he chafed, how he longed to assert himself! It was intolerable that he had no rights that were not granted to him by his wife and that (as he told Prince William of Löwenstein) he was 'only the husband not the master in the home'. So much in England was defined by law, yet Blackstone had not a word to say on the consort of a queen regnant.

Pride forced him to play the insignificant part allotted to him impeccably. At his first Drawing-Room as the Queen's husband he created a sensation with his good looks, his amiability and his assiduous care of his wife, whom everyone agreed love had transformed. Her manner to Tory guests was less brusque, her smiles not solely reserved for her Whig friends. Well aware of the Queen's hostility (Greville roundly condemned such impudence in 'a chit of nineteen'), the duke of Wellington grumblingly obeyed a summons to the palace. Expecting insults, he returned completely mollified by Albert's polite attentions. But he could not please everybody. Ernest's friends accused him of being stand-offish; why did he not come with them to play cards at White's or gamble at Crockford's? When he did not, society wrote him off as a prude. They expected to see fireworks the day Mrs Norton turned up at a Drawing-Room – did the Prince know that she had been Lord Melbourne's mistress? – and were astonished to see him single her out and talk to her pleasantly for some time. How little they knew him! The fact that, although innocent, this woman had endured the horror of a public examination in a court of law made him her champion at once; although he knew very well that there would be talk behind his back, this did not deter him for a moment.

To avoid seeming to hang about his wife's skirts when ministers called for an audience, he went hunting and shooting or for long walks with George Anson, as unemployed as his master. Although the relationship had started off on such a bad footing, Anson soon became Albert's prop and stay, a close and loyal friend from whom little was hidden. It had not been easy for the two men to get to know each other. The great obstacle had been Ernest's jealousy – he never missed an opportunity to vilify Anson, and continually reminded his brother that Anson had been 'thrust upon him', had a 'poor opinion of all Germans' and would 'isolate him from his friends' – and it was not until Ernest left London that friendship began to develop between them.

The old royal family showed their displeasure at the marriage by scarcely speaking to Albert and by being very touchy about their rights, particularly in the matter of precedence. The duke of Cambridge made his position clear from the start; he refused flatly to walk behind any 'young foreign upstart' and no one should make him do so. They were on safe ground here, he told the family, because he had it on good authority that there was 'nothing in writing', and off he went to Apsley House to consult the one man whose opinion no one would have the temerity to dispute. The duke of Wellington's answer put the old royals into a rage. Only a few months earlier, before the marriage, he had said that Albert would only take precedence in front of them 'over my dead body', but now he

decided that the Queen had a perfect right to give her husband whatever precedence she pleased; if Cambridge were wise he would not
let the family make difficulties. It is not quite true that 'common
sense prevailed' after this ruling, as Greville said, for they still took
every opportunity to make Albert look small. When he left a City
banquet early so that the Queen should not be alone to receive the
news of Princess Augusta's death, Cambridge referred in his speech
with many lewd winks to the new husband's eagerness to return to
'a very fine girl'. At a dinner given for the young couple by Queen
Adelaide, the duchess of Cambridge did even better; with a coolness
that Albert could not help admiring, she remained seated when his
health was drunk. The furious Queen retaliated by striking her son
George's name off her dance list. Two days later, the duchess came
across Albert at the head of a squadron of Life Guards in Windsor
Park, and put it about that he looked ridiculous trying to ape the
soldier and that he knew nothing of English drill and the English
words of command. Her brother-in-law the duke of Sussex had
already made a boorish fuss when his Garter banner in St George's,
Windsor, was moved one foot to make room for Albert's; in return,
Albert magnanimously persuaded the Queen to do what the duke
had long wanted, making his morganatic wife respectable by creating
her duchess of Inverness. The old royal family were still at it three
years later. At the wedding in June 1843 of Princess Augusta of
Cambridge to the Grand Duke of Mecklenburg-Strelitz, Albert only
prevented the King of Hanover from taking precedence over him by
roughly shouldering the King down the altar steps, and the Queen had
to outmanoeuvre him at the signing of the register by nipping round
the table, signing with her elbow on the book, and handing the pen
to Albert.

Only the gentle Queen Adelaide stood out against Cambridge's
bullying. She invited her niece and her new husband to her famous
children's party at Marlborough House, and dropped the Cam-
bridges. Sitting between the two queens Albert forgot his ill-humour
and laughed uproariously at the antics of the young dancers. The
day was oppressive and hot and that night he earned the Queen's
displeasure by falling asleep at the opera and missing two whole
arias of Grisi's.

Albert's musical abilities were becoming known, although he was
exceedingly modest about them. One morning Lady Lyttelton
heard through the open door of her room at Windsor Castle a beautiful chorale, superbly played, and discovered that Albert was trying
out the new organ specially built for him. When, later that day, she

ventured to ask him what he had been playing, he evaded the question and talked instead of the organ 'that first of instruments', never once mentioning that the music she had so much enjoyed was a composition of his own. In March 1840 he was invited to become a director of the 'Ancient Concerts' which had in George III's day been considered the height of sophisticated entertainment but were now going out of fashion. Although he knew very well that he was only asked because no one else wanted the job, Albert accepted and bravely set about planning a completely different kind of programme – Bach, Beethoven, Mozart, Liszt, Glück and Purcell – and hoped to induce Mendelssohn himself to give a recital. The Queen flatly refused to attend; people would only come to stare at her, and besides there was bound to be a lot of 'that tiresome old Handel'. Just before the wedding, Stockmar had warned him that the Queen could not be coerced but might sometimes be persuaded, so without telling her whose music she was going to hear, Albert took her to a performance of Handel by the Philharmonic Society, selecting the programme in advance himself. The evening was a huge success; Victoria loved it all and could barely believe that it was really Handel's music that she had enjoyed so much.

Albert got it into his head that he must be successful in everything he undertook; only in this way could he gain the Queen's confidence, but his belief in himself was often at a very low ebb. Besides, it was not easy for him to adjust to living with a strong-willed and emotional woman. Her tears unnerved him; he was willing to give up all that he had gained after a battle of wills, if only she would stop crying. Afterwards he could not help feeling resentful that she had gained her point by trickery. Every married man feels this at times, but his problem had an extra twist to it. Hitherto most of the women in his life had been elderly and had spoiled him atrociously; this was no school for dealing with a wife who could turn Queen the moment it suited her.

Those who were invited to the palace did not think Albert henpecked, but they did not think that he often looked happy either. There could be only one answer: the Queen was more in love than he. After all, Coburgers only married for ambition, but this one did not know what to make of his new status. The duchess of Bedford, the Mistress of the Robes, who had felt the lash of the Queen's tongue, got her own back by letting it be known that she had it from duke Ernest himself that the prince had had to be persuaded into the marriage and 'would never have enough resolution and firmness to control such a high-spirited woman'. The Tories, too, seizing the

51

chance for a stab at the young couple, put it about that the Queen was glad that 'the Prince's allowance had been reduced, since it gave her more power over him'. But he did not lack champions, and several ladies sprang to his defence: Lady Palmerston recognised the signs of true love and indignantly contradicted the rumours. Lady Lyttelton, the Woman of the Bedchamber, was one of the fortunate few who saw the lovers at their best, and often intercepted adoring looks between husband and wife; at a grand review she noticed that he had eyes only for the Queen as he rode past at the head of his regiment, and remarked that if he had been hunting, he had to find out where she was, before he changed. As Albert himself wrote to Ernest, 'I wish you could be here to see in us a couple united in love and unanimity. Victoria will now give up something if it is for my sake; I everything for her sake.'

With the uncompromising hardness of youth, Albert made it plain that he did not think his wife's friends worth talking to; they reminded him too painfully of his boring cousin Augustus, of whom Lady Lyttelton remarked that he said not a word at a dinner-party until bear-hunting was mentioned, after which nothing could stop him from holding forth on technical details. Even the household were silent at table except for remarks about the weather and tomorrow's drive. As a result intelligent people became tongue-tied when dining with the sovereign and assumed a vacuity that they would have been ashamed to show in their own homes. Even experienced men of the world caught the habit. Dining at Windsor in 1840, Guizot, the French Foreign Minister, was surprised to find that neither Melbourne nor Palmerston had a word to say beyond a few inanities; they did not touch on politics, yet a discussion of political affairs in a congenial atmosphere had been the object of the visit. King Leopold and Stockmar knew that the quality of royal conversation was poor, but had hoped that Albert's presence would be enough of itself to improve things. But the fault was partly theirs; they had so impressed the Queen, during her engagement, with Albert's exceptional erudition that they had terrified a young girl who already doubted her own capabilities, and made her dread competition with her husband. She had once confessed that when confronted even with people she knew quite well she could think of nothing to say; how could she now challenge a giant at his own game? Every woman likes a husband cleverer than herself, but not too much cleverer if she is a Queen.

As early as the middle of May Albert was asking Melbourne to help him raise the standard of dinner-table conversation by inviting literary and scientific men to the palace, for he had already found out that the Queen would not hear of it. Melbourne's laconic 'she will come round to it by and by' was cold comfort to a young man of twenty bored to distraction, having no one of his own intellectual level to talk to night after night. Under pressure from Leopold the Queen relented enough to invite his old friend Sir John Hobhouse to dine. Hobhouse was surprised to find how well-informed Albert was and how skilfully he conducted a conversation. The informality of the occasion charmed him too: after her own health had been drunk, the Queen jumped to her feet to propose Albert's, with a loving look which he found touching. Hobhouse was not particularly learned himself, but he knew all the most intelligent men in London, and this dinner-party marked the beginning of Albert's success in raising the intellectual tone of the palace. When Guizot next dined, two years later, he was astonished at the change which had taken place: the guests were congenial, the conversation lively and un-flagging, and the Queen played her part animatedly. The atmosphere was so relaxed (the chairs were more comfortable than before, there were bowls of spring flowers everywhere, and a warm fire blazed because it was a chilly evening) that Guizot found it easy to lay aside his role as statesman and discuss his historical study of the English Revolution of the seventeenth century with Albert.

At the end of February, duke Ernest (who had stayed on in England after the wedding) returned to Coburg, leaving the Queen in tears at the departure of this 'dear, good man, so beloved of us all'. In fact, the household saw Albert's father go with relief. Most of the Queen's ladies had suffered from his attentions, and Lady Lyttelton's eyes had to be everywhere to keep a watch on virtue. It had been hard work preventing even the merest whisper of his lecherous behaviour from reaching the Queen's ears. The household's habit of protecting the Queen harmed her more than it helped them. Sooner or later the truth always leaked out, shattering her carefully guarded illusions. Albert was the worst offender of them all, not by telling her direct lies (that would have shocked them both), but by leading her away from the truth because he was afraid of upsetting her. It was the worst mistake he could have made.

He had only himself to blame if the Queen misunderstood his manner to his father. On the morning the duke left for Coburg he went through all the conventional motions of regret that he knew were expected of him. In this way the demonstrative Queen did not realise that hers was the only genuine grief as, sobbing, she clung to 'dear Uncle's' hand. Albert never did anything to correct this erroneous picture of his father, and so when later he took her in his arms and told her tenderly that she 'made up to him for everything', she assumed that he was referring to the 'loss' of his dear Papa, whereas he was thinking of the many unhappy incidents in his child-hood which a loving marriage could wipe out.

On the other hand, his grief was real when his brother Ernest left at the end of May for a holiday in Portugal with their cousin, Ferdinand Kohary, now King Consort of Queen Maria. During his three months in England he had managed to drag the Coburg name in the mud (or, as Albert dramatically put it, he had given the Coburg reputation 'its death blow'). While under the Queen's roof, he had been laid low by an attack of venereal disease, which he had contracted in Dresden the previous year. Dr Clark, the Queen's physician, was called in and the cat was out of the bag. Albert took it very much to heart, and he begged Ernest to get cured before he married, otherwise he ran the risk of a 'sick heir, thus destroying your wife's happiness'.

Ernest could not go without the brothers prolonging the agony. On the last morning they were singing a duet together when all of a sudden Albert stopped and broke into the Bonn students' farewell song. 'Such things are hard to bear', he muttered, choking with tears, as he watched his brother's carriage disappear from sight. It was pure anguish to remember that the bond between them was loosened by his own happiness with another human being. If his behaviour appears over-emotional and extravagant, it must be re-membered that a strong natural attachment was increased by a feeling of something like guilt that he was forsaking Ernest. He knew that his brother was weak; what would he do without his protection? The Queen seemed not to need him as much as Ernest did. If she had asked for his help, even in a small way, this would have made up for the loss of Ernest's companionship and lessened his guilt. His unhappiness at Ernest's going left him too unresponsive to turn to good account the Queen's tender promise to do everything she could to repay him for the sacrifice he was making. 'I was hardly able to recover all day,' he wrote sorrowfully that night. But in three days the gloom had miraculously lifted, and he was off with George Anson on an expedition to the London docks.

He turned first to hunting as an outlet for his energies (riding for its own sake bored him – 'es ermüdigt mich so'). Since the Master of the Horse refused him a mount from the royal stables, he spent money he could ill afford on a horse which had taken his fancy in the park, wearing the owner down until he sold it to him. But could hunting not pay for itself if he kept a stud? Flush with the £3,000 annuity from Coburg which had just come in, he bought a thoroughbred mare and stallion and then, impetuously, the winner of the Ascot Gold Cup as it was brought in steaming and sweating after the race. Shortly afterwards, he set about repairing some of the royal stables which had fallen into disuse. Stockmar was horrified at recklessness reminiscent of his father, but Albert paid no attention because he had at last found something to occupy his mind. He wrote excitedly about scientific horsebreeding to Ernest and persuaded the Queen to go to Epsom races. Having been insulted by cries of 'Mrs Melbourne' at Ascot the year before, she hesitated at first, but was delighted when they received a rapturous welcome. This time it was Leopold's turn to protest, urging Stockmar to stop Albert playing to the gallery for cheap publicity. He even disapproved of Albert's riding about London, with only one equerry for company, to visit bookshops and artists' studios ('it does not do to get close to these people'), not realising that the serious purpose behind it was to meet his wife's subjects informally and, quite simply, to buy books and paintings.

One day, while riding about London thus, he and Anson lost their way near Piccadilly and suddenly found themselves in the slums. The contrast shocked Albert: 'Palaces and slums side by side'. What plans were there, he asked, for building houses for the labouring classes? Incidents like this served to reinforce his gloom at lacking a sense of purpose, but he was too proud to admit to Victoria that he was bored and unhappy. Instead he reverted to the habit of years, said nothing, and let her remain in a fool's paradise: a masochistic attitude that brought its own satisfaction. In some respects he had only himself to blame if he gave the wrong impression. He would dash upstairs the moment he returned from one of these expeditions, eager to tell Victoria all that he had seen and done, pouring out his impressions – 'are they so very wrong', he would ask, for he still did not know enough about England to be confident of his opinions and needed her reassurance. Of course the Queen was deceived. How could she guess that he was deeply disturbed about his future? At such moments they seemed close, but were really far apart. Once or twice he came near to blurting out his anxieties, but the fear that she might repeat them to Lehzen made him hold back. In turn, this made him hate himself for not trusting her and for not believing that she put him first.

His nature did not adjust easily to change: different food, climate, customs, even language – for he tried very hard to speak German as little as possible – took their toll, and there was always the additional strain of battling with hostility and the feeling that, as a foreigner, he was under a cloud. In November 1839, when he was first thinking how best to help Victoria, he wrote Stockmar a serious letter: 'I will not let my courage fail. With firm resolution and true zeal on my part I cannot fail to continue "noble, manly and princely" in all things.' Although this may sound sententious when translated into English, it gives some indication of the high principles with which he faced his new tasks.

At the end of March, Albert knew that he was to be a father. With her fear of childbirth ('the only thing I dread'), the Queen turned to him for comfort and reassurance. Her need gave him patience to endure uncomplainingly her tears at finding herself pregnant so soon, although it could not give him understanding. As a countryman, he looked on birth as natural and not to be feared; when Victoria's time came, it was her sufferings that unnerved him and not the thought that she might not survive. None of his relations had succumbed in childbed, while she was haunted by the tragic fate of Princess Charlotte of Wales.

Despite his youth and inexperience, he handled the situation with commonsense and kindness, singing and playing to her or reading aloud while she rested on her sofa. The coming child gave him the excuse to persuade her to spend more time in the fresh air of Claremont and less in smoke-filled London, which he hated because it made him sleepy and unwell; the country would not be boring once she learned how to live in it. Spring was warm enough that year to risk sitting out of doors in a sheltered corner of the castle gardens at Windsor, both of them sometimes sketching the same view for the fun of competition; Albert would keep ennui at bay by inventing all kinds of amusing games that appealed to the juvenile side of the Queen's nature – each would draw one half of a turret, and they would then put the two together and ask the household to guess who had done the right, who the left. When the sun went in, they would run hand in hand back to the warmth of a fire and an evening spent with music or reading, then early to bed. After a week, Albert looked better, felt better and said that he had not been so happy for a very long time. Almost imperceptibly the Queen discovered that the country held a fascination that she had never noticed before. Boring old drives took on a new charm if Albert rode alongside her carriage, breaking away every now and again to gallop ahead, 'leading the drive through every beautiful turn, which he knows as he does every tree'. Albert was in his element, relaxed and happy, calling her to look at that fine swarm of bees, those wild flowers or that curious tree. When his painter's eye was caught by some magnificent scarlet geraniums glimpsed through the glass of a conservatory, nothing would satisfy him until the

Queen got down from her carriage to see for herself. In his own way he was teaching her how everything grows in value when it is shared. Despite its sad associations, Claremont was a happy place. Albert loved it as a precious part of his uncle's youth and because in its beautiful and unspoilt garden he could dig and plant to his heart's content, spurred on by hopes and fears, haunted and yet calmed by thoughts of the marriage that had been happy there too, more than twenty years ago. But he loved Claremont above all because it was the one place that Lehzen detested; she never went there if she could help it – the pollen, she said, gave her hay fever and made her ill. He was determined to spend the Queen's twenty-first birthday there, in a style befitting 'a young wife and prospective mother rather than a queen', for there would have to be another celebration in London later on, 'among the world at large in a long and boring Drawing-Room'.

At Easter they received the Sacrament together for the first time. Albert took it for granted that they would follow his custom of withdrawing from society twenty-four hours beforehand, dining alone and spending the evening quietly together, and the Queen did not question it for an instant. She lay on her sofa listening to Albert playing a Mozart Requiem, which put them into a tranquil mood, at peace with each other and the whole world. Before they went to bed, Albert drew up a chair and read passages from a German devotional work and an article on self-knowledge. Next morning they saw no one but walked quietly in the garden, retiring to the Blue Room until communion in St George's Chapel at three o'clock. It was Christmas before they took the Sacrament again. This short time completely alone together was the happiest Albert had spent since his honeymoon; his worries and frustrations fell away, and he felt closer to his wife than ever before.

The Queen's pregnancy meant that he had her more to himself than usual; she no longer wasted time in Lehzen's room, but preferred to take drives with her husband in an open carriage every afternoon. The duchess of Kent had moved out of Buckingham Palace and was living just across Hyde Park at Ingestre House, lonely and sad. Victoria had been as determined to get rid of her mother from under her roof as Albert was to heal the breach between mother and daughter. Soon after the wedding he had tentatively raised the question of the plight into which the estrangement had thrown the duchess of Kent. The truth was that Albert liked having his aunt in the palace because hers was a friendly face in a world of strangers. He saw no reason why she should not stay; Victoria saw no reason why she should not go, and of course she had her way. As it turned out, however, the move brought advantages which Albert had not foreseen. What more natural than that the daily drive should take them past Ingestre House and that they should stop for a while and converse with Mama? Under her own roof, the duchess was less nervous and the Queen more kind. Yet it was not easy with a wife who sulked and pouted – did they have to go to Belgravia every day? Gradually he found that a cool stare and a surprised 'not go to see Mama?' was answer enough (never to argue when he was in the right was one hard lesson he had learned), and he soon persuaded her to invite her mother to luncheon or dinner several times a month: it touched him to see how pathetically grateful his aunt was for these invitations, taking him aside to whisper that she had not had so much attention paid to her for years. Thus a regular routine was established; wet or fine they never missed a visit to her and before long Albert realised that the the Queen was storing up items of news that might interest or amuse her mother, and was even impatient if they were late starting out.

Warm spring soon changed into hot oppressive summer and London sweltered in a heat wave; June was particularly heavy and damp with intermittent haze that hung over the city like a pall. On the morning of 10 June the Queen awoke feeling unwell. Albert postponed the drive until six o'clock, when they tried out a brand-new phaeton drawn by four beautiful grey and brown horses, all exactly alike, which Herr Meyer had recently bought for them in Germany. They had gone barely one hundred and fifty yards up Constitution Hill and were still between the palace wall and Green Park, with the horses already going at a spanking pace when Albert, who was sitting on the right, noticed a small misshapen youth leaning against the park railings close by. Suddenly a shot rang out, so loud that the horses shied and the coachman had difficulty in pulling up. 'Victoria had just turned to the left to look at a horse and could not therefore understand why her ears were ringing, as from its being so very near she could hardly distinguish that it proceeded from a shot having been fired.' Deathly pale, Albert seized the Queen's hands, asking her if she was all right – would the fright harm the unborn child? The Queen reassured him, and again Albert looked at the youth – standing now with his arms folded and a pistol in each hand – just as without warning he fired again. At first the crowd was too petrified to move; then someone seized the culprit and at once a tremendous commotion broke out, the crowds shouting 'kill him, kill him'. With no thought but for the safety of Victoria and her child, Albert ordered the coachman to drive on at once. Shocked at what had happened, the evening riders in the park closed round the carriage in protection and escorted it back to the palace through cheering crowds. Once safely indoors, Albert felt overcome; taking Victoria in his arms, he kissed her again and again, praising her courage and self-possession. With tears in his eyes, an aged palace servant said that the Queen was 'just like her grandfather', George III, who had never been known to turn a hair when fired at.

The assailant was soon revealed as Edward Oxford, a half-witted barman of eighteen. Public and press demanded instant retribution: 'hanging is too good for him', 'send him to Botany Bay'. Even responsible statesmen like Melbourne, Grey and Sir James Graham regretted the recent change in the law which had abolished the death penalty for the insane, but Albert surprised them by saying that on the contrary he welcomed it.

The popularity of the young couple soared directly after their escape, and this solved one pressing problem. From the moment that he had known of the Queen's pregnancy, Stockmar had been working behind the scenes to get Albert made Regent in case the Queen died in childbirth. By the time of the attempted assassination only one question remained: should he be Regent with a council, or Regent alone? The shooting and Stockmar's tact now persuaded Wellington to come out in favour of Albert's being sole Regent, and the Bill passed both Houses without opposition and was enthusiastically welcomed by the newspapers. The only objections came from the old royal family, and Albert took particular pleasure in telling Ernest how little ice they cut: 'You will understand the significance of this matter and that it gives my position in the country a fresh importance. Sussex moved Heaven and earth against it and declared it to be an affront to the rightful family.' It was a slap in the eye too for duke Ernest, who liked to maintain the fiction that the Queen kept Albert in his proper place – right behind her. Melbourne congratulated him warmly on the passage of the Regency Bill, going out of his way to tell the Queen that it was due entirely to the 'golden opinions' her husband had won since his arrival in England: 'Three months ago they would not have done it for him,' he said, 'it is essentially his own character.'

But their failure over the Regency Bill was not enough to daunt the old royal family. Led by the duchess of Cambridge, and with the connivance of Lehzen and the earl of Albemarle who, as Master of the Horse, had jurisdiction over the State Coach in which the Queen drove to open or close a session of Parliament, they asserted that Albert had no right to ride with her in the royal coach when the Queen drove in state on an occasion of this nature, or to sit by her side in the House of Lords. Victoria naively let this out, telling him that she had asked Melbourne to discover what Queen Anne's husband ('that infernal George of Denmark', Melbourne called him) had done nearly a hundred and fifty years earlier. 'Not George of Denmark again,' Albert replied coldly, deeply wounded by Victoria's inability (or unwillingness) to defend him, and bitter at seeing her hesitating to take his part. Why could she not remember who was Queen? How differently he would have acted were their positions reversed! A few days later they were at luncheon when a box arrived from Melbourne. Opening it, the Queen read the Prime Minister's letter; then, blushing deeply, said, 'I asked Lord Melbourne about the House of Lords, for I was very much concerned about it and I see George of Denmark went with the Queen. . . . I thought it had not been so, but I am very pleased. You will lead me in and sit there.' 'I don't mind about going there,' Albert answered in a low voice. But he did mind. In some elation he wrote to Ernest 'In spite of Lehzen and the Master of the Horse, I shall drive with Victoria in a carriage to the House and sit beside her on a throne specially built for me.' It was a feather in his cap when the duke of Wellington took the trouble to come to the palace to say how pleased he was to see the Prince in his rightful place. 'Let the Queen put the Prince where she likes,' he said, and made short work of the Master of the Horse : 'The Queen can make Lord Albemarle sit on top of the coach, under the coach, behind the coach or wherever Her Majesty pleases.'

Hints to handle the Queen more firmly continued to come from Stockmar, and Albert was only sometimes able to take them up. He would not let her stay by Princess Augusta's death-bed – no place for a pregnant woman – and whisked her off to Claremont. Another time he used the same tactics, but was sharply put in his place. A box arrived from one of the government departments, marked 'Sign immediately'. Albert was outraged at such rudeness and asked her to delay signing for a day or two. Instantly she was on her high horse – she would not allow interference, she knew that he was opposed to everything she did and there and then seized her pen and signed. Crestfallen, Albert felt that his hastiness had lost him all his recent gains. He might as well face the fact that he was of no consequence whatever and go back to learning constitutional law with Mr Selwyn of Lincoln's Inn, who at least valued his opinions and had commended the 'masterly way' in which he had grasped the intricacies of Hallam.

But he was too young at twenty to be unhappy all the time. Husband and wife shared a love of music, especially of Italian opera. They loved to sing and play duets, sometimes together and sometimes with Lablache, her music master, and although Albert's skill on the piano was far greater than hers, he was careful not to choose pieces that were too difficult. Apart from Shakespeare, the Queen had seen comparatively few plays; so, when Albert's cousin Victoire arrived at Windsor with her new husband the duke of Nemours on a private visit, Albert arranged for Charles Kemble and his company to perform a series of light plays at the castle, as well as *King Lear, Richard II* and *Twelfth Night*. On Melbourne's recommendation they all went to see *The School for Scandal,* 'the cleverest comedy in the English language'. The next night they were in the royal box at Drury Lane, the Queen and Victoire Nemours applauding Fanny Ellsler's wild and exciting tarantella until they lost their heads and threw flowers from their bouquets onto the stage. A performance at Windsor by the famous Astley tumblers (whom Albert had first seen in Coburg) was a surprise arranged for Victoire's birthday, and sent the royal ladies into ecstasies. When it was over, Albert went backstage and brought Mr Astley and his troupe to be presented to the Queen. Later the same evening he had the satisfaction of hearing the Queen tell Victoire that she had never enjoyed herself so much before.

The young couple proved to be the most congenial of companions. Victoire Kohary had been Albert's playmate at the Rosenau, and had married the duke of Nemours, one of Louis Philippe's sons, only a week after their own wedding. In a dispassionate way Albert admired her statuesque beauty, but she could not touch his heart or hold a candle to his own Victoria. While the two brides were being painted by Ross, romantically posed on a garden seat, Albert took Nemours off to the paddock to inspect the Arab horses which the Queen had now handed over to his care. He drew the Frenchman's attention to the neglected state of the grounds and asked for information about aquatic birds at Versailles (he was planning to have some in their own gardens), partly to cover up his lack of occupation and partly to avoid discussing politics, about which Nemours was far more knowledgeable than he. Forced at last to talk about the Eastern Question,* he confessed that he

---

* The 'Eastern Question' comprised a loosely-linked series of problems arising from the decline of the Turkish Empire. Some, like the struggle for Greek independence in the 1820s, grew out of the national aspirations of the Balkan peoples. Another arose in the 1830s when the Turkish province of Egypt revolted under Mehemet Ali and his son Ibrahim, France fished in troubled waters, and Palmerston intervened against them both to save the Turks in 1840. Underlying all was Russia's agelong aim to expand into the Mediterranean at the expense of the 'sick man of Europe' (as Czar Nicholas I called the Sultan of Turkey), which was the seed of the Crimean War.

found it 'dry as dust'. For what it was worth, it was his opinion that
the Ottoman empire was not yet done for; given a long period of
peace under the enlightened Sultan Mahmud II she could become a
force to be reckoned with again. Nemours took the opposite view;
he did not think much of the Sultan, Turkey was rotten to the core,
Egypt was the rising star, the Egyptian Pasha, Mehemet Ali, the
coming man. On one thing they were agreed – Russia must be
watched. With great daring Albert sounded him out on Thiers'
foreign policy, too pro-Egyptian and anti-British for his taste;
would it not be well if France were to join England in protecting
Turkey? Was it not the only way to prevent war? Smiling, Nemours
shook his head; he would not be drawn – at least one of the family
should be discreet. Albert, for his part, was discreet, not to say
secretive. Much as he liked Nemours, he did not yet know him well
enough to be sure that Nemours would not give an uncomfortably
candid picture of his situation to his brother-in-law, King Leopold.
He had already been inundated with advice which showed that his
uncle was very put out by the Queen's unforeseen obstinacy, and
he had been forced to read long descriptions of the king's expert
handling of his first wife. Apparently her nature had changed for the
better after only a few weeks of firm treatment by her husband!
It was hard to swallow stories like this, and he did not want to risk
a repetition.

In August King Leopold came to Windsor, bringing Queen Louise
and raising his elegant eyebrows at the frivolous life Albert was
leading. Had he nothing better to do than potter round the garden
and play with horses? Alone with his uncle, Albert poured out the
whole sad story. The King was sympathetic and not nearly as
pessimistic as he expected; it would all come right, he was sure,
cheering Albert very much by saying that he had been successful
in one quarter at least; Victoria was immensely improved. Queen
Louise, too, took him aside and said that the transformation was
amazing. Three weeks before, Victoria's half-sister, Princess Feodora
Hohenlohe, had paid them a flying visit and had told Albert the
same thing, but he had not dared to believe that it was he who had
brought it about.

More important things than Albert's affairs had been the cause of
Leopold's journey to England that summer. The anti-French policy
of the Foreign Secretary, Palmerston, was upsetting King Louis
Philippe so much that he had travelled all the way to Antwerp in
the heat, to catch Leopold before he sailed and beg him to intercede
with Victoria for him. England, Austria, Russia and Prussia had
let him down, the old man complained. In July they had gone behind

his back and signed a four-power treaty to preserve the sovereignty of Turkey; and because his government had been unwilling to suppress Mehemet Ali, England had turned hostile and the Czar had humiliated him by cancelling a state visit to Paris – 'it is not convenient this year'. Leopold was statesman enough to realise that Palmerston's partisanship was a political necessity while France's independence was political suicide, but he had an important stake in the quarrel that was raging that summer between England and France over Turkey. Albert, he knew, was very much taken with Palmerston, but he did not know whether they had discussed foreign politics or not. So after dinner one night he tested him by bringing up the subject of France and praising Louis Philippe: 'a more charitable man never breathed, he could say that from the bottom of his heart'. Sorrowfully, Albert had to assure his uncle that, much as he would have liked to help, he had no influence.

A week later the Queen came to Albert in tears. What would happen to Uncle Leopold if England went to war with France? Albert replied that he did not know, because he saw no papers, and comforted her by saying that he did not believe that Palmerston would risk war with France for a semi-barbarous people. Unnerved by Leopold's alarming letters, Victoria said that if he would find out for her, she would be glad for him to see all the papers at once. It was the first time she had suggested anything of the kind.

A talk with Palmerston, very willing to instruct, showed Albert how much he had to learn (Louis Philippe had behaved foolishly, and was now imploring England to come to his rescue) and taught him to admire the panache with which Palmerston handled foreign affairs. But Palmerston's cool audacity and the risks he had taken in ordering the fleet into Syrian waters in the teeth of his colleagues' opposition alarmed Albert; this first experience of 'gunboat diplomacy' quite took his breath away. And so when, after the crisis had passed, Palmerston received a letter from the Queen pointing out the dangers of taking risks with an unpredictable nation like the French, he could easily detect its real authorship. Though anonymously, Albert had written his first State paper.

Although it was his twenty-first birthday, Albert was homesick and full of fruitless regrets on 26 August: 'my birthday is over, but in a manner totally different from before [it was the first birthday he had spent in England] . . . Kurt, with his embarrassed congratulations in the morning . . . and good old Eos were the only familiar and accustomed faces.' As so often, the real cause of his depression was something quite different. A letter had come from Ernest in

Portugal cutting across his happiness like a knife. Ferdinand was every inch a king, Donna Maria a paragon of wifely compliance and virtue, it ran: 'Such an affectionate surrender is rarely to be seen. She knows nothing of obstinacy, moodiness, etc., and lives only for her family.' The tactless Ernest knew perfectly well, of course, that things were very different between Albert and Victoria. But even on that score, though he did not know it, the situation was now a little better; Albert could truthfully tell Stockmar that during the last three weeks Victoria had not once been hot-tempered and only twice had the sulks.

It was fortunate for Albert's bruised feelings that the week was a busy one. The Goldsmiths had chosen his birthday to admit him to membership (it was his first connexion with one of the London City companies) and a deputation came to Windsor Castle to see him take the oath and to lunch with the Queen. Two days later he was made a Fishmonger; the following day he became a Freeman of the City of London, and had to eat a lot of indigestible food at an enormous banquet in his honour. How he groaned! But he was pleased too, and a certain pride can be detected in the letter in which he described all this to Ernest, now back in Coburg, kicking his heels with nothing to do and feeling as he enviously read his brother's letter that life had passed him by. Albert was not above getting his own back!

In September he was given another small sign of public confidence – a seat on the management board of the duchies of Lancaster and Cornwall. In high glee he dashed off a letter to Stockmar full of this excellent news; he did not doubt that it would be welcome. Stockmar quickly disillusioned him. Did he suppose that he had married a queen only to become a petty official? There were plenty of them already, and he was 'wasting himself in dissipation of the mind on worthless affairs', a bad habit that could be fatal to 'one on whose faculties there are so many claims. I advise you to avoid going too deep into details which will only bewilder you. It is for you to give the impulse only.' The severity was undeserved (Stockmar could not expunge from his mind the erroneous idea that Albert was a replica of his mother, and too easily satisfied) and, feeling Albert's unhappiness, he soon relented. The Prince must not take his rebuke too much to heart; 'mistakes, misunderstandings, obstructions are always to be taken for what they are, namely a natural phenomenon of life which represents one of its sides and that the shady one. In overcoming them with dignity, your mind has to exercise, to train, to enlighten itself; your character to gain force, endurance and the necessary hardness.' Ruthlessly he warned Albert never to relax in 'logical separation of what is great and essential from what is trivial and of no moment, never to relax in keeping yourself up to a high standard – in the determination, daily renewed, to be constant, patient and courageous.'

Reading these sermons – for that is what they were in effect – one can sense the real but unnecessary concern that motivated the man. The trouble was in Stockmar himself; he would look on his Prince as something more than mortal. But Albert took everything in good part as a rule; trust and affection made him believe that there was no sting in these strictures. He understood Stockmar a great deal better than Stockmar understood him.

One thing the baron did understand however: he could not afford to allow Albert to lose confidence. Back in May, he had consulted Melbourne to see how matters in the palace could be improved. Reluctantly they concluded that there was no quick solution to the Lehzen problem (this was a change of heart for Stockmar, who had been chafing at Albert's inertia over it). The Queen admitted to Melbourne that her husband complained that she did not give him her confidence 'in trivial matters' – a curious understatement – 'and in all matters connected with the politics of the country'. She defended herself by pleading 'indolence', agreeing that she was at fault, but adding that for the precious time she and Albert were alone together she preferred talking of 'other matters'. Melbourne thought this very natural, but not quite true; he believed that the Queen was afraid of touching on controversial subjects with the Prince in case she spoiled the harmony between them – an idea which originated with Lehzen. With the sad experience of his own marriage before him, he told the Queen that differences between husband and wife were better aired, otherwise distrust was sure to follow. Stockmar's conclusions were blunter: the Queen was afraid of disclosing her ignorance and losing face in front of the man she loved – she had a bad habit, he knew, of not listening when the Prime Minister explained something to her and so would naturally not be able to discuss it with her husband. On the other hand, Stockmar had repeatedly weakened Albert's self-confidence, warning him that on many subjects he did not yet know enough to have a worthwhile opinion. If, therefore, he offered his advice and disaster followed when it was taken, it would not be asked for again and he would lose in the long run. But this, as Stockmar well knew, was to ignore the real source of the present trouble – Lehzen. Albert must have hidden his real feelings very skilfully, for even Melbourne did not realise that Lehzen was behind the Queen's lack of openness with her husband and that therefore she was the true source of his lack of confidence.

Early in the morning of 21 November 1840 the Queen awoke feeling unwell. Dr Locock and Mrs Lilley, the midwife, were called, but her child was not born until after a twelve-hour labour in which she suffered severely. Albert remained with her until the actual moment of the birth, supporting and encouraging her until, at a sign from Dr Locock, he retired behind a screen; there, waiting with the duchess of Kent, he heard his daughter's first cry. It was natural that he should have hoped for a son, but his disappointment lasted only until Mrs Lilley brought the baby to him, screaming lustily. One look, and he was captivated; regret vanished, never to return. It was the beginning of a father and daughter relationship almost without parallel. Two weeks later, already a doting parent, he was ashamed to be reminded that he had said that he would have preferred a son.

His first glimpse into the mysteries of childbirth had been daunting. The pain the Queen had endured so heroically sickened him; it cut him to the heart that he was helpless to alleviate it. He was one of the first to welcome the invention of chloroform, and he gladly allowed it to be administered to the Queen for the birth of their eighth child, Leopold.

Two hours after her delivery the Queen was sitting up, happy and eating with appetite. Albert was delighted but dumbfounded. 'It is hardly to be believed,' he wrote in real bewilderment to Ernest, 'that only a few hours before she lay in dreadful pain.' Although the Queen felt 'as well as though nothing had happened,' Albert followed Stockmar's instructions to the letter; she must be kept 'as calm as possible, so all political affairs must be kept from her.'

Light-hearted at the amazing fact that he was now a father, he swallowed a hurried luncheon, and dashed off at three o'clock to hold his first council, where he gave his consent for prayers of thanksgiving for the safe delivery of the Queen to be said in all churches. (Without consulting anyone he had prohibited prayers before the event as unnecessary and as liable to create apprehension in a woman in the sensitive state of pregnancy – a far more mature view than that held by Wriothesley Russell, a canon of Windsor, who tried to rush him into permitting them.)

Albert's first concern was to nurse his wife back to health; no one but he was allowed to carry her from her bed to her sofa, and he would come instantly when called for to do this. It was the same after the birth of each child, even though at great inconvenience to himself as the burden of work increased with the years, for he never grudged anything which could make up to her for all that she endured in bearing his children. While she was recovering he did everything possible to keep her amused. He read through a selection of

novels, opening up a world she had never discovered for herself –
for in her desperate efforts to bring up her daughter properly, the
duchess of Kent had banned all novels from Kensington Palace
on the ground that fiction was trash – and refused to go to the
theatre or opera without her, preferring to dine alone with his aunt,
a sacrifice very gratifying to a young wife. It was during these cosy
evening meals that the duchess unburdened herself and told him
a great deal about the past that he had not known before. The deeper
knowledge of her sufferings which he now gained hardened his heart
against 'a certain person'. Amongst other things, Albert discovered
that the duchess had a talent for composing. To surprise her he
tinkered with one of her forgotten military marches, and later on it
was always played on the birthday of the heir to the throne and came
to be known as the 'Prince of Wales quick-step'.

Driving to Windsor for Christmas, Albert refused to entrust his
child to anyone, but held her on his own knee. With the radiant
Queen by his side, he was filled with 'quiet satisfaction' (a favourite
expression to denote extreme happiness) that Providence had been
so good to him. This year his 'dear festival time' held a special
meaning – he was now the father of a family. This meant three
present-tables (the duchess was not forgotten), the Queen's magnificently decorated by Albert himself with a huge arch of laurel and
multi-coloured chrysanthemums entwined to form her initials,
which made her speechless with delight. An extra surprise was the
enormous tree, gay with candles and decoration, which he had had
sent from Germany.*

At Windsor, Albert was in his element, revelling in the beauty of
the castle, the magnificent trees, the river (where in summer he
loved to swim) and the quiet park where, free from prying eyes, he
enjoyed long gallops with the Queen. He gave the place his highest
accolade: 'I feel as if in Paradise in this fine fresh air.' But how
woefully neglected everything was! It cried out to be restored, and
he determined to answer the cry. That Christmas he made plans to
rebuild George IV's cottage (later Royal Lodge), which was still
delightfully pretty although tumbling down, and the temple on
Virginia Water, now in an awful state. If he did this well, he thought
he might be allowed to restore the grounds completely and make the
castle one of the show-places of England. If he were remembered for
nothing else, he would like to go down in history as the man who
made Windsor fit for a queen to live in.

* Albert may not have been the first to bring Christmas trees to England (in the
eighteenth century there was a huge one every year in the hall of Stafford House) but
he certainly popularised them.

67

4

'Everything I do
is for the Queen'

SOON it was 10 February again. Albert could hardly believe that they had been married a year and were parents. To mark the occasion the Princess Royal, now nearly three months old, was baptised in a room in Buckingham Palace with water from the same golden font which had been used for her mother twenty-one years before. The child was given the names Victoria Adelaide Mary Louise but was usually called Pussy or Pussette until, at seven years old, she thought herself too grown up for such a babyish name and became 'Vicky' for the rest of her life.

The Queen's pliable mood came to an end as soon as she was up and about again. But condescendingly she still allowed Albert to have his head over the arrangements for the baptism and the preparations for the banquet afterwards. She liked his idea of making this an occasion to show off the royal treasures, and allowed him to make any other innovation his inventive mind suggested. But on one point she would not be moved: no Tories must be present at her child's christening. It was to be an entirely private affair, and she would invite whom she pleased. She did not like Tories, would have nothing to do with plans to show that the throne was above party, and did not care a jot about being too scrupulously fair. Eventually she was persuaded to include just two Tories: the duke of Wellington and Lord Liverpool.

With this Albert had to be content. Yet long ago – only a month after his wedding, in fact – he had come to realise that Stockmar had not exaggerated when he said that the Queen was heading for disaster if she insisted on her partisan treatment of the Whigs. A letter from King Leopold early in the New Year had repeated the baron's warnings: he would not answer for the consequences if Albert delayed in showing Victoria the grave mistake she was making; the Queen's political education had been narrow, administered in tiny, easily-palatable doses by Whigs, for Whigs; she had lived in an atmosphere of such total Whiggery that if she was not careful she would find that they had lost her the throne.

Albert already understood the Queen's mind far better than either Stockmar or her uncle. The Whigs were her friends. If she withdrew her support she would be disloyal to them, to her Prime Minister and to dearest Lehzen. Although her character was by no means simple, it had simple overtones, and friendship was not a thing she could value lightly. This belief burned so strongly in her that it almost consumed her duty to country and throne. But the throne as Albert saw it was something entirely different; to occupy it was to occupy the highest position of trust in the land, and a monarch had but one duty, which was as clear as the water in the brook behind the Rosenau: to serve God and his country. His own opinion had been settled long ago: a 'Queen's party' had no place in the modern world, and a young woman who still held enough power to damage the monarchy beyond repair must not seem to lead one – it had already done her harm to be called 'Queen of the Whigs'. He laid most of the blame for this upon her advisers, who refused to listen to Stockmar's warning against showing the slightest trace of partisanship. In April 1840 Albert put on record his views about the English party system in the first of his many political memoranda, the forerunner of thousands of such papers.

'I do not think it necessary to belong to any party; composed as a party is here of two extremes, both must be wrong. The exercise of an unbiased judgment may form a better and wiser creed by extracting the good from each. The Whigs seek to change before change is required. The love of change is their great failing. Tories, on the other hand, resist change long after the feeling and temper of the times has loudly demanded it, and at last make a virtue of necessity by an ungracious concession. My endeavour will be to form my opinions quite apart from politics and party and I believe such an attempt may succeed.'

Gossip about the Queen's blatant parade of her Whig bias at her daughter's christening soon reached Coburg. Determined to make himself heard, Stockmar wrote Albert a scolding letter, unfairly blaming him for not controlling the Queen, and full of the foreboding that to exclude the Tories was inflammatory and might easily provoke party warfare. Albert ought to have known better: 'more havoc can be caused by offended feelings than by an earthquake.

The Prince must see that the Queen be more judicious in future.'

King Leopold put all his pent-up irritation into a letter from Laeken on 24 February. Albert felt very ill-used when he read pages of criticism of his alleged supine conduct. Why was he not doing more? Pride and obstinacy could be as ruinous as Victoria's silly behaviour. Did he not understand that it was his duty, as the husband of a Queen Regnant (by which of course Leopold meant the dominant partner), to re-establish the proper role of a constitutional monarch, a task for which his uncle had at one time thought him ideally suited? King Leopold was far too wise to give the impression of meddling in English politics, but as an uncle and as (in his own opinion) the only other constitutional king in Europe he felt he had the right to offer advice. There was more to his letter, however, than Albert could possibly realise. Leopold had never explicitly said that one of his objects in encouraging Albert's marriage to Victoria had been to assure small unprotected Belgium a strong and powerful ally, but this had in fact been the case; he had never been able to believe that a young and inexperienced girl could control Palmerston's anti-French proclivities and was convinced that Albert possessed the qualities which would enable him to do so. But now it began to look as if Albert could not even control Victoria: so he complained, and Albert, not understanding what it was all about, felt aggrieved, for he knew that he had done his best.

If he had seen the correspondence between Laeken and Stockmar in Coburg in March 1841 he would have been still angrier. King Leopold demanded to know why Albert did not 'insist on his rights'. If the Queen tried to shut the door in his face when she received her ministers, he should walk in boldly; if she locked her boxes, he should seize the keys; if she changed the subject when he expressed a political opinion, he should not give up but continue speaking: waiting to be invited was a lot of nonsense. He should assert himself more; it was the only way with a woman like Victoria. Stockmar's reply brought Leopold little comfort. Ever since he had left England relations between the young couple had been unsatisfactory. Nothing had changed for the better – except the royal stables, which were now grand beyond belief, but the money spent on this enterprise (Albert's Coburg allowance, in fact) was without rhyme or reason. Both men underestimated Albert's difficulties. Although they had once shown a sympathetic understanding for his plight, they were now impatient that he would not act out of character, throw his weight about and crack the whip – behaviour quite unthinkable to a man of Albert's temperament. Here they were very wide of the mark.

Yet they were right in guessing that Albert was unhappy and needed help. George Anson knew that Albert was downright miserable. In his kindly way he tried to keep up his master's morale by composing a paper in which he reviewed the progress made in eighteen months of marriage. He put everything in the best possible light, but Albert knew that there was no truth in the statement that 'the Court, from the highest to the lowest, is brought to a proper sense of the position of the Queen's husband', or in the assertion that 'the country has marked its confidence in his character by passing the Regency Bill . . . ministers treat him with deference and respect'. He could agree that art and science looked up to him as their 'special patron', but this really meant no more than lending his name to a few committees, not that either his services or his novel ideas were valued for their own sake. The real position was very different, as they both knew; nevertheless, Albert was grateful.

During the Queen's confinement, keys of the Cabinet boxes had been cut for him and every day he had diligently studied State papers, writing a note on each so that she could more easily keep abreast of events. At the time she had seemed grateful, and had even written to King Leopold to say what a help Albert was being. The slightness of the work had astonished him; there was scarcely enough to keep him occupied for an hour or two every morning. In December he confided in his brother how little there was (Ernest had seen her sighing over the cares of state): 'I have been carrying out all her duties, and have thereby convinced myself how little it is. I have made extracts from all the despatches, and there are not many of them, so that Victoria can bring herself up to date.' But now the Queen was up and about again, the keys were still on his watchchain, but what good were they without the boxes? His privileges, although not expressly withdrawn, were of no further use since the Queen made it plain that she could manage without him. This was all the greater shock because, soon after Vicky's birth, Lord Melbourne had made him very happy by telling him that the Queen proposed that he should henceforth see all foreign despatches 'as a matter of course.' But as soon as she was at her desk once more Victoria had deliberately forgotten all about it, and he was back where he started – unwanted, unemployed and depressed.

He was far too loyal not to be upset when King Leopold and Stockmar blamed Victoria for the sorry state of affairs. Victoria was a naturally fine character, he knew, and he felt she was being led astray by those whom she trusted. So he set about looking for a scapegoat, and cast Melbourne for the part; Victoria relied on him so completely that it was only natural for her to think his advice best.

Brutally Stockmar disabused him. The Queen had always been able to twist him round her little finger, and Melbourne had never succeeded in dissuading her from a course she was set upon; he had wanted the Prince to have his way about George Anson's appointment, for instance, but the Queen had overridden him.

Stockmar knew who was really to blame, but did not want to do Albert's detective work for him. He preferred that matters should unfold themselves in their own good time. It exasperated him that Albert was so obtuse that he would now have to act against his own better judgement and tell Albert in plain words since he seemed unable to see it for himself, that the Queen was too much in the pocket of her lady companion for her own good and certainly for that of her husband, who should be 'her friend and counsellor in everything'. Albert should long ago have realised how great a threat to Lehzen's security his arrival on the scene represented. A woman who had once been all in all to the Queen could not be expected to take with equanimity the intrusion of a husband into a home which she had long looked upon as her own, where she had reigned supreme since the accession and from which, she was confident, the Prince had no power to turn her out.

No one had ever questioned Lehzen's devotion to her young mistress. But over the years that devotion had become such an all-consuming passion that it had destroyed even her love for Victoria. She had battled her way to power by very dubious means, was determined that at all costs she would retain what she had won, and to this end she had endeavoured to make the Queen believe that love and politics did not mix. She had interposed herself between husband and wife and shared secrets that should have been theirs alone; she was thus insidiously corrupting both their relationship and the Queen's character, which, as Stockmar noticed early in 1841, was becoming less ingenuous than formerly. The canker was spreading from day to day; until it was cut out, they could never be really happy, although Albert had not yet been able to make her understand this.

In a mood of despair, Albert told Stockmar that 'Victoria takes everything about the baroness so much to heart, and feels she ought to be her champion'. Stockmar deplored so hopeless a tone; instead of 'shutting himself away' (a reference to Albert's habit of retiring to his room when things became too much for him) Albert should strike at once and get rid of Lehzen before she got rid of him. This was easier said than done; rather than crediting a boy of twenty-one with the authority of a seasoned statesman, Stockmar should have remembered the realities of a very difficult situation.

How was a newly married husband to break the bond which time had forged between the two women? Victoria's accession should have weakened it, her marriage should have broken it; instead, Lehzen had taken good care to draw it still tighter by making herself in effect the Queen's private secretary – and now tried to draw it tighter than ever by convincing the Queen that her husband, like her, should hold no official position.

Coming from outside the narrow confines of the Court, Albert could see (what even Stockmar for all his wisdom did not) the lowering effect of Lehzen's presence. Although the daughter of a Lutheran pastor, Lehzen was so ignorant that she once asked Stockmar whether immortal souls would be allowed to meet in Heaven. She was so snobbish that she undermined the Queen's trust in the Conservative leader, Sir Robert Peel, by dwelling on the fact that his father had made his money in trade. 'Nothing will induce me to send for that bad man Peel who behaved so wickedly': the voice was the Queen's, but the words were Lehzen's. The degrading effect of behaviour like this was plain enough to Albert when he saw courtiers showering the baroness with flattery and doing her bidding as if she were the Queen herself. It was surely wrong that distinguished visitors showed far more respect for her than for the Queen's husband, whom they barely noticed. He had been utterly taken aback when, not long after the wedding, he saw baron Brunnow bow low before her. But attentions to her favourite pleased the Queen and she flared up when Albert pointed out that they were most improper. Lord Albemarle, the Master of the Horse, had been 'a charming and reasonable man' until Lehzen reduced him to such a state of servility that he became little more than her lackey; it was really Lehzen who prevented Albert from riding the Queen's horses or keeping his own in the royal stables, although Albemarle issued the orders.

Perhaps Albert was wrong to expect defenders. But where were they to be found? This was what he hinted to Stockmar, for the truth cut so near the bone – that he was afraid to act because he feared that the Queen would not back him up. He longed to fight, but remembered Stockmar's warning to reserve his anger for the important occasions and not to waste it on trifles. This was the important occasion all right, the kind of situation Stockmar was supposed to be so expert at dealing with, but his own hands were tied and he was getting no help; he agonised and suffered, hurrying to Stockmar's room every evening with a face as long as his list of troubles. Secretly he blamed Stockmar for being so meek where Lehzen was concerned, yet could not bring himself to say so outright. How angry he would have been to know that in 1839 Stockmar had declined the Queen's offer of the private secretaryship on the ground that such an important position should not be held by a foreigner, for if he had accepted Lehzen would never have been able to get such a hold over the Queen.

Lehzen's all-pervasive presence had been a perpetual irritant to Albert since the wedding-day itself. He and Victoria had made a pact that day to have no secrets from each other, yet before long he was hiding a very large secret indeed – his desire to get rid of Lehzen. It was outrageous that on the first night of the honeymoon she had expected to remain in the bedroom next to Victoria's (the connecting door had been removed long ago), so that he had to have her bundled out before they could have any privacy.* He had caught her padding round the private apartments at night with the transparent excuse that it was her duty to lock up, but he knew that it was this spying of hers which fed the old royal family's spiteful gossip. Even their afternoon rides were ruined because the Queen insisted on slowing their pace to suit that of Lehzen's pony phaeton; Albert was glad to leave the Queen's side to canter beside the duchess of Kent's cob, reflecting cynically that Victoria had announced that 'Dearest Daisy shall stay with me always as my friend' in the same breath as 'Ma must go'! Their first serious quarrel had arisen suddenly one day when, maddened by jokes between the two women in what was almost a private language, he found himself hurling accusations at his wife; outraged, she would not speak to him for several hours, and he was more lonely and miserable than ever. Many of Albert's letters to Ernest in 1840 and 1841 contain acid references to the *Blaste* (old hag), which was what the two brothers called Lehzen. One of these letters has become widely known, but only because a piece of careless editing has made it seem evidence of Albert's romantic attachment to Victoria instead of a sarcastic comment on Lehzen's appearance: 'yesterday at table she looked most charming, very décolleté, with a bouquet of roses at her breast which seemed as if it was going to fall out.'† 'It made my

* It was not until August, and then only with Anson's help, that he got the door put back. 'I have managed to wall her out,' he told Ernest.

† Immediately before this sentence, Bolitho *The Prince Consort and his Brother*, p. 24, omitted 'the old hag has conceived a terrible hatred for you and takes you for the author of all ill. She said as much to Anson only yesterday' from the German text (*CA* 22 August 1840), but gave no indication that he had done so. In consequence the words 'yesterday at table she looked most charming' have always been taken (e.g. by Longford p. 145) to refer to Victoria (who is mentioned in the preceding sentence of Bolitho's version) instead of to Lehzen, to whom Albert was in fact applying them. The words have therefore been understood as a lover's doting instead of the scornful mockery Albert intended. The German original of the passage quoted above is 'Sie war gestern bei Tische gar lieblich anzusehen, ganz decoltiert und mit einem Rosenbouket im Busen, das unter Kleide herauf wollte.'

blood boil', Albert exclaimed, to encounter Lehzen emerging from the audience chamber, where he was not allowed, and it maddened him when she turned the maids of honour against him. The Queen denied that she ever did this and turned a blind eye to Lehzen's real shortcomings (as when Albert found that she had left confidential papers lying about in the Long Corridor at Windsor) because she knew that Albert was always on the look-out for faults in her favourite. He scored one success in the summer of 1840, and gained it by swift and decisive action. Buckingham Palace was so infested with Lehzen's toadies, the Paget clan ('the Paget club-house', the Press called it) and their mistresses, that Albert was shocked at the prospect of bringing up a young family in an atmosphere of such immorality. The Queen continually consulted Lehzen's pet among them, Lord Alfred Paget – affectedly, Lehzen called him 'son' and he called her 'mother' – who, Albert felt sure, had once presumptuously hoped to use Lehzen's influence to marry the Queen. Albert, on the other hand, found him insolent and offensive, and when one day he overheard Paget's loud remark that 'foreigners are inferior and Germans are dregs' he suddenly saw red. Enlisting the help of Melbourne, Anson and Duncannon (whose Commissioner-ship of Woods and Forests gave him authority over accommodation in the palace) he had got rid of the whole pack inside a month. It was 'a masterstroke', timed to perfection, which Lehzen – in bed with jaundice – was powerless to prevent. 'I have done it,' he crowed to Ernest, 'with Duncannon's help they are gone, and are not coming back.'

Albert's trust in Melbourne was growing. Jealousy had at first made him believe that Greville was right when he said that association with the Queen and her ladies had made Melbourne 'like a twaddling old woman', but his opinion began to change the day he heard him discussing the peculiarities of Anglican theology with evident learning. Now he would have been more inclined to agree with what Sydney Smith, abandoning his witticisms, told Croker after Melbourne's death: 'I am sorry to brush away the magnificent fabric of levity and gaiety he has reared, but I accuse our Prime Minister of honesty and diligence; I deny that he was careless or rash.' Stockmar had encouraged Albert in this direction by showing him the shrewd and businesslike letters he had exchanged with the Prime Minister since the Queen's accession, letters which belied Melbourne's outwardly indolent attitude to politics. Gradually, Albert came to appreciate how hard the Prime Minister laboured for the monarchy, and to realise that Melbourne's fatherly style of conversation was designed to flatter the Queen by making her seem clever, whereas his own unfortunately only managed to draw attention to her ignorance. It was partly for this reason and partly because, although unhappy himself, he was quick to sense Melbourne's happiness in guiding the Queen, that he put aside his own feelings and did nothing to change the familiar routine whereby Melbourne still rode next to the Queen, still sat at her right hand at dinner and still had his favourite chair placed next to hers afterwards, just as it had always been before Albert and Victoria were married.

Nevertheless, as he grew older Melbourne was more and more inclined to leave things alone to get better by themselves, and although he sincerely wanted Albert to have his due he did nothing to secure it for him and lent no support to Anson's attempt to get him 'started on a right course'. Without Melbourne's active assistance, progress was bound to be slow.

It is not true, as has often been asserted, that Melbourne belonged to the Lehzen clique; he only worked in harmony with her when it was expedient to do so, for they were totally incompatible. He found her intrusions insulting because of her ignorance and presumption. She was, for instance, in the habit of arrogantly dashing off little notes, signed simply with a bold 'L', giving her orders to the Prime Minister as if he were no more than her page. (Two of these, undated, in the Stockmar-Wangenheim papers, tell Melbourne and Stockmar to be 'ready at 3.00 to accompany Her Majesty on a drive'.) Her confidential manner towards the Queen was a constant source of annoyance to him. The untidiness of her person grated on him, and he found her habit of chewing caraway seeds quite disgusting (Stockmar believed that she did this to take away the smell of alcohol from her breath). As Prime Minister, Melbourne naturally enjoyed certain privileges in dealing with the Queen, but of course always showed the greatest respect towards her; Lehzen, he observed, accepted privileges but showed little respect.

Recurrent money troubles, made worse by constant demands from Coburg, further disturbed Albert's peace of mind during these difficult first two years of marriage. Half his English allowance was eaten up before he saw it by the salaries of his staff, obligatory subscriptions to societies and patronage of one kind and another. He had begun to invest his Coburg annuity in horses and in repairs to the stables at Cumberland Lodge but was compelled to divert some of it back again to meet the insatiable demands of the two Ernests. A servant-girl in Dresden claimed that his brother had got her with child (Ernest denied it), and Albert's soft heart made him guarantee her an allowance. Bills poured into Buckingham Palace after each of Ernest's many visits, and they had to be met lest the monarchy's reputation suffer. Beagles and racehorses were in turn Ernest's passions, and since both could be best bought in England, Albert was left to pay. When he remonstrated, Ernest pleaded with crocodile tears that unless his rich brother helped him poverty would force him into an unwanted marriage with a Russian Grand Duchess. To cap all, duke Ernest asked Albert to secure an allowance for both of them from Queen Victoria. This was the one thing Albert would never do. By mid-November his irritation boiled over: 'I am sending papa's letter back to you again', he wrote to Ernest, 'the principles he declares in it are really most deeply hurtful. Always money, money, money.'

One evening in the early spring of 1841 soon after Stockmar's return to England from a short visit to Coburg, Albert rushed into his room in a fury: he had just caught Lehzen in the nursery dandling little Pussy on her knee. Instead of showing his indignation, Stockmar brushed Albert's complaints aside. He was preoccupied with worry that the exhausted Whig ministry might soon collapse – Melbourne had just told him that it was 'exposed to all sorts of casualties' and that he saw 'no guarantee anywhere of its stability'. If Melbourne fell, Peel was the only possible successor, and this in turn meant the risk of another Bedchamber crisis* and, as Stockmar foresaw, untold damage to the monarchy. Albert had never understood what all the fuss over the Queen's ladies had been about. To him this bunch of women had no place in a man's world, they were merely her personal friends. Her only mistake had been to choose them from a single party, but he knew that she was as ardent a Whig as ever and would resent every attempt to 'sell' Peel to her. Both men saw that there was trouble round the corner.

Stockmar tried to remedy Albert's inexperience of English politics by explaining to him the difference which was growing up between the two parties. Too arrogant and self-satisfied to see that they had shot their bolt of reform and were now without a purpose in government, the Whigs were on the decline. By contrast, the Tories under Peel's leadership were developing a professional approach to politics which made it certain that they would win the next election. It was

* In 1839 Peel had made it a condition for assuming the Prime Ministership that the Queen demonstrate her confidence in him by dismissing all Whig ladies of the Bedchamber. She refused to sacrifice personal friendship for a party she detested; Peel therefore refused office and Melbourne remained Prime Minister. *See* Appendix I.

therefore essential, Albert felt, that he should get to know their leader; yet how could he do so without drawing undesirable attention upon himself? Peel was never invited to dine at the palace, and Albert had not set eyes on him since their brief encounter in June 1840. While he was still puzzling over the problem, Melbourne brought them together at a Trinity House dinner in February 1841. The warmth of Albert's handshake instantly melted Peel's shyness. The vital first contact had been made, but how was he to persuade the Queen to ask Sir Robert to dine? With tact and patience, he managed it in a week or two. The dinner passed off well. The Queen hid her antipathy to Peel better than she had done on the last occasion (as long ago as 1838), so that Peel could relax instead of freezing into immobility. Alone with him for a moment, Albert managed to convey his intention of supporting him when the time came, and directly afterwards pleased Stockmar by saying how delighted he had been with the meeting. Things had moved faster than Stockmar had dared to hope, and before he left for Coburg in April (leaving Albert feeling strangely bereft. He went to Stockmar's room one evening, only to find the curtains drawn and dustsheets everywhere; as usual, the old man had crept away without a word of farewell) he impressed the immensity of his task upon Albert, playing ruthlessly upon the younger man's sense of duty. There must be no hesitation, no giving way, if the Queen refused to listen when he brought up the subject she so much dreaded, a change of government: 'You must do it, and it is your duty to your Queen and country.' He kept up the pressure when, back in Coburg, he saw signs of the old weakness, apathy: he had long detected in the Prince 'a tendency to rest satisfied with mere *talk*, where *action* is alone appropriate', and was determined to eradicate it. But, as Albert later pointed out, he could hardly have much interest in politics if he never saw state papers, or help Victoria if she told him nothing, but he showed the requisite energy by quickly following new instructions to arrange confidential talks with Peel through Anson.

Anson was already preparing a memorandum about a possible change of government when Albert stirred himself to action and added the heading 'A Ministry in Jeopardy' in his own hand on 4 May. Five days later, on Albert's orders, Anson began a series of four conversations with Peel which soon resolved the whole difficult problem of the Queen's ladies: Peel would not insist on his right to remove them if the Queen would undertake that they would resign if there were a change of government. Honour was satisfied all round, and Albert's tact seemed to have removed a constitutional obstacle

Melbourne once thought Peel's 'doggedness and pertinacity' might make formidable.

While these discussions were going on Cabinet and Queen had been considering whether or not to dissolve Parliament. Melbourne was against it, warning Victoria that the result might be a House 'smack against' the Crown, and that he did not want to expose her to such an affront. 'This is very true', she wrote in her Journal, but she was nevertheless pig-headedly set on a dissolution as a last hope of keeping Melbourne in office. Mindful of King Leopold's description of dissolution as a card to be kept in reserve up the monarch's sleeve, Albert agreed with Melbourne and felt that the crown should not interfere on behalf of a doomed ministry.

On 12 May, at Melbourne's insistence, Albert was present for the first time (to his own surprise, he was not nervous but 'cool, calm and collected') when the Queen received her Prime Minister in the Blue Room. The Queen cut Melbourne's opening words short with the furious interjection that Albert had pressed Sir Robert on her without mentioning other names, and proposed Wellington in his place. Wearily, Melbourne repeated once more that she ought to make up her mind to send for Peel – Albert noticed with compassion how tired and drawn the old man looked – but roused himself to emphasise that above all she must let the Prince assist her.

The Queen wanted time, not Albert's help. Albert, however, was more than ever uncertain whether he possessed her trust; it had crossed his mind to take Melbourne's hint and assume the lead, but he hesitated to do so because he sensed that he must first obtain her co-operation; if there was to be a lasting partnership between them it must rest on a solid foundation. So he was sick with dread as he waited for Melbourne to break to her the news of the Anson conversations and to reveal his part in them. To his great joy, she felt no resentment at the 'liberty' he had taken and the deception he had practised, but was touchingly grateful. To match her 'exemplary conduct', Albert decided that his household as well as hers should change with the administration and in addition that those members of it who were also MPs must either give up their seats or resign from his service. But although, now that the tension was broken, he could joke to Stockmar that the Queen was not sulking and they were still on speaking terms, he somehow felt that they were not out of the wood yet. His instinct was right. The Russells, the most powerful of the Whig families, were at work behind the scenes to persuade the Queen that for her ladies to resign on a change of government was to imply that she had been wrong in 1839 and was being bullied into submission by Peel now. In mid-June Lord John

Russell got his brother the duke to write to the duchess of Bedford (who was one of the Ladies of the Bedchamber) a letter which, as intended, Lehzen showed to the Queen. In effect, it raised all over again the whole tiresome question whether those appointments were personal or political.* Albert exploded, particularly at Lehzen's part in the affair – 'it bears the stamp of her cunning and malicious mind' – for he knew that Peel must have his way this time if a serious constitutional crisis was to be avoided. He explained to Victoria in no uncertain terms that she would put the monarchy itself in peril if she denied Peel now; but it put him somewhat out of countenance to discover that, when she shortly decided to dissolve Parliament, she took almost everyone's advice except his; and it was still not clear whether she would send for Peel when the House reassembled if – as seemed likely and proved to be the case – the Tories were returned with a majority at the election.

In June, shortly before the dissolution, they went on a round of country-house visits which the Queen had arranged without consulting Albert. They stayed mainly at great Whig houses – Panshanger, Woburn and Brocket – and this made Albert think that the tour had been instigated by Lehzen to boost Whig prospects in the coming election. Taking the painful lessons of the past to heart, he had made two conditions before accompanying the Queen: that the house-party for Ascot must contain several Tories and that Lehzen remain at home. He managed to make the Queen believe that the baroness's first duty was to look after the Princess Royal, and this put him in excellent spirits: 'The moon is on the wane', he wrote gleefully but prematurely to Ernest. But the high spirits did not last long. On edge lest politics were discussed in his presence, he was shy and not at his best; the incessant rain depressed him, as it always did, but gave him an excuse to stay indoors and examine the treasures in the Whig picture galleries: 'such Raphaels, Correggios, Rembrandts and Carlo Dolcis', ran his letter to Ernest, 'and so many excellent English painters I have not seen before, though how badly hung most of them are, often in dark corners so that their beauty is obscured.' (The following year, on a similar tour, he persuaded the Queen to look at the pictures with him, so that he could explain them to her, for he did not like to see her at a loss for an answer when her opinion was asked. Lady Lyttelton suspected that she preferred to go alone so that her ignorance should not be shown up; Albert, on the other hand, knew that he was still ignorant about many things in England, and was always asking questions and eager to learn.)

* For details *see* Frank Eyck, *The Prince Consort*, pp. 26–9.

A visit to Tory Oxford for an honorary degree followed, but he was hissed and booed by the undergraduates because he was in the company of Whig ministers. At luncheon afterwards he sat next to Lord Ashley, the famous reformer, and turned the occasion to good account by asking Ashley (an intimate of Peel and other Tories) and his wife to join the royal party at Ascot. Ashley accepted, but somewhat unwillingly, for he had always sneeringly called Ascot 'the annual exhibition of the sovereign to the people' and was anxious lest hobnobbing with royalty at a race-meeting might tarnish his image and be 'productive of mischief to the slight influence I may have in the world of carrying forward measures and designs of good to mankind.' Albert, blissfully unaware of his guest's discomfiture, was delighted to be seen in public with a man of such high reputation.

The late summer months of 1841 were among the most decisive and important of Albert's married life. The Queen's parting from her adored Prime Minister would be painful; he knew that she would need all the comfort he could give her, and that the way he handled events would make or mar their future, and was therefore determined that in her distress she must turn to him and no one else. He must preserve 'infinite calm', for by self-control alone could he hope to counter Lehzen's excitability, which often caused Victoria to do in haste things which (he suspected) she later regretted although she would never admit as much to him. At this critical moment he felt desperately alone, and longed for the comfort of Stockmar's presence. There was no one like him, no one could take his place – small, wizened, coolly analytical and infinitely dependable as he was. 'Stockmar is the only person we could need,' he wrote to Ernest, deliberately using words that included the still aloof Victoria, 'and yet he has not said whether he will come.'

5

'Let us be better and everything will be better'

(passage often quoted by Stockmar from
Coburg hymn-book)

By the end of August they were at Claremont seeking peace and
quiet. Albert's first real taste of politics had been enjoyable, but the
nervous strain of acting against the Queen (although in her interests)
had taken a lot out of him. After the anxieties of the last weeks he
needed the tranquillity of the country to restore his sense of proportion.

His first experience of a rowdy English election was more unpleasant than exciting to one of his peaceful nature, but a ceremony
after his own heart was the handing over of the seals of office on
3 September; for the Tories had won an overwhelming victory and
Peel became Prime Minister. As the Queen (winning everyone's
admiration by her control) received the oath of allegiance from each
new minister, Albert stood a little behind and to the side, quietly
self-effacing, yet silently giving encouragement. William Ewart
Gladstone, a member of the Cabinet for the first time, was struck
with the solidity of the royal partnership and sensed the power that
was to leave its mark on history. Four days earlier the parting from
Melbourne had been emotional and exhausting, for Albert too felt
his departure keenly. During the summer, in a burst of frankness,
Melbourne had told Albert that he thought the Queen so ill-
equipped and immature that she needed advice on every subject.
Now, with his hand on Albert's arm, he turned to the Queen and
said quietly that he was leaving her well cared for, since she had the
Prince to advise and guide her, and begged her to put her trust in
him: 'He understands everything so well and has a clever, able

head. You said when you were going to be married that he was perfection, which I thought a little exaggerated then, but really I think
now it is in some degree realised.'

More than he knew, Albert had come to lean on Melbourne.
Subconsciously he had looked to the older man to interpret the
Queen to him. Consequently it now seemed quite natural for him
to invite Melbourne, through Anson, 'to continue to him and to the
Queen his advice and assistance, especially on measures affecting
their private concerns and family concerns.' In the delicate constitutional situation of the moment this was the height of folly, and
presents a strange contrast with the political insight he had shown in
recent weeks. As it happened, Albert and Peel became at once so
friendly that his correspondence with Melbourne lapsed almost as
soon as it began, although the Queen continued hers for some time.
Their letters were innocuous enough, but Melbourne allowed himself
an occasional indiscretion, as when in January he passed on Palmerston's opinion that Aberdeen, the new Foreign Secretary, was weak
and timid, and likely to let the country down.

If Albert was soon on good terms with Peel, the Queen had not
yet made her peace with the new Prime Minister. But he had
magnanimously made it with her; he told Greville that she had
behaved perfectly to him and that 'he considered it his first and
greatest duty to consider her happiness and comfort.' In spite of
this, she almost precipitated a serious incident shortly after Stockmar's return to England. Early in October she let her longing overcome her scruples and, without consulting Albert, invited Melbourne
to Windsor. Albert was at first uncertain what his attitude should be,
for he had never seen any harm in correspondence with Melbourne,
but Stockmar sensed danger and at once took charge of the situation.
Stockmar saw that so public an endorsement of Melbourne's privileged position was an affront to a Prime Minister who had been only
a month in office, particularly as Melbourne had just established
himself as leader of the Opposition by a strong speech in the House
of Lords. It was unfair to involve Albert, he felt, because 'he had
not the means to cause his opinion to be either regarded or complied
with', and was certain that the Queen ought to meet Melbourne
'only on the terms of general society in London.' Stockmar sent Anson
to him with a sharp memorandum, and it was perhaps the suggestion
in it that Melbourne's own sense of right should tell him what to do
which prompted his exclamation 'God eternally damn it. Flesh and
blood cannot stand this.' Stockmar had cut uncomfortably near the
bone, since Melbourne seems to have at any rate envisaged the
possibility of using his position to Peel's disadvantage, but Stockmar's

intervention was enough to ensure that Melbourne did not go to Windsor and that everything passed off smoothly.

Albert was delighted to find that Peel's views on both foreign and domestic affairs coincided with his own – peace and good relations with France on the one hand, mild tariff reform to stimulate the economy on the other. But he was so new to English politics that it shocked him when the Radical, John Bright, attacked the new income-tax as 'a vile system of slavery designed to maintain the corn laws'; and it is easy to understand why he told Ernest that Cobden and Bright were 'two of the most irresponsible men in England'. It was fortunate that it was from Peel that Albert received his first serious instruction in politics, and doubly fortunate that he soon came to like and admire him so much. Their temperaments were so compatible that the difference in their ages (they were twenty-three and fifty-four respectively) did not matter at all. Peel's idealism attracted a young man with high ideals himself, who was glad to follow a leader of such outstanding integrity and devotion to duty, and together they formed a working partnership which neither cost the one his neutrality nor made the other a mere reflection of royal opinion. Albert respected Peel's refusal to compromise on matters of principle, and found him a man 'determined either to stand or fall by his opinion. In such hands the interests of the Crown are most secure.' He soon came to realise that there were few men as willing as Peel to put nation before party, while his own failure yet to understand the virtues of the English party system made him even too inclined to overrate this quality in the Prime Minister.

He particularly admired the professional efficiency with which Peel ran the Cabinet, and consequently began to model himself on Peel, for 'what better man can be found to guide England through a time of such grave crisis?' More ominous for the future was his lavish praise for the way Peel tirelessly superintended every government department himself – for a refusal to delegate and the exhaustion which overwork induces were the undoing of both men. It was a pity that the Queen did not see that the similarities between them and their almost father-and-son relationship might have this consequence, but still continued to lament the fate which had deprived her of Melbourne and quite failed to realise the good fortune which had given her husband the desire to learn from a mentor willing and able to instruct him in the art of ruling a constitutional country.

Albert showed no rancour for the part Peel had so recently played in restricting his allowance. Nor does Peel seem to have regretted his action, but it was to make some amends for past lack of generosity that he asked Albert to head a Royal Commission on the Fine Arts which he set up in 1841. Albert tried to utilise this to introduce fresco-painting into England, but met a great deal of ignorant opposition, and the most valuable consequence of his chairmanship was that it made him better known in political and artistic circles and was, in particular, the origin of his friendship with the painter Charles Eastlake. One reason for the ineffectiveness of the Fine Arts Commission was a conflict of purpose: Albert did not realise that he had been appointed merely to be a figurehead, and that initiative and action on his part were unwelcome. It was a situation which was to recur again and again. Leopold and Stockmar were critical of this latest activity; to mingle in the art world was, in their opinion, to downgrade himself and to mistake his true function of assisting the Queen in her constitutional duties (and 'assist' had a very special meaning to them; 'govern' might have expressed it better). Instead of rejoicing that his shyness had been reduced and his confidence increased by presiding over the Commission, they scolded him for wasting his time. Albert was shaken to discover that they intended him for a purely political rôle and wished him to avoid everything inconsistent with their narrow views of his proper field of activity.

He had shown his interest in wider areas of national concern by a speech on the Slave Trade in June 1840. Because it was his first public speech, he was exceedingly nervous and learned by heart everything he intended to say; the extent of his anxiety can be gauged by his telling Ernest that it was a 'very long speech', whereas in fact it took less than five minutes to deliver. It was not so much what he said, however, as the fact that he said it, and to a packed meeting in the Exeter Hall, which lent the occasion significance. His speech was crisp, clear and concise, and his audience was astonished to realise that he cared deeply and sincerely about injustice. Again, the contrast with the old royal family was striking; the last two kings and all the royal dukes loved speaking in public, but they rambled on unintelligibly.

Peel's speeches on slavery took the same strong line, and Albert noticed how different was Palmerston's lukewarm attitude. It was as well that he did not know that in 1839 Palmerston had voted against the Abolitionists and had announced that flogging slaves did not worry him at all. This was the second occasion Albert had had for distrusting Palmerston, whose conduct of the Opium War with China confirmed his feeling that Palmerston was a man of too few principles and too much cynicism. Nevertheless, on the surface

85

their relations continued to be good. At the end of July 1841 he and Victoria spent a most agreeable four days with the Palmerstons and the Cowpers at Panshanger. Seen in the bosom of their family, the Palmerstons were at their best; despite 'reservations', Albert felt himself drawn to them both. Palmerston's marriage in 1839 to his old flame, the widowed Lady Cowper (a sister of Melbourne's) had vastly amused the newly-engaged Victoria and Albert – 'they make up a century between them', he had written laughingly at the time. How much Albert could relax and enjoy himself in an English country-house atmosphere is shown by the letter he wrote to his hosts after the visit: 'I hasten to fulfil my promise in sending you the scripts of my composition, begging you not to consider them as the work of an artist but as the result of a leisure hour's occupation. I was so much pleased with your eldest boy's verses that I felt tempted to put them to music, and I venture to add this song to the rest.'

Aberdeen's appointment to succeed Palmerston at the Foreign Office in the autumn of 1841 marked a big change in Albert's life which was not at once discernible; it raised his spirits to find that here was a second politician with whom he felt himself in complete rapport. Aberdeen was an elderly man with a tragic past: his first wife and three young daughters had died of consumption, misfortunes which touched the heart of one who had so recently become a parent himself. Suffering had not made Aberdeen bitter or soured his view of life. In their very first conversation Albert learned a great deal about the new Foreign Secretary, notably that he abhorred violence and war and would always try conciliation first. To work with Aberdeen was to work with a man who had none of the dark and dismaying recesses of Palmerston's mind. Aberdeen possessed that quality which the Queen and Albert appreciated above all others – he was safe; and they were never tempted to say, as Albert did of Palmerston 'Someone ought to tell him to resign', although Victoria took a long time to forget that Aberdeen had criticised her behaviour in 1839.

From Albert's point of view, however, Aberdeen possessed one supreme quality: he treated the Queen and her husband as one. Were the doors opening at last? Victoria was certainly becoming more willing for Albert to act for her, and raised no objection when Peel gradually developed a habit of dealing with her through him, and it was increasingly plain that her interest in politics was declining while his own was growing. All the same, he wondered whether it was a real change of heart or whether, under the new regime, she was finding it too difficult to shut him out. In the hope it would prove to be the former, he drew his links with Peel and Aberdeen ever tighter. Aberdeen, incidentally, introduced him to a totally new interest: by following the disputes over slavery and the North-West Frontier he became more aware of the New World and acquired a life-long interest in it.

After this promising start, however, to Albert's chagrin progress once again slowed down. A couple of despatch-boxes disappeared on the way from the Foreign Office and were eventually found, gathering dust on Lehzen's desk.

This was very nearly the last straw. Albert longed to snatch the keys that dangled so impudently from the chatelaine at Lehzen's waist, and one hot night that summer his irritation burst out into complaints about the 'low patronage' which made the Queen's Drawing-Rooms like a cattle-market. Victoria perfectly understood what he meant and flared up at once, and he dared not risk more scenes because she was pregnant again. But he realised through this incident more clearly than before how Lehzen was the real brake on his progress, and from that moment he was certain that he had to get rid of her or be prepared to accept for ever a secondary position in Victoria's confidence. His mind was made up, and he determined to take action against Lehzen as soon as the baby was born. Meanwhile, without consulting Victoria, he invited Ernest for another visit, making the excuse that he needed Ernest's advice about some songs he had composed, but only as a cover for the loneliness that he still sometimes felt when deprived of his brother's company. One morning, shortly before Ernest was due, Victoria burst into his room white with rage and shouting that Lehzen had just told her that Ernest had insulted her on his last visit, three months before; if he could not be more respectful, he should never stay with them again as long as he lived. As she collapsed on the sofa in tears, the truth suddenly dawned on him: she was afraid of Lehzen. The realisation chilled him. His wife afraid of her own servant! For the first time he fully understood why she had never given him her complete trust, and why he had been so miserable. But his hands were still tied by her condition, and her tears distressed him deeply. The only thing he could do was to put Ernest off at once, telling him the reason: 'the fear that you might stir me up against her during the next month would completely take away the trust which she must have in me so that I can exercise a good influence. Don't send me any answer to this.' The secrecy, and the scribbled postscript 'a drowning man clutches at straws' makes clear how the 'good influence' was to be exercised: against Lehzen.

That autumn a piece of good fortune – though he could claim some of the credit for it – gave him for the first time evidence against Lehzen outside court circles. During the spring he had used his influence with Count Bülow to get Prince William of Löwenstein posted to the Prussian Legation in London (he had clashed over this with Ernest, who favoured another candidate and wrote him an abusive letter). Keenly as he anticipated the arrival of this old friend ('another door is open to me, and one that is congenial in every sense'), Albert can hardly have expected to learn so much from him about Lehzen's past. Prince William's father had been a friend and confidant of the duchess of Kent, and his son was able to tell Albert the inside story of the plots and intrigues in Kensington Palace before Victoria's accession. It was a saga of malevolence, jealousy and hate.

Briefly, the duchess of Kent was neither strange nor possessive, but simply a lonely and penniless woman who tried to bring up a wilful girl as well as she could on the chance that she might one day be Queen, and kept her away from the Court only because of its immorality. Sir John Conroy, the Comptroller of her household, had never been her lover, as had been rumoured; so foolish a mistake was not in her nature. The charge that she was harsh and cruel to Victoria was a calculated lie of Lehzen's. Lehzen had got rid of the duchess's lady-in-waiting, baroness Spaeth, because she was too fond of Victoria, using Conroy as a stalking-horse, and had then turned against Conroy, persuading Victoria to dismiss him. With these two out of the way, she had found it easy to widen the gap between mother and daughter. Lehzen had been behind Victoria's harsh treatment of Lady Flora Hastings.* It was Lehzen who had put it about that King Leopold was afraid of his sister† and who, by working on the poor judgement of George IV and William IV, had ensured that the duchess was never invited to court, never consulted, and ignored by her own daughter, while she herself came and went freely. The furore over Conroy had obscured Lehzen's evil machinations, making her position unassailable and the duchess's eclipse total by the time of Victoria's accession.

The pieces of the puzzle now began to fall into place. Albert's long-held belief that it was the duchess of Kent who had formed the better parts of his wife's character and Lehzen who had corrupted

---

* Lady Flora Hastings, an unmarried lady-in-waiting of the duchess of Kent, was for some weeks in 1839 suspected of being pregnant, to the great scandal of the court. Later she was discovered to have a stomach tumour, from which she eventually died.

† Albert knew that it was not her fear but Leopold's selfishness, and wrote in 1861 'Mama would never have fallen into the hands of Conroy if Uncle Leopold had taken the trouble to guide her.'

it was confirmed by Prince William's revelations, and further corroborated by others who had good reason to know the truth and no
axe to grind: Lady Sefton, Lady Portman and Lady Ashley give
the duchess all the credit. Lehzen may have been a suitable governess for the untalented Feodora (the duchess of Kent's daughter by
her first marriage, whom she was originally engaged to teach) but
there is no evidence that she was qualified by knowledge or discretion to instruct a future queen, and much to show that she was
not. Stockmar, for instance, suspected that she encouraged Victoria
to drink because she was so fond of wine herself, and noted with
undisguised disapproval how much the young Queen drank at
dinner: 'A Queen does not drink a bottle of wine at a meal' ran one
of his little notes of admonition. What particularly enraged Albert
was the way Lehzen claimed undeserved credit for her pupil's
knowledge. 'She was praising herself for all she was worth,' he wrote
at about this time, 'by showing what a thorough education she has
given Victoria.' He had heard her give accounts of the Queen's
literary tastes which bore no relation to reality, and had found
Victoria far less well-read than his cousin Lynette Reuss-Ebersdorf –
who had been very well educated although not destined to be a
queen – and many other German girls. He had even started to
instruct Victoria himself, but gave it up six weeks before the confinement on Stockmar's orders. Anxious that too much stimulation in
this delicate state should not bring out symptoms of the madness*
he always feared she might inherit from George III, Stockmar
forbade study along with his favourite three Ps – pork, port and
passion.

Public rejoicing at the birth of an heir on 9 November 1841 was
greater than might have been expected. *The Times* called Victoria
the 'model of a female Sovereign' and even accorded some praise to
Albert, whose own interpretation of this unexpected popularity was
that the stricter moral life of the court was becoming known and
was welcomed.

For the first two days of the Queen's confinement her boxes were
not delivered to Albert. Irritated at this omission, he spoke to
Aberdeen, who corrected the mistake at once, and thereafter sent

---

* For the last thirty years of his life George III was intermittently subject to
attacks of what was then believed to be madness, and his son George (subsequently
George IV) was Regent for long periods at a time. It has since been discovered that
George III suffered from porphyria, a deficiency disease which causes symptoms
closely resembling madness. Stockmar's fears were therefore not unreasonable at the
time (although he laid too much stress on the dangers), however unfounded they are
now known to have been.

him the nightly reports on Parliamentary debates. Albert sum-
marised the most important papers, but was astonished to find that
Victoria often fell asleep while he was explaining them to her. Anson
also noted this decline of her interest in affairs even after she returned
to normal life; he put it down to the cares of motherhood, Albert
to an increased confidence in himself. Its first practical consequences
had been manifest just before the birth of the Prince of Wales over
the choice of a new Governor-General of India. She favoured Lord
Fitzgerald, while he preferred Lord Ellenborough because of his
superior knowledge of the country and its problems. Victoria meekly
gave way, and before she could change her mind Albert informed
Peel of their decision. It was the first time she had yielded to him on
an important matter; a small beginning, but to Albert a promising
step forward, which increased his self-assurance and helped to give
him the courage to disagree with those older, more experienced and
supposedly better informed than himself.

The court moved to Windsor for Christmas and the New Year.
Victoria arranged for German music to accompany the festivities,
in the belief that it would make Albert happy; in fact, he did not
suffer from homesickness half as much as she imagined, and the
woebegone look he sometimes wore was due rather to present
grievances than to regrets for the past.

As soon as he heard that the new baby would be heir to the throne,
King Frederick William of Prussia had hinted that he would like to
be a godfather. The royal parents were delighted with the idea, but
it raised a delicate problem at that particular moment. Only a month
earlier, a joint Anglo-Prussian Protestant bishopric had been established in Jerusalem by the two governments. Most of the initiative had been Frederick William's, but although the motives of both
countries were mainly political (to establish some kind of foothold
in Turkish territory), there had been a good deal of criticism from
the High Church party in England. Albert had been involved in the
affair as president of the Church Missionary Society, and Stockmar
now pointed out that it would be undesirable for him to arouse
public antagonism again. King Leopold took the opposite view – to
invite Frederick William might wean him away from Russia and
bring him more into the western European circle – and so did
Albert, for the complementary reason that a Prussian alliance might
be useful to England against France. They had their way, but
Frederick William's eccentric behaviour at Windsor, and his evident
instability, made it certain that their schemes would come to nothing. The christening did Albert good in two small ways, however;
his new lighting scheme at Windsor was much admired, and his

neat solution of a delicate question of protocol at the service won enormous praise.*

The Princess Royal had been ailing since the autumn, and the more everyone tried to reassure him that there was nothing really wrong with her, the more alarmed Albert became. He had no faith in Sir James Clark, whom he had only reluctantly accepted as his medical adviser, for Clark was uncomfortably like their incompetent family doctor in Coburg; he always told the Queen what he knew she wanted to hear, and Albert suspected that he took a rake-off from the firms which supplied the expensive medicines and diets he prescribed. Moreover, Stockmar, himself a physician, had warned Albert of Clark's incompetence. The cause of Pussy's ill-health, Albert became increasingly certain, was slackness and ignorance in the nursery. The room was kept too hot, because Mrs Southey, the superintendent, was anaemic and suffered from poor circulation, and refused to allow the nurse, Mrs Roberts, to contradict her. Worse still were the constant intrusions of Lehzen, who had no place in the nursery but whom he often found gossiping with Mrs Southey over a roaring fire. He was powerless to prevent Lehzen's interference, and he hated the way she breathed caraway seeds all over Pussy as she nursed her. As the child's health failed to mend, he became really frightened and blamed Lehzen for fears which were magnified by the wicked rumours in London that the little girl was blind and too delicate to live long, and by the letters of a madman threatening the lives of both children. As recently as last August, there had been a chance to remove Lehzen; Stockmar and Melbourne had both advised Albert to use the change of government as an excuse to persuade the Queen to get rid of her, but the opportunity had been let slip because Leopold – who had always been Lehzen's champion and was staying at Windsor at the time – could not face the embarrassment of seeing her dismissed.†

Before long Albert's fears for Pussy and his hatred of Lehzen precipitated the final crisis, but only by bringing on a dreadful quarrel between himself and Victoria. He had no sooner taken Victoria to Claremont for a much-needed change in January 1842 than they were recalled by an urgent message from Stockmar;

* Was the Prussian Minister to be regarded as in attendance on his Sovereign and placed near him, or lower down in accordance with his rank in the diplomatic corps? Albert averted something like an international incident by proposing that ambassadors and ministers be placed after Knights of the Garter and members of foreign governments.

† At the height of the Conroy affair, Leopold had even tried to get Lehzen naturalised so that she could attend Privy Council meetings and become Victoria's public as well as her private adviser, a foolish plan foiled only by Stockmar's intervention.

Pussy was worse. Rushing straight to the nursery directly they reached the palace, Albert was terrified to see the change in her, and was gripped by the appalling thought that she must have consumption and would die like so many of the English nobility's children. His muttered criticisms of the nursery made Mrs Roberts flare up; Victoria flew to her defence and accused Albert of wanting to drive her out and as good as murder the child. Albert turned ashen with horror, shouted 'I must control myself', and banged out of the room. The note he wrote to Stockmar a few minutes afterwards read 'I went quietly down the stairs and only said I must have patience'; Stockmar's disbelief was shown by the exclamation-mark and the even larger question-mark which he pencilled in the margin. Later that night Albert's anger burst its bounds and there was a violent scene between husband and wife. Victoria, distraught, flung 'I wish I had never married' at him. Albert countered, when as usual he ran to Stockmar for consolation, with the charge that this quarrel, like all their others, could be traced back to Lehzen, who undermined Victoria's will. They would never be happy, he stormed, until Victoria saw the old hag as she really was. He could bear his own sufferings with patience, but he could never allow his marriage to be wrecked or his children's lives endangered by the same evil influence which had done Victoria so much harm. Victoria could not herself be blamed for 'the mess we are in', for Lehzen had brought her up to be completely dependent upon her. The only way to break the spell was to separate them.

What began as anxiety about a child's health (Pussy soon recovered, of course) had now become transformed into a renewed quarrel over Lehzen – Albert was right when he saw Lehzen as the source of everything that came between him and Victoria – and it was their worst quarrel yet. For the next day or two the only contact between husband and wife was by letter; Stockmar had taught them that they would avoid serious quarrels if they put their feelings on paper, but by doing this he had also prevented the one thing which could clear the air – a confrontation. Victoria 'forgave him his thoughtless words of yesterday' and begged him not to believe all the stories he heard. Albert dismissed this as Lehzen's work, and told Stockmar that he could not answer for the consequences if he were goaded in the same way again: it had been a shock to discover how irrational and violent he could become. The Queen had evidently not weakened, and he was determined not to do so either until the cause of all the trouble had been removed.

When Stockmar saw that Albert had had all he could stand, he decided to bring Victoria to her senses sharply. Further quarrels like this, he pointed out in a carefully drafted letter, could only inflict the greatest misery upon them both and would make his own position at court untenable. He banked (quite rightly, of course) on her realising that she could not do without him, and felt that he could therefore speak bluntly without risk to himself. Next morning there were signs that she was beginning to give way, for she wrote a note explaining that she often said stupid things without meaning them and that she discussed only very little with Lehzen nowadays, following this with another note swearing that Albert was her only confidant. Full of remorse as soon as he read this, Albert began to weaken, but Stockmar held him firm : there must be no compromise. Albert had his reward when Victoria capitulated a few hours later, accepting the condition that Lehzen must go.

Albert had won; but though the battle had cost him much in anguish and nervous exhaustion, it ended up by bringing husband and wife closer together in a deeper understanding of each other. Albert was generous in victory, and when the reconciliation occurred he willingly offered his share of concessions, promising to try to break the secretive habit of years, and to be more open about things that upset him. He made the promise sincerely and with a full heart, but it is doubtful how far he was ever able to carry it out. He never realised how large a part of himself he always kept hidden even after this quarrel was over; many of his deepest feelings would always go unshared, except now and again in later years with his eldest daughter.

Two questions call insistently for answers before the Lehzen affair can be finally dismissed.

Why did Stockmar not act sooner? On the one hand, the relationship of trust in which he stood towards both Victoria and Albert would have made it very easy for him to do so; on the other, to leave his intervention so late meant risking the Princess Royal's life, although he examined her carefully himself, concluded that there was nothing seriously wrong, and agreed with Lady Lyttelton that too rich a diet had caused the mischief. What excused Stockmar's delay in his own judgement – and surely in a later and more impartial judgement too? – was that it was better for the tribulations to last a little longer until they produced a crisis which would put a final end to all that Albert had endured for the past two years. Not until Albert's exhaustion compelled him to find a quicker solution would he intervene himself: to have put pressure on the Queen at an earlier stage to get rid of her favourite would have been to do Albert's job for him and so to have lowered his prestige in his wife's eyes. 'I am only the husband, not the master, in the house,' Albert had written to William of Löwenstein soon after his wedding. Both Melbourne and Palmerston had predicted that Albert could not be kept down for long because he was a born leader, but only Stockmar knew that he would not steel himself to the decisive step, break through the obstacles and really become master until his peace-loving nature was pushed beyond endurance and he was forced to rouse himself to strong action. Anxiety about the health of the child he adored gave him the necessary impetus.

Secondly, why did Albert detest Lehzen to what seems an abnormal extent? Stockmar loathed Lehzen, but he was careful not to prejudice Albert (or Leopold either) against her, content to wait until the pressures built up so much inside Albert that he was forced to act. Albert's detestation went deep, far deeper than the usual explanation that he was maddened by Lehzen's muddle and incompetence. Albert saw something in Lehzen which has since been overlooked: that her well-known lust for power, love of intrigue, downright dishonesty and wicked gossip's tongue hid a far more dangerous quality – an unlimited capacity for hatred.

She hated the duchess of Kent because she was her adored pupil's mother, with claims on the young princess which she could never match, and for this she consigned her to outer darkness for ten long and lonely years. She had even tried to go further and banish her for ever by putting it about that Victoria disliked her mother because she had taken Conroy, her Comptroller, as a lover. When the story reached Buckingham Palace it broke up the life-long friendship between Queen Adelaide and the duchess and estranged her from King William, who should have been her natural protector. Lehzen hated baroness Spaeth as soon as she saw that Victoria had become too fond of her mother's lady-in-waiting, and got rid of her by making it seem that she left after a quarrel with Conroy; it was probably true that Conroy opened the door, but it was Lehzen who pushed the baroness through.* Lehzen's starved maternal instinct was fed on love for Victoria, whom she came to look on as her own child, and whom she would share with no one, particularly not with a husband. When Albert turned her out of her accustomed bedroom next to Victoria's, when his desk had replaced hers next to Victoria's in the Blue Room, her malevolence knew no bounds. Finally, Albert was all but certain that two mysterious and very nearly fatal accidents which he had suffered could be explained by her desire for revenge and her determination to remove him. On 20 April 1840 he was given a horse to ride to a meet of staghounds at Ascot; it bolted

---

* After Lehzen's departure for Germany, baroness Spaeth returned to serve the duchess of Kent until her death.

and threw him against a tree, and Albert discovered later that every stable-boy knew it to be so unmanageable that only its own groom could safely ride it. On 9 February 1841 the ice gave way while he was skating in the grounds of Buckingham Palace, and he had to swim for several minutes before he reached the bank. Several of his palace staff knew that this particular spot was dangerous, and Lehzen must have known too – Victoria did not skate, she regularly did – yet no one had told him. The coincidences were too remarkable not to be suspicious. It had to be war to the death between them, and he had to win.

Victoria seemed to regret her former governess very little. The royal train passed through Bückeburg (where Lehzen had settled) on its way to Berlin when Victoria and Albert visited Vicky in 1858, and a small black-clad figure stood on the platform waving a handkerchief, but the Queen did not order the train to stop. Next year they met Lehzen briefly in Coburg. Albert had a few minutes' conversation with her, and was astonished to find that he felt nothing at all.

Another and happier result of Lehzen's departure was that the Queen and her mother were reconciled at last. The past was wiped out when Lehzen, with her baggage of twenty years, drove out of the courtyard never to return. Not long afterwards, Albert was entirely successful in reconciling his aunt with the dowager Queen Adelaide. It was not easy, however, and Albert told Ernest that it had required 'the skill of a diplomat and the delicate touch of a tightrope walker, but patience and perseverance have won the day.'

Part Three

Apprenticeship 1842-1851

6

'The first link
has been forged'

THERE was now no reason why Albert should not become the Queen's unofficial private secretary; indeed, he soon became a great deal more than that, for to her surprise she found it easy and natural to lean on him. 'I depended on him for everything', she wrote in her widowhood, 'and had absolutely no will of my own. He told me when to go to bed and when to get up; he ordered all my actions, all my thoughts.' There is of course some exaggeration in this. She was too strong-willed to be a puppet and his dominance could not become complete until he gained more experience, but with Lehzen's departure there began nineteen years of leadership by Albert.

He had first to overcome her reluctance to accept Peel completely. She complained that his shyness made her shy and that a man who handled her so badly must have bad judgement in other things too. Albert told her bluntly that it was up to her to break the vicious circle, and that she would never get the best out of Peel until she changed her attitude. For his part, Peel felt her hostility so keenly that he asked Albert how he should handle her; the answer 'through me' was only meant as a temporary measure, but it proved so satisfactory to all three that it was never changed. When Peel wrote in February 1842 'it would give me great satisfaction to have the opportunity from time to time of apprising Your Royal Highness of the legislative measures in contemplation . . . and of explaining in detail any matters in respect of which Your Royal Highness might wish for information' the period of Albert's mastery had begun. The golden key to the despatch-boxes which Victoria gave him, together with her complete trust, also opened the door to a new life. Queen and country were never better served.

In place of his former diffidence, Albert now handled her with greater skill and firmness and therefore got his way more easily. Working closely with her, he realised how immature dependence on Lehzen had kept her – it was ridiculous that a woman who had been on the throne for five years should have warned him to keep the Tories at a distance because of the way they had treated him. She learned some lessons quickly, however: when the earl of Munster (natural son of William IV) shot himself in March 1842, she accepted without a moment's hesitation Albert's advice to continue the pension to the widow, although Melbourne protested that there was no reason for it, thereby showing that she had already lost some of the hard, unyielding attitude which Lehzen had taught her.

Increasing power brought its temptations. It would have been easy for Albert to take advantage of her remorse for his two years of unhappiness and encroach imperceptibly until he became not just her deputy but sovereign in all but name. To his great credit, he never yielded to the temptation but kept to the rule he had made himself – that they must act together: consequently he spent long hours explaining papers that she did not understand, encouraging her to offer her opinions and with great fairness always making sure that she understood the implications before he drew out their joint conclusion. As he explained to the duke of Wellington ten years later, he had long acted on the principle of sinking his own individual existence in that of his wife. It was the carefully thought out resolution of a highly honourable man. Albert kept to it rigidly, but since only those closest to him knew of his resolve it was natural that at times his behaviour should be misunderstood and his reserve called pride and censoriousness. Most unjust of all was the accusation that he demanded a high degree of homage, more than his right, and that he set great store by etiquette and formality. Those in close contact with him knew differently, but since it was a rule never to discuss the matter, this calumny was seldom contradicted. Strangely enough, a part of Albert was embarrassed by homage, particularly if it came from older or distinguished men; it was Ernest, whom everyone thought so easy and informal, who was the stickler for etiquette and who often criticised the English court for lack of it. In their home life, Albert and Victoria were natural and informal; Mendelssohn, a regular visitor to the palace, was astonished one day in 1842 when, a gust from an open window having scattered the sheets of music from which he was playing to them, they both bent down without a thought to pick them up.

That same spring Ernest suddenly announced his intention to marry. After chasing all sorts of eligible girls from a Russian Grand

Duchess down ('why does Ernest have to over-price himself?', Albert wrote to Leopold), he had settled for a simple German princess, Alexandrine of Baden. It is sad to read of the delight with which Victoria and Albert greeted the union of the innocent and sensitive Alexandrine to a man suffering from venereal disease, and Albert's long letters, packed with anxious advice, do nothing to remove a feeling of distaste. A brush with France over Tahiti, which provided the first of his new lessons in foreign politics, prevented Albert from attending the wedding, so their present, the latest thing in travelling carriages (which Ernest had asked for in place of the silver centrepiece they had suggested) was trundled across Europe in solitary state.

Albert's eyes were being opened to domestic affairs, too. There had been a number of riots but, as he said, men do not rebel for nothing; he studied conditions in the mines and found them 'terrible', like those in the iron and steel industry where whole families could barely eke out a living, and like the London slums which he found 'abominable stinking holes, fit neither for man nor beast.' Military force had been used to put down some of the riots, and he was shocked and nauseated by the heartlessness of the authorities. His concern for the poor found no echo in government circles, and it was for want of guidance that he made one bad mistake. In order to help the unemployed Spitalfields silk-workers, he and Victoria gave a ball at which all the guests had to be dressed in silk. The Press failed to see the kindly concern beneath the glittering surface, and it was rumoured that his own costume had been specially woven for him at £15 a yard (in fact it was made from an old curtain). Even Albert was not satisfied : 'there must be some better way of helping the poor,' he said, and it upset him, for instance, when he was expected to eat a large plateful of beef at a charity lunch in order to remember that the starving poor were thankful for a crust. But it baffled him that some of the poor did not at once respond to the workings of his social conscience and instead almost rejected help. The neat little family houses he designed for workers on the royal estates were by no means invariably popular, and a labourer once confessed to him that if he were forced to leave his tenement and live alone with his wife and children he would not be able to stand it.

Like Lord Ashley, Albert drew the inspiration for his humanitarian work from his religion, but he was free from the fanaticism which made the older man so difficult and unrelenting. Ashley made an excellent impression when invited to Buckingham Palace, but did not share Albert's desire for co-operation; he considered royalty fit only for formal tasks like waving good-bye to the first emigrants to Australia, and this led to friction between them over Ashley's Ten Hour Bill, which did not go far enough for Albert's taste. Worse shocks were in store: such dissimilar characters as Peel, Cobden and Bright all came out against the bill, and Ashley made the horrifying admission that legislation of the same sort had already been enacted in backward Prussia. There was soon another reason too for the lack of understanding between the two men. Encouraged by Stockmar, Albert set his heart on Ashley for an appointment in the royal household. To recruit England's foremost reformer, a man universally respected for his high principles, would be the best possible way of furthering his aim to have about him 'men who have done great deeds and who have come to peace with themselves and mankind in general' in order to raise the moral tone of the Court, and Ashley's age put him the class of those wise and genial father-figures (Leopold, Stockmar and Melbourne, for instance) by whom he had been surrounded throughout his life and to whom he had always turned for guidance. Peel had offered Ashley such a post in 1839, and Ashley had been ready to accept it in the hope that it would advance his reforming cause to have the ear of the sovereign; but when Peel did not take office the plan fell through. In January 1843 Albert asked Peel to renew the offer, but Peel's approach was so clumsy that Ashley suspected (quite wrongly) the offer was only made to get him out of the way, and tried unsuccessfully to strike a bargain – his acceptance against Peel's committing himself to factory reform. Albert next tried to achieve the desired result through other intermediaries, only to receive a sharp rebuff; Ashley thought it a 'crude and unnecessary insult' to be asked to give up his political activity 'just for the pleasure of ordering dinners and carrying a white wand.' Young and self-centred, Albert did not understand that distinguished men could not be expected to sacrifice so much simply for the privilege of improving the mind of the Queen's husband.* Had Stockmar been at hand, his tact might possibly have persuaded Ashley and would certainly have prevented the coolness which now arose between them; but Stockmar was in Coburg at the time.

Christmas 1842 at Windsor was less lavish than usual because Albert's newly-awakened social conscience insisted that they give a good example (he made an exception for Victoria's present, an enamel and emerald necklace which he designed himself). There

---

* 'I was to be cajoled and persuaded, to sacrifice my public honesty, to lower myself by taking an inferior place on the grounds that my morality was necessary to please the country and facilitate this government,' Ashley wrote in his diary.

were fewer courses and less wine at dinner, and his new dominance was also shown in the way their daily routine was gradually approximating more closely to his Coburg habits – unlike her, he preferred to get up early and could not do without sleep. He worked right up to Christmas Eve, preparing a memorandum to help Victoria understand the complicated question of patronage in the Scottish Church, and was soon anxious to get back to London. During the holiday it was for the first time becoming noticeable that he was less eager than formerly to push Victoria's ice-chair round the frozen lake or act as coachman for their family sledge, less inclined for card-games or charades in the evening so that he could go back to his study to catch up with his work on state papers.

Not all of Albert's energies were devoted to official business, however. At about this time another initiative, already undertaken with Stockmar's support, began to gain momentum. For the next two or three years he was intermittently occupied with the Herculean task of completely reorganising the royal household, which had for half a century or more been sinking deeper and deeper into the mire of inefficiency and corruption. So far as there was any single cause discernible for this appalling state of affairs, it was muddle and confusion, and this infuriated a man whose own study was always in apple-pie order. To be compelled to work in the midst of others' muddle was a continual irritant to his nerves; but he had come to realise there might also be a danger to health.

His first assault was upon the externals of life at Windsor. There was an almost total lack of privacy. In George III's reign it was considered a splendid day's sport to crowd on to the terraces and stare at the Royal Family as they took their daily walk: the novelist Fanny Burney has left a vivid description of sightseers rudely pressing against the King and Queen and of the royal children's complete unconcern at thus being on show. Albert found this intolerable, and put a stop to it (though only against fierce opposition) by closing the roads through the Home Park and by laying out paths so that he and Victoria could walk or drive considerable distances completely unobserved. When he examined the ground for this purpose in 1840 he found bare patches in the grass, piles of litter, broken statuary, crumbling buildings, and George III's favourite sunken garden overgrown with weeds and smelling vilely. Victoria had never noticed anything amiss, but good-naturedly gave Albert a free hand to make what improvements he wished.

The extravagance and inefficiency of the household clamoured even more loudly for attention. Extravagance did not mean comfort;

103

Albert was miserably uncomfortable and longed for his spartan existence in the well-run Rosenau. It humiliated him that dinner was late and cold, that whenever they moved some of their luggage was 'lost', that food and stores were stolen wholesale, that different departments were responsible for cleaning the inside and the outside of windows, so that it was a matter of chance if both were ever clean at the same time, and that security was so bad that an intruder like the boy Jones could spend several nights undetected near the Queen's bedroom and confess to having often sat upon the throne.* Victoria's casual attitude towards all this astonished her husband; like her predecessor William IV, she thought it the unavoidable penalty of being royal. Albert, on the other hand, was horrified that all Europe seemed to know of the squalor in which they lived – stories of it were in fact still circulating in Berlin to be picked up by his daughter Vicky twenty years later. The chief sources of trouble, he found, were division of responsibility and lack of supervision; two-thirds of the servants were not answerable to a head of department, and when one day he called for the Surveyor of Furniture to interrogate him, no one knew who he was. Stockmar provided the solution in one of his memoranda: a clean sweep and the introduction of central control. So drastic a reform could not be accomplished without treading on toes. Peel warned Albert to have a care – so soon after the Bedchamber incident (*see* Appendix I below) the household was still treacherous ground – and told Stockmar that a young German might not be aware how much the English venerated tradition. The job of completely reorganising the household took several years, but the better part of it had been done by 1845.

The health aspect had been particularly worrying. It was disconcerting enough to find unemptied cesspools all round Windsor Castle and a blocked and foul-smelling drain beneath their bedroom window, but absolutely nauseating to have food prepared in filthy and rat-infested kitchens. The 'delicate stomach' which the Queen and others mentioned so often in these years, the sore throats and swollen glands from which he suffered so much in early married life, can no doubt all be traced to one or other of these sources. The pure air of Thuringia and the superior hygiene at the Rosenau had given Albert no immunity against infection, so he succumbed immediately. The only way to prevent this sort of thing from happening, he saw at once, was to modernise the drains and kitchens.

---

* In the middle of one night during Victoria's first confinement a boy named Jones was found curled up underneath a sofa in Victoria's dressing-room.

There was a certain restlessness about Albert during these early years in England which was due to the restrictions which his position imposed on him. He had not done the Grand Tour (his six months in Italy with Stockmar had taken its place) but he knew the Continent well and often longed to widen his horizons. His imagination had been seized by the maiden voyage of the steamship *President* to New York in 1840, and he read every account of her fifteen days at sea; thereafter, America always fascinated him. His enormous physical energy needed a better outlet than hunting and shooting – and long walks in the hills at home had given him a chance to think as well, instead of just concentrating on the next fence or how many birds he would bring down. However, hunting at least gave him exercise and it was only an affectation when he pretended not to enjoy it. He rode so recklessly that the Queen was often terrified; grumbling, he agreed to ride to hounds less often. Shooting she considered downright dangerous, and with good reason; Uncle Ferdinand had once winged the greyhound Eos, and not many years later Lord Canning only just missed the Prince of Wales.

In the circumstances, Scotland was 'discovered' only in the nick of time. Stalking replaced hunting, and Albert's wanderlust was eventually diverted into the building-up of the Balmoral estate. His interest had first been aroused when duke Ernest spent a week in the Highlands in 1836 and reported the country 'beautiful beyond words', but it was a struggle before he and Victoria were allowed to cross the Border, because some ministers feared that riots in Glasgow and Perth might endanger the Queen. Peel eventually settled it by saying that Scotland was as safe as England and they could as easily be killed outside their own front door; in the event, the voyage in the unseaworthy *Royal George* proved the only serious hazard. The Highlands captivated Albert: 'the country is full of beauty of a severe and grand character – perfect for sport of all kinds, and the air remarkably pure and light in comparison with what we have here.' They were back again eighteen months later, but this time in the new royal yacht *Victoria and Albert*. The expense of building her provoked criticism – the royal quarters were luxurious, said Greville, but the ship's company was 'crammed into wretched dog-holes with not enough room to move' – and Albert tried to meet this by pointing out that the yacht would pay for itself if used for state visits, thus saving the cost of other transport.

Albert still had a lot to learn about England. He was shocked by the Camden Town duel of July 1843, but even more by the way society still condoned so barbarous a custom. A Colonel Fawcett had so provoked his brother-in-law, Lieutenant Munro, that Munro had felt bound to challenge him. Fawcett was killed in the duel; but Munro, who would have been called a coward if he had not fought, was now branded a criminal, and his army career was ruined. An indignant request to Peel to stop duelling was met, to Albert's surprise, by the conventional defence that the disgrace of refusing a challenge could never be lived down, and by the erroneous supposition that Albert, as a former student at a German university, was accustomed to it. (Peel seems not to have known that duelling and secret societies had not had time to take a stranglehold on student life in Bonn, which was still a very new university in Albert's time.) Thus checked in one direction, Albert tried another: could not Wellington at least prevent duels in the army, perhaps by substituting secret courts of honour? Wellington thought the mere question betrayed Albert's ignorance of English traditions, and would have nothing to do with anything secret. Undeterred by this double rebuff, and convinced that the law afforded too little protection to the innocent, at Christmas 1843 Albert composed a paper entitled 'Honour and Duels' which Wellington put before the Cabinet. He made out a powerful case, and although the only immediate result was an alteration to the Articles of War a few months later, he had given additional impetus to a change which was already beginning to get under way. It was an example of that 'perfect timing' which Stockmar was always advocating. Albert realised this himself; 'quiet perseverance', he told Stockmar in April 1845, 'has given duelling its death-blow'. The pace of change accelerated rapidly in that decade; Cardwell believed that he could have been forced to fight a duel in 1841 but would have been 'regarded as an idiot' if he had accepted a challenge ten years later.

In April 1843 Stockmar returned to England, bringing a long recital of Ernest's misdeeds. They were both scandalised at the way Ernest was gallivanting all over the Continent with his racing friends, spending Alexandrine's money like water; Albert's immediate impulse was to go off himself and drag his brother back from Rome, but Stockmar restrained him by pointing out that the exhibition of fresco-painting which Albert had arranged in Westminster Hall would collapse without his guiding hand. The exhibition was to be something of a test case of Albert's theory that the working-classes would come if the entrance price was low enough. He had encountered ridicule and hostility (some even said that the Hall would stink), and had staked his growing reputation on success. He was proved right; working-men of all sorts came in droves, and his only mistake was to suppose that they would prefer the special penny abridgement to the illustrated sixpenny catalogue. Encouraged by success, he wondered whether they would be equally interested in an exhibition of pictures from the royal collection. The idea appealed to the Queen, who, under Albert's guidance, was learning to take pleasure in caring for the under-privileged, and had never realised how much she had to offer.

Albert was opening doors which she never knew existed, in art, literature, music and service to her people. He was showing her how to develop the resources within herself and how to share some of her new interests with wider circles. It brought her closer to the life of England when he persuaded her to read Dickens's latest novels, and closer to her personal staff when, in 1842–3, he organised a series of private concerts in which members of the household were joined by professional singers and musicians, or when he built the new chapel at Buckingham Palace in which they could all worship together (the short sermons he insisted on made the services more popular, but placed unwelcome restraints upon visiting preachers). The construction of the chapel was also a successful experiment in architecture, but the new summer house in the grounds was a failure; not only did he attempt the impossible by seeking to combine the classical and romantic styles, but he conceived it on too grandiose a scale and spoiled everything by crowding eight temperamental artists together to decorate the walls of the tiny building. He and Victoria came down to inspect progress every day, and Charles Eastlake, one of the artists, was impressed with their anxiety that as many people as possible should know that they were not haughty and aloof in an ivory tower but two human beings anxious for the welfare of those over whom they ruled.

The summer of 1843 was in some ways a bad one for Albert. With the death of the duke of Sussex a whole new series of irritations flared up. Sussex's brother, Ernest, King of Hanover and duke of Cumberland, came over for the funeral and promptly attacked the Queen for not vetoing Sussex's request to be buried in Kensal Green public cemetery (she approved his wish for his morganatic wife to be buried beside him later). Next, the King tried to wrench the Hanoverian jewels (the best she possessed) from Victoria, alleging that his mother Queen Charlotte had bequeathed them to him. He saw through their attempt to soften his heart by making him god-father to Princess Alice (born April 1843) and demanded a ridiculous price when Albert offered to buy the jewels. Parliament refused either to buy them or to lend money for the purpose: Lord Clarendon, the government spokesman, told Albert that the Queen's popularity 'was due to her own judicious conduct; the country did not mind whether she was decked out in fine jewels or not.'*

By staying on for the London season the king of Hanover created continual embarrassments for his niece and her husband. They could not possibly let him come with them to Ascot, because his scandalous reputation would lower the moral tone they were labouring so hard to raise (the duchess of Cambridge had just placed them in an awkward position by presenting at Court a lady-in-waiting supposed to be pregnant by her son, Prince George of Cambridge), yet it would look strange if they went without him. He stirred up the old royal family again so that they refused to attend the levées Albert held when Victoria was indisposed – for him to take her place was an insult to them and to the Crown. Albert did not mind whether they came or not, but Victoria accused him of a lack of pride and retaliated by having an exact replica of her throne (in place of the makeshift seat he had been using) set up beside hers in the House of Lords ready for the next Queen's Speech. How Greville's tongue wagged! He spread the story that ministers no longer saw the Queen alone and that the royal 'We' now meant 'both of us'. This did not make Albert more popular, he commented; but he was wrong – Albert's new throne made him both more popular and more powerful, as Victoria had instinctively known it would.

Shortage of money was troubling him all that year. Because Parliament had refused a dowry to Princess Augusta of Cambridge on her marriage to his friend Prince Fritz of Mecklenburg-Strelitz, he gave them a larger wedding present than he could afford, and this left him too short to send Ernest his fare along with an invitation to stand godfather at Alice's christening (Ernest always expected his fare to accompany an invitation to stay). To save expense, he then asked Prince Fritz to act as proxy – which sent Ernest into a huff: 'I see I am not wanted.'

To cap it all, he caught influenza that summer when an epidemic struck England, and insisted on getting up to arrange the christening in June before he had properly recovered. No doubt the arrangements would not have been made so well had he not directed them, but this was an early illustration of what was to become his fatal weakness – an inability to delegate anything. George Anson caught 'flu at the same time, but instead of calling for a temporary replacement, Albert took on Anson's work as well as his own and thereby delayed his recovery; by the end of August he was very tired and told Ernest that all this work was more than he could manage. His

* Victoria was eventually compelled to hand them over in 1858.

febrile state was dangerously exaggerating that tendency to be over-eager for work which Stockmar had already noticed that summer, although he interpreted it only as a sign that Albert had cast off his former intellectual lethargy.

In a gloomy mood induced by post-influenza depression, Albert looked back on more than three years of marriage and felt that he had made little progress. He particularly longed to immerse himself in foreign affairs, but had been given little opportunity to do so – mainly, of course, because there had not been much activity in this field lately, but also partly because Peel and his colleagues had not yet learned where his usefulness lay. It was only when he thought of his happy home life that he could genuinely feel 'quiet satisfaction'.

From the time of his marriage, Stockmar had warned Albert against allowing his correspondence with his continental relations to draw him unwittingly into their affairs; their welfare might clash with English interests, and he must remember that both could not be served with equal fairness. Leopold agreed, and no one had at first worked harder than he to drive the lesson home: if Albert did not take care, every petty state in Europe would soon be asking for English aid. It was therefore ironical that Leopold himself was the first to ask for it, and as early as November 1841, when he begged his nephew to get the Foreign Office to help prevent 'cut-throats and vandals' from infiltrating into Belgium from Holland. Albert found the appeal flattering, but it took Stockmar's pressure (Albert having tried in vain) to extract from a reluctant Aberdeen the guarantee that England would come to her assistance if Belgium were attacked. A year later, in changed circumstances – free of many former constraints though still considering himself insufficiently occupied – Albert tried his own hand at a little diplomacy with the object of benefiting his uncle. Prussia had not yet recognised Belgium and, since he was on good terms with Frederick William, Albert now suggested that she should do so. Fearing that a strengthened Belgium might ally with France against him, Frederick William asked what was the precise relationship between the two countries, an inquiry which Albert had to pass on to Leopold. When Leopold's reply was evasive, Albert discomfited him by asking further searching questions, and went on to lecture his uncle – which was to turn the tables with a vengeance, for both Leopold and Stockmar had continually stressed that it was essential never to evade difficult issues but to go to the root of every problem. It was remarkable how easily Albert changed roles and became the adviser: Leopold

109

had to swallow his pride, listen and appear grateful. Irritated by Albert's evidently very strong anti-French prejudice, however, Leopold tried to make him see at any rate the French King in a better light by ensuring that Louis Philippe invited them to the Chateau d'Eu in Normandy, where he spent every August quite informally with his family.

Aberdeen welcomed the plan, because he might be able to use the visit to discover France's intentions in Spain, and Victoria and Albert set out for Eu on 28 August, amid much criticism at home and abroad from the many who were opposed to Anglo-French friendship. Unfortunately Albert had already been fishing in dangerously troubled Spanish waters by proposing a marriage between his cousin Leopold Kohary and the young Queen Isabella, and the trip to Eu compelled him to reveal this to Aberdeen. The *Victoria and Albert*'s course from Southampton took her close to the Isle of Wight* and they reached Le Tréport on 2 September. The Prince de Joinville, Louise Philippe's sailor son, made a particularly good impression with his hearty handshake and steady gaze; here was a man they could trust, they told each other, not realising that he was deaf and had to stare directly at them in order to lip-read. Victoria had pored for hours over materials and pattern books, with Albert's help, in order to look her best before the fashion-conscious French, but the result was not happy. Her purple dress and black bonnet enlivened by a blue ostrich feather and tied with yellow ribbon were not youthful enough and did not set off her light-brown hair and rosy cheeks. Although the French welcome was enthusiastic and the arrangements superb, Albert could not rid himself of an uneasy feeling that these were only a façade, as flimsy and unreal as Louis Philippe's professed warmth towards England. The King's empty and inconsequential chatter wearied Albert, and he longed to join the two Foreign Secretaries, Aberdeen and Guizot, who were walking up and down on the other side of the garden discussing, as he thought, fascinating problems of politics; had he but known, their conversation was entirely about philosophy. Only once during the whole visit was a serious political issue raised: Louis and Guizot both gave an assurance that there was no truth in the rumours that one of the French princes was to marry Queen Isabella of Spain. Because of the prevailing mood of distrust for France the tone of the British Press had been hostile before the visit, but Victoria and Albert returned to a chorus of praise for their efforts to bring about a rapprochement between the two countries.

* Close enough for Albert to get his first glimpse of Osborne House, which he was to buy in a few years' time.

Lithograph of Prince Albert after a miniature by Ross, 1840

Albert's mother—Louise of Saxe-Gotha-Altenburg, after Ruprecht

Drawing of Prince
Albert by Lane

Leopold I, King of
the Belgians, by Dawe.
Uncle to both Albert
and Victoria

Albert's father—Ernest I, Duke of Saxe-Coburg-Gotha, by Dawe

Within a few days they were back on the Continent at the express invitation of King Leopold, who was impatient to know how they had got on with Louis Philippe. While they were in Brussels, Albert took the opportunity to continue Victoria's cultural education by explaining the Rubens 'Crucifixion' and 'Descent from the Cross' in the cathedral, and to demonstrate the difference between the Roman Catholic and Lutheran faiths by pointing out the contrasts between the interiors of two neighbouring churches. It was disconcerting to be rebuked for this innocent expedition by a Cabinet reluctant for too close a connexion with Leopold, whom they looked upon as a sinister figure who spent his time at Laeken hatching plots.

By now they had acquired a taste for travel; Windsor seemed very dull after the excitements of Eu and Brussels, and it was Albert who suggested that they visit Cambridge, which he had never seen. Dr Goulburn, the MP for the University, told him that Cambridge was far superior to Oxford, particularly because it was not tainted by the High Church tendencies to which Albert's Lutheran conscience objected. The visit was hastily arranged soon after they returned from Brussels on 21 September, and they only gave a fortnight's notice of their intention to arrive on 25 October. Innocently, Albert imagined that they could be treated almost like ordinary sightseers, and did not foresee the commotion into which their presence would throw everyone, particularly the Master of Trinity (in whose lodge by tradition the Sovereign would stay). Mrs Whewell, the Master's wife, was made quite ill by the prospect of finding enough rooms for the Queen and a train of servants, and everyone trembled because of their ignorance of protocol. Whewell himself and Romilly, the Registrar of the University, read the little they could lay hands on about the last royal visit, but with far less rewarding results than Albert derived from his own researches. In 1728 George II had dined in Hall at a table by himself while the Master and Fellows stood around and gaped: Whewell announced that he had no intention of playing the waiter, and despairingly told the Fellows that they could only do their best and trust in Providence.

The reception was comic in its clumsiness. In his capacity as Vice-Chancellor of the University, the portly Dr Whewell first welcomed the Queen and Prince outside the gates of Trinity in a much-rehearsed little ceremony (the Senior Tutor had stood in for the Queen) and with a short speech handed the Queen the keys of the college. Then he turned abruptly on his heel and doubled back to the middle of Great Court, elbowing his way through the throng

111

and crying 'Give way there', to greet the Queen and Albert a second time as Master of Trinity. 'We were very glad to reach the safety of the Lodge on the other side of the court,' Albert wrote to Stockmar, 'for the crowd was overpowering and at one time we thought we would be knocked down where we stood.' Whewell excused the Fellows' undignified rush for seats in Hall as the result of excitement and the desire to welcome the Sovereign; and Albert's after-dinner speech was punctuated by the banging of plates and rude shouts of 'Speak up'. Conversation at High Table during the meal was so constrained that Dr Goulburn was reduced to giving an account of the college buildings which Albert recognised as coming word-for-word from the guide-book. Albert wished he knew what went on in the minds of these dons who had so little to say to him. Secretly he envied them – for nature had intended Albert to be an academic, and he often longed to return to a life which had satisfied him so completely at Bonn – but they could not know this and looked upon him as an exotic being to whom they had nothing to offer. He told the undergraduates who fetched candles to give him enough light to see Newton's bust in the ante-chapel that they were lucky to live in a place of such beauty and learning and to have lodgings far superior to those of his own fellow-students, and he found their friendly politeness a great contrast to the bad manners he had encountered at Oxford.

They both carried away the pleasantest of memories with them, and the visit was the subject of lively conversation for several days. For his part, Dr Whewell was left with some misgivings. The Master's Lodge at Trinity had often been loosely called a royal residence in the past, and judges (as representatives of the Queen) regularly stayed there on circuit. Was the reward for his part in making the visit a success to be the disturbance of frequent repetitions, whenever the royal family needed a change of air? Mrs Whewell had no such fears; she gave her mother a rapturous account of their 'naturalness, good humour and intense satisfaction in all they saw'. The royal coachman had the last word; he had driven Her Majesty to many places, but to none where the ale was so good.

Dismay greeted Albert's next proposal – that he should visit all the manufacturing centres in turn, beginning with Birmingham at once. 'The mayor is a hosier of extreme political views, in fact a Chartist,' warned Peel, and the Home Secretary, Sir James Graham, pointed out that police precautions were not infallible and gloomily predicted that he would be blamed if Albert were shot. Blank and uncomprehending opposition of this kind was regularly put up against any unconventional proposal Albert made in these years, and he had to keep beating it down; long afterwards he told Leopold that if he had hunted all day, gambled all night and drunk himself silly, ministers would have known how to deal with him, but that they were baffled by anything which did not fit their preconceived notion of how a prince should behave. Determined that it was his duty to make himself known to the people and undeterred by the possibility of demonstrations against him, but with a quite new freedom from inhibition, Albert cheerfully assured the Cabinet that the first time was the worst and that they would get used to it. Less than a month after their return from Cambridge, he and Victoria set off to stay with Peel at Drayton, and from there Albert visited Birmingham alone on 20 November. The extreme warmth of his reception vindicated his attitude completely; there were none of the expected republican demonstrations, the mayor pledged the loyalty of all Chartists with three rousing cheers, and the atmosphere was so relaxed that, handling a dish in an electro-plating factory, Albert could remark jokingly, 'Now everyone can live like a king.' Leopold deduced that the visit had been a useful counterbalance to the prevailing view of Birmingham manufacturers that royalty was useless and that it would be preferable to have an elective head of state like the Americans. Stockmar's comment was that by going to Birmingham Albert had unequivocally shown that the monarchy was above party, to which Albert replied that 'the first link has been forged between crown and people'. Even Peel admitted, after the event, that the Prince had been right to insist on going, adding with great generosity that Albert was 'a man with unquestionable status, whom the workers can look up to, yet a human being who lives his life to a pattern they can understand and copy.' The Birmingham visit had only lasted a few hours, and could therefore in one sense be no more than a symbol, yet in another sense it was of tremendous significance. His insistence on making it, and the welcome he received, released forces in Albert which were to increase in momentum for the rest of his life, and the change he sensed in himself was clearly evident to others. Harriet Mundy had thought him solemn and uneasy in manner when she met him in 1841; meeting him at Chatsworth now, two years later, she was astonished at the difference: he was smiling, animated and confident, and she particularly admired the 'indescribable mixture of dignity and deference' with which he conversed with the duke of Wellington, 'quite perfect to an old and distinguished man'.

7

'To me, Prince Albert is King'

CHRISTMAS at Windsor was marred by a hunting accident which kept Albert on crutches and renewed the terror the Queen had felt when he 'rode like a demon' with the Belvoir earlier in the month. She need not have worried; hunting was beginning to lose its charms as his interests widened, and he had less time for it as political and family affairs preoccupied him more and more.

Ever since their marriage, his father had bombarded him with demands for money to make up for his own improvidence and extravagance, looking upon his younger son as an inexhaustible source of supply. 'If I proceeded like Papa', Albert wrote to Ernest, 'I should be sitting before the Queen's Bench in no time,' and although he sent whatever he could afford, it was like dropping coins into a bottomless pit. He had to make considerable sacrifices to do it but the only thanks he ever got was 'Why isn't there more?' In turn duke Ernest 'ordered' his son to demand his 'rights' as soon as the Tories came to power in 1842 – an increased allowance so that more could be passed on to him – used blackmail by suggesting that he would have to mortgage Coburg to Russia if England did not supply all his wants, and pledged his son's credit for bills he incurred at watering places. Albert had not even been married a year when he confessed to Stockmar that he was afraid to open letters from Coburg.

There had been pressure of another kind too. Within a year of the marriage, duke Ernest had conceived the bright idea that his son's wife could confer the title of Royal Highness on him and thus raise his standing among the other German princes. Albert thought the idea absurd, but entertained it simply for the sake of peace, and consulted the Foreign Secretary on an essential point which seemed to have escaped his father's notice – even if the Queen conferred the title, the German states might not recognise it. (Prussia and Austria both refused, adding that they had no influence over the others but that in any case they would not want to encourage the ambitions of the house of Coburg.) Pressure from duke Ernest continued none the less, to Albert's mortification, and he was still more humiliated when in the autumn of 1843 his father approached Aberdeen direct, thus converting the question of his title from a family matter into one of British foreign policy. This not only made Aberdeen cool towards Albert, but also provoked Leopold, who testily ordered him to control his father; as some concession to the old man's egotism, Leopold offered to try to get Louis Philippe to address him as 'Altesse Royale' at court. Duke Ernest's sudden death on 29 January 1844 effectively put an end to this annoyance, although his elder son maintained the claim for some months after his succession.

Those nearest to him thought that Albert was overwhelmed with grief at his father's death. Anson collapsed with migraine at the sight of his sorrow, and Queen Victoria wrote 'My darling stands so alone, and his grief is so great and touching.' Albert's own letters pull out all the stops, but no doubt this is partly because current convention obliged him to use phrases which would now be thought extravagant. Anson's sensitive nature always over-reacted to the sufferings of others; he worked himself up to fever-pitch with nerves, and his collapse was the natural consequence. Similarly, for Queen Victoria other people's feelings were frequently clouded by the richness and exuberance of her own emotions, and she always wrote in terms of hyperbole – King Leopold, who knew his brother's real worth only too well, must have allowed himself a cynical smile when he read that she was 'bowed down by the loss of one so universally beloved'. There are so many stock phrases in the almost identical letters Albert wrote to his brother, his uncle, Stockmar and the king of Prussia that they do not ring true: 'The trunk has fallen, and now all the branches which are spread about the world must strike their own roots and create their own worlds; this is an awesome thought. ... Poor Mamma! Dreadful annihilation of her former life. ...' He cannot really have grieved like this for a parent who had always been so selfish and heartless towards him; he knew that duke Ernest had neglected his stepmother shockingly, and it cannot have surprised him when within six months she threw off her widow's weeds and set out to enjoy herself in Paris.

Duke Ernest's death did not in the least diminish the irritations which beset Albert; it merely changed their source from father to

115

son. Although the new duke was the elder brother, Stockmar committed him to the care of Albert, who replied with passionate intensity 'I will help Ernest with heart and hand in the difficult task to which he is called.' He was as good as his word, though constantly provoked by outrageous demands. Meanwhile, the two brothers exchanged mementoes of the dead: a silver fruit-knife, a leather hunting-jacket, a white waistcoat and garters arrived at Buckingham Palace, where they were wrapped in a shroud like their former owner and put into a wooden box which was taken to an attic and forgotten. Albert seldom mentioned his father again.

At Easter Albert travelled to Coburg to try to bring some order into his father's affairs, Ernest having proved quite unable to cope with the muddle he had left behind and having bombarded his brother with cries for help. It was painful to leave Victoria for two whole weeks; they had scarcely been separated since their marriage. He was conscious of the sacrifice she was making, and touched by her dependence on him, which he had unconsciously encouraged. By now she could not even write to a relation without telling him first; he composed all her letters to the Prime Minister or Foreign Secretary, and she merely copied them out; she could not fulfil an engagement alone; and all her bonnets and dresses bore the stamp of his taste – and very bad it was. In her own words, his care of her was like a mother's. The letters they exchanged during his absence reveal this dependence; although his are stilted in comparison with her lively style, she was very satisfied with them. He told her that she was never out of his thoughts, and he was hardly on board ship at Dover before he was in his cabin scribbling away. 'Bear up, and do not give way to low spirits, but try to occupy yourself as much as possible. You are even now half a day nearer to seeing me again. By the time you get this letter you will be a whole one.'

Coburg received Albert like a reigning king. Because of court mourning there were no flags, no bands and no processions, but everybody came out to line the streets and every window displayed a picture of the Queen and Albert wreathed in laurel and black bows. Under a bright sun, the effect was curiously gay, but the meeting with the family opened the floodgates afresh and they enjoyed a good cry together. All Coburg was anxious to meet the boy who had made good, and against his will Albert was obliged to hold a levée. Misplaced loyalty made him decree that it must be all male since his wife was not with him; this at once caused his popularity to wane, but instead of reproving him the Queen was delighted.

116

He dreaded going to Gotha because his father had lived there so much in recent years, but when he steeled himself to do so it was a shock to find that some of the palace servants did not recognise him. Though he would not yet admit that he had changed in the last four years, this did make him realise that 'home' now meant England, where wife and children eagerly awaited his return. But he raided the attics of the Rosenau for lithographs of Thuringia to hang in his study at Windsor; mementoes of the old to adorn the new.

On Good Friday, just before he began the return journey, he had the chance to revitalise himself with one of Pastor Genzler's sermons. The old man had lost none of his fire: he did not once mention duke Ernest's virtues, but dwelt forcefully on the remission of sins. By 11 April Albert was back in London, bringing with him a surprise for Victoria: baron Stockmar, huddled up in rugs and shawls against the treacherous spring weather. Victoria was in the sixth month of her fourth pregnancy, and Stockmar had come as usual to give unofficial advice and moral support. Albert was thankful to be back. The beauty of Thuringia still had the power to stir him, and always would, but it no longer tugged at him in the old painful way. The spell was broken; he had outgrown his native land, and the ties were to become frailer with the years. He was at his desk almost as soon as he was indoors, catching up with all that had happened at Westminster during his absence, the fourteen days in Coburg already forgotten.

Before long he had thrown off all traces of mourning and was sitting to Thorburn for a miniature which, to satisfy a romantic idea of the Queen (who had admired the portrait of one of his ancestors) was of himself in armour. He had often postponed this, and only sat now in order to assuage his feelings of guilt at buying a picture by Lukas Cranach the Elder, in whose work he was particularly interested because – Cranach being a native of the district – many of his paintings hung on the walls of the Coburg Veste. Like most collectors with little money, Albert was always trying to find excuses for what he bought; this time the excuse was that, Cranach being little known in England, he had been able to buy cheaply. Despite George IV's acquisitions, there were still gaps in the royal art collection, particularly among early German and Italian paintings, and he was set on filling them. He began with two Cranachs (ten of the fourteen in the royal collection today were bought by Albert), a Memlinc, a Dürer and an Italian landscape, as well as a van Eyck. This called for some sacrifices: 'I have often to refuse myself every little wish in order to keep my head above water', he told Ernest, who had complained that he ought to have first call on all Albert's spare money. As the pressure of political business increased, he was compelled to forgo the excitement of the saleroom himself and to employ Professor Ludwig Gruner, a well-known art expert, to bid for him. Gruner was extremely skilful, and frequently picked up a bargain for Albert when buying extensively for rich clients in Paris, Brussels, Dresden and Frankfurt. It soon became common practice for dealers to let the palace know of forthcoming sales, and it was in this way that Albert was able to secure for as little as £190 a triptych of the Madonna and Child, then ascribed to Duccio but now thought to be more probably by Fra Angelico. When the Nicholls collection came up for sale in 1844, Albert sent Gruner to bid for several Italian primitives. He never bought for investment, thinking this a soulless attitude, but only for enjoyment; if his purchases proved to be worth more than he paid, so much the better.

The need to make space to hang his new purchases gave Albert the excuse to rearrange the pictures at Windsor. He put all the Winterhalter portraits together in the white drawing-room, where they at once took on an importance they had lacked before, and everywhere got rid of disorderly muddle by grouping works of the same period together. These alterations made William IV's heavy Empire furniture look out of place, so it was gradually removed and replaced by eighteenth-century pieces which the Prince Regent had kept at Carlton House.

The plight of living painters often weighed on his conscience. Every year he set aside a small sum to buy a work by a contemporary artist, in the hope that this would encourage others to do the same; it seldom did. As early as 1841 he had tried to raise the status of artists in England by asking the Queen to confer a knighthood on Landseer, and was upset when Landseer refused it on the ground that 'the time was not auspicious'. His efforts in similar fields were more successful. The concerts by Mendelssohn which he promoted were a huge success, and jewellers did a roaring trade when society followed the fashion he set by designing for the Queen a necklace of golden oakleaves and semi-precious stones.

Because Victoria was in the seventh month of her fourth pregnancy, they sought quiet at Claremont in May, but their peace was broken by the publication of the Prince de Joinville's violently anti-British 'Note sur les forces navales de la France'. This shocked them profoundly; they had received him as a friend less than a year before, and he had also been their guest on the royal yacht. Albert gloomily prophesied that the pamphlet would be a best-seller (if it were, commented Stockmar, this would show how gullible the public could be) and would knock Aberdeen's *entente cordiale* on the head, but he was determined to prevent what need be only a minor incident from becoming a major crisis. He drafted a note for Victoria to send to Louis Philippe which was far more moderate in tone than the angry letter she had wanted to dash off, and took the same line with Aberdeen who, in the face of mounting indignation in the Press and calls for war with France, was preparing to demand a formal apology from the French government. While he would not for a moment deny Joinville's imprudence, he told Aberdeen, he felt sure that he had written the pamphlet not in a spirit of hostility to England but to show how immensely superior the English forces were. Albert's counsels of moderation prevailed, and the incident passed off without serious political consequences; but it enabled him to drive home to Victoria the lesson that it was vital to suppress private feelings in the interests of public advantage.

Not long before this Albert had boasted to Peel of the good he and Victoria had done to Anglo-French relations at Eu, including their new friendship with Joinville, in order to counter a reproof from Peel, who had discovered a private correspondence they had been carrying on with Lord Ellenborough, the Governor-General of India. Albert had jumped at Ellenborough's offer to write to them occasionally, because it would enable him to learn more about Indian affairs. He had never agreed with Stockmar that the Queen's correspondence with Melbourne was unwise, and failed to see that his attitude was sheer folly while the Bedchamber affair was still so fresh a memory. Indeed, his behaviour towards Ellenborough throws into sharp relief his stubborn refusal to believe that it was either wrong or imprudent for the court to seem to receive advice on public affairs from sources outside the Cabinet, and the reproof Peel gave him on this occasion did not deter him from acting during the next few years towards the royal families of Spain and Portugal in a manner more typical of the ruling houses of central Europe than of the constitutional conventions which England had long accepted. His political education was not yet complete, and his actions could still betray his inexperience. There might well have been serious friction with the Prime Minister when Queen Victoria let the cat out of the bag in April 1844 by showing Peel a letter from Ellenborough suggesting that she might assume the title of Empress of India, but for the mildness of Peel's reaction. By rebuking them in measured rather than in angry tones he wiped away the last shreds of the Queen's antagonism to him, and by accepting the rebuke they

119

substantiated the opinion he had already formed that they would always listen to the voice of reason. The incident was closed when Albert engineered a meeting between Peel and Ellenborough over dinner at Windsor – something which could never have been successful but for the friendly and congenial atmosphere he had created there in place of the old regime of cold rooms and unappetising food.

Albert's new domestic arrangements passed a still severer test in June when Czar Nicholas descended on them almost without warning; the rooms allotted to the king of Saxony, who had long planned a visit for the same time, had to be changed at a moment's notice and space made in the best suite for the truckle-bed with which the Czar always travelled. Victoria was self-conscious about her pregnant condition, but Albert begged her not to be prudish, to join in the social functions and to leave the politics to him, for he had guessed that the Czar had only come to find out what they had been up to at Eu and to insist that the Joinville pamphlet proved the French were not to be trusted. The absurdity of the visit became clear when Nicholas misunderstood everything – for example, he construed Aberdeen's dislike of war to mean peace at any price, and would not listen when Albert explained that all England required from France was the maintenance of the Orleans dynasty. His charm made him a success with women although his former good looks had vanished, but when he tried to talk politics at the duke of Devonshire's garden party Albert whisked him off to see the giraffes. He struck the right note with Victoria by praising Albert extravagantly, although once he had gone Albert had to open her eyes to his obstinacy and ignorance: he neither knew nor cared what went on in his own country and really believed that the serfs had been born merely to serve their Emperor.

No sooner had Nicholas left than there was a three-day government crisis following the defeat of Peel's motion to reduce the sugar taxes. It was becoming clear to Albert that Peel's increasingly liberal tendencies were making him enemies within his own party and even threatening his political future. The sympathy showered on him when he came to Windsor reflected the close rapport that had grown up between them, and Peel unbent enough to say that it put new heart in him to find them both so calm and confident.

From the moment that Alfred ('Affie') was born on 6 August Albert's interest in Coburg intensified, for it had been agreed between the brothers that if Ernest died childless Albert's second son should inherit the duchy. After three miscarriages it did not now seem likely that Alexandrine would bear Ernest an heir, and Albert began to feel that he had a right to see that affairs in Coburg were properly conducted, so that Affie should inherit something more than a mountain of debt and his uncle's soiled reputation. But when he sent Stockmar to find out details, Ernest was furious and had to be placated by money, sent to bring Alexandrine to stand godmother at the christening. The fact that Affie was only a younger son made Albert hesitate to take up Stockmar's suggestion of asking the prince of Prussia to be godfather, although he was anxious to establish ties with a man whom he believed to be a liberal and who seemed likely to succeed his ailing brother the king before long. When the invitation was accepted, he was instantly charmed by his new acquaintance and almost ran out of superlatives in describing him. It is difficult to understand how he can have been so mistaken. William was in fact cold, hard and autocratic, the very antithesis of a liberal; his one love was the army, but the Berliners said that he would never have reached commissioned rank if he had not been born a king's son. Nothing would have dragged him away from the barracks if Prussia had not been in need of allies against the menace of Austria, but he now played up to Albert in the hope of winning England's support, even praising constitutionalism but omitting to add that he would not have it in his own country at any price. Albert discussed German unification with him – the first time he had done so with anyone but Stockmar; William listened attentively but gave no hint that if it became a serious issue he would fight it tooth and nail.

A short holiday in Blair Atholl, lent by Lord Glenlyon, involved a tiring journey which Albert said would be cut in half when the railway came. Albert wore the kilt for the first time and was outdoors in the crisp mountain air all day. He and Victoria returned more in love with the Highlands than ever, and fortified against the tedium of entertaining Louis Philippe, who arrived on 8 October to find out what Czar Nicholas had been up to at Windsor. Louis Philippe was full of facile but unconvincing explanations of his son's *faux pas*; he wished the 'stupid pamphlet *au fond de la mer*' and said gaily that it was of no account. At Eu Albert had never been alone with the king, but now made a point of having some private conversations (after which Louis Philippe remarked to Victoria *'le prince Albert, c'est pour moi le roi'*); he was astonished to discover that Louis' mind was full of trivia 'ill-assorted and of no use to man or beast'. To please the French king, Albert took him to all the places he remembered from the period of his father's exile, and added an expedition to Claremont, which he had never seen. Tired, and

121

anxious to return to the comforts of Windsor, Louis was not impressed with Claremont, dismissed it peevishly as too insignificant for a king and expressed surprise that Leopold was so fond of the place. Less than four years later it was to become his refuge for the remainder of his days!

Both Victoria and Albert felt the need of sea air before the winter, so in October they impulsively decided to go to Osborne in the Isle of Wight, which had aroused Albert's interest as they sailed past on the way to Eu. They rented a house and were delighted with its intimacy and cosiness. Though Albert missed the mountains he liked the climate and found the island as secluded as Blair Atholl. Their visits to the Brighton Pavilion had always been ruined by rude crowds, as had a holiday at Walmer Castle, lent to them in 1841 by the duke of Wellington. 'I have found a second paradise,' Albert wrote excitedly to Ernest, '. . . we have rented a small house, which we shall probably end by buying. It is situated in a remote and attractive spot, and we very much feel the need to own a place of our own.' Still hypersensitive at being 'on show', Albert longed to be able to withdraw to a private retreat away from the society of people who, however kindly and discreet, made him feel positively ill when they pressed upon him in great numbers. He had accepted that marriage to Victoria entailed many appearances in public, but was transforming his bachelor love of solitude into an overmastering desire to escape from prying eyes occasionally in the company of wife and children. Therein alone lay security.

Drayton Manor, Peel's country house in Warwickshire, was the model for the Osborne House which Albert soon set about creating. Peel knew of and sympathised with his wish for a place of his own, and advised him to buy Lady Isabella Blandford's estate (the 'little house' they had just been renting) when it came up for sale in the spring of 1845. The site was ideal for a holiday home – pure air, a wonderful view, golden sands (from which Victoria later took her first bathe) and above all, privacy. But the house was too small for a growing family, and even before the deed of sale was signed Albert was making sketches of a larger building. For the design and construction work, he employed the firm of Cubitt, whose recent development of Belgravia, Bloomsbury and Pimlico he had admired. He insisted that local labour should be used as far as possible, and on his frequent visits to oversee progress gained his first direct contact with the British working man.

Albert's personality is stamped all over Osborne, interior and exterior alike. The outside is as strange to our eyes as the Brighton

Pavilion was to Albert's, its flat roofs, campaniles, arcades and flag-towers as odd a mixture of styles and personal idiosyncracies. He fondly imagined that he had copied an Italian villa in a part of the British Isles which resembled the Bay of Naples in climate and appearance; but when Ferdinand Kohary saw it in 1846 he complimented Albert on reproducing a perfect German Schloss in an English setting, pointing out to Queen Victoria that the terraced gardens were an exact copy of those at the Kallenberg and that the flowered paper on the bedroom walls reminded him of the Rosenau. No space was wasted indoors. The L-shaped drawing-room encouraged informality by enabling gentlemen to play billiards out of sight of the Queen and her ladies but yet in the same room. The huge wardrobe constructed along one wall of their bedroom was not only quite modern in conception but delicately disguised the entrance to one of those 'little rooms' which Albert, as usual in the van of progress, was busy constructing in great numbers at Windsor and Buckingham Palace. But much of the interior decoration was frankly German; the chandeliers were copies of those at the Ehrenburg, the colour-scheme came from the Rosenau, and a set of horn furniture (specially made in Frankfurt from the antlers of stags he had shot himself) was Albert's own tasteless variation on Bavarian themes. Prints of Coburg and Gotha in 1812 hung on his study walls, and were joined later by some of the Italian primitives he was so fond of collecting.

From the start Albert intended the Osborne estate (the original 800 acres grew to 2,300 in a series of shrewd purchases) to be run as a profitable farming complex. He adopted the up-to-date equipment he had seen at Drayton, and was never afraid of trying out newly-invented implements and machines. Some of his experiments were unsuccessful: a steam-driven thrashing machine proved uneconomical and a new sewage plant had to be abandoned because the effluent could not be purified satisfactorily.* In a part of the ground set aside for the children he erected a model fort so that the boys could practise military tactics and a Swiss chalet with a kitchen where the girls could learn to cook. In everything, the aim was self-sufficiency. Life was uncertain, revolution an ever-present possibility to a man brought up on the Continent in the 1820s and 1830s; none of them should be caught unprepared. Working on his own land, providing for his family's needs, was for Albert a most satisfying experience. Osborne tells us a great deal about Albert's character, more even than Balmoral; at Balmoral he simply adopted a Scottish

---

* In 1858 similar plant was installed at Wellington College at Albert's suggestion, and worked reasonably well.

laird's way of life, while Osborne was his own creation. When he stood on the terrace with the Queen, or walked with her in the woods imitating the song of the nightingales and hearing their answering call, life could not be better.

Osborne made them dissatisfied with their other homes, and gave renewed impetus to Albert's schemes for modernising Buckingham Palace and Windsor Castle. There were so few rooms that if they had any more children they would soon be sleeping in attics. When the king of Prussia came to Windsor in 1841, Victoria's maids of honour had to move into the servants' quarters because there was no other way to find proper accommodation for his suite, and it had been humiliating to discover that only the king of Saxony's forbearance had prevented awkwardness when the Czar of Russia's visit coincided with his own. Further, if they were to do their duty properly, it was essential to have a room at Buckingham Palace large enough to entertain two thousand people at once. The government, however, pretended not to understand and thought the rebuilding schemes too expensive. Peel put on his 'wooden face' when Albert appealed to him; but a newspaper's suggestion that Buckingham Palace looked more like a public house than the home of the Queen of England eventually made him yield. Albert devised an ingenious new plan to save money by utilising corridors and landings to enlarge bedrooms and replacing skylights by mansard windows (windows were a great feature of Albertine houses), and he paid particular attention to the servants' accommodation: only two beds to a room, for overcrowding might lead to epidemics. To reduce the danger from fire, several narrow staircases were replaced by a single broad one for which space was found by getting rid of a landing. The façade was to be improved by the master-stroke of creating the balcony looking up the Mall which has since witnessed so many historic scenes; it was ready in time for Victoria to wave to her people after opening the Great Exhibition in 1851.

All this may have justified the Queen's entry in her Journal that Albert had 'a wonderful turn for architecture', but the vital things were his persistence, his precise estimate of cost, and the care the two of them took to present their plan persuasively in a letter which, Albert insisted, must be 'short, crisp and explanatory', where the point was not obscured with words but could 'jump out of the page'. This letter was finally sent off on 10 March 1845. Peel did better for them than they had dared to hope. In mid-August Parliament grudgingly granted £20,000 for the alterations, but asked the Queen to contribute to the cost by selling George IV's extravagant Pavilion at Brighton to the town corporation. The place was no loss; it was haunted by uncongenial ghosts, and was even more inconvenient than their other two houses. Albert had already selected the best pieces of furniture for Buckingham Palace and Windsor, and many were in the hands of expert restorers who were repairing the havoc wrought by thirty years of sea air. How thunderstruck George IV would have been to know that a member of the detested Coburg family was alone in thinking his treasures worth saving.

8

'I wish that he should be
equal in rank to me'

FIVE years after his marriage Albert could not help noticing a change in the attitude of the Press, which was slowly beginning to be more friendly towards the monarchy; *The Times* and Palmerston's *Morning Chronicle* commented favourably on the fact that the last two State visits had cost the country nothing, and noted that it was Albert's careful management of the royal household which had enabled the Queen to pay for them. The public, too, received them far more warmly than earlier. Two years before, the Queen would not have bothered whether her subjects cheered her or not, but now she was on the look-out for every mark of respect or disapproval. Perhaps her previous indifference made her err in the opposite direction, and Albert scolded her for being pleased at the sight of the duke of Buckingham bringing him a cup of coffee when they dined at Stowe, saying that she should have taken such a mark of respect for granted. It did not pay to be humble, he told her, but it did pay to be constitutional; the duke's deference was to the throne, not to him personally. It was a new attitude on the part of the crown which had brought about this change; at her express wish, Albert had let the Cabinet know that she regretted her past mistakes and was determined to be impartial in future. That this new attitude had been sensed outside the confines of Westminster was evident from the applause which greeted a speech at Northampton by the Liberal Lord Spencer in November 1844; starting from the top, he said, the new outlook would sweep the country into more prosperous times; the Queen and her husband were pointing the way, let others follow. Albert wrote triumphantly to Stockmar 'There, after four years, is the recognition of the position we took up from the first. You always said that if the monarchy was to rise in popularity it could only be by the sovereign leading an exemplary life, keeping quite aloof from and above party.' As the newly-emerging constitutional genius of the Queen, Albert was beginning to practise the ideal which Stockmar had put forward in 1840, namely that the crown should possess a 'superintending responsibility' over government, instead of either being an active partisan (like Victoria in her early days) or confining itself to the acquiescent nod of a 'mandarin figure'.

On a visit to radical Northampton in November, Albert was cheered by name, and this remarkable indication of his popularity set Victoria's mind running along old lines again – could she make him King Consort? His status as Privy Councillor (still his only title to a voice in English affairs) and occasional regent did not measure up to the responsibilities he now bore, particularly since in her view 'He ought to be above me in everything really, and therefore I wish that he should be equal in rank to me.' In January 1845 she asked for Stockmar's opinion, and was astonished to discover that he was strongly opposed to the King Consort idea. Peel and Aberdeen were equally emphatic in their dislike of the proposal. Perhaps because he liked Albert so much, Peel bent over backwards to be impartial and ended up by being unfair; even a personal appeal by the Queen could not melt him. He fell back on the threadbare excuse that to elevate Albert would be unfortunate because it would remind the public that he was a foreigner, and he was pusillanimous in his replies to questions in the Commons.

The Queen's instinct was almost certainly right. An exalted personal title – though probably 'prince' would always have been more acceptable than 'king' – befitted the influential position Albert now held and would have impressed his image more sharply on the public mind; any initial hostility would soon have died down. The lack of it preserved the anomaly of his constitutional position and lent it an undesirable vagueness, as well as laying him open, when travelling abroad, to the regular pin-pricks of Grand Dukes who insisted on taking precedence over him. Stockmar would never have dismissed the proposal so lightly ('You have the substance . . . do not suffer yourself to be seduced even by the wishes of affection into bartering the substance for the show.'). But of course Albert might have found it hard to reconcile the title of King Consort with the ideal of sinking his own personality in Victoria's.

For her birthday that year Albert gave Victoria models of their children's hands and feet in marble – an idea that had come to him after seeing a model of Princess Charlotte's hand at Claremont. In melancholy moments his mind would often turn to this tragic girl, and he would begin to wonder what would happen if he too were to die young before Victoria was ready to take over. An attempt on his life in March 1845 was one such occasion although, since the Queen was not with him, he took it calmly and was only afraid that the Press would make too much of the affair and alarm his grandmother, the duchess Caroline, who regularly read the English newspapers. To spare her anxiety, he wrote to Ernest that same night, begging him to make light of the incident: 'It is a very exaggerated story. I met a young man with a pistol on the bad spot, Constitution Hill. *Voilà tout.*'

Children were the best remedy for melancholy. Albert excelled as the young father of a growing family: affectionate, patient and understanding, the inventor of endless nursery games. He was entirely free of the hurtful sarcasm with which his own father had so often wounded him as a boy. There is simply no evidence whatsoever that his children feared him,* and much to show that they did not. Both Victoria's letters and his own reveal him playing hide-and-seek, turning somersaults, chasing butterflies, flying kites or building a house with wooden bricks on the nursery floor. It was Albert who taught the children to swim and skate and who acted as coachman of the gay little sledge which gave Londoners a sight of a Royal Family as homely as their own. Holidays with the children were frequent and always exciting, and they all adapted themselves easily to the 'semi-gypsy life' which Stockmar and Lady Lyttelton frowned on because it interrupted lessons. At a time when the children of well-to-do families often hardly knew their parents, the royal children were sailing in the *Victoria and Albert* to Scotland, Wales and Ireland, watching the first races for the Americas Cup in 1850, or learning navigation from their father. He was never tired of watching his children at play, rehearsing them for amateur theatricals and *tableaux vivants*, enlivening their appreciation of Shakespeare by inviting Charles Kean to bring a company to Windsor, or introducing them to wild animals at Wombwell's menagerie. Self-possessed and assured, the children met everyone who came to Windsor, from foreign potentates to General Tom Thumb, the dwarf from Barnum's circus who received them standing on a table.

Like the Queen, the children looked up to Albert as the master of the house. 'Papa is an oracle' was something Vicky believed all her life; the others echoed her – 'Papa knows how these things are done',

---

* As has more than once been suggested, e.g. by Woodham-Smith.

128

'Papa will do it', 'I will ask Papa'. But in some ways the Queen herself was one of them. Albert's instinctive desire to shield her from the buffets of life, to make allowances for her 'fidgetiness', her moods and her strong temper – these things tended to create a relationship which at times resembled that of father and daughter. On the rare occasions when they were parted, his letters always began 'Dear Child', and many years later the Queen told Vicky 'Papa is my father, my protector, my guide and adviser in all and everything, my mother – as well as my husband.' Set on a pedestal as a god, Albert sometimes found it hard to come down to the level of ordinary mortals. As time went on, he gradually came to resent criticism even from within the charmed circle of King Leopold and Stockmar, and to disregard it.

Shortly after the Princess Royal's birth, Albert began to consider how he should educate his family. It was unfortunate that Stockmar, to whom he naturally turned, marred his German thoroughness and usual good sense with too much academic theorising and the alarming premiss that their position was more difficult than that of any parents in the kingdom. But when it came to something practical, like selecting a governess, his judgement seldom failed. Lady Lyttelton was his choice, and was clearly right for the job : she combined a love and understanding of children with a natural ability to teach and won the affection of the nursery from the start. For the boys, particularly the heir to the throne, there had to be a different plan. Here Stockmar's judgement deserted him. In three successive memoranda he propounded the far-fetched theory that children are born 'pure' and must be kept so by surrounding them with those who are 'pure' themselves, and drew an unnecessary parallel between the present situation and George III's neglect of his family. Paradoxically, Albert wanted his eldest son – just because he was also Prince of Wales – at one and the same time encouraged towards freedom of thought and yet hedged in by restrictions. It might have been better if he had paid less attention to Stockmar's elaborate theories than to Lord Melbourne's downright advice not to be over-solicitous about education : 'It may be able to do much, it may mould and direct character, but it rarely alters it.'

Both men knew what they wanted; but a second Florschütz was not to be found in England, where tutors were looked down on and employed to teach only quite young children. The poor teaching, bullying and neglect from which English schoolboys suffered horrified Albert, and he did not for a moment consider subjecting any son of his to such an experience. Instead Bertie (whom Albert habitually referred to as 'the nation's child'), was to be moulded by a carefully-designed scheme of private education into one of the 'enlightened princes' who were to save Europe from 'the danger inherent in a democratic age', a 'perfect man', as archdeacon Wilberforce put it. The only way to achieve this miracle, according to the Queen, was for the boy to grow up under his father's eye. Baron Bunsen (for they canvassed outside opinion widely and even bothered to read a condescending pamphlet) was more practical; he suggested that they appoint the Reverend Arthur Stanley as a tutor, a suggestion which Stockmar vetoed because a cleric might turn the boy against science. Albert himself wanted to educate his son at home and pass on the 'treasure of political knowledge' which he was accumulating because it would be the 'best endowment for his future kingly office'. A picture of the person to hold this office was gradually emerging: wise, just, and deservedly beloved, he would keep the monarchy safe. In 1845 Albert could not foresee how different the reality would be, or that the task of handling a difficult and backward boy would strain him to the utmost. He and the Queen wanted Bertie 'to be accustomed early to work with and for us, to have great confidence shown him, that he should early be initiated into the affairs of state,' but their plan was to be frustrated by the boy himself.

Early in 1845 the mayor and corporation of Dublin asked for a royal visit, and Albert was eager to go. He felt ashamed that he had not yet set foot in Ireland and felt that he ought not to evade his duty any longer. But Peel was adamant that he could not allow the risk, now that Daniel O'Connell's movement to repeal the 1801 Act of Union with England was gaining ground, and at the very least the Queen might be insulted. Macaulay agreed; he had just returned from Dublin full of horrifying stories about shootings, murders and daylight robbery, and had himself only escaped molestation by a hair's breadth. Had a visit by him alone been acceptable, Albert would willingly have defied the Government, for he thought they made too much of the 'troubles', but he would not lead the Queen into danger. In his view religious intolerance – anathema to his Lutheran conscience – was at the root of the disturbances, and he set his face against Wellington's recent proposal to send troops to quell the troublemakers; far from restoring order, he thought, soldiers would only serve to inflame feelings, and at all costs England should 'not make martyrs of the Irish'. To him O'Connell was not an agitator but an honest man who 'longs for his poor country to rise again', and his sympathy with the causes of discontent led him to draw misleading parallels between Ireland and Coburg. Opinions of this kind made ministers uncomfortable when they dined at the palace to bring him up to date about Irish affairs, and they displayed much ingenuity in directing the conversation into safer channels. Even the irrepressible Palmerston shifted uneasily under a barrage of painful questions, and Albert interpreted this as inability to take a moral stand where his own interests were at stake.

The Queen's Speech of February 1845, outlining future Government legislation, proposed a three-fold increase in the subsidy to a training college for Roman Catholic priests, which came to be known as the Maynooth Grant. Albert thought it 'courageous' because of England's economic difficulties at the time. He agreed with Peel that important decisions ought not to be postponed simply because they are unpleasant, but nevertheless warned the Queen that this was an explosive issue. Peel was 'right to cut across prejudice', he wrote, although three-quarters of his party were against him; but he was shocked at the Protestant reaction, noting that only one solitary Presbyterian minister had the courage to say 'bigotry is more common than shame', that even Gladstone deserted Peel on a point of conscience, and that the Ashley whom he so much admired could not agree to 'assistance for popery by the state'. When Peel stood firm against the Parliamentary opposition to his proposal, Albert became more convinced than ever that he was 'a giant among Prime Ministers' and was sorry when he refused the Garter with the words 'I do not covet honours' and told the Queen the only reward he wanted was the knowledge that he had done his duty. But they both noticed how exhausted he looked, and were distressed when he fainted one morning while talking to Anson and Albert, who took the unusual step of calling at his house next day to inquire after his health.

On 26 April 1845, at the height of the Maynooth controversy, the Queen and Albert gave a fancy-dress ball; costumes copied from Hogarth's engraving *Marriage à la Mode* were to be worn. There were several novelties – Albert's new subdued lighting, the buffet supper, the two of them mingling with the guests. Criticism came from the uninvited (it was a small ball, to prevent the crush Albert hated), and from those who thought the very low-cut, figure-revealing dress he designed for Victoria far too *risqué* (some said she would never have dared to wear it if Peel had been present), but no one seems to have been in the least surprised that it was all Albert's doing; up to 1845, at least, he had not acquired his later reputation as a prude. The Press even cooked up the story that he gave extravagant dinner-parties at which a great deal of rich food was wasted and fed to the pigs; in fact, all that had been enriched was the conversation – Sir James Graham said of one dinner that the talk over the port was so absorbing it was three-quarters of an hour before they joined the ladies.

At Osborne in May he began planning a visit to Coburg, which Victoria had never seen. They longed to get away, yet everything seemed against them. A spell of bad weather disinclined them for travel; Lord John Russell made trouble about a Regency; and Ernest turned awkward and unwelcoming (he castigated Albert's plan to call on the king of Prussia on their way as 'kow-towing to the king of an inferior country while ignoring his own flesh and blood' just because Albert had expressed a wish for a quiet holiday in Coburg). All this aggravated Albert's usual bout of travel-nerves, and the Queen became alarmed at the thought of leaving the children. He had just begun to realise how much his moods affected Victoria's: if he was depressed, she did nothing to raise his spirits but was instantly low herself and this in turn reacted on him – so that he began to wonder whether it was worth going at all. In order not to over-awe little Coburg, they took only a very small suite; a serious mistake, as Albert should have known, for the Coburgers were expecting to be overawed and were badly disappointed when they were not. Chopping and changing plans to win more time for the Rosenau did not improve Albert's mood and they were already nervously exhausted when they embarked at Woolwich on 9 August.

During their brief stop at Brühl, Frederick William IV set out to flatter them and, through them, England; he succeeded better than he could have expected. His heavy-handed speech at the State dinner (on the theme 'Victory at Waterloo/Victoria') made a vivid impression upon Albert; his usually cool rationality deserted him and he was so overwhelmed with emotion that, as he confessed to Stockmar later, 'I had such a lump in my throat that I could not trust myself to speak.' The effect was tremendous and it lasted throughout his life. But it was the country, Prussia, rather than the man Frederick William that henceforth filled his vision. His *idée fixe* that Prussia must take the lead in the movement towards German unity dates from this moment, and it survived an immediate shock which might have been enough to make a peaceful and unmilitaristic man like Albert discard it before it was properly formed. In a twice-repeated display of his army's might, Frederick William had 4,000 men on each bank of the Rhine firing volleys across the river until the hills re-echoed with the sound; Albert was stirred to thoughts of the glorious past and of Luther's proud defiance: 'It was as though the spirit of Germania was come forth visibly and audibly, proclaiming "Here I stand, and from this place no one shall drive me".' Emotion of such intensity was proof against all evidence of Prussian militarism present or past, and no suspicion that her development was making Prussia an incongruous ally for England seems ever to have entered Albert's mind; even the gradual revelation of William I's despotic tendencies scarcely disturbed his later dream that his daughter and William's son were to lead Prussia along paths of peace towards German unity. The paradox is as puzzling as it is plain; and in this one fatal respect Albert was undoubtedly blind.

Since he had particularly asked that there should be no fuss, Albert was annoyed that Ernest received them in Coburg with a guard of honour and his little army on parade. Because it was bound to be an emotional experience to take Victoria to the Rosenau, he arranged for them to be alone when he showed her his old bedroom under the roof, with its wallpaper still pockmarked from fencing practice, and the wide book-lined landing where he had spent many happy hours reading. In the Veste he took her to see the Cranachs, the new Ernst-Albrecht Museum, the chapel with the pulpit from which Luther had preached and the marvellous view from the terrace. Everything was as it always had been, except that he now had a wife by his side. Yet he himself had changed, although he seems not to have realised it. He was amazed that he had never noticed that the peasants lived in hovels, that their wives worked in the fields even in the last stages of pregnancy, and that there were no schools to speak of. It was a shock to find the contrast between Coburg and Gotha far greater than he remembered. There was much more evidence of culture in his maternal grandfather's palace than in all his father's houses put together; Rembrandts, Rubenses and Holbeins, a splendid library, a magnificent coin cabinet, a collection of scientific instruments which he was not surprised to be told were the finest in Europe, and a Chinese-Japanese museum which people came from far away to see. The contrast with duke Ernest was only too clear; Albert had not realised how many of his own interests were inherited from duke Frederick Francis, and how much his four years in England had done to develop them.

On their way home Victoria said it would be rude to sail past the Chateau d'Eu without calling on Louis Philippe. But the king was thrown into a great state of consternation by their visit, and so were the ministers whom they were surprised to find with him in his holiday home. Albert sensed that something was up and that they were not welcome. His suspicions grew deeper when, at dinner on the one evening they spent at Eu, Louis Philippe separated them by a manoeuvre so adroit that it passed unnoticed at the time and persuaded Victoria to show him over the new royal yacht. Once on board, the king and Guizot talked lightly about the future of Spain. Louis Philippe said that he would like his son to marry Isabella's sister, but not until the young Queen herself had married and had children. In return, Victoria and Aberdeen promised not to press Albert's cousin Prince Leopold Kohary as a candidate for Isabella's hand. By the time he managed to rejoin them, Albert had become very uneasy. Something told him that Aberdeen had been tricked into undertaking more than he knew, but it was not until later that he was sure. Their unheralded call at Eu had interrupted a meeting at which the final plans for the notorious 'Spanish marriages'* were being made, and Louis Philippe's embarrassment was mainly due to his fear that Albert's acute intelligence would discover what was in the wind.

That summer they began regularly attending the little parish church at Whippingham near Osborne, and were delighted when their presence caused no more fuss than if they had been the squire and his wife at morning service. It was pleasant to feel that they were not 'on show', something which made Albert in particular feel uncomfortable; a respectful bow and nothing more suited him to perfection. Genuine devotion and a real liking for the simple country service took them there – in complete contrast with the duke of Wellington, for instance, who shocked them by saying that he only went to the Chapel Royal out of a sense of duty, and that the sooner it was over the better.

By the end of July the weather broke and it began to rain continuously. A wet summer following a cold spring soon began to threaten a bad harvest, and before long Albert was dismayed at the sodden condition of the fields round Osborne, worse (he was told) than anything in living memory. Peel had smelled danger as early as June, and by mid-August an article in the Horticultural Society's Journal confirmed Albert's worst fears that if the rain continued there would be a grain shortage by winter. Sir James Graham wrote of potato blight in Cumberland, and soon the news was that the entire Irish potato crop had failed. Albert quickly realised that the situation was 'fraught with the greatest political complications;

* See below, pp. 144–6.

it will be impossible to argue with a famished people', and was astounded to be told that his plan to ship quantities of rye and wheat to Ireland was useless because the Irish would only eat potatoes. A visit by Peel to Osborne in October to discuss the grave state of affairs made Albert feel inadequate because he knew nothing, and angry that he had not followed his instinct and gone to see Ireland for himself a year ago. Concern for the Irish was soon making him inconsiderate towards Peel, who was already so overwhelmed with work that summonses to the palace at inconvenient times were an unfair additional burden. The Prime Minister was always assiduous in keeping Queen and Prince informed about events by daily reports written with his own hand, including things like the conference of scientists which he summoned to advise him, for he knew how near the marriage of science and politics lay to Albert's heart. By December a food shortage all over Europe was certain. For some weeks now, Peel had been urging the Cabinet to abolish all tariffs on food-stuffs, but without convincing them. The Queen and Albert were disgusted, and did not know whether to laugh or cry when a man like Brougham said in the Lords that the famine was God's way of keeping the population down. (Albert's sarcastic comment was that evidently Brougham thought it was the Almighty's duty to keep his chosen ones in affluence.)

Lord John Russell's famous 'Edinburgh letter' of 22 November 1845* was an attempt either to hurry Peel down the road to aboli-tion of the duties on imported corn or to force him to resign. The strength of protectionist opinion within his own party inclined Peel to resign, but before he did so on 6 December he paid a special visit to Osborne, where Albert saw him alone. The meeting affected both men deeply; Peel found the prospect of parting from them 'one of the most painful moments of my life' and regretted that by not moving faster towards tariff reform he had missed his chance of retaining office. Russell, with a minority party, faced real difficulties when he set out to form a government, and Peel's understandable refusal to commit himself in advance to support all the details of a programme he had not seen certainly contributed to them, but an important ingredient in the story of the next fortnight, ending in Peel's return to office on 20 December, was the attitude of Albert.

When Lord John reached Osborne on 11 December, Albert began by seeing him alone, just as he had received Peel; once more, Victoria only joined them later. But in all other respects the two

* So called because written from Edinburgh to his constituents in the City of London.

meetings were quite different. Albert was stiff and unhelpful towards Russell, and inclined to make conditions: Palmerston must
not have the Foreign Office, and if he objected 'must be made to
understand that the Foreign Office is a department of government
and not his private concern'. (Victoria added that Palmerston would
be sure to endanger the good relations they had recently established
with Louis Philippe.) The explanation was not, as Russell thought,
that Albert disliked the tone of the Edinburgh letter, but that he
wanted Peel to remain Prime Minister and knew that obstruction
by him would make it still more unlikely that Russell could form a
government – in which case, of course, Peel would stay in office.
To lose Peel would be to end the happy relationship between
Buckingham Palace and Downing Street which had been built up
during the last few years, and to let the monarchy decline into the
'mandarin figure' against which Stockmar had warned. Peel had
kept them informed of everything and had regularly listened to their
opinions although he did not feel bound to act in accordance with
them; Russell was unlikely to do anything of the kind. Thanks to
Peel, Albert had recently begun to feel himself 'inside' government,
and was reluctant to be thrust out again. The prospect filled him
with as much anguish as the Queen had felt when Melbourne
resigned, and he acted very much as she had done four years earlier –
yet in the interval he had continually preached to her that the crown
must be above party and that private feelings must not affect public
conduct! Albert's consequent behaviour towards him made Russell
realise with a start how much things had changed since 1841. He
could manage the Queen well enough, he thought, but both together
would be too much; it was no longer 'I' but 'we', and as Greville
said (not for the first time) it was really Albert who was discharging
the functions of the sovereign – 'he is king to all intents and purposes'. Within a week Russell had 'handed back the poisoned
chalice to Sir Robert.'

'We are now standing exactly as we stood before – on our feet',
Albert wrote cheerfully to his stepmother on Christmas Day,
'whereas during the crisis we were very nearly standing on our heads.'
Soon he began his usual stocktaking: what had been lost and what
gained? The throne seemed to have been strengthened, for the
radical *Examiner* praised the Queen's conduct throughout: 'there is
one part which, according to all reports, has been played most
faultlessly: that of a constitutional sovereign.'

Sympathy for Peel prevented Albert from understanding the
Protectionists, whom he now began to despise with something of the
vehemence of the Queen's one-time rancour against the Tories, nor

136

was he as careful as he might have been in hiding his feelings. He thought them selfish, muddle-headed, unpatriotic and leaderless ('one of their chief members admitted the other day that they were quite divided and very jealous of each other'); moreover, they belonged to a class he and Victoria detested as wastrels, young men who had never paid any attention to public business and were only interested in hunting. Stanley, who passed for the chief among them, seemed to have little control over the others and less political insight; 'I begin to think that the *Spectator* is right, who said . . . Lord Stanley should be sent back to Eton again.'

When the House met in January Albert waited for 'a great statesman to take through Parliament one of the greatest bills in history', and declared Peel's first speech – in which he stated the public interest and the public safety as his only objects – to be 'unanswerable'. It was thought strange that Peel did not immediately reply to the 'gibes and bitterness' of Bentinck and Disraeli, his chief foes already and the cruel architects of his downfall six months later. Albert believed he knew the reason – a mixture of pride and contempt for baseless accusations, such as he felt himself – but he was partly wrong: at one moment Peel was so furiously angry that he considered challenging Bentinck to a duel. On 27 January Albert was in the House to hear Peel introduce his proposals in detail, and an observer noticed that he did not take his eyes from Peel's face for an instant but sat in rapt attention for the whole three hours. He had thrown caution to the winds by going, drawn by the historic nature of the occasion, but it is not surprising that his presence was taken to be a deliberate show of support for the government and incurred severe criticism. The bitterness with which Peel was attacked astonished him; he could not understand why the Protectionists talked of betrayal because he rated the importance of party too lightly and thought that in an emergency, party loyalty should give way to the national interest. Even Peel rebuked him for underestimating the necessity of a party system for a healthy Parliament, and it is clear that, in spite of the close affinity between them, Albert misjudged Peel's attitude over the Corn Law bill. One reason why Albert was so shocked by the attacks on Peel was that he had not yet managed to understand English society well enough to grasp how outrageous, how revolutionary, the abolition of the Corn Laws was bound to seem to the landed interest, who derived so much of their income from growing cereals. Peel, of course, knew this, and once told Albert that he would have liked to give them more time to get used to the idea but that this was impossible because of the Irish famine: in some cases, he said, the opportune moment never arises naturally and must be forced. Albert, on the other hand, had long been well prepared for this moment by Stockmar (who had told him five years earlier that to untax the poor man's loaf was inevitable and right in a world becoming daily more humane and conscious of social inequality), and could not understand why others did not see the issues in the same way as he did. He liked to think himself an ally of the new reformers, and prayed that he would not become reactionary with old age, like Melbourne, who was reputed to have said that 'Sir Robert had disgraced himself to all eternity'.

It was the same during the great Corn Law debates in the Commons during the spring of 1846. Albert was stunned and bewildered by the violence let loose against Peel. How could so compassionate a bill produce so hostile a reaction? How could responsible men talk like this while the Irish were starving? It seemed to him beside the point to demonstrate the obvious fact that Peel had changed his mind; surely Peel was unquestionably right to do so, since the circumstances had so completely changed? But he indignantly repudiated Croker's malicious suggestion that Peel's conversion was due solely to fright at the activities of the Anti-Corn Law League.

Cobden and Bright, the leaders of the League, were naturally a great success with the palace. Bright's remark that when Peel resigned he was the head of a party, but when he returned to office a fortnight later he was the minister of sovereign and people, fitted Albert's own ideas exactly; so did Cobden's denunciation of the attacks on Peel as merely a cover for the hollowness of the opposition case. The warmth Albert and Victoria showed to them was balanced by the coldness they showed to the duke of Richmond when he and the Protectionists presented a petition against repeal. The insensitive duke quailed before the young couple's freezing stares and was suddenly anxious not to prolong the audience he had sought. But the omens for repealing the Corn Laws were not good. In a moment of despair (deepened by the success of Smith O'Brien's anti-British Young Ireland movement) Peel told Albert that there was nothing to do except sit it out with as much patience as he could muster. Albert agreed; it was no solution for the government to resign. The strain on both was terrible; Albert felt it particularly, for Victoria was pregnant again and needed constant reassurance against what might happen 'should the knife fall'. The palace was elated when the bill passed its second reading in the Lords at the end of May, but Peel warned them that the battle was still only half won, predicting that he would be defeated on the Irish Coercion Bill as soon as the repeal became law. He was proved right on 23 June. It was the end.

Albert never forgot parts of Peel's resignation speech, though he dared not go down to the House to hear it. The words 'I have every disposition to forgive my enemies for having conferred on me the blessings of the loss of power' exactly expressed his own life-long feeling that power is not a proper object of ambition. But although he never admitted to any change in this opinion, from about this time on he was – unconsciously, it is almost certain – deceiving himself into supposing that he still held it. For as his power increased, so did his enjoyment of it and his reluctance to surrender it. The paradox persisted for the rest of his life, and has sometimes obscured historians' understanding of him – the paradox of an unambitious man who came to wield enormous power and to relish what he had once despised.

The other passage he always remembered was Peel's tribute to Cobden, which puzzled but pleased him by its generosity: 'The name that ought to be associated with the bill is that of Richard Cobden; his appeals to reason, expressed with an eloquence the more to be admired because it was unaffected and unadorned.' Later on, Peel explained how Cobden had helped him 'behind the scenes, striving to hold the heterogeneous repeal movement together in support of a Tory who in all else stood for everything they loathed.'

Peel's last visit to Osborne as Prime Minister proved distressing for both men. It was many years since sovereign (which Albert was to all intents and purposes by now) and first minister had been so temperamentally compatible, and the prospect of parting moved them both. But the chief element in their strange relationship was that of master and pupil: Albert liked to think of himself as one of the young 'Peelites', and fresh memories of the respectful attitude adopted towards professors at Bonn led him naturally into the role of student. Peel found it more difficult to play the part of teacher. Albert could forget, what Peel could not, that a Prime Minister was hampered by the constitutional delicacy of the relationship, and his desire for instruction did not always square with the niceties of the necessary conventions – he even embarrassed Peel by making a written record of one of their last conversations, forgetting how easily a new government could misconstrue it.

As he walked up and down the terrace at Osborne waiting for Peel to arrive for this last visit, Albert began to realise that he was undergoing the same kind of emotional upset Victoria had suffered in 1841 when she contemplated losing Melbourne's guidance and that he had been unduly hard on her then. It had taken an uncannily similar experience to make him understand the depth of the emotions she had felt.

9

'There is no turning back the clock'

PEEL's departure seemed to Albert the end of an era, the termination of the first stage of his apprenticeship to politics. He was not far wrong; never again were he and Victoria to enjoy so lengthy a period when both Prime Minister and Foreign Secretary were as ready to listen to their opinion. Yet in another sense – although he could not yet see this – it was to mark the beginning of the years of his increased authority and assurance. Between 1841 and 1846 Albert had grown up, and he was now ready to apply the lessons he had learned. The shy diffident boy had vanished, his place taken by a sophisticated young man full of confidence and strong views which he was not afraid of expressing but which he now knew how to put forward with tact and cogency enough to get his own way. The transformation had revealed a humanity in him almost startlingly well-informed and realistic in one so close to the throne; the effect was to be far-reaching. Under Peel's stern but kindly direction his character had matured amazingly, and although still so young (he was barely twenty-seven when Peel resigned) his opinions were already respected and he was beginning to be consulted not just because of his position but because of the intelligence which gave point to his ideas and because of the thorough preparation and balanced good sense upon which they were grounded. Peel and Aberdeen had shown with what attention they expected his views to be treated in public life, as Victoria had done in the home; his early struggles for a recognised position – without which he would never have been happy – were over and done with. There was now not a state paper he did not see, a minister he did not deal with directly. As the Queen's private secretary and privileged adviser he held a key position, writing minutes of her meetings with ministers and drafting letters for her to sign. It is scarcely an exaggeration to say that the Tory Cabinet were by 1846 coming to regard him as the sovereign, though Albert always remembered that he was not.

His chief weakness was in foreign policy, where he was short of experience because there had been so little opportunity to gain it. During the five years of Tory rule, home affairs had held the centre of the stage and Aberdeen's conciliatory methods had solved such foreign problems as did arise (such as the Tahiti affair and the Oregon boundary dispute) quickly and peacefully. Indeed, Albert had admired Aberdeen's conduct of foreign policy so much that it had been natural to let him, as well as Peel, step into Stockmar's shoes at a time when Stockmar was usually in Coburg. Now both Peel and Aberdeen were gone; who could take their place? Albert's first thought was that no one could do so, and therefore – just like Victoria five years before – he suggested that he continue to write to Peel about political matters; Peel assented as Melbourne had done, and for the same reason – he too dreaded breaking off all contact with the palace. As soon as the elections were over, Albert sat down to compose a paper on the general state of parties and sent it to Peel for comment. The reply arrived with commendable speed, but although long it prudently avoided giving a direct answer to any of Albert's questions. On reflection, Peel was not going to be led into constitutional maladroitness; disconsolate, Albert took the hint and never wrote again.

To brace themselves for the ordeal of facing the prospective Prime Minister, Lord John Russell, Albert and Victoria went to Osborne for a few days. At the height of her anxiety at the prospect of losing Peel, Victoria had given birth on 25 May 1846 to a 'blue baby', Princess Helena; the child quickly recovered, but worry increased her tendency to post-natal depression. A year earlier she had laid the foundation-stone of the new Osborne House, and they now moved in on 16 September, although the building was not finally completed for another five years. 'Our island home' was opened with a little ceremony of the kind Albert loved: after the singing of a German anthem, an old shoe was hurled into the house by one of the Queen's ladies just as she crossed the threshold. They had paid for the place with their own money, and both of them thought it 'perfection'. Greville condemned the 'monstrous expense', yet thought it lacking in dignity and quite unfitted for a royal residence, and this annoyed Albert so much that he sent Anson to tell him that he had put the Queen's private affairs into such good order that she had been able to meet the entire expense out of her own pocket. Anson went further, and with sly malice let fall a hint that Albert's business acumen had also made it possible to provide the prince of Wales with an income out of the duchy of Cornwall estates, which had barely paid their way before. This extraordinary flair for business which Albert was beginning to develop was already showing remarkable results. The care he had lavished on modernising the home farm at Windsor was paying dividends, just as he had predicted; the school he had built in the Great Park for the labourers' evening classes was profitable in another way. But he was not free to do what he liked at Windsor, where the Department of Woods and Forests was always looking over his shoulder. For far too long the Department had been a sinecure for retired politicians with no qualifications for the work, and this state of affairs persisted until the appointment of Charles Gore as Commissioner in 1851; Gore understood Albert's ideas and supported them, and thus for the first time proved that Albert and a government department could get on well together. That summer at Osborne brought him into closer contact with another department too. He had never yet taken much interest in the navy, but the sight of the experimental steam squadron at Spithead revealed interesting mechanical innovations, and he soon adapted some of the new ideas for his own little steam yacht, the *Fairy*.

They had not been at Osborne more than a few days before politics began to catch up with them. On 30 June Lord John Russell arrived to let his sovereign know that he was quite ready to form a government. Although Albert thought Lord John too temperamentally unreliable to make a good Prime Minister, and too much in the pocket of his brother the duke of Bedford, he tried to accept him with as good a grace as possible. A clannish man himself, Albert distrusted clannishness in others, and was particularly suspicious of the way the Russells always stuck together. Moreover, Lord John's lack of height embarrassed him. He was always ill at ease looking down on this pint-sized politician, and although he knew he was being unreasonable found it hard to believe that so small a man could be efficient. Nothing of the sort spoiled his relations with the duke of Bedford, who was of normal height but was neither as able nor as likeable as his brother and had just those vices of inefficiency and vacillation that he thought he detected in Lord John.

The interview went reasonably well, although it was plain that Lord John would have considerable difficulty in holding his mixed crew together: he needed Peelite support in order to stay in office,

Baroness Lehzen

The wedding of Queen Victoria and Prince Albert,
10 February 1840, by Hayter

Viscount Melbourne

Meet of the French Imperial Hunt at St Germain

Prince Albert, 1848

Queen Victoria and Prince Albert, 30 June 1854

Grey was already rocking the boat in Parliamentary debates about the Irish Church, and after Peel's eulogy Cobden presented an awkward problem – could an agitator safely be given office? Albert saw a welcome solution in the news that Cobden was going abroad for a year for health reasons. Most of Albert's misgivings about the new Cabinet centred on the figure of Palmerston, however; it would be hard to accept a man he could not trust in Aberdeen's place. Albert's dislike of Palmerston is usually supposed to have been based on moral disapproval, dating back to an incident in 1839 when Palmerston tried to force his attentions on one of the Queen's ladies while staying at Windsor; but it does not seem likely that he heard this story until much later (he used it for the first time in July 1850), and he was criticising Palmerston as a man of no principle as early as 1840.

As soon as he took office, Palmerston sensed the change that had come over Albert since he was last Foreign Secretary in 1841, and was taken aback. Then, he had looked on the Queen and her husband as naive, inexperienced children; but now (like Lord John) he saw at once that they had developed minds and wills of their own and might be formidable opponents. It is strange that Palmerston was so surprised. Although he had spent most of his time at Broadlands, his country house in Hampshire, and on his Irish estates during the last five years, he had of course heard Albert talked about with growing admiration and respect and had read in the newspapers of his increasing public activities; but he had dismissed all this as exaggeration. Never in his wildest dreams had he expected Albert to become a man of importance, and it was a shock to find how much he had underestimated him. Nevertheless, he did not feel that Albert was more than he could handle – how could a young man of only twenty-seven, and a foreigner at that, stand up against his own long experience? It was in this relaxed and comfortable mood that he wrote a jocular letter about a goodwill visit by Ibrahim Pasha to London: 'Your Majesty may perhaps have heard that Ibrahim Pasha learned to write while Your Majesty's messenger was waiting with Your Majesty's album, and that when he had written his name in the book he threw away the pen, saying that, as the first time in his life that he had written his name had been for the Queen of England, so it should also be the last, for he would not write it again for anyone else.'

The new government was divided from the start between the followers of Grey and Russell; their own indiscreet talk made no secret of disagreements, and the Press stirred the pot vigorously (Albert even accused *The Times* of trying 'to rule the Government with a rod of iron'). Listening to these discords, Albert could not help gloomily contrasting this government with the last, Russell with Peel, Palmerston with Aberdeen. The Tory Cabinet had given Victoria and Albert what they needed most from their ministers – a sense of security, but this was now sadly missing, and they were to feel its lack more and more. Nostalgically they looked back to the Peel era; there had been occasional troubled waters, but 'however hard the row, we always knew that he would bring us safely to shore.' Now, with these 'two dreadful old men' as their only defence against the Protectionists, they feared for the future, and would have been more than human if they had not favoured the Peelites. This naturally drew unfriendly comment; Bentinck spitefully wanted to go as far as repealing the Regency Act, and the court crowed openly when he found no backers.

Life was moving into a new but not very idyllic phase, in which Disraeli gradually became as much of a *bête noire* to Albert as Gladstone later did to Victoria. Quite apart from his distrust of the bizarre quality in Disraeli, Albert could not forgive him for the part he had played in the fall of Peel. If Disraeli had shown himself to be kindly, Albert would have swallowed his comic-opera appearance without a murmur, but the man's deliberate cruelty sickened him, and when he wrote 'he has not one particle of the gentleman in him' he was not (as is often supposed) thinking of Disraeli's Jewish origins, but of his savagery towards Peel.

In spite of his necessary preoccupation with home affairs in recent years, Albert had found the time to keep up a regular correspondence with his relations abroad. One reason for this was that the family had come to treat him as their head, now that he had greater resources than the rest of them, and had no hesitation in appealing to him for help whenever they felt in need. Among his most assiduous correspondents were the Mensdorff and Kohary cousins, and the latter were now to be the cause of two unfortunate initiatives which he took in the Iberian peninsula. His mistakes in the course of these complicated affairs, and their ignominious outcome, show how relatively unskilful he still was in foreign politics; even more, they throw a glaring light upon his stubborn reluctance to admit that royal relations were as fallible as anyone else and that instinctive support for them might lead him into very deep waters indeed.

Ferdinand Kohary had been King Consort of Portugal since 1839. As early as 1841* Albert had suggested Ferdinand's youngest brother

* See p. 134 above.

Leopold as future husband for the young queen Isabella of Spain. Leopold's more equable temperament might counterbalance Ferdinand's irascibility, he hoped, promote good relations between Spain and Portugal and benefit England by preserving stability in the peninsula and giving additional security against France. Isabella, now sixteen years old, was so sexually precocious that her mother was anxious to get her married as soon as possible. In this situation Albert tentatively renewed his proposal that she should marry Leopold, but of course with the proviso that neither of them should be pushed into marriage unwillingly. There matters rested when Ernest put the cat among the pigeons by going to Madrid in May 1846, letting himself be fêted there as if he were the cousin of the successful suitor, and giving the impression that the marriage was being engineered from England – his insistence (about which Albert complained bitterly) on travelling home via London looked as if it were to report on a diplomatic coup. The French Press was immediately up in arms; assumed, quite erroneously, that Ernest had been negotiating on Victoria's behalf, and wrote that 'her English Majesty had broken her word' (a reference to the undertaking supposedly given one year earlier at Eu).* Palmerston now compounded Ernest's wilful stupidity by sending a list of possible candidates to Madrid in July: it was headed by the name of Leopold Kohary. This clumsy provocation precipitated French action: Isabella was promptly married to her cretinous cousin Francisco and her younger sister to Louis Philippe's son the duc de Montpensier; since Francisco was impotent, France would eventually inherit the Spanish throne. Between them, Ernest and Palmerston had given the French the loophole they were praying for; as Guizot said years later, it was all too good to be true.

Albert and Victoria, with Palmerston in attendance, were cruising off the south coast and knew nothing of all this until they picked up their mail at Penzance on 8 September. Both were more outraged by the human cruelty than annoyed by the diplomatic affront. Albert was particularly upset by a gloating letter from Louis Philippe giving sordid details about Francisco's impotence; it preyed on his mind to such an extent that it completely ruined a day's shooting! Peel had never seen him so distressed, and had to dissuade him from trying to invoke the Treaty of Utrecht of 1713. Victoria was soon ready to forgive Louis Philippe and forget all about it, but Albert was not. Usually conciliatory, he was now implacable. The most likely reason is that he felt responsible for letting Leopold down and reducing his career to ruins; there was an

* See p. 134 above.

uncomfortable similarity with what he had feared might happen to himself if in 1839 he had consented to a three-year engagement to Victoria and nothing had come of it in the end.* For the young queen and her sister he felt nothing but pity, and when Isabella shortly divorced her husband and took a succession of lovers he did not condemn her. 'What will Louis Philippe not have to answer for in Heaven?' he wrote.

The part Albert played in Portuguese affairs about this time is far more open to criticism than anything he attempted in Spain. According to Palmerston, he was beginning to regard the Foreign Office as his own special province – he and Victoria returned the compliment by accusing Palmerston of acting as if he owned it – but there can be no doubt that Albert was sometimes indiscreet in letting his relations know the opinions of the British government. This was particularly the case when civil war broke out in Portugal towards the end of 1846, so much so that Palmerston accused Albert of hampering his efforts to bring it to an end. Stockmar had often warned Albert not to let emotion and family loyalty sway his judgement, but his cousin Ferdinand, King Consort of Portugal, knew him well enough to notice that he regularly disregarded this advice. Indeed, Ferdinand had so often benefited from his kindness in the past that now, in the stress of emergency, he expected Albert to pull all his chestnuts out of the fire. Just before the Tories left office Albert had succumbed to the extent that, having failed to get certain customs duties modified at Ferdinand's special request, to favour Portuguese trade, he had indiscreetly passed on the information that both Peel and Aberdeen had urged the change upon their Cabinet colleagues but without success. Now, upon the outbreak of civil war, he sided unquestioningly with his relations, shutting his eyes to *The Times*'s charge that Donna Maria, the Queen, was guilty of bad faith, intrigue and cruelty, an autocrat who disregarded constitutional forms. Unfortunately, he had swallowed all Ernest's favourable accounts, and had never taken the trouble to discover how reactionary both Maria and her chief ministers really were. He blandly suggested that constitutional rule did not suit all countries (his words were flung painfully back at him a dozen years later when he urged it on the Prussians) and expected even Palmerston to understand that he and Victoria were naturally bound to support every monarchy, however despotic; rebels against lawful authority must be crushed, he said, quite overlooking the disgraceful oppression of the Portuguese crown and his own affinity with the liberalism

* See p. 29 above.

the rebels professed. Stockmar easily demolished his argument that Maria's harshness was to be excused on the ground that she had not been educated with the words 'then she must give way to someone who has'.

Publicly, Albert preached a policy of non-intervention, but he endeared himself to no one by doing so. Ferdinand cried loudly for instant help. Palmerston also spoke of non-intervention, but did not really mind whether the Portuguese throne tumbled or not, and laughed heartily over Albert's solemn double-talk – where his family was concerned, he told Greville, he was as resistant to reason as Cobden over the cheap loaf. Palmerston was right. When the situation in Portugal deteriorated in the autumn of 1847, Albert asked Palmerston for 'unconditional help' for the monarchy, claiming that Ferdinand and Maria were 'not just royalty, but relations'; at this, Palmerston allowed a long silence to fall. At last Albert began to see that his relations might not be perfect and that England could not do everything they wanted. His cousin Alexander Mensdorff, upon whose opinion he knew he could rely, had kindly gone out to Portugal the previous winter to see what could be done, but had written indignantly to say that he found Ferdinand and Maria as obstinate as mules and unwilling to listen to a word of advice. A few months later his own equerry, Colonel Wylde, went on the same mission but met with no better reception. With the growing success of the rebels, it would be necessary to rescue the royal family. Palmerston agreed to send a warship, provided that an amnesty was granted and the constitution restored. Donna Maria and Ferdinand were outraged that anyone should impose conditions on two people whose conduct had been 'perfect throughout', but had no choice but to accept Palmerston's terms or lose the throne.

The tremendous unpopularity of the Portuguese royal family with the British Press was by now beginning to rub off on Victoria and Albert, whose partisanship was well known, and they were forced to take notice when respected figures like Lord Clarendon called their behaviour 'stupid and irresponsible'. Greville abused the palace openly, blaming Aberdeen for allowing them to poke their noses into government affairs during his time at the Foreign Office: now they could not give up the habit. Albert himself did not realise that Palmerston had saved his face as well as Donna Maria's throne, and gave him as little thanks as he got from Ferdinand, who complained petulantly that his health had broken down under the strain! But although loyalty still compelled him to defend his cousins to Palmerston, in private he criticised them bitterly for their refusal to learn: he could find no greater condemnation.

In the end, circumstances forced him to accept the fact that the gulf between conditions in England and Portugal could not be bridged, and that ideas which might apply well enough in the government of the one would have disastrously different consequences in the other. The Queen of Portugal and her advisers, he had come to realise, were incapable of understanding constitutional government; 'they have not the least idea of what it means', he wrote to Stockmar in August. His initial partisanship for his royal cousins had blurred his judgement, usually so objective; but his undoubted flair for foreign politics was never again seen at such a disadvantage. For his experiences in the Portuguese affair taught him a lesson which he never forgot. In future, he allowed his head to rule his heart; this was really the natural approach for one of his temperament, and he seldom had much success if he disregarded it.

In 1847, Cambridge provided relief from a series of disappointments, and gave a welcome boost to Albert's confidence just when it was being sapped by events abroad. On 12 February the duke of Newcastle, Chancellor of the University, was found dead in bed at Alnwick. Albert scarcely knew the duke, although he had received an honorary degree at his hands in 1843, and his only reaction to the news was that it would be troublesome to replace him as a member of the Order of the Garter. He was entirely unprepared to receive next day a letter from Dr Whewell, Master of Trinity College, asking permission to nominate him for election to the Chancellorship, but so delighted that his immediate inclination was to agree. But how would the throne be affected? Stockmar assured him that a connection with the university would do the monarchy nothing but good, and that Cambridge would gain from having a Chancellor young enough to remember his own student days vividly and to transfer something of the scholarly outlook of the modern German universities to England, where academic reform was long overdue. They both well understood that circumspection would be required when dealing with so conservative a body as the university, but took it for granted that Albert's role as Chancellor would be an active one. They did not realise that by convention the Chancellor was only a figurehead who had no voice in the formation of policy, and that Whewell was risking considerable opposition in Cambridge by proposing a foreigner without a seat in the House of Lords from which to perform the Chancellor's one function – the defence of the university's interests. On Stockmar's advice, Albert consulted Lansdowne, Lord President of the Council and an old Trinity man, who thought it an excellent idea that Albert should be Chancellor.

Albert's letter accepting nomination stipulated that he must be the university's unanimous choice. At exactly the same time, however, but unknown to either Albert or Whewell, the Master of St John's proposed a member of his own college, Lord Powis. Although Albert's leading supporter, Lord Monteagle, dismissed Powis as 'a deaf old woman , he appealed to many because he was English, a sound Tory, a Cambridge graduate and a noted Tractarian sure to get the votes of all who disliked Albert's criticisms of the established Church and his hostility to the Oxford Movement. Powis might have withdrawn, out of deference to the Queen's husband, but the London *Evening Standard* had already published news of his candidature on 15 February. With the prospect of a contested election, Albert's euphoria of the last forty-eight hours vanished, and difficulties he had not thought of before suddenly loomed large; perhaps the Chancellorship might after all embarrass the monarchy, perhaps he could not really spare the time, perhaps Cambridge only wanted to use him for its own ends. In this situation, it was a tense and white-faced Albert who received the Vice-Chancellor (Dr Philpott, Master of St Catharine's) when he brought the formal request to accept nomination to Buckingham Palace on 20 February; because he cared so deeply, and because he was so divided in mind, he behaved with uncharacteristic stiffness and abruptly handed the Vice-Chancellor the prepared refusal which it had cost him so much pain to compose. Yet even before the sad news was being digested in Cambridge that evening, Albert was hinting to Colonel Phipps, his new private secretary, that although he could not accept nomination for a contested election, he would not object if nominated none the less. This news was quickly transmitted to Cambridge, and Whewell circulated a manifesto in Albert's favour on 22 February. The election campaign was short but very sharp. Whewell, who had never bowed the knee to anyone, was branded 'the most contemptible of cowering sycophants' and bombarded with abusive letters by the country parsons: Albert was 'unworthy as a man to be Chancellor', 'a foreigner ignorant of university affairs', 'so the Prince wants my vote? Well, let him want.' But some voices were favourable. Many M.A.s were prepared to vote for Albert to save the Queen embarrassment; one Fellow of Trinity had a short answer to the 'foreign' charge – 'The Prince is an Englishman' – and another supporter believed in counter-attack: 'It is true that Prince Albert was not educated at Cambridge, but Lord Powis has not been educated anywhere.'

Thursday, 25 February, the first of the three days appointed for the election, was miserably cold, and Albert's spirits sank still lower when he heard that Powis's backers had chartered special trains to transport non-resident M.A.s to Cambridge to vote, something which his own side had not thought of: one elderly man, who had to fight for a seat, had never seen 'so many militant dog-collars' since watching the departure for Lourdes of a party of young ordinands. 'Bedlam let loose' was the way one observer described the effect on peaceful Cambridge of this invasion and of riotous undergraduate attempts to disrupt the voting. While feigning indifference, Albert felt a compulsion to read every word the papers printed about the election – and they were full of it, since other news was scarce that week-end. Voting was extremely close, and the poll very heavy, but Albert drew slowly ahead each day, and on the Saturday afternoon he was declared elected by 117 votes.

Misgivings rose once more in Albert's mind as he began to fear that, far from being the university's unanimous choice, he could expect to win by only a small majority. If this proved to be so, should he still accept? Paradoxically, this renewed hesitation masked a deep longing to become part of the academic world. (Whewell had detected it when he said that talking to Albert was like talking to one of the younger Fellows of Trinity, and so had one of them when he lamented that such a good candidate for High Table was unobtainable.) As usual when in a quandary, Albert turned to Stockmar, who had no real doubts but felt that only an Englishman could advise on so English a matter, and referred him to Peel. Peel was strongly in favour of acceptance, and so was the Queen, who pointed out after the result was declared that to refuse now would give great offence to the many distinguished men who had voted for him. This was enough, but the formal signifying of his assent was an awkward affair. The Vice-Chancellor and the Senior Esquire Bedell, who brought the Latin letter containing the university's request, were shown into Colonel Phipps's room on the ground floor of Buckingham Palace as if they were inferior beings, fit only for the servants' hall. To make matters worse, Albert's manner was bleak; he had conquered his diffidence where his public capacity was concerned, but his elation at being given the opportunity of taking a hand in academic affairs was entirely personal and private and brought on an attack of paralysing shyness which made him stiff and awkward. The interview was stilted and formal. The dons clumsily thrust into his hands the blue morocco box containing the invitation, and he as abruptly gave them his reply. After they had gone, he read the Latin letter and found fault with a phrase in it; he instructed Phipps to point out that, although it was 'great presumption to criticise Cambridge Latin', his official title was *dux Saxoniae*, not *dux de Saxe*: 'it is not a matter of the slightest consequence, except that in case there is any record kept of the document, it might as well be altered.' His final word on the whole affair, which gives a hint of the seriousness with which he would take his new office, was given in a letter to his brother Ernest: 'It is my first chance to do something in my own name for my adopted country.'

Albert's ceremonial installation as Chancellor took place in mid-July. Two new signs of the country's industrial progress were at once evident, although it was only four years since their last visit to Cambridge: this time the journey was made on the newly opened railway, and gas lighting had been installed in the Senate House (it cost £45, and its harsh glare turned the Vice-Chancellor such a ghastly colour when he went to inspect it that a rumour soon spread that he was dying.) Another improvement – due entirely to Albert's insistence – was some rehearsal of his part in the ceremonial: but the university officials rehearsed nothing, and most of them did not know what to do when the time came (should one kiss the Queen's hand, or shake it? With glove on, or glove off?). The Public Orator's long Latin speech of welcome evoked cries of boredom and disapproval. Albert's was short, sweet and much applauded: 'My Latin proved a success', he told Stockmar afterwards. The new Chancellor had been looking forward to dining at Trinity High Table in the company of distinguished scholars, and was vexed beyond measure to find himself placed at a separate table and surrounded by his own household and foreign princes, just as if he were dining at home; his annoyance at the unruly crowds which pressed round him as he entered was equalled by his irritation after dinner at the antics of the drunken Lord Hardwicke, who called again and again for 'three cheers for the new Chancellor'. As he and Victoria took a quiet stroll along the Backs (she would call it 'the waterside') on their last evening, a happy thought struck him: there ought to be a bridge linking the neighbouring gardens of Trinity and St John's: it would enable next summer's Honorary Degree garden-party to make use of them both, and might lessen the ancient hostility between the two colleges which had lately been manifested in their quarrel over the Chancellorship.* The idea of thus acting as a peacemaker put him into such a good humour that he saw beauty in everything, and felt that the scene lacked nothing but music.

It did not take Albert long to sense that intellectual standards were far lower in Cambridge than in Bonn, (as Bunsen told him that

---

* The present iron bridge was not erected until 1874, however.

summer 'the humbug of Cambridge customs and ceremonies masks a poverty of thought and spirit') and from the moment he became Chancellor he determined to do all he could to arrest a decline which was eroding the university's part in the life of the state. Though there had been several attempts at reform since the beginning of the century, none had gone far enough; the systems of teaching and examining were in great need of improvement, far too few under-graduates spent much of their time in serious study: it shocked Albert to learn that a medical graduate could 'use the knife for the first time on a living human being'. Dr Whewell, whom at first he knew better than any other Cambridge resident, had offered to initiate him into university affairs and had sent him his recent book *Of a liberal education*; but a reading of it showed him how widely their views on reform differed over the promotion of the study of science, for instance. He soon became well acquainted with men whose views corresponded more closely with his own, notably two successive Vice-Chancellors Dr Philpott and Dr Phelps, and entered into a kind of conspiracy with them to introduce improvements quickly enough to ward off the already imminent threat of a Royal Commission of inquiry into both the older universities. After much furious debate, several of these changes were accepted on 31 October 1848. 'My plan for a reform of the studies at Cambridge is carried by a large majority' he wrote in his diary next day, and was astonished at the sudden popularity which the event brought him. *The Times*, which had often criticised him, now said that the nation owed him a debt of gratitude, and the radical *Examiner* was pleased to see that he had weighed Cambridge in the balance and found it wanting.

But a few educational improvements proved insufficient to avert the eyes of Lord John Russell (who had been educated at Edinburgh University and was therefore not troubled by sentiment) and many others, from the out-of-date way in which the university and colleges governed themselves, nor from the suspicion that their considerable wealth was being selfishly used. A committee to draft revisions of the statutes was appointed in March 1849, but wrangled long and bitterly; for where privilege was at stake, prejudice was profound and resistance to change obdurate. It is hard to discern what part Albert played in encouraging the deliberations of this very necessary committee, but the Prime Minister's extraordinary behaviour shows that he at least believed him to be behind them. It was only a few hours before he announced on 23 April 1850 the appointment of a Royal Commission on the universities that he let Albert know of his intention. The Queen was furious at Russell's rudeness, but Albert behaved with commendable self-control in public and only let himself go to Victoria: for Russell, who was notorious for mislaying State papers, to justify the Commisssion on grounds of efficiency was, he said, 'enough to make a cat laugh'. His dilemma was painful: he could not criticise the actions of a minister of the crown without constitutional impropriety, yet to keep silence was to seem to let a hurt and angry university down.

Albert seems to have played a smaller part during the next three or four distressful years in Cambridge, when the university first failed to do much about reforming itself and at last suffered the indignity of having reform imposed upon it by Act of Parliament. Doubtless he had been able to spare more time from the Great Exhibition than he could later from his preoccupation with the Crimean War. However, he urged the need for reform on the Vice-Chancellor in 1853, and it was his mediation which prevented worse conflict in 1856; in this way he judiciously combined his own wish for modernisation with the due discharge of his duties as the university's protector.

10

'Prince Albert
has the right ideas'

WITH Albert a new concept of royalty was born which was individual and owed nothing to precedent. Stockmar noticed the first distinct signs of it when, after an absence of nearly a year, he came to England for his last long visit in the spring of 1846; the signs multiplied during the twelve months he was in the country. Albert had lately worked out a way of life for himself beyond anything Stockmar had envisaged – he was now completely self-reliant, for instance, the 'passions' which had been so deplorably uncontrolled during the Lehzen years were now held on a tight rein, and he had developed a remarkably sure judgement of men and events. Stockmar had only a few trifling reservations – 'his natural vivacity leads him at times to jump too rapidly to a conclusion and to act occasionally too hastily' – but, noting that Albert was bringing out all the good qualities hitherto latent in his wife, he felt at last that he could safely leave them to manage their own lives.

The essence of the new concept was a closer link between the crown and the common man. Albert was the first royal prince to be well known to the working classes, to take an interest in them which was neither patronising or officious, and to speak to them in language which they could understand, using none of the high-flown phrases and complicated arguments which prevented the speeches of contemporary politicians from moving their hearts. He made them feel that he really cared about their welfare, and was not simply mouthing platitudes when he expressed concern for their lot. No royal personage before him had managed this; George IV and William IV had consorted only with riff-raff, and most of the others had held themselves aloof from all but aristocratic circles. It was no wonder that London society was baffled by Albert's brisk and businesslike attitude towards classes from whom little but deference was expected.

Albert went wherever the workers were to be found in large numbers – building sites, coal-mines, factories, but especially ports and dockyards, all drew him like a magnet. The sea meant little to him until his marriage brought him into contact with the English naval tradition, but he soon came to realise that it was the men who made the navy great, and was shocked to discover that no care was taken of sailors when they were discharged and came ashore; they lived in perpetual fear of the workhouse, and an old sailor told him that they would rather die in battle than in solitude and poverty. He had already founded and opened a sailors' home in the port of London by May 1846. It was the first of many, and the design, combining privacy with common recreational facilities, was all his own; Stockmar praised him for this entirely new idea. A one-day visit to Liverpool in July 1847 to open another home shows how much effort he was prepared to make on the sailors' behalf and how close a young German could now come to the English people. He was loudly cheered for his unexpected and spontaneous toast to British commerce at the official luncheon, surprised everyone by his technical knowledge, and left behind him the impression of a cheerful, relaxed and well-informed young man, alert and anxious to learn. Occasions like this did a lot to revitalise the monarchy.

His new position as Chancellor of Cambridge gave him a standing in the learned world and lent new impetus to the purpose of serving scholarship which had long been in his mind. Herr Meyer, whom he appointed librarian at Windsor in 1846, was a distinguished anti-quarian and bibliophile who set out, under Albert's direction, to reorganise the royal library and make it one of the best in the country. The huge but chaotic collection of papers was classified and catalogued and made available to scholars, but Albert probably did not realise what a Herculean task this was nor how much his own lengthy memoranda were already beginning to add to it. Nor did he confine his attention to the written word. The royal collection of Velasquez and Raphael drawings alone, he felt sure, would be of the greatest interest to art historians, for no one outside royal circles had ever seen them. As early as 1841 he had designed show-cases to display some of them, taking care to provide them with green baize covers to protect the drawings from damage by light. Seven years later he engaged Professor Ludwig Gruner, who had already bought Italian primitives for him,* to make engravings not only of the Raphael paintings in the royal collection but also

* See p. 118 above.

of those in private hands and in museums all over England and the Continent; he took the general idea from the enterprise of Woodburn the printer who had recently made reproductions of the Raphael drawings in Sir Thomas Lawrence's famous collection.

Towards the end of the 'forties Albert devised a scheme for the exchange of photographs of paintings between Windsor and other great houses, so that students could compare several works of a single artist. Only the duke of Devonshire welcomed the scheme at first; others thought it bizarre, and a thoroughly puzzled Palmerston spoke for them all when he inquired 'What on earth for?'. By 1849 Meyer's work had progressed far enough to attract students in increasing numbers. Albert was so often in the library himself that he met most of them, including the historian Macaulay, who had criticised him as 'too Teutonic' and had voted for Powis in the Chancellorship election; Macaulay was astonished at his enthusiasm and at his precise and detailed knowledge of the contents of English museums and libraries.*

Intense as his interest in art was, however, music was Albert's first love, and here too his influence was presenting the monarchy in a cultural aspect it had not shown for a whole generation. Music and the theatre were taken very seriously by the royal family. To go to a play or a concert was not simply a way of passing an evening, but a means of enjoying the skill of great musicians or actors – and the politician who insulted them by talking during the performance was soon dropped. Albert idolised Jenny Lind, Victoria stayed loyal to Grisi, both were so devoted to Mendelssohn that he was frequently invited to the palace and became almost a personal friend. Their attachment to both the man and the music was publicly shown by the unique spectacle of the sovereign and her husband attending a memorial concert – 'a kind of requiem' Albert called it – on Mendelssohn's death in November 1847. Music, too, kept him in touch with his German countrymen in London. Learning that many of them had nothing to do in their spare time, he encouraged the Prussian minister to form a male voice choir to keep them out of mischief. The Lutheran church in the City provided a focus, and the choir was such a huge success that Albert thought of promoting amateur theatricals as well, but was frustrated by the elders of the church, to whom the theatre was an invention of the devil (since Luther, even the most innocent amusements were suspect, he told Bunsen with a wry smile).

---

* Although he knew of Macaulay's hostility, Albert had offered him the Regius Professorship of History when he lost his seat in the House of Commons in 1847. Macaulay refused it.

An unforeseen side-effect of the prominence he was now openly giving to himself as a patron of the arts was an attempt by his relations to exploit it for their own ends. He seemed to them to have a bottomless purse. In April 1847 Ernest wrote that he would soon be forced to sell family portraits to raise money, thus giving a broad hint that Albert should stop them from falling into the hands of strangers. Albert of course fell into the trap; 'I cannot imagine how anyone could think of doing such a thing,' he wrote in real bewilderment, bought the pictures, and generously allowed them to remain in the Ehrenburg palace. Next in the field was their cousin, the impoverished Prince Ludwig Ernst von Oettingen-Wallerstein, who sent a hundred paintings to be auctioned in England, expecting that Albert would buy them instead. The Queen's half-brother Charles of Leiningen and others followed suit, and soon a regular flow of pictures and objets d'art was directed towards him. He bought as many as he could, but there was a great deal of grumbling when he could not afford them all.

Albert could turn his hand to most things, and one aspect of the new-style monarchy was that he made a point of informing himself about matters which had previously been left to departmental specialists, and of supervising them all. For five years before the retirement of Sir Dennis Wheatley, Keeper of the Privy Purse, Albert did a great deal of his work because he was fond of Wheatley and saw that the complexities of the royal finances were getting beyond him; Anson only replaced Wheatley in 1848. The skill and good sense with which Albert handled the business side of the Osborne estate at that time made Peel exclaim one day that he wished his Chancellor of the Exchequer were as capable. Albert himself explained his financial acumen as something he had been forced to learn in order to unravel his father's chaotic affairs.

The decision to buy a place of their own in Scotland, also taken in 1848, soon turned out to have been far more momentous than it can have seemed at the time, since from it stemmed a novel and eventually dominant part of the new mystique of royalty – the popular image of the Queen and her husband, dressed in kilts, striding across the heather. They had paid regular visits to Scotland since 1844, but Albert found Ardverikie, which they had rented, lowering to the spirits; it was cold and too remote, and the sport was poor. Above all, Sir James Clark (whom the Queen always listened to) loathed it and cleverly played on Victoria's fears for her husband's health by implanting the idea that Albert needed a bracing climate for his rheumatism, not wild mountain gales. Sir James knew a far better place, Balmoral, conveniently near his own Birkhall, which was set in beautiful countryside on the banks of the river Dee, possessed an abundance of game, and was for sale. They both fell in love with Balmoral as soon as they saw it – Albert said it reminded him of Thuringia, and always felt as brisk and energetic there as he had done at home. The one drawback was that the house was too small for a growing family, but that was soon remedied when Albert designed a larger mansion on a better site a hundred yards to the north-west of the old one. Even before this was completed, he was also building cottages for the tenants which astonished Sir Edwin Chadwick, the Poor Law Commissioner and public health reformer, into remarking that houses like these would reduce the death-rate in the east end of London by a third, and was soon putting up schools at Crathie and Glen Girnock and a library to serve the whole district. For a time *The Builder* became his favourite reading. By 1849 he was consulting Ashley about the best way to cope with the needs of the labourers who flocked to the building-site in search of work, arranging for a shop to serve them, and setting up a cottage-based weaving industry and a savings bank. Even he was surprised at the satisfaction all this paternalistic care for the welfare of others gave him and how much these new contacts with the lower classes in an unfamiliar part of the kingdom were teaching him in his self-imposed task of making the monarchy real to the people.

To go to Balmoral was, for both of them, 'to enter a better world'. Albert had always craved intervals of peace and quiet in the country to regenerate himself and regain his strength for another period of intense activity – for the struggle to keep and increase his foothold in politics had now become just as essential to him – and by about 1850 Balmoral was doing for the man what the Rosenau had always done for the boy. If the Highlands had one drawback for the Queen, however, it was the attraction that field sports held for her husband. In fine weather he was out all day, following the deer with the same singlemindedness as that with which old duke Ernest hunted boar. Victoria became so incensed with his late home-coming that she converted two ghillies' huts above Loch Muinch into a miniature hunting-lodge where they could both stay overnight with the minimum of attendants. At Alt-na-Giuthasach there was a heavy old boat in which Albert rowed the Queen round the loch, until at dusk the wail of the pipes called them home. It was a simple way of life which Albert loved, and one which Victoria might never have known if she had married one of her other suitors; he was always cheerful and fit in Scotland, never complaining (as he constantly did in London) that he 'could not breathe'. To capture for ever the memory of this happy life, Albert invited Landseer to paint the family quite informally, and enjoyed keeping the children amused while the artist was at work.

Among the first official visitors to Balmoral was Charles Greville, who limped his gouty way to the Highlands to see for himself exactly what this strange royal pair were rhapsodising about. He soon understood, and grudgingly admitted that they were at their best in conditions of great simplicity – though he hardly felt safe when he discovered that the whole place was guarded by only a single policeman. His opinion of Albert took a turn for the better when he saw him at close quarters. In his hasty fashion, Greville had hitherto written him off as stuffy and formal, a typical unbending German; but when he now showed himself easy, relaxed and gay as well as highly intelligent, Greville was quick to say that he had always known it. It says much for Albert's personality that this arch-critic was struck by his knowledge and thorough grasp of affairs and impressed by his naturalness: he was 'without the least stuffiness or air of dignity'. A day at the Braemar Games showed the same thing. They set off in two pony-carriages like any other family party, and Albert unself-consciously joined in some of the competitions, modestly disclaiming praise for his success with the discus as beginner's luck.

At Balmoral, as at Osborne, Albert was as much master of the house as he could wish. When the new building was finished, the Queen was content to leave the furnishing and decoration in her husband's capable hands and found no fault with the 'tartanitis' that amazed and dazzled visitors. Albert's idea was to give a fillip to the declining Scottish woollen industry by showing how useful and versatile tartan cloth was, capable of being used for walls, floors, chairs and curtains.

'Life in the Highlands fits me like a glove', Albert wrote happily to his brother in the autumn of 1849, but before long it was the Queen who was reluctant to leave the peace of the countryside and Albert who chafed to return to affairs. Politics were already taking him away from her more and more, and there was some truth in her complaint that he was becoming 'a terrible man of business'. Her jealousy was sharpened by the realisation that he now very much enjoyed the work itself, although he had undertaken it in the first place only to spare her. Like a good many devoted wives, she wanted it both ways: to have him all to herself, and yet to see him with the respect of all for his excellent management of her country's affairs. She was delighted that he was so much in demand, but illogically wished that he could make some of his public appearances by proxy. With a little help from Sir James Clark, she devised a new reason

159

why he should not leave her side so often – his constitution was delicate. When writing to Stockmar she never failed to complain that he was 'fagged out', 'looked pale and yellow' or 'needed rest'. She talked so often of him 'never having been strong' that even the household came to believe it, and she certainly convinced herself that this fiction was truth. Instinct made her play on his hypochondria and nervousness, just as his doting grandmothers had done when he was a child, so that he should never want to leave her. What he really needed in these low moods was not sympathy but bracing; Colonel Phipps acutely noted that if a crisis arose or there was something exciting afoot his malaise soon vanished.

A good example of what was becoming a regular pattern occurred while they were at Balmoral for a spring holiday in April 1849. Albert caught a chill while out deerstalking, and the Queen tried to make this an excuse for him to cancel an engagement to open a new dock at Grimsby. There was a flare-up – 'If you will not do your duty, I must do mine' – but Albert won, as he was now beginning to realise that he always must. Besides, the new docks were of special importance to him, for they had been built to handle trade with Germany, and he was not going to miss the chance of promoting this. Similarly, his wish to see everything for himself often exasperated the Queen. During a brief overnight stop in Glasgow a few months later, they had not been at the George Hotel a minute before Albert was off to inspect the prison.

Nor could he any longer leave politics behind while they were on holiday. The first really large-scale example of this had occurred while they were at Balmoral in the spring of 1848, when the noise of revolution was first heard on the Continent and the English attitude had yet to be settled. Greatly to the Queen's annoyance, Albert spent as much time in the study as in the open air. The fact that he felt obliged to do so – more, perhaps, than any actual influence he had on government decisions – was the best indication yet of the new position he had won for the crown. Its co-operation had become indispensable to the formulation of policy in a way scarcely known since the early years of George III.

Something which might almost be called Albert's theory of the new royalism comes out in his opposition to the Tractarians of the Oxford Movement with their High Church inclinations and their apparent tendency to drift back towards Rome. He was a Lutheran by birth and upbringing, he had been educated in the Continental tradition of liberalism, and he had been deeply influenced by the teaching of the younger Fichte at Bonn, with its strong emphasis on conscience, moral freedom and strenuous activity as the essence of true religion and its outward manifestations. These firmly rooted beliefs made him distrustful of the introspection and dogmatism of the Tractarians, whom he no doubt misunderstood but repeatedly accused of wishing to turn the clock back – whereas in his own opinion the Reformation had never yet gone far enough in England. Their love of ritual and formalism seemed to him evidence of this, just as their stubborn defence of their position appeared a sign of bigotry rather than of true conviction: he would not be drawn into the excitement and controversy which the publication of their writings engendered, and stood somewhat contemptuously on the side-lines, refusing either to admit that any good would come from the Movement's influence or to show any curiosity about its leaders. He declined opportunities offered him by Ashley to meet Keble and Pusey, although he would have had much in common with the latter, whose humanitarian views were as strong as his own. No doubt he was much influenced by Peel, who held Puseyism in horror, and by Ashley, who never let slip a chance to pour scorn on the Tractarians, despite his affection for his cousin Edward Pusey. Indeed, Albert, although no evangelical himself, applauded the evangelical Ashley's part in fighting the Movement, congratulating him on one occasion for 'the bold stand you have taken up against the influence and pretensions of Puseyism and popery'. The paradox of advocating toleration for Jews in one breath* and demanding the suppression of the High Church party's popish practices with the next did not disturb him in the least, for one of his most strongly held and often repeated views was that there could be 'no compromise in religion'. Yet he was full of sympathy for those who, like Newman and Manning, felt compelled to go the whole hog and join the Church of Rome, for he felt that this was the only honest course to take. On the other hand, any sign of broadmindedness in his own chaplains delighted him, as for instance when Wriotheseley Russell took communion, along with one hundred and fifty Dissenting ministers, from a Baptist pastor in Berlin whose invitation a number of prominent Tractarian clergy had refused the year before.

An emotional creed like that of the Tractarians could never have made much appeal to Albert because it was in fundamental conflict with his own rational and scientific outlook. But it was particularly repugnant to him because it sought to modify the established religion, and was therefore in some sense a revolt against the throne. He could not in his heart applaud the Established Church in all its aspects, and indeed criticised some of its clergy and many of its

---

* So that Jews elected to Parliament could take their seats, Albert wanted them to be allowed a special oath.

practices, but he whole-heartedly approved of the Establishment itself as one of the pillars of the monarchy and the state. Thus his dislike of the Tractarians was but the negative which corresponded to a far more important positive: the stabilising influence which an upright, moral and hard-working royal family could exercise over the whole of society, by giving a good example in its own private life and by ensuring that the established Church was not debased by the infiltration of corrupting practices.

High Churchmen welcomed the appointment of Samuel Wilberforce as one of Albert's chaplains in January 1841, holding him to be about the only man who could wean Albert away from his Lutheran predilections. On the surface, Wilberforce possessed just these qualities; he was young, witty, broadminded and a noted humanitarian. But in those days too little was known about the Queen's husband for anyone to realise that his views could only be changed by strong and convincing argument based on even stronger belief, and these were qualities which Wilberforce emphatically lacked. His first sermon in the Chapel Royal, on 26 September 1841, did not make a good impression, and a conversation with him the same afternoon led Albert to note that he was far too inclined to sink his own opinions in order to please. This was a weakness which Albert despised, and in all probability Wilberforce's chance of promotion to Canterbury was prejudiced from that moment. So far from being able to change Albert's views, Wilberforce was soon disconcerted by them and became not the attacker but the attacked. During a series of conversations in 1843 Albert made him very uncomfortable by bringing up the question of the gloomy English Sunday which denied well-deserved relaxation to men and women who worked hard all the week, pointedly comparing England with Coburg where the ten thousand inhabitants celebrated Sunday in thirty-two public gardens with bands and beer. It had shocked him to discover that in England even the innocent games of children were forbidden on Sundays: 'It is not thought proper if people do not put on a Sunday face; I have not heard a real shout on a Sunday since I came here.' One Sunday evening a year later Albert invited Wilberforce to play chess, and laughed openly at his discomfiture when he accepted the invitation but played with a sense of guilt which his glum expression and unwontedly unskilful moves betrayed. Mischievously, Albert asked him to explain why a game of chess was so much more wicked on a Sunday than on any other day, twitting him for the pleasure of seeing him squirm. Wilberforce consoled himself with the reflection that the Queen did not care for Albert to play chess on Sunday, but quite misunderstood her reason: she objected because chess deprived her of her husband's company – whether he played on Sundays or not was immaterial to her.

The character and pastoral activity of an ideal bishop were set out in a letter Albert wrote to Wilberforce in October 1845, at the time of preferment to the bishopric of Oxford. From it can be deduced fairly closely the part Albert believed the established Church should play in the life of the state, and therefore the qualities to be looked for when the crown's right of patronage to the highest offices in the Church was exercised. The letter has usually been interpreted as Albert's instructions for future conduct issued to his former chaplain upon his elevation to a bishopric, although the inherent unlikelihood of such an action on Albert's part is left unexplained.* The circumstances in which it was written (Wilberforce invited it, and Albert at first decided not to write, lest he appear presumptuous), and the closing words of the letter itself ('I have spoken as thoughts have struck me, and am sure you will be better able than I am to take a comprehensive view of the position') almost rule this interpretation out. Moreover, the form of the letter closely follows that which Albert often adopted for his memoranda, notably one on the duties of the Queen's consort which he wrote for Stockmar at the time of his marriage, in that in each case Albert set forth his opinions not as orders which the recipient is to obey but as propositions upon which he seeks comment so that he may himself become better informed. Albert had had a voice (perhaps a decisive voice) in Wilberforce's appointment to Oxford, knew him better than any man who had been raised to the episcopal bench since 1840, and had a considerable regard for his general abilities. What more likely, therefore, than that he should seek enlightenment from him upon the manner in which the established Church regarded the duties of its prelates?

After a conventional distinction between a bishop's duty not to get mixed up in politics but to speak out boldly against social evils, and a simplistic antithesis between 'Christian' and 'Churchman', Albert warms to his theme. The Church has duties towards people and country, and must be zealous in performing them. A bishop

'ought to be uniformly a peace-maker, and when he can, it is his duty to lessen political or other animosities, and remind the Peers of their duties as Christians. He ought to be a guardian of public morality, not, like the Press, by tediously interfering with every man's private affairs, speaking for applause, or trampling on those which are fallen, but by

* e.g. Fulford, *Prince Consort*, p. 189, Newsome, *Parting*, p. 306.

163

watching over the morality of the state in acts which expedience or hope for profit may tempt it to commit, as well in Home and Colonial as in Foreign affairs. He should likewise boldly admonish the public even against its predominant feeling, if this be contrary to the purest standard of morality (reproving, for instance, the recklessness and wickedness of the proprietors of Railway Schemes, who, having no funds themselves, acquire riches at the expense of others, their dupes).'

He had always stressed the connexion between private and public morality, and was shortly to draw the Queen's attention to it again. Within a few years, his condemnation of Palmerston's adventures in foreign policy would be based on the same criteria. The episcopal bench, he now came to realise more clearly than before, ought to be a reservoir of moral power from which good influences radiated outwards for the public benefit; the moral force of a regenerated Church – 'the Church of the Land, the maintenance of which is as important to the country as that of its constitution or its throne' – should drive the nation in the direction of a pure morality: Church and crown joined in a common cause.

One of the talents Albert most envied in Wilberforce was that, although not specially learned himself, he was quick to recognise learning in others. Albert sought to cultivate the same talent himself, and put it to good use when he secured a canonry at Westminster for the Syriac scholar William Cureton in 1847. Less happy was his choice of James Prince Lee for the new diocese of Manchester in the same year, overriding the objections of Lord John Russell, by now Prime Minister. Prince Lee had been a Fellow of Trinity at twenty-five, and an assistant master under Arnold at Rugby before becoming headmaster of King Edward's School, Birmingham, where Albert met him in 1843. He had a great reputation as a classical scholar and teacher (Arnold's testimonial claimed that he was the best in England) and this reputation together with his genial manner so commended him to Albert that Lee became his ideal of a headmaster – most uncharacteristically, after only a single meeting. But the ideal headmaster proved an undistinguished and unsuccessful bishop, bogged down in the petty routine of administration and on bad terms with his clergy. Albert got a good deal of the blame for a mistaken appointment, and deserved it: Lord John Russell vowed that in future he would not allow royalty to interfere in such matters.

The choice of R. D. Hampden as bishop of Hereford later the same year was Russell's own, and it is doubtful whether Albert had even heard his name before the limelight was thrown upon him for the second time in his career. There had been a furore in Oxford when Hampden was appointed Regius Professor of Divinity in 1836, because of allegations that his theology was unorthodox, and the Crown's rights had been brought into issue. The same questions were now raised again. Stockmar warned Albert not to engage in religious controversy, for all it did was to stir up mud better left to settle. Yet when he heard that the bishop of Oxford was pressing for Hampden to be tried for heresy, Albert's distress that a man whom he respected as much as Wilberforce could behave so foolishly was very great – perhaps partly because he knew that Wilberforce was quite well aware that he shared some of Hampden's views about the priority of Scripture over tradition – and he took up the cudgels on Hampden's behalf. It would no doubt have been wiser to stand aloof, but he was so outraged that he let his feelings get the better of him and had only himself to blame when he was charged with actively promoting Hampden's cause. Greville believed that he bombarded Russell with letters every day until the appointment was confirmed. Whether or not this was so, he certainly told Russell that Wilberforce had 'shown the cloven hoof'. To Stockmar he complained that Wilberforce had shown 'a lack of prudence and a contentiousness unseemly in a bishop', and he rebuked Wilberforce himself for bringing the royal supremacy into jeopardy by 'waging war upon a minister of the crown and the sovereign'. What most alarmed him about the Hampden affair, however, was the fear that the clergy were magnifying beyond reason what were really quite trivial matters ('perhaps the next suggestion will be that Hampden should be burned at the stake', he told Stockmar) while leaving greater grievances to go unchecked.

The same fear of bigotry running riot underlay Albert's attitude towards Pius IX's re-establishment of the Roman Catholic hierarchy in England in 1850 and his appointment of Cardinal Wiseman as Archbishop of Westminster. It was possible to conclude that Rome was challenging the Reformation Settlement at a well-chosen moment (Wiseman had long been arguing that the logical goal of the Oxford Movement was Rome), and anti-popery became rife – the headmaster of Rugby even demanded the removal of a local postman because he was a Roman Catholic. To Albert's horror, Lord John Russell stoked the fires of intolerance by referring to Roman Catholic ritual as 'mummeries of superstition'. Strong critic of Rome though Albert was, he hated intolerance a thousand times more and determined to do his best to stem the wave of religious persecution which seemed to be breaking over the country and as far as possible to present the monarchy as more tolerant than its subjects. But as the husband of a Queen who had sworn to uphold the Protestant faith it was not always easy for him to act as he wished, and his official position sometimes placed him in a serious dilemma. A party of Oxford and Cambridge dons ('as ridiculously worked up as a pack of old women', he contemptuously told Ernest) arrived at Windsor one dark December day to present the Queen with a petition for the expulsion of Wiseman. Albert was frozen with cold when he and Victoria received them in an unheated St George's Hall, but sarcastically remarked later that the dons were no doubt kept warm by their own fervour. As Chancellor of the University, he had to deliver the Cambridge address; all he could do to tone down its anti-Catholic phraseology was to read with what the Queen called 'well-marked emphasis', although she feared that this was lost on everyone but herself. On the other hand, by refusing to accept the Roman Catholic Lord Edward Howard's offer to resign his position as equerry, the Queen and Albert signified their disapproval of narrowmindedness. An attempt by Albert to use King Leopold's good offices with the pope came to grief against the stubborn opposition of Palmerston and the Cabinet, and so did his proposal to send a formal mission to induce the pope to change his mind, but he was the first to propose a postponement of the Ecclesiastical Titles Bill (designed to prohibit the establishment of the Roman Catholic dioceses), and so contributed in no small measure to its ultimate abandonment. His actions throughout the affair were constantly directed towards cooling the overheated atmosphere, and he was not afraid to endanger the crown's prestige (there were cries of 'No popery' at the state opening of Parliament in February 1851) in a cause which touched his conscience so nearly.

Ireland had long attracted Albert's attention – in 1847 he had planned a visit *incognito*, so that he could see things for himself and not simply be shown what others thought he ought to see, but had abandoned it when the secret leaked out – and the spring of 1849 seemed, in Clarendon's words, 'a politically propitious moment', since the people had quietened down after the Corn Law disturbances. But a state visit to a country plunged in the depths of poverty would scarcely do, and Albert ingeniously suggested that they should save expense by calling at Cork, Dublin, Belfast and other ports on their way to Scotland by sea; it was a poor reward to be criticised for downgrading a state visit into a yachting excursion. They received a tumultuous welcome when they landed at Cork on 2 August and took it for an indication that loyalty had survived the troubles, not sensing that the Irish were merely using their presence as an excuse for merry-making. The splendours of the Viceregal Lodge at Dublin delighted them; they were enchanted by the servants' brogue and charmed by the beauty of the scenery and the women, and although Albert was well aware that these impressions of a ten days' visit were necessarily superficial, he nevertheless began for the first time to feel that Ireland's problems might not be insoluble now that he had seen the place for himself.

Unfortunately he quite failed to comprehend the depth of Irish hatred and rancour towards England or to realise that his usual remedies for distress – better housing, new industries, railways and education – which might have had a chance in the days of Daniel O'Connell, could not possibly work now that the revolutionary Smith O'Brien led the nationalist movement, although they were more desirable than ever because of the continuous fear of a 'stab in the back' by a Franco-Irish assault which had haunted him during the Chartist riots. One of his gravest misconceptions was that if the Irish once realised the horrors of civil war they would cease to support such a firebrand as O'Brien, but like others after him Albert did not understand that in Ireland rational conclusions do not apply. If he had fathomed the nature of the Irish better he would not have been so quick to blame Lord John Russell for doing too little for Ireland. It was all very well to say, as he did to Ernest, that it would soon be too late as it already was in France; he did not make enough allowance for the fact that the government had to grapple with the consequences of past mistakes as well as with the difficult Irish temperament. He was in the right, however, when he complained of prejudice and neglect of the fundamentals of the Irish problem, and had already proposed several solutions of his own, all of which had proved abortive. The 1849 visit served to stimulate his interest afresh and to confirm him in his refusal to regard Ireland as a lost cause. The ignorance and waste he saw everywhere alarmed him: not nearly enough use was made of natural resources, potatoes were grown where wheat would have flourished (what could one make of a country, he said, where a farmer actually ploughed in his wheat in order to emulate his neighbour's fine crop of potatoes?), few of the people were literate and the children ran wild. The don in Albert set to work on the educational problem, proposing to bring all the existing colleges together in an all-Ireland university, conducting examinations and conferring degrees, to prevent the various institutions from degenerating into Roman Catholic seminaries in the south and Presbyterian schools in the north; if this was too elaborate to be realised at once, at least it would provide a good

167

target to aim at, and might help to break down the barriers of misunderstanding.

In all this, Albert's object was to keep Westminster on its toes and force the government into productive activity. He went to Ireland more like a minister of the crown on a fact-finding mission than a sovereign on a state visit, and some of his memoranda read like the reports of a member of the Cabinet to his colleagues. Not surprisingly, Westminster was somewhat disconcerted, for Albert was the first to see that the English approach to the Irish question was psychologically wrong and so could only make matters worse. Most disconcerting of all was his determination to proclaim that the welfare of Ireland was the responsibility of the throne.

Just as few monarchs had visited Ireland, so few had shown an interest in social conditions at home, but there had never been so great a need for such interest as in the second generation of the Industrial Revolution, nor a member of the royal family so fitted to display it as Prince Albert. Working-class unrest, caused by the economic depression of the late 1830s and expressing itself, sometimes militantly, in the Chartist Movement's strident demands for Parliamentary reform which culminated in the monster petition and the riot of 1848 (see p. 174 below) had shown him how near violence was to the surface of society; poverty, unemployment and the callousness of employers were to him the roots of discontent, and the way to forestall violence was to eradicate them. The dismissal, during a government economy drive in 1850, of workmen engaged on repairs to Westminster Hall and Buckingham Palace gave him the opportunity for a little direct action. Dismissals of this kind were the best way to revive the Chartist cry 'Why should we pay for the Queen?', for the public could not be expected to know that she had no hand in them, and he said that it made his blood boil when men who had given years of faithful service had nowhere to go but the workhouse. He had been brought up in Coburg to take it for granted that the sovereign would care for such people in sickness or old age. He hammered away at Lord Morpeth, Commissioner of Woods and Forests, until the work was resumed and the men reinstated. But his interest extended far beyond this immediate case. He ordered Lord John Russell to instruct the Chancellor of the Exchequer to produce a scheme for joint employer/employee savings to provide pensions for the aged; but although he held that the government should be responsible for such things he wanted to avoid going as far as Louis Blanc's national workshops in the Paris of 1848. He was shocked by the conditions under which so many of the poorer classes worked and by the inadequacy of their earnings – witness his support for Ashley's Factory Bill* – and was already being influenced in this direction by Cobden and Bright.

The only permanent remedy, however, was for the poor to be taught to help themselves, so that by their own efforts they might increase their comfort, protect their health and rise in the social scale, and he harped upon this theme repeatedly over the years. But by doing so he annoyed successive governments, which did not want his name associated with the workers' cause lest it seem that the Queen's husband was a socialist. If helping one's fellow-men was socialism, Albert replied, he was all for it and made no secret of his commitment. In 1844 he had become president of Ashley's Labourers' Friends Society, and in this capacity was asked to chair a public meeting in the spring of 1848 to celebrate the opening of the first model lodging-house, a project in which he had played a major part. Prime Minister and Home Secretary rushed to the palace as soon as they heard he had accepted the invitation, seeking to dissuade him because there might be 'incidents'. No words of theirs could make him go back on his promise, for he felt it his duty to preside and to show 'interest and sympathy for the lower orders'; a copy of an anonymous pamphlet attacking the royal family for living in luxury upon the earnings of the people, which Russell sent in a final effort to deter him, served instead only to strengthen his resolve. Flanked by Russell and Ashley, he made a strikingly successful speech, and was rewarded when the next morning's papers praised it with the words 'Prince Albert has the right ideas'. The public was, already, within eight years of his marriage, beginning to recognise how much he had changed the image of the monarchy and enabled the people to look up to it for help and guidance.

* See p. 102.

169

11

'Like a series of dissolving views'

From the first weeks of 1848 the news became gradually grimmer for the crowned heads of Europe. Albert was less sanguine about even the English monarchy's future than his uncle Leopold, who wrote in February that although the English throne might be temporarily rocked 'it could rest on its new foundations with an easy conscience, and no harm will come to it'. He brought out and carefully studied a series of warning letters which he had received from Stockmar but not heeded at the time. One of them, written in the autumn of 1847, full of gloomy forebodings about Germany ('The political horizon grows darker and darker'), had seemed unreal and scaremongering when read in the peaceful sunshine of Balmoral. Read again in wintry London, when the news in the papers was worse, it looked rather different – indeed, not strong enough. To prove to Stockmar that he had not completely disregarded the warnings, Albert sent him a copy of a memorandum he had written for Lord John Russell in August 1847, in which he had attempted to define England's attitude towards the liberal movement in Europe and called for a declaration of non-intervention in other countries' affairs: 'Civilisation and liberal institutions must be of organic growth and of national development if they are to prosper and to lead to the happiness of a people. Any stage in that development, any jump made in it, is sure to lead to confusion and to retard that very development which we desire.' Summoned to discuss this paper, Lord John (who had seldom been good-tempered since returning to power with a much diminished majority in July) was so obstinate and uncomprehending that Albert wondered whether he had lost the memorandum before reading it, since his carelessness was well-known.

On this occasion, as on many others, his battle with Russell was fought as bitterly as his many battles with Palmerston, although so much less openly that its seriousness was less widely known. There were two chief causes of conflict between them: Russell did not believe that small states like Coburg could survive anyhow, and was therefore averse to helping them; and he was anxious not even to seem to knuckle under to the palace, since he had so often accused Peel and Aberdeen of doing so. He broke into what he called Albert's 'lecture' to announce abruptly that he was sending his father-in-law Lord Minto on a fact-finding mission to Italy before making any declaration of policy. The Minto mission set off, but was soon overtaken by the swift progress of revolutionary events and, though with the best of intentions, intervened in Italian affairs more than Albert liked. His real difficulty over all this was his own ambivalence and the awkward fact that in half Europe constitutional change meant opposition to Austria. He was inclined to support every monarchy almost on principle, yet he disliked the Austrian monarchy because it was Catholic and hostile to Prussia and because he favoured the constitutional reform (granted no outside intervention) which Austria was bound to oppose.

The drawback of this ambivalence was soon apparent. In November 1847 the king of Prussia wrote an agitated letter to Queen Victoria soliciting help in keeping control of the Swiss canton of Neuchâtel, of which he was sovereign. On the principle that crowned heads must stick together, Albert was inclined in his favour; yet Frederick William seemed interested in Neuchâtel only for the revenue it could produce, and Albert wrote to him pointing out that therefore his troubles were largely of his own making, for he had 'given the people the cold shoulder' instead of 'taking them into his confidence' by incorporating them in the structure of government. It was even harder to uphold the king of Greece, whom Albert always referred to as 'that detestable Otto', who was as great a despot as the Czar in spite of his coronation oath. All Albert's sympathies were with Otto's 'poor oppressed people', yet he felt bound 'on principle' to do his utmost to prevent Palmerston from sending a fleet to support them, for the whole monarchical system would be destroyed, as water washes away a stone, if popular revolution against even someone like Otto were permitted.

It was not just the inconsistencies of monarchs or his own ambivalence on a vital issue which weighed Albert down at this time. Two deaths in the family during the winter had shaken him badly. His adored grandmother, duchess Caroline ('She was an angel upon earth', he wrote brokenly) died in February, and he had found it

171

even more difficult to assimilate the death of his own contemporary, Hugo Mensdorff, who had suddenly 'gone out like a light' three months earlier. Gloom overcame him, and he suffered a return of his old obsession with the shortness of life and the transience of things. There seemed so little time to accomplish all that he wanted to do, so he rose earlier and worked later in order not to leave a mass of unfinished business if he too were suddenly taken. He was not in a resilient enough mood to face the political disasters which overwhelmed him in the spring. Soon 'stretched to the full' with foreign affairs as the revolutionary flood gathered momentum, he was denied an Easter holiday, but noted wryly that his relations gave the oddest excuses for not accepting the usual invitation to Osborne – Ernest could not afford the fare and Alexandrine could not travel alone, Princess Hohenlohe pleaded ill-health, the Leiningens were 'too busy', King Leopold could not leave Belgium but gave no reason, his stepmother was frightened of the sea-journey.

The sudden fall of Louis Philippe in February 1848 was a blow struck at the sensitive heart of his ambivalent feelings. Far from rejoicing at the overthrow of a man whom the Spanish marriage affair had made him distrust, Albert was alarmed at the prospect it opened up for all the crowned heads of Europe, and wondered whether it was the beginning of the end for them all. He had half foreseen that revolution would be the consequence of the corruption in French society, remarked 'What has happened is a terrible indictment of the King's self-imposed isolation', and felt it only a just retribution when Louis Philippe fell a bare three days after he had boasted 'if the Parisians are resolved to have a struggle with me . . . I am quite prepared for them and shall give them a good beating.' This remark had been an uncomfortable reminder of the ostentation with which Louis Philippe had worn the crown; the most shocking example was the way he had entertained them at Eu with a description of how he handed out decorations at an investiture – 'You see, I know how to play the part pretty well.' They comforted themselves by reflecting that they had always worked hard to deserve the respect of the British people and had led moral and upright lives. This might be their only protection against the storm which seemed about to break.

What astonished Albert, however, was the insularity of Londoners throughout the revolution in Paris; they were more concerned with the possible defeat of the government in a Commons debate over the income tax than with the dreadful events across the channel. The violence of the Parisian mob made him fear for the French royal family's safety, but at the same time convinced Albert more strongly than ever that the monarchies must close ranks and present a united front, however strongly his sympathies had once been with the constitutionalist cause. Summoning Stockmar to his side, he listed the woes of the royal refugees, and was despondent at heart although he felt that the Spanish royal family, for instance, were only getting what they deserved. The face of the Continent was changing every day like 'a series of dissolving views'. But Victoria and Albert had a warm welcome for all the exiles, no matter how reprehensible their conduct had been nor how ironical it was that they now sought safety in England – Metternich, he noted, soon began to use the freedom of speech he had so vigorously suppressed in Austria to say uncomplimentary things about his benefactors. Buckingham Palace was soon so full that Bertie, Affie and Alice had to sleep in attic rooms; never before had Albert seen so many pregnant women together at one time, and the sight added greatly to his responsibilities. Yet his concern for the exiles was so great that for days on end he had a carriage meet every train from the coast arriving at London Bridge Station until Louis Philippe and Amélie finally appeared. He was exasperated, however, when the foreigners refused to adapt themselves to English ways, and were rude and unmanageable. Their servants quarrelled and were caught trying on the Queen's dresses, their children bit Miss Skerret's hand as she held them to allow Mrs Moon, the seamstress, to take measurements for the new clothes she was to make on Albert's latest acquisition for the nursery, a treadle sewing-machine. Worst of all was the contemptible lethargy of the French king and queen, who refused to settle down at Claremont. Three weeks after a first quick visit to ensure that they were properly looked after, Albert found them 'the picture of shipwreck' surrounded by the kind of muddle that made him shudder. He could not imagine himself and Ernest not taking off their coats and getting to work, but the young French princes were lounging about, reading the papers, and had not even bothered to open the boxes which Queen Victoria had had specially packed at Buckingham Palace with everything needed for the family's comfort; they were all simply clinging to the hope that someone would put Louis Philippe back on the throne which he had given up so easily but in his mind had never vacated. They grumbled in spite of all Albert's kindness. Although they did not know it, in addition to everything else Albert had arranged through Palmerston for an anonymous gift of money to Louis Philippe 'from a well-wisher' and had begged the revolutionary government not to confiscate his personal property; yet because he did not pour out sympathy in an unending stream they complained that he was 'hard and un-feeling'.

Amidst all the pandemonium, Victoria's fourth daughter, Louise, was born on 18 March. Confined to her room in enforced idleness, Victoria fretted herself into such a state of groundless alarm that she began to doubt the security of even her own throne and imagined herself 'trapped' by the condition of childbirth.

Revolution almost seemed to have come to England too when a mob rioted outside Buckingham Palace on 6 March, shouting 'Vive la République'. The Home Secretary reassured them that it was just a flash in the pan, and Albert put the rioters down as merely 'people who sympathise with the French and break windows', but Victoria, still awaiting her baby and worked up by the refugees, was frightened and tearful. Therefore when he learned of plans for a monster Chartist meeting on Kennington Common on 10 April and heard that public buildings were being barricaded against rioters, Albert kept the news from her and quietly set about boarding up the windows of Buckingham Palace. But whereas Palmerston was in his element fortifying himself in the Foreign Office and preparing for a long siege, Albert did not enjoy the job: the defences could only be makeshift, and he had a host of anxious women and children to protect. Wellington, as Commander-in-Chief, was reassuring about the prospect of successful resistance because he had troops posted at strategic points, but told Albert that his task would be a good deal easier if Buckingham Palace were empty. Albert would have en-joyed a scrap, and was exhilarated at the prospect of serving under the great duke's command, but he soon realised that the Queen's husband could not fight the Queen's subjects and came to the half-reluctant conclusion that it was his duty to evacuate the women and children before blood was shed. Would this seem like cowardice, however? He need not have worried; not a single newspaper even hinted that the orderly departure from Buckingham Palace on 8 April was running away. No sooner had he settled the Queen and her three-week-old baby at Osborne than news came that the great Chartist demonstration had ended in anti-climax, whereupon Albert immediately wondered whether he had not left the scene of action too precipitately – after all, he reflected, they had twice before threatened to plunder London but each time had dispersed at the first show of firmness by the government. He congratulated Lord John Russell and Wellington on the way they had handled the situation, and brought his family back to London before the end of the month.

Albert's cheerfulness throughout these trying weeks won Victoria's admiration, and so did his patience in helping her back into harness again. Work was the only antidote to 'lowness', he had assured her as he laboured over State papers at Osborne, and she envied his ability to keep himself interested under any conditions when he turned in the evenings to composing a chorale for the baby's christening.

As revolution spread through Germany, Albert grew concerned for the fate of Coburg and Gotha. He hoped that the state would survive unscathed, but feared that his brother was courting disaster by refusing to adapt his methods to changed conditions. Two years earlier he had advised Ernest to give way to reasonable demands before he was compelled to concede them, but Ernest, bewildered by a situation he could not understand, blustered and paid no heed. Now the danger was upon him; unless he made concessions at once, Albert wrote on 17 March 1848, Ernest would soon lose his throne. Only at this critical moment did Albert realise how detached from Coburg affairs King Leopold had become – 'he has found a safe haven elsewhere', said the prince of Prussia. However, Leopold was roused to indignation when he heard that Ernest had planned to give up the struggle, abandon his wife and flee to Russia, but had been frustrated by Stockmar. Albert was speechless with fury and racked with anxiety that his brother's shame might become known outside the family and perhaps do harm to the English throne.

Even so, disillusionment with Ernest did not extinguish his hope that the latest stirrings of liberalism might fruitfully shape the national future of Germany; 'it all depends on throwing in the right yeast when the brew is fermenting', he wrote in April. But events moved too fast. Though he disliked Austrian autocracy as heartily as he hated the radical excesses in France, the revolts against Austrian rule in Italy put him in an awkward dilemma. Not only were many of his relations serving in the Austrian army against the Italians, but over the years he had always taken the line – for once contradicting Stockmar – that Austria must be the leader and saviour of the Germans. So he was soured by the Austrian defeats in Lombardy, and paradoxically feared that they might lead to the disintegration of a monarchy whose 'rotten moral fibre' he had often condemned. The astonishing course of events in Berlin put him in an even more awkward dilemma. He thought Frederick William of Prussia must be out of his mind when he heard that he had joined the revolutionaries, and was disgusted at his tergiversation when later on he asked for help against them. Yet he kept finding excuses for him, because kings must always be given the chance to come to their senses. The future of Germany was in the melting pot, now was the moment when her destiny might be moulded – yet both Austria and Prussia were letting her down. To whom could the Germans (the only people really worthy of freedom, he once outrageously remarked, and was perhaps lucky not to damage his reputation in England by saying it) turn for leadership and salvation? There seemed only one small ray of hope: the prince of Prussia, Frederick William's brother and heir. Their slight acquaintance had been enough to make Albert decide upon William as the future constitutional leader of a united Germany, and from this time onwards he sided with Prussia rather than Austria in consequence. He had picked the winner, for William became German Emperor in 1871, but Albert never realised how completely mistaken he was about William's character.

When William arrived in England at the end of March, therefore, a refugee in flight from Berlin, it seemed a heaven-sent opportunity to persuade him of the advantages of life under constitutional government. William had come to save his skin, but for some reason Albert convinced himself that he had deliberately chosen England because England was a free country. He set about indoctrinating him with constitutional ideas, supposing him to be an avid listener and taking William's frequent silences to indicate agreement rather than – as it really did – complete repudiation tempered by the necessary politeness of a refugee. Their conversations about German unity followed the same pattern; William remained silent while Albert explained his vision of a federal German national state – 'a modern constitutionalist industrial version of the medieval Holy Roman Empire', he called it – under the joint leadership of Austria and Prussia, incorporating classes hitherto excluded from a share in government but yet preserving the rights of the princes. It was an impossible amalgam which he expounded in letters to Leopold and Ernest. Never for a moment did William, a typical Prussian militarist at heart, let on that he disagreed with every word his host uttered and cared little for anything but the power of the Prussian army. It is perhaps not really very surprising that Albert managed to blind himself in this way. He was so full of enthusiasm for German unity that he saw only what he wished to see, and gave himself no chance to escape self-deception. William looked more intelligent than he really was, had certainly behaved with more prudence in recent weeks than his brother the king, and listened attentively when Albert held forth on his favourite theme; but this was no sufficient ground for the conclusion that 'Germany cannot do without men like William', particularly since William had never spoken a word in favour of either unification or constitutional reform.

Early in April a Polish national and democratic revolt against their Prussian rulers broke out; it led to some brutality but was suppressed with even greater savagery. Sickened by the atrocities, and bewildered that Germans could commit them, Albert still felt bound to stand up for Germany whenever the English criticised her. It irritated him that Palmerston disliked the Prussian military system and correctly prophesied that a wave of reaction would follow the suppression of the Polish revolt (he told Ernest that Palmerston knew nothing about Germany and that his handling of her affairs was 'wretched'), and he felt it unreasonable that the atrocities should bring German prestige in England so low, for no one took the trouble to understand German politics before denouncing them; thus honour required him to put up the best defence he could. But he was greatly comforted by the reflection that since Prince William had been in England at the time of the massacres – he did not return to Berlin until 30 May – even the prejudiced English could not hold him responsible for them or blacken his name with a charge of complicity. It never occurred to him that William would cheerfully have commanded the Prussian troops had he been on the spot.

Meanwhile the German population of Schleswig and Holstein had rebelled in March against the king of Denmark, who ruled both in his capacity as duke, and called for help from Prussia. The Prussian invasion set off another outburst of anti-German feeling in England, and Albert's embarrassment was the greater because, like most Germans, he favoured the Augustenburg claimant to the Danish succession and not, like Palmerston, most of England and the Danes, the Glücksburg claimant. Thus he was the target of innuendo or attack in Press and Parliament. Although he assured Russell that he tried to be completely objective, he was in fact never able to free himself from understandable prejudice, and by the summer of 1848 the Schleswig-Holstein affair had led to another clash with Palmerston – who had judged England's interests more accurately – the effect of which lasted several years. What filled Albert with horror, however, was the thought that Schleswig-Holstein might lead to war between England and Germany. In May he feared that it was only a matter of days before war was declared and believed that the English would be glad to 'see Germany wiped off the face of the earth'. Anxiety made him so depressed that Victoria feared that he was going to be seriously ill. In fact, as Greville noted, he was suffering from a severe attack of 'Prussianitis';

it was many years before he recovered, and the most distressing symptom was the unpopularity it brought him. Prussia's humiliation at Olmütz in 1850 destroyed the last vestiges of his respect for her king, but he retained his faith in Prince William and the future of the Prussian kingdom. 'I honour the reserve you have shown till now,' he wrote to William in December 1850, 'and charge you with all the warmth of friendship . . . to hold yourself ready for better times, in order to become the sheet-anchor of the ship which is now at the mercy of the storm.' 'Prussia must be the upholder of constitutional freedom in Germany', when William succeeded, he told Radowitz the Prussian Foreign Minister; Radowitz knew William too well to swallow so gross a misjudgement, but hid his scepticism in silence, and thereby helped to ensure that Albert remained in his fool's paradise.

12

'The drop which made the cup overflow'

———

THE duke of Bedford had assured Victoria and Albert in September 1846 that his brother, Lord John Russell, would see to it that Palmerston conducted himself at the Foreign Office with more restraint as a member of the new government than he had done in Melbourne's day. But Lord John was quite unable to do so, although several of his Cabinet colleagues begged him to exert his authority, and in effect Palmerston went his own way as he had done before: he knew only too well that he was the strongest member of a weak government and that he was therefore beyond the Prime Minister's control. In the five years since Palmerston had last been Foreign Secretary, however, there had been a change in Albert. Under Aberdeen's kindly tuition he had learned a great deal more about foreign affairs than he knew when they crossed swords over Mehemet Ali in 1840, and the 'new monarchy' which he was now well on the way to creating could no longer tolerate the independence which was Palmerston's natural way of conducting foreign affairs.

This was one reason why 1848, the year of revolutions, with its swiftly-changing pattern of events all over Europe, saw the opening of a serious rift between the two men. But there was another reason too, subtler but even more fundamental. The revolution in France in February 1848, and the proclamation of a republic, started a European conflagration; by midsummer almost every country on the Continent was up in arms against the repressive monarchs who had held sway everywhere since the peace settlement which followed the defeat of Napoleon thirty years earlier. The revolutionaries' creed was a mixture of national feeling (for many of the monarchs were foreigners, imposed by force or diplomacy on the lands they ruled) with the demand for a more liberal and more representative form of government, and it was mild in comparison with either the nationalism or the socialism of the later nineteenth and twentieth centuries. To the kings and the aristocrats who had been supreme since 1815, however, it seemed to go to the limit of revolutionary extremism. They resisted, counter-attacked, and in most countries eventually triumphed – with the result that many of the oppressed, having failed to liberalise the government of their native land, sought a new and friendlier home across the sea in the first great wave of emigration to America.

Palmerston's ostentatious hatred of oppression put him on the side of the Continental liberals and their uprisings; but this attitude was combined with a shrewd assessment of his country's interests – notably in what was to prove the decisive case of France, where he saw that England must recognise the self-declared Emperor Napoleon III whether she liked it or not, since he had clearly come to stay. Albert too was a liberal, and Albert too was devoted to England's interests. But Albert was the son of the absolute ruler of a small German state, and he was the husband of the most powerful monarch of them all. To Albert, monarchy seemed self-evidently the best form of government – not least, of course, because when well-conducted it could ensure that liberal laws prevailed – and anyone who opposed monarchy seemed in consequence hateful. Thus Albert repeatedly referred to the revolts of 1848 as 'red republicanism', disliked them even though in his heart he sympathised with many of the revolutionaries' demands, and gave comfort and shelter to the kings they exiled even though he knew some of the kings had been oppressors.

Albert's intellectual dilemma in 1848 was sharper than perhaps he realised, but by word and deed he was as unhesitatingly on the side of royalty as Palmerston was on that of the liberal revolutionaries. The gulf between them was wide, and it widened as revolution spread across the Continent that summer. But if the immediate cause of the rift was political, its deepest origins were to be found in a disharmony of temperament so great that neither would make the slightest concession to the other's point of view. Palmerston's natural mode of action was primarily intuitive. The consequence was that his unpredictability, his sudden decisions, the risks he took and the nonchalance he displayed when dealing with grave matters, his refusal to take advice or to confide in others – all these gave an impression of recklessness when confronting situations which might easily become uncontrollable, and made Victoria and Albert feel that they were sitting on the edge of a volcano. They could not help seeing Palmerston as a bull in a china shop, utterly insensitive to the feelings of others and quite devoid of principle. Albert's leading qualities were almost the complete opposite. He had a naturally orderly mind and a professional outlook learned from Peel, and he liked to believe that he always proceeded by logical and rational steps from evidence to conclusion. Temperamental differences on this scale were bound to cause friction.

Thus Palmerston found the new Albert a nuisance because what he called his Germanic anxiety to be well-informed made him too inquisitive. Yet Palmerston was himself the greater sinner. His age and experience should perhaps have made him more tolerant of the younger man's transparently sincere longing for information, and he was almost childishly possessive about the Foreign Office, which he regarded as his own by prescription. Consequently Albert's efforts to keep himself abreast of foreign affairs seemed an intolerable invasion of his rights, and but the prelude to taking over his job or at best curtailing his power. To his mind, Peel and Aberdeen had allowed the part played by the monarchy to be so transformed during the last five years that the Queen now looked upon herself as a kind of permanent Prime Minister with Albert as her Foreign Secretary; between them, he feared, they would soon be running the country. There was a grain of truth in his fears, no doubt, but he completely (even deliberately) misunderstood Albert's real motive, which was simply to be of the greatest possible service to his adopted country; the intimate knowledge of Europe which he had gained at first-hand since boyhood qualified him uniquely, he felt, to perform this service in the field of foreign affairs. The very extent of this knowledge posed a further threat to Palmerston, however; he was just as capable of assessing Albert's talent at its true worth as Peel and Aberdeen, but lacked the generosity to admit it because the talent was to be exercised at his own expense and because he more than half feared that he had met his match. The better side of him recognised Albert's selflessness, his high sense of principle and his sincere desire to serve the community, but he feared for his own position too much to acknowledge their usefulness in practice by surrendering his monopoly of foreign affairs.

On the other hand, Palmerston positively welcomed Albert's interest in Germany, because he hoped that it would keep his nose out of other things, particularly Italy. He was entirely mistaken. Although Albert was now giving up his former predilection for Austria as the leader of a revived Germany, Austria was none the less a German power and many of his relations were serving in the

Austrian army. Moreover, everything that happened in Italy directly concerned Austria, since Austria occupied so much Italian territory; and in consequence the battle over Italian freedom (in which Palmerston hoped to enlist republican France, which was of course anathema to Albert) was fought as fiercely in London as on the plains of Lombardy. All the best cards were in Palmerston's hands; almost insolently he blocked Albert's desire to know what was going on, sending off despatches (often very insulting to foreign governments) on his own responsibility alone and even deceiving the palace by accepting their amendments while suppressing the fact that the text had already been transmitted. Even Greville thought this was going too far. Another of his tricks was to confuse the royal pair by giving them unrelated scraps of information out of context. On the rare occasions when he showed them the drafts in time for them to scrutinise the wording minutely and alter it beyond recognition, he got his own back by sending the original version instead. Albert's anger, when he discovered the deception, strengthened his resolve to get the better of Palmerston. It became a trial of wills, which Albert eventually won. The vein of iron so conspicuous in Queen Victoria's character was by no means missing in Albert, as many have assumed, but he was all the more formidable because he was willing to bide his time and to wait for the right moment to strike the decisive blow. Palmerston found Albert an enigma. Surely he must be carrying on a treasonable correspondence with his foreign relatives – yet the translations which Albert showed him were so innocuous that Palmerston felt sure he was suppressing something and tried to catch him out. In May 1848 he opened a letter addressed to Albert which had come in the diplomatic bag, but found nothing in it to which he could object. He had the effrontery to claim that he had done so by accident. Albert and Victoria did not believe this for a moment, but Albert was probably quite right, as well as very generous, when he said that Palmerston had 'yielded to a sudden impulse', and that because he was not a man of principle there was 'no inner voice' to stop him.

Their first serious clash in this year of revolutions came over Italy. Long before, Palmerston had heard Albert say that Austria was his 'second fatherland', and in consequence had convinced himself that Albert was prejudiced against the Italians; yet Palmerston expected his own violently pro-Italian sentiments to be treated as the product of rational and impartial judgement. He kept Albert as short of information about the Italian revolts as he dared, justifying his conduct by the palace's alleged pro-Austrian bias. If Albert had not heard regularly every week from his cousin Alexander Mensdorff in Vienna he would have been entirely in the dark about the march of events.

Palmerston never hesitated to wave the red flag of Italian liberalism under Albert's nose. He rudely demanded to know how the Austrian occupation of so much Italian territory could be justified, and rejoiced when the armies of liberal Sardinia-Piedmont drove the Austrians out of half their north Italian possessions, when Sicily rose against her oppressive king and when a republic was proclaimed in Venice. Albert, of course, saw no reason why a north Italian state should be set up at Austrian expense, and went over Palmerston's head by drafting a letter to this effect for the Queen to send to the Prime Minister.

Anxious to stop the fighting if possible, Albert had sketched out a peace plan as early as May 1848, and successive re-drafts, to keep up with the wildly fluctuating situation, occupied him at intervals all through the summer. He did not manage to be nearly as objective as he supposed – accusing Palmerston of being 'absurdly' pro-Sardinian, for instance – but suggested a compromise peace which was overtaken by events when the Austrians defeated Sardinia-Piedmont at Custozza on 22 July and regained all that they had lost. This meant that Austria's hold on Italy could not be loosened unless the Italians sought outside help and the new republican government of France came to the aid of the liberal king of Sardinia-Piedmont. But three evils would follow if this happened, Albert considered: a widening of the conflict, more danger to Austria, and (if Palmerston had his way) English applause for the Parisian revolutionaries. A revised version of his plan, which Albert promptly drew up, earned nothing but scorn from Palmerston; without ceremony, he drew his pencil across it. His own solution would be quicker and more effective – Austria must surrender all her Italian territory and take her soldiers home. This confirmed Albert's worst fears, as he had made the Queen say in a note he had drafted in a fit of anger at the beginning of the month: 'She cannot conceal from Lord Palmerston that she is ashamed of the policy which we are pursuing in this Italian controversy in abetting wrong.' A similar letter three weeks later ('the establishment of an *entente cordiale* with the French Republic, for the purpose of driving the Austrians out of their dominions in Italy, would be a disgrace to this country') brought a declaration by Lord John Russell that the whole Cabinet was solidly behind the Foreign Secretary and revealed an unexpected ally in Disraeli, who exactly expressed their own feelings when he told the House of Commons that 'joint action with French Jacobins is to be deplored. It commenced with fraternity and ended with assassination.'

Fury with Palmerston and frustration at his own helplessness before long led Albert into indiscretion. Overworked and irritable, he began writing a series of letters to King Leopold, sending copies of them to his cousin Alexander Mensdorff in Vienna and to Charles of Leiningen, the Queen's half-brother, in Frankfort, reviling Palmerston and in effect offering secret advice to the Austrian government which contradicted everything Palmerston was telling them through ordinary diplomatic channels. Such inexcusable conduct can only be explained by the strength of his feelings and by his and Victoria's need to find abroad the sympathy which was denied them at home. It is clear that he intended his views to be leaked to the Austrians, but it was extremely foolish of him to trust Leiningen, who had the reputation of being far too free with his tongue, particularly since he was careful to say nothing to his brother Ernest, a well-known gossip. Leiningen soon abused his confidence by talking too openly in Frankfort, so that the prince of Prussia, with whom Albert was anxious to foster good relations, never wholly trusted him again.

Before long, Albert and Victoria were soon plotting to get rid of Palmerston. But how to do it? They fantasised so wildly about the wonderful relief that his departure from the Foreign Office would bring them that they even concocted an absurd scheme to make him Lord Lieutenant of Ireland – quite overlooking the fact that Palmerston had never been known to do anything against his will and that Russell would never have let him go. There was a curious blindness in the Queen and Albert which prevented them from understanding that others did not always want the same thing as themselves. They thought their plan for getting rid of Palmerston quite excellent, and were put out when the Prime Minister flatly refused to accept it, showing an obstinacy which forced Lord John to defend Palmerston with more vigour than he really intended. But they refused to give up, invited Lord John to dine, and rounded on him after an awkward and uncomfortable meal with 'Palmerston must quit'. He had lost their confidence, they said, and his letters to the governments of Europe's kings ('bitter as gall' was Albert's description of them) were endangering the peace of the Continent. Next they produced the ridiculous charge that he had made too much fuss about the Spanish marriages, thereby increasing the animosity of the British public against Louis Philippe's France; of course, they went on, they fully recognised his skill, but came up with the preposterous suggestion that his abilities fitted him to be Lord Lieutenant of Ireland (perhaps he would like time to see to his large estates there, Albert added for good measure). Poor Lord

John! They had no mercy, so he had no choice but to oppose them. To remove Palmerston from the Foreign Office, he said, was sure to make him turn against the government and so cause dissension at a highly inconvenient moment. The Queen piped up with 'there are greater interests at stake than offending one man', adding with deliberate menace that she might one day find herself unable to put up with Palmerston any longer, 'which would be very disagreeable'. Watching Albert's stony face, Lord John wondered whether he really believed that the crown still retained the right to dismiss a minister at will. Just let them try it on!

Anger with Palmerston mounted during the autumn. His Austrian despatches were more than ever 'unworthy of a gentleman', and by refusing to mediate when the Austrians had the upper hand in Lombardy but doing so when the situation was reversed he had, from Albert's pro-Austrian point of view, sacrificed an advantage and got 'very bad terms'. Albert's one-sided emotional involvement seems to have blinded him to Palmerston's sincere desire to prevent a general conflagration; his abhorrence of a delay which so obviously favoured the Italians is of course more easily understood. By December the palace itself was feeling the direct consequences of Palmerston's attitude. Albert's worst fears were realised when foreign governments failed to distinguish between the Queen and her Foreign Secretary. The new Austrian Minister-President, Schwarzenberg, so much disliked England's foreign policy that he omitted to send an envoy to the court of St James's to announce the accession of the Emperor Francis Joseph II, although he sent one to every other European court. Summoned by Albert and blamed for the slight upon the Queen, Palmerston brushed the rebuke aside; he took the snub as a compliment, he said, since it came from a despotic government.

Although frequently angered beyond endurance by the Foreign Secretary, Albert was diplomatic enough not to force an open breach, yet could not allow himself to be overridden without a word. In mid-December he most unwisely asked King Leopold to let the Austrian court know of his sympathy for their cause, and went on to criticise Palmerston sharply: 'I consider Austria's *rancune* against Pilgerstein* quite natural, and I am glad that one expects better and more loyal feelings from Victoria and me than from this heartless, obstinate and revengeful man.' It was fortunate that no harm came of this indiscretion; the luck that he so often bemoaned when it favoured Palmerston smiled on him for a change.

* The nickname Victoria and Albert used for Palmerston when they were in an angry mood.

185

By the new year of 1849 Palmerston had become an even greater liability. Though they believed themselves to be prepared for anything, it was still a shock to read in *The Times* that the Foreign Office had secretly allowed a British contractor to ship arms from a royal arsenal to the Sicilian rebels in flagrant violation of Britain's policy of neutrality in the struggle between them and their pro-Austrian king. They were at Windsor at the time, and sent a peremptory summons to Lord John Russell to come and give an account of himself. He did not dare refuse. On 24 January he had to undergo the humiliation of a two-hour carpeting by the Queen and Albert, both beside themselves with anger. The previous day Palmerston had brazened it out with Lord John; for Lord John to brazen it out with the sovereigns was impossible. Albert produced records of conversations, memoranda and letters, all in apple-pie order, to confound him. The Prime Minister did his best to defend his colleague, but his every move was checkmated by Albert's infallible memory and the papers in his hand. It was intolerable, the accusing voice went on, to have to apologise over and over again for actions which Palmerston had taken on his own responsibility alone and for which he ought now to pay the penalty by resignation or dismissal. The most the Prime Minister would concede, however, was a promise that when the court went to Scotland in the autumn Palmerston would not be left alone in London with nothing to do – it was only boredom which caused him to make mischief.

So obsessed had Albert by now become with the man's misdeeds that he more than half believed that Palmerston blew up the famous Don Pacifico incident of 1850 to outsize proportions in order to irritate the Queen and himself. A Greek mob had sacked a house in Athens which belonged to Don Pacifico, a British subject though a Portuguese Jew from Gibraltar, and the Greek King and government refused redress. The king of Greece was Otto of Bavaria, and Palmerston had long persisted in believing that Albert favoured German princes wherever they were found simply because they were of the same blood as himself. Thus in bringing the country almost to the brink of war by sending the fleet to demand compensation for Don Pacifico he was dealing a sidelong blow at Albert as well as giving free rein to his sense of the dramatic and to his anti-German prejudices. He had badly misjudged his man. Albert more than once referred to the king of Greece as 'that loathsome Otto', but nevertheless felt bound to take his side because he was a king, not because he was a German; it was the threat to monarchy posed by Palmerston's action which aroused him. But the Foreign Secretary's action had caught the country's mood, and 'the people's Palmerston' was jaunty at his sudden popularity. Albert, on the other hand, wondered whether he had gone too far and hoped that this time he had played into their hands; 'Give him enough rope', he had often urged on the impatient Queen, on fire for her minister's head. Now perhaps he was at last about to hang himself, though at the cost of placing the country in a terrible predicament. Palmerston had not taken the Cabinet into his confidence, but had acted entirely on his own. Would this be enough to bring him down? Once more mercilessly interrogated by Queen and Prince in turn, the Prime Minister stood his ground, refusing to disown Palmerston in spite of the harm he was doing. He could not possibly be moved from the Foreign Office – where else could he go? Not out of office altogether, for that would bring the government down at once. He had refused the Colonies in 1845, and would do so again. Albert would not hear of his becoming Leader of the House of Commons, for this would not clip his wings enough (he might even use his position to seize the premiership, Albert feared; Lord John countered unconvincingly by saying that he was too old at sixty-five) and very strongly pressed Russell to take the Foreign Office himself. Worn down by the pressure, Lord John supposed he could manage both offices; but nothing could be done until Parliament rose. When the Prime Minister had left, Albert remarked bitterly that if only Russell had shown as much resolution towards Pilgerstein years ago as he was showing towards them now, their lives might have been easier.

The enormous popularity which Palmerston's actions had brought him was a source of real bewilderment; he was cheered wherever he went – in the streets, at the opera, even in Parliament itself. Only in the palace were there frozen looks and cold hearts. On 25 June Palmerston faced his critics in the Commons, where the opposition of several of the ablest men, led by Peel, encouraged Albert and Victoria to hope that their enemy was about to meet his doom. Night had fallen by the time Palmerston rose to speak; five hours later, as dawn was breaking, he sat down after one of the most remarkable performances the House had ever witnessed. Not once searching for a word, not once consulting the half sheet of notes which he held in his hand, he mesmerised his audience with his fluency and ended with a piece of patriotic bombast which has become notorious: 'As the Roman in the days of old held himself free from indignity when he could say *Civis Romanus sum*, so also a British subject, in whatever land he may be, shall feel confident that the watchful eye and the strong arm of England will protect him against injustice and wrong.' Oratory had rescued him from disaster, and Albert had underestimated his instinct for self-preservation. 'It will be more difficult to remove him now,' he wrote gloomily to Ernest next day.

Because of their position the Queen and Albert were quite unable to understand the power of public opinion; they had no idea how to court it nor how to handle it and they were no nearer understanding it after reading an account of Palmerston's speech, although Albert was generous enough to call it a masterpiece. They managed to convince themselves that much of his apparent popularity was manufactured, a weapon designed to intimidate rather than a genuine expression of feeling. How easy it was to become the idol of the people! But what did it profit him or his country if he had 'no very high standard of honour and not a grain of moral feeling.'

It was his total lack of principle that really damned Palmerston in Albert's eyes. Victoria had given birth to her third son, Arthur, on 1 May, and had still not fully recovered. How would she stand up to still further provocation from Palmerston, Albert wondered, particularly since the Prime Minister did not protect them. Lord John Russell was far too irresolute to be capable of mediating between two such strong characters as Albert and Palmerston; instead, he would timidly agree with the one and then go back and fall in with everything the other said – but it was usually Palmerston who had the last word. Indeed, Russell was not altogether unhappy to sow discord between the palace and the Foreign Office, and sometimes even fanned the flames; when in July Albert unworthily revived the old story of Palmerston's nocturnal wanderings at Windsor*, he could easily have scotched it, instead of saying that he knew other ladies in society who had suffered in the same way. There was so much to criticise in Palmerston's present actions that it was foolish of Albert to rake up the past, and he would have done better to stick to his record as Foreign Secretary.

Albert turned to Stockmar for advice, but got less than he had hoped for. In his old age, Stockmar had taken to encouraging the autocratic tendencies in the Queen which Albert was always trying to damp down. It was Stockmar who had put into a head which was very ready to receive it the idea of regarding herself as a permanent premier, and he had done nothing to check her sneaking belief in the Divine Right of Kings (except when the boastful Prussians made use of it). Fortunately, the last word was always Albert's. On the increasingly frequent occasions when Albert gave her unpalatable advice, she turned to Stockmar for solace and for confirmation that

* Before the Queen's marriage, Palmerston had burst into the bedroom of one of her ladies-in-waiting, supposedly in error.

she was right and Albert wrong; sometimes this meant that Albert had to take them both on at once, and formidable adversaries they made. She appealed to Stockmar now and got the answer she wanted: 'Palmerston is mad and should be dismissed'; dangerous advice, which Albert was too sensible to heed but which the Queen took literally because it fitted in with her own inclinations. Five months earlier Stockmar had drawn up a memorandum on the sovereign's rights, a piece of work as confident as it was inaccurate. According to him, the Queen held the trump card, the right of dismissal:

'The least the Queen has a right to require of her Minister is (i) that he will distinctly state what he proposes in a given case, in order that the Queen may know as distinctly to what she has to give her royal sanction (ii) having once given her sanction to a measure, the Minister who, in the execution of such measure alters or modifies it arbitrarily, commits an act of dishonesty towards the Crown, which the Queen has an undoubted constitutional right to visit with the dismissal of that Minister.'

This was too much for Albert's taste, and he tried to persuade the Queen to delete 'an undoubted constitutional right' before Lord John saw it; unlike Stockmar, he was far from certain that it was correct. In any case, his experience told him that to dismiss Palmerston (whether she had the right to do so or not) was to take a direct hand in politics, and that this – particularly in view of Palmerston's popularity – would be the height of folly and might endanger the crown itself. When Lord John received her only very slightly amended version of Stockmar's document on 12 August he was appalled but conceded that it demonstrated her right to dismiss a minister; Palmerston, he considered, could not possibly continue in office after this.

Neither Albert nor Lord John need have lost a moment's sleep; the culprit caved in at once and without a word of protest agreed to everything. He asked for an interview with Albert and was granted it on 14 August. Their meeting was very different from what Albert expected. Gone was the bland smile, the jaunty air and the easy self-confident explanations; in their place were tears and an agitated manner as he stammered 'What have I done wrong'? He could not describe his horror at being accused of lacking in respect for the Queen, to whom he was bound by every tie of duty and gratitude; in future he would obey her commands without question. It all came out very pat; Albert had perforce to be satisfied, but he was only half convinced. Was Palmerston after all capable of turning over a new leaf? Perhaps he was. But Palmerston had gained one useful insight: during the whole interview, he noticed Albert used the third person ('The Queen thinks . . .', 'The Queen says . . .'), but he saw plainly that it was really not the Queen at all but Albert himself who thought and said and commanded. In future, he knew, it was Albert who had to be reckoned with.

The fear that Palmerston might still be unrepentant persisted all through their holiday at Osborne; he dominated their conversation by day and made such an uncomfortable bedfellow that they could not sleep at night. Albert admitted to Stockmar that they felt themselves so blinded by passion that 'we can no longer see the picture clearly. The game is Pilgerstein's and how he enjoys playing it!' It was a pity that the Queen's fidgety nature could not let the matter rest, for the inescapable consequence was that she worked Albert up too and that the affair so filled their minds that they could enjoy nothing – neither the garden nor the children's happy shouts as they played on the beach. Resolutely, they tried to raise their spirits by taking short 'marine excursions', reading new novels to each other and dipping into the poetry of the young Alfred Tennyson, which Albert enjoyed. This year Albert persuaded the Queen to bathe in the sea for the first time; shocked by a report that women were bathing at Mediterranean resorts in costumes which showed every curve of their bodies when wet, he had designed a heavy black garment for her which did not show a single scrap of plump queenly flesh. When she drooped in the evenings Albert persuaded her to study Ashley's new emigration scheme, which was to bring hope to hundreds. Recently he had gone with Ashley to wish God Speed to a party of young people bound for Australia and a new life. 'Was there room for her'? the Queen asked. Pilgerstein made her too feel like emigrating, and Albert's mood was so black that he could not savour the good news from Germany to the full. The king of Prussia had roused himself from his lethargy sufficiently to dismiss his reactionary Minister-President Manteuffel and replace him by the liberal Brandenburg: the exulting Stockmar had written 'Prussia is saved, Germany too'. But who would save them from Pilgerstein?

They had hardly been back from Osborne a day before he struck again. The draymen at Barclay Perkins' brewery had recently hit the headlines through the mauling they gave an unwelcome visitor, the Austrian general Haynau, when he came to London soon after taking a prominent part in the unnecessarily cruel suppression of the liberal revolts of 1848 in the Hapsburg empire. Horrified, Victoria and Albert demanded that Palmerston send an apology to Vienna. He agreed without demur, but delayed three weeks before sending it and then could not refrain from adding a postscript: 'The general's visit was most unwise.' It seems never to have occurred to Palmerston to explain to the Queen that there was some justification for the public's dislike of General Haynau, in view of his many brutalities, and that he shared it himself. Had he done so, he would have found a surprisingly warm welcome. Even after the rough handling he had received a month before, there was no need for him to give way in everything; as Peel had discovered long ago. Albert and Victoria were always open to reason and would listen to a good case so long as it was presented calmly. But Albert was still bedevilled by his inability to understand public opinion, and it was up to Palmerston to explain its strength to him. Albert took it for granted that the draymen and the newspapers were wrong when they attacked Haynau, simply because they were the voice of public opinion, but it would not have been difficult to persuade him otherwise. Palmerston did not attempt it, and so Albert was still in the same frame of mind when he drafted for the Queen a demand for a second apology, which Palmerston tried to counter with a threat of resignation on 13 October, relying on the fact that it was a bad time for him to go. But backed up by his father-in-law, Lord Minto, with whom he was staying, Lord John was adamant and insisted that the second apology must be sent. Once cornered, Palmerston gave in without a murmur and sent an amended despatch. Strangely enough, Albert was relieved; he did not want the Foreign Secretary to resign over a matter on which he was just beginning to change his mind and to show the sympathy which Palmerston could easily have awoken in him if he had done his duty at the beginning. Since the incident he had received a letter from Alexander Mensdorff in Vienna putting Haynau in his true light: 'he is a thoroughly bad character and richly deserves what he got.'

The next trial of strength came just a year later, with the arrival in England during October 1851 of Kossuth, the patriot who had led the 1848 rising in Hungary, who came to render thanks to Palmerston on his own behalf and that of thousands of others for saving them from Austrian and Russian vengeance in 1849 and ensuring their safe passage to America. Kossuth received a hero's welcome, but when from English soil he denounced the governments of Austria and Russia the Queen forbade Palmerston to proceed with his plan to receive him, lest this give the impression that Britain endorsed what Kossuth had said: a rare letter from the prince of Prussia made this very point. After a moment of blustering defiance, Palmerston once more gave way, thus earning Albert's contempt for again preferring to retain office rather than stand up for his principles.

Only a week or two later, the luck of the 'devil's son' ran out at last, and Albert saw the English proverb 'Give a rogue a rope and he will hang himself' once again fulfilled in his fall. On 2 December 1851 Louis Napoleon, the president elected after the republican uprising of 1848 in France, declared himself Napoleon III, Emperor of the French. Although Palmerston's instructions to the British Ambassador in Paris were quite correct in requiring a non-committal stance at this moment of tension, in private conversation with the French ambassador in London he gave warm support to the *coup*, and his contradictory behaviour soon became known. To Albert, this was 'the drop which made the cup overflow'; the Queen scarcely needed his persuasion to demand that Russell dismiss Palmerston, and Russell was not at all reluctant to comply. It was done at last (save that Palmerston failed to keep his appointment to hand over the seals of office and later wrote with cool effrontery to apologise for what he called a 'misunderstanding') and the relief was enormous. Albert's New Year letter to Ernest dwelt with equal satisfaction on the success of the Great Exhibition and on the 'happy circumstance' that the man who had embittered their lives by facing them with the 'infamous alternative of either approving his misdeeds all over Europe or letting him lead the Radical party into open conflict with the crown, thus throwing into utter chaos the only country in which freedom and the rule of law exist side by side' had been the agent of his own destruction.

The Foreign Secretary's humiliation was not yet complete. Two days after his dismissal Lord John, smarting from one of Albert's rebukes ('We have known for some time that you could not control him') read the Queen's letter of August 1850 to a packed House.* The effect was devastating as it gradually dawned on Palmerston's colleagues that he had eaten humble pie in order to retain office. It gave Albert great pleasure to see that, now the facts were known, 'Lord Palmerston is not coming off well with public opinion', and Stockmar rejoiced at the disappearance from the political scene of the 'self-willed lord'. 'Pilgerstein is finished', Albert crowed to King Leopold, and Disraeli spoke the funeral oration: 'There *was* a Palmerston.'

It is ironical that Palmerston was dismissed on the one occasion when he was right; it was necessary to recognise the new regime in France, although Palmerston went about it in the wrong way. But in the moment of triumph neither Albert nor Stockmar realised that they would soon be paying tribute to Palmerston's foresight; for Palmerston had already recognised the first signs of the Russian aggression which was soon to culminate in the Crimean War, and

* See p. 189 above.

had seen that an Anglo-French alliance was necessary to counter it.

The words with which Albert described, in his letter to Ernest, the cruel dilemma in which Palmerston's behaviour had placed the crown were not written lightly, for they represent the core of his reasoning about Palmerston. Behind Victoria's far more intransigent attitude (which seems to have persisted right to the end) loomed the shadow of Stockmar, sometimes thought a dangerous adviser whose 'ignorance of the British constitution was equalled only by his belief in his own perspicacity.' This may be too harsh, although it is certainly true that as he got older and his correspondence with British ministers virtually ceased, Stockmar's views on the monarchy became narrower and more fixed; but in any case by this time Albert had often disregarded Stockmar's advice and went his own way. Albert's natural caution and his deep knowledge of constitutional law overcame his strong personal desire to get rid of a thorn in his side, and this comes out clearly as soon as his actions are understood. It was he, not Stockmar (as Greville supposed), who forbade the Queen to dismiss Palmerston on her own initiative and made her bide her time and allow events and Lord John Russell to do the work for her.

When Palmerston stalked off to Broadlands, accompanied by his outraged wife, the Queen and Albert breathed a sigh of relief. Happily for their peace of mind, they were unaware that this was by no means the end of the old enemy, and that he was soon to rise again wearing another and (to Albert) more congenial hat, that of the Queen's first minister. With the passing of Pilgerstein the Foreign Secretary, the jealous guardian of his own policies overseas, there disappeared also the need to keep Albert at arm's length; the Prime Minister of 1855 could judge the Prince's potential at its proper worth and appreciate, as Peel had done, how much he could help him in dealing with the more volatile Queen.

The clash between them would have been less serious if Palmerston had recognised from the start how useful Albert's flair for foreign politics could be, and how much he could learn from the private information contained in the correspondence with his relations abroad which Albert willingly offered to show him. But Palmerston's years of foreign travel had not obliterated his English prejudices: Albert was a foreigner and therefore could neither understand England nor see foreign affairs with English eyes. It would have helped, too, if he had known of the vow Albert took in 1841 to sink his own personality in that of the Queen and as far as possible to play only an unobtrusive part himself, for this would have prevented him from suspecting that Albert's ultimate objective was to make himself Foreign Minister in all but name. Behind and beyond all this, however, lay the unbridgeable gulf between two contrasting personalities which looked at life in totally different ways. Conscience, which was the key to Albert's view of politics, scarcely troubled Palmerston at all; he was left unmoved by social injustice and cruelty, which enraged Albert and drove him to seek remedies, and never came anywhere near an understanding of Cobden's or Bright's passionate concern for their fellow-men, which struck an answering chord in Albert almost at once. If he had shown any sign that he really cared for the welfare of the peoples he befriended abroad, Albert would have been the first to respect his motives. But he acted as if they were merely instruments of policy, and seemed to have an almost complete disregard for right and wrong, which shone out to Albert as the statesman's lode-stars.

Part Four
Fulfilment 1851-1861

13

'A monarchy that was a myth has become a reality'

ONE day in the spring of 1848 Albert travelled to Suffolk to visit a friend who was thinking of selling his farm because he could not make it pay. Inspection revealed that the implements and buildings were out of date, that the manager had not kept up with modern scientific methods although he was willing and energetic enough and the soil was rich. A bargain was struck; Albert would supply some modern farming equipment if in return the owner would give him a detailed report on the difference it made. Fourteen months later he received a glowing report; the improvement in his return was far greater than the farmer expected. The incident brought home to Albert the lamentable fact that all over England farmers were lagging behind for lack of proper scientific knowledge, and made him determine to remedy the situation. He had searched for years himself before he had found a first-class implement maker in Ipswich, but the firm employed so few men that orders were never fulfilled on time, and when he had mentioned expansion the head of the firm had said that he did not do enough business to make this economically feasible. Nevertheless he had managed to have some of their farming implements exported to Ernest in Coburg, and when an estate in Bohemia came on the market cheaply had vainly tried to persuade his brother to buy it in order to conduct agricultural experiments.

From the time of his Suffolk visit in 1848 he began to turn over in his mind the idea of holding an exhibition of farm equipment to advertise modern agricultural methods and stimulate British farmers to persuade the government or the Bank of England into giving financial assistance to firms which lacked the resources to

197

develop their inventions. Recollections of the Frankfort trade fair, which he had known as a boy, and of its profitability, soon led him to extend his idea to include inventions in fields other than the purely agricultural and to develop it along lines which had become familiar through the exhibitions held in Paris, Dublin and elsewhere during the last half-century. A visit to the National Gallery added another element to his design. He noticed that there was hardly anyone about, and remembered that he had seldom seen more than a handful of visitors in any of the museums and art galleries of London. Why not remind the public of the treasures they possessed by adding an exhibition of pictures to his plan? He was to explain the combination of these separate elements into a single whole two years later in the following words: 'Science discovers the laws of power, motion and transformation; industry applies them to the raw matter. . . . Art teaches us the immutable laws of beauty and symmetry, and gives our productions forms in accordance with them.' Meanwhile, during the spring and summer of 1848 the idea gripped his mind with increasing force, as he worked through the reports of the commissioners for the triennial exhibitions held in Dublin since 1829 and accounts of similar events.

Unlike other royal princes, Albert was inside the art world; he was by now a well-known collector in his own right, frequently consulted by experts, and he had been the very active President of the Society of Arts since 1845 (his predecessor, the duke of Sussex, could not tell one picture from another and used to say complacently 'Royal patronage is enough'). As President, Albert had guided the society through a critical stage, raising badly needed money and offering prizes for design-work which promoted the union of the arts and manufacturers. This acted like rain on parched soil, and there was a huge response from commercial artists pining away for lack of encouragement and funds. In his speech at the annual prize-giving on 14 January 1849 Albert sounded the members of his plan for a national exhibition of British goods, and to his great joy the proposal met with tremendous applause.

One member of the society responded to the speech more eagerly than the rest; he was Henry Cole, a former clerk in the Public Record Office, a self-confident, almost pushing man. From the start his dynamism attracted Albert, who marked him down as a man he could use. Here, ready-made, was the ideal second-in-command – resourceful, quick and able to translate Albert's ideas into commercial terms, tactful and energetic. But there was also another side to Cole's character, not at first discernible: he was a snob, and he ingratiated himself with Albert in order to forward his ambitions through royal patronage. When Cole was invited to Buckingham Palace it was difficult to tell which of the two men was the more impressed with the other. They discussed the exhibition as though it were something already settled. To Cole's first question 'How big?' Albert replied 'Big enough to attract important people', and in response to the question 'What?' thought that the exhibits ought to range from paintings to machines for making butter-milk, embracing all the inventions of the industrial age on the way. When Cole inquired where the exhibition was to be held, Albert suggested Leicester Square but let himself be persuaded to accept Cole's alternative proposal of Hyde Park because it would give greater prominence although it would be more expensive. It has become fashionable to credit Henry Cole with the whole idea of the Great Exhibition, and his autobiography (written forty years after the event) shows that he had almost come to believe it himself. One instance of this is his claim to have proposed for the first time at this meeting that the exhibitions should be international; always a man to give credit where credit was due, Albert does not say anything about this, but takes it for granted that it was his own idea. It seems likely that he had been thinking along these lines for some time, and that Cole's warm response to his speech (in which he had not used the word 'international') led Albert to try out this still larger scheme on him.

A few months later he invited Cole and three other members of the Society of Arts to Buckingham Palace to go into the project further, and gave each one a separate part to play. Cole was allotted the most important – to travel on the Continent and advertise the exhibition. He was able to report, on a visit to Balmoral in the autumn, that his mission had been highly successful in awakening interest abroad, and that he had secured many promises from potential exhibitors. At a large public meeting in London on 21 February 1850, a smack in the eye was administered to Lord Stanley and the Protectionists by the announcement that all foreign goods for the exhibition were to be admitted free of duty. (It seems to have been a highly successful meeting. Lord Morpeth, who presided, quoted Pope with resounding effect to applause so enthusiastic that it reminded Lord Malmesbury of the last day of the half at Eton – 'All that was missing,' he said, 'was something to throw.')

Everything depended on a speech Albert was to make at a Mansion House banquet on 21 March at which the exhibition was to be formally launched. With so much at stake, his old nervousness of public speaking returned, and so far from being able to calm him, Victoria was as agitated as he, for she knew how close to his heart the project lay.* But his fervent belief in the project lent him courage, and he spoke for half an hour with vigour and effect.

'Nobody . . . who has paid any attention to the peculiar features of our present era, will doubt for a moment that we are living at a period of most wonderful transition, which tends rapidly to accomplish that great end, to which, indeed, all history points – the realisation of the unity of mankind. . . . The distances which separated the different nations and parts of the globe are rapidly vanishing before the achievements of modern invention, and we can traverse them with incredible ease. . . . Gentlemen, – the Exhibition of 1851 is to give us a true test and a living picture of the point of development at which the whole of mankind has arrived in this great task, and a new starting-point from which all nations will be able to direct their further exertions.'

There was no doubting the tremendous success of this speech, or that now the exhibition would certainly take place. Caught up at once in the general excitement and too busy to brood self-pityingly on Albert's imagined neglect of her, the Queen forgot the anxiety about his health which she had only lately expressed to Leopold ('He spares himself too little and others too much') and now told him 'Albert is indeed looked up to and beloved as I could wish he should be, and the more his rare qualities of heart and mind are known, the more he will be understood and appreciated. People are much struck by his great power and energy.'

But there was as yet no money. The government had refused to shoulder the cost of 'frivolities' and for some time there were no subscriptions to the guarantee fund which was opened directly after the Mansion House banquet. Then one day Cole by chance met a businessman with social aspirations, a Mr Peto who, on discovering that no one had been brave enough to start the fund, wrote a cheque for £50,000 on the spot. The size of the figure made Albert whistle when Cole told him the news; 'this will stir others', he said excitedly. At last they were in business.

The building committee was full of famous names but so entirely lacking in taste that Albert rejected all its designs out of hand.† John Grace, MP, was quite unjustified in branding one of them, which had been leaked to the Press, as 'exactly the kind of hideosity the palace likes' and in saying that public opinion would never allow it to be built in Hyde Park. Albert had always known what

* Peel's kindly nature was revealed when, as soon as it was clear that Albert's speech was being well received, he slipped away in order to bring the good news to the Queen at once.
† The best it could do was a dome 200 feet in diameter built with 19 million bricks; it reminded Albert of a prison.

kind of building he wanted, and at this moment recalled Joseph Paxton's great glass conservatory at Chatsworth, which he had first seen in 1844. So impressed was he with this unusual structure that he had at once minutely cross-examined Paxton about its strength and durability. Later in the same year, during a tour of a glass factory, he had come across a new substance which would bind glass and steel together and would not crack under pressure. At the time he had merely been considering the erection of a similar green-house at Buckingham Palace, but now there dawned upon him the possibility of adapting this method of construction for the exhibition building. At midsummer, while the controversy over the designs was still raging, he invited Paxton to inspect the Hyde Park site and to say whether he would take the job on. (It says much for the duke of Devonshire's faith in Albert that he made no comment on this extraordinary request and at once gave his head gardener leave to go to London.) Unlike most countrymen, Paxton found London entrancing, and during a moonlight walk inspiration came to him in a flash. He sat down at once and described it to his wife; the building would be 'the same length as Portland Place, three times its breadth, and the same height as that great street.' Albert was delighted, but wondered whether the public could be persuaded to accept so revolutionary a design in the short time still available. Encouraged by the enthusiastic opinion of the pernickety Grace, to whom Cole showed it, he had the design published in the *Illustrated London News* for 5 July. The warmth of its reception was as startling as the design; the public clamoured for it, and soon almost came to believe that they had thought it out for themselves. Only the build-ing committee remained obdurate, and it cost Albert three meetings and endless patience before he could bring them to see any merit in it.

Just at this critical moment a dark shadow was suddenly cast over the whole plan by Peel's riding accident on 29 June and his death a few days later. Not only had he been one of the first com-missioners of the exhibition, but Albert's closest friend and adviser for many years, and the shock of his loss was almost enough to put Albert off the project altogether. It deprived him of his long-time guide and friend, the one Englishman he could talk to without reserve, just when he was most needed; for it was directly after a meeting of the Commissioners of the Great Exhibition – at which Peel had worsted those who opposed Albert's views about the Hyde Park site – that Peel's horse stumbled and threw him as he rode up Constitution Hill. Albert was one of the few who knew how really ill Peel had long been, how debilitated by insomnia and continuous headaches, and it seem likely that the explanation of the horse's stumble is to be found in a fainting-fit or sudden stroke on the part of its rider. Gladstone had already seen the effects of ill-health reflected in poor performances in the Commons. Only two nights before the accident, Peel had dined at the Palace, and it had distressed Albert to see how little he ate and how unusually silent he was. Yet his speech at the Great Exhibition meeting was quite in the old style, full of fire and strength – so much so that Albert for a time felt that he could not carry on without him. In answer to his first anxious inquiries, he was told there was hope: Sir Robert had fallen into a deep sleep and awakened in less pain. But this alarmed Albert. Was the sleep anything more than the onset of coma? The later report that the patient was weaker seemed to confirm this, and made him so uneasy that he could not settle down to work, yet felt too restless to go to bed, and the news of Peel's death was brought to him just before midnight as he sat in his study trying to read. Deep emotion compelled his pen for once to reveal his true feelings: '. . . Peel, the best of men, our truest friend, the strongest bulwark of the throne, the greatest statesman of his time'. The intensity of Albert's affection for Peel had been brought home to Gladstone a few hours earlier. He called at the Palace to give Albert the latest bulletin, and was amazed to find that he had already gone out, alone and on foot, to seek it himself.

If Peel's death caused Albert's enthusiasm for the Exhibition to wane for a moment, the warm reception given to Paxton's design made him rouse himself, and he felt it his duty to carry on now that he had got so far. He invited Richard Cobden to take Peel's place as Commissioner, but it was only with the greatest difficulty that he got Cobden to sit at the same table with Protectionists like Stanley 'for the Prince's sake'. Most people thought Cobden an extraordinary choice, and were amazed and critical when it leaked out that Albert had been so keen to secure the Radical MP that he had delivered the invitation in person. Albert's reasons were not in the least devious; he needed a man whom he could rely on to work hard, a man whose proven fund-raising abilities would be of tremendous value in the coming months. It was not realised how much Albert liked and admired Cobden, particularly for the help he had given Peel behind the scenes in 1846 and for the way he always stood out for principle – even when doing so led him to wear his ordinary black suit for dinner at the palace (when Albert did not mind in the slightest, Cobden said defensively that he had dined in it with several other crowned heads).

Difficulties soon arose about a site. Albert had come to the con-clusion that the south side of Hyde Park would be best, and intended to achieve a 'natural effect' by enclosing some of the standing trees within the building. This novel idea was greeted with howls of incredulity, but the objections were just as loud when he ordered a few small trees to be cut down – he was charged with vandalism and people who had not set foot in Hyde Park for years screamed that it would soon be a desert at this rate. When Paxton's glass house at last began to go up, it was derided as too weak and in-substantial, and Ruskin likened it to a cucumber-frame. Objections of this sort were not entirely silenced even when the flimsy-looking structure rode out two severe storms without damage, for Sir John Airey, the Astronomer Royal, wrote a pamphlet to prove that it was bound to collapse. The wildest and most prejudiced accusations were current; Colonel Waldo Sibthorpe, who had not raised his voice in the House of Commons since he had opposed Albert's grant ten years earlier with the words '£20,000 is too much for pocket-money' now asserted that Albert was concealing 'terrible ambition' behind the project and prayed Heaven to send hail and lightning to destroy 'this den of vice', in which foreigners would undercut British trade, rape British women and plot revolution.

Nonsense like this had little more than nuisance-value, however; internal dissensions among the committee members were far more dangerous. One group was seldom on speaking terms with another, and there were constant accusations of tale-bearing. An atmosphere of tension developed as one man jockeyed with another for royal favour in the hope of being rewarded with a title. Cole took too much upon himself; he threatened Fox and Henderson, the building contractors, that unless the work was speeded up he would let the newspapers know that their firm was useless, and without consulting anyone suddenly announced that the exhibitors would have to pay for admission every day, thereby causing such an outcry that Albert had to issue an immediate denial. There were fierce disputes about the catering contract until Albert insisted on awarding it to the highest bidder (Messrs Schweppes, at £5000).

To get away from anxieties like these, Albert took a brief holiday with his family at Osborne in March, and returned refreshed to oversee the final preparations. Pessimists still abounded, and there was too little money in the kitty, but Mr Fox, of Fox and Henderson, cheered Albert by saying that his name was guarantee enough, and refused additional payment as an inducement to his men to work faster. Those who had hung back rallied when the duke of Welling-ton was seen daily on the site talking to the workmen and raising the spirits of those who shared Albert's secret fear that the work would never be finished on time by the brisk words 'I know it will be ready. Paxton has said it will'.

When he could tear himself away, the soldier in Wellington took over. For fear of riots, certain roads must be kept open to facilitate the passage of troops, he said, and he wanted to draw up emergency plans for the placing of men and guns, until persuaded by Albert that it would be a mistake to have a soldier in sight. Albert's instinct about crowd reaction was surer than the duke's; the presence of soldiers would have struck a jarring note out of keeping with the whole tone of an exhibition which, he had laid it down in the Mansion House speech, was to celebrate 'peace, love and ready assistance not only between individuals but between the nations of the earth'.

The only concession he would make towards preparations for keeping order in an emergency was to make use of the scientific inventions which it was the purpose of the exhibition to show off: the electric telegraph would be demonstrated to visitors by a detachment of royal engineers, whose line was connected also to the nearest police station, and a black ball was to be hoisted over the transept, after the fashion of a storm-cone, as soon as the building became dangerously full. Another invention which was put to practical use was the improved gas-lighting which, on one overcast day, was acclaimed 'almost as good as sunlight'. Albert's own fascinated interest in technology was shown not only in the prominent place allotted to the photographic stand but also in an idea which struck him suddenly one day during the building period – the crowds of onlookers showed that others shared his fascination, so why not rope off an enclosure for them and charge a small entrance-fee? Later, in a curious anticipation of the routine at 'stately homes' today, he extended this to include conducted tours of the model dwellings erected for the construction workers, in the hope that a speculative developer with plenty of capital would see them and want to copy them elsewhere on a large scale: Albert had a remarkably sharp eye for business! Among the thousand other details he had to attend to, some needed very delicate handling: Pugin had to be tactfully persuaded to remove an enormous crucifix from the Tractarian stand before evangelicals like Ashley spotted it and jumped in with all guns blazing, and his diplomacy was taxed to the utmost before he persuaded Cole to revise his first obscure and long-winded draft of the catalogue. Through all these troubles and travails, Victoria was his greatest support, for she never had the slightest doubt that the exhibition would be a great success. She came on eight different occasions to see the work in progress, (Cole reckoned that each visit cost £20 in lost working-hours, but that the men worked with more vigour after a sight of their sovereign) and kept up his spirits so well that everyone found his confidence infectious.

Most Continental rulers had shown some initial interest, but as time went on all in turn got cold feet and withdrew their promises to attend. Those who had survived the revolutions had no wish to be finished off in a foreign land by some trigger-happy terrorist; that 'dear friend' King Frederick William of Prussia, for instance wrote to say that his brother's life was too precious to risk by a visit, that he had heard the Crystal Palace was unsafe and that great crowds pressed together might bring a new outbreak of the Black Death.* Remembering how overjoyed the king had been in 1848 to know that his brother was 'safe in England', Albert replied sarcastically that he could 'give no guarantee against these perils, nor assume responsibility for the possibly menaced lives of your royal relatives', but put a sharp sting in the tail of his letter: 'It is probable that any sudden postponement of the visit, and the reasons for it, would create a very serious sensation among the public.' This soon brought Frederick William to heel, for he feared the loss of one of his few allies: his brother and his family would come, with a 'small suite' of twenty-nine. The decision was a momentous one; the Prussians stayed four weeks, finishing up with a few days in the domestic atmosphere of Osborne. Walking up and down on the beach in the sunshine, Albert and Princess Augusta settled Germany's political future to their entire satisfaction; Stockmar had just done the same with Prince William, and had reported to Albert that he found Prussia's future king (whose whole outlook was totally opposed to everything the two of them stood for) 'firm as ever in his constitutional views and highly indignant at what had taken place in Berlin.' Most momentous of all was the first meeting between Vicky and her future husband, Fritz.

---

* He had been scared by a letter in the following terms from King Ernest Augustus of Hanover: 'I hear that the Ministers as well as Prince Albert are beginning to jibber with anxiety over this rubbishy Exhibition in London. I beg you, if you have time, to get read to you the speech of one of the most prominent and cleverest statesmen that we have, Lord Lyndhurst, a former Lord Chancellor, who gave a complete exposé in Parliament last Thursday of the infamies, plots and menées of the excommunicated of all lands, who are now in London. It is really a masterpiece, and not merely as a speech, but in the clearness with which he explained to the Lords and Ministers how things are in London at the moment. I am not easily given to panicking, but I confess to you that I would not like anyone belonging to me exposed to the imminent perils of these times. Letters from London tell me that the Ministers will not allow the Queen and the great originator of this folly, Prince Albert, to be in London while the Exhibition is on, and I wonder at William's wishing to go there with his son.'

The grand opening day, 1 May, began with a fine drizzle which happily turned to sunshine before the royal carriage reached Hyde Park. There had been a 'pretty little ceremony' in the palace courtyard before they set off. Vicky, all in white, with roses in her hair, had presented the prince and princess of Prussia with a copy of the catalogue specially bound in satin and gold; the first verse of Psalm 24 on the title-page – 'the earth is the Lord's and all that therein is: the compass of the world and they that dwell therein' – expressed her father's belief in this 'mighty project', his fervent prayer that peace and plenty should come to 'this storm-tossed world'. The significance of the cheers that greeted the procession were not lost on the Prussians, who rightly took it for a sign of the respect in which the monarchy was held in Britain. But even Victoria and Albert were startled by the reception which met them when they entered the exhibition hall. The organ crashed out Albert's own oratorio as he led the Queen – in her favourite pink watered silk, the Koh-i-Noor diamond blazing in her hair – up the aisle towards the dais, with its canopy of blue and gold; she was more deeply touched, she said, than she ever could be by a church service. Albert, too, only hid his emotion with difficulty, but let nothing disturb his triumph – not even a stupid quarrel over precedence started by the Prussian minister (it completely ruined the procession of the Diplomatic Corps) which he dismissed as 'terrible trouble over the arrangements'. It was left to the Queen to sum up the day's achievement: 'God bless my dearest Albert, God bless my dearest country, which has shown itself so great today!'

The first of many eulogies of Albert as creator of the Great Exhibition was pronounced by Sir Charles Eastlake at the Royal Academy dinner on 3 May, and Albert's reception of it was typical. He turned the praise aside as soon as he could, congratulating Eastlake upon his appointment as President of the Academy instead. This was always his way; outside the family circle, praise was to him almost indistinguishable from fawning and flattery, and he was sparing with his own praise – all he said to Peel when the Corn Laws were repealed, for instance, was 'Well done', although he regarded the event as one of the most momentous in history. Yet paradoxically his nature needed a certain amount of praise to bolster up his tendency to pessimism: it was only the Queen's unstinting support which had kept him cheerful through the ups and downs of planning, and the eulogies he now received from all quarters had a permanent effect in raising his self-confidence, however lightly he appeared to value them. He swallowed all that the gushing Princess Augusta said about the Great Exhibition, however, for he was quite uncritical of everything to do with the Prussian royal family and could never view its members objectively. He saw them not as they were, but as he wanted them to be, disregarding warnings in the Press and the lessons of his own experience in dealing with Frederick William IV. Augusta, he was convinced, would now sing the exhibition's praises to her previously sceptical brother-in-law, and from Berlin news of its success would spread all over the Continent, making doubters look foolish and enhancing England's reputation in Europe.

The real importance of the Prussian visit was not this, however, but the way in which it had opened Augusta's eyes to the strength and stability of the British throne and the opportunity it gave for the beginning of a friendship between Albert and her nineteen-year-old son Fritz William. After noticing how even to walk round the exhibition hall exhausted Prince William, and how his appearance had deteriorated since they last met, Albert was now discarding his former faith in William as the future saviour of Germany and turning instead to his son, who had clearly inherited Augusta's liberal ideas. In a series of long evening conversations he poured out his hopes for German unity to the young man, and found him a ready listener, particularly to severe warnings about Russian power, Austria's anti-German attitude and the way Habsburg and Jesuit influence was opening the door to red republicanism. All this was going too far and too fast for Fritz, who, untravelled and with a purely military background, did not know what to make of this strangely different society – he was really alarmed, for instance, when the duchess of Kent became accidentally separated from their party in the Crystal Palace and astonished when the Queen and her children went into peals of laughter at the idea that she could possibly come to harm in a place like London.* Fritz was surprised, too, that the Queen was delighted with a trick handkerchief which turned into a bouquet as soon as she touched it, instead of treating its presentation as a mark of disrespect. So, floundering and ill at ease, Fritz was relieved to be able to take refuge with the ten-year-old Vicky, who talked to him in fluent German and helped him buy one of the marvellous new English electric clocks to take back home as a present.

Victoria could not attend the closing ceremony on 15 October – the Commissioners were to occupy the platform for the final speeches, and Albert had reluctantly to persuade her that, while she obviously could not sit with them, it would be even more improper for her to sit elsewhere, lower than her own subjects. So the two of them paid

---

* A policeman, who did not know who she was, took care of her and found her a good position from which she could see the Queen!

a last nostalgic visit the previous day. She could hardly keep back her tears at the thought that 'this glorious project that has brought happiness to so many' was coming to an end. Not one of the predicted disasters had occurred – the Crystal Palace had not fallen down, the roof had not leaked, not a pane of glass had cracked, not a board splintered; everyone had been orderly and the sun had shone its blessings on them all. This last day proved no exception to the rule that each visit brought some new excitement: as Victoria made her way up the central aisle she was greeted by an old woman who had walked all the way from Cornwall to see the exhibition and her sovereign, full of joy that she had arrived just in time to fulfil her dearest wish. The incident proved to the Queen's satisfaction that their reputation for leading a model family life had spread far and wide, and combined with the cheering crowds on her way back to the palace to console her for missing the Great Exhibition's final moments. Her happiness overflowed when Albert did not allow the exacting business of the next day to prevent him from giving her the bracelet of gold leaves which he had designed specially to mark the twelfth anniversary of their engagement. That night she wrote a letter to Stockmar, who had been back in Coburg since September, and could not resist ending it with a dig at all those who had been too craven to risk a visit to the scene of Albert's triumph: 'We regret for their own sakes that so few princes have come, here again dividing themselves from their people. Deeply will they repent it when it is too late. . . . He stands so high; all the people feel he wishes them well, and thinks of them; and depend upon it, this will never be forgotten.' She could afford to be a little superior, for the cheers still ringing in her ears proved the truth of Albert's reiterated teaching – never to separate herself from her people.

Long before the exhibition closed, it was widely known that Paxton, whom success had made ambitious, was dropping hints everywhere that the terms of the charter under which the use of the Hyde Park site had been permitted should now be modified so that the Crystal Palace could become a permanent winter garden to house his favourite tropical plants; *Punch*, for instance, which had poked such fun two years earlier at the idea of holding an exhibition in a home-made conservatory, now plugged the winter garden scheme for all it was worth – 'It could become a source of instruction in botany and ornithology.' Ignorant of the obligation to remove the building, and conveniently forgetting his own earlier opposition to the Hyde Park site, Greville took the same line, affecting to believe that 'the Prince was bent on demolishing it from the start'; even

City aldermen had become so fond of it that they begged Albert to leave it where it stood. To Albert himself, this was a mistaken view. Quite apart from the legal obligation to remove the building, its future ought to be consistent with the objects of the exhibition it had housed and

'we have distinctly pledged ourselves to expend any surplus which may accrue towards the establishment of future Exhibitions or objects strictly in connection with the present Exhibition. The purchase of the Crystal Palace for the purpose of establishing a Winter Garden, or a Museum of Antiquities, or a public promenade, ride, lounging place, etc. etc., has, in my opinion, no connection whatever with the objects of the Exhibition. Our connection with the building has been an incidental one, namely, as a covering to our collection, and ceases with the dispersion of that collection.'

He was therefore well pleased with the decision to re-erect the Crystal Palace on a site in the south-eastern suburbs at Sydenham, but the main purpose of the memorandum from which these words are taken was to advocate a particular method of turning the unexpectedly large surplus of £500,000 to good use. Four museums of the arts and sciences could be built on a twelve-acre site in South Kensington (it was on the market for £50,000), thus prolonging the exhibition's aims indefinitely and filling a serious gap in the cultural life of London. He invited the Commissioners to Osborne to discuss this imaginative and far-sighted proposal; because he knew how easily decisions are postponed on the plea that more information is required, he had gone carefully into every detail of the four museums (finance, construction, nature of the collections and so on) and was most emphatic that they should settle quickly on some such grand plan rather than fritter their money away on a series of smaller and worthless schemes. Cole raised silly objections, more to manifest his independence than because he believed in them, and so Albert adjourned the meeting for ten days to give time for reflection and to avoid all appearance of overriding his fellow Commissioners. Unanimity came sooner than he expected. At a second meeting on 2 November, Cobden put all his weight behind Albert's scheme, and his advocacy carried the day. The foundations of the South Kensington Museum (later renamed the Victoria and Albert Museum) were laid soon afterwards.

Cobden had ended his speech with the words 'considering the enormity of the job he has done, the Prince has the best title to have his own way.' How times had changed! Only a few years before, Cobden had referred to Albert in the most scathing tones as 'an appendage to the throne', closer acquaintance had begun to change his views even before he became a Commissioner, but since working intimately with Albert over the Great Exhibition he had been too honest not to acknowledge his good fortune in getting to know him better and to admit that although he was a hard taskmaster he never spared himself for a moment. For his part, Albert had looked on Cobden with affection ever since Peel had opened his eyes, and had found him almost the only completely disinterested Commissioner.

Cobden was one of the only two (Eastlake was the other) who held themselves aloof from the indecent scramble for honours, which began even before the success of the exhibition was assured. When would they come? What form would they take? – these were questions canvassed almost hourly. When opening day passed, and still nothing had happened, some of the Commissioners began to wonder whether they were to be cheated, and to murmur that they were entitled to a reward for their labours. Their complaints make sickening reading in the pages of Cole's diary. Cole himself treasured every scrap of praise from important people, listed it in his journal, and took good care that it was known all over London, presumably in the hope that it would come to Albert's ears and that it would weigh heavily in his favour: only three weeks after the exhibition opened he recorded how Macdonald, an official of the royal household, promised that he would 'take the opportunity of pointing out that my services ought to be recognised', and followed this entry with a remark by Fox (the head of the contracting firm) to the effect that without him there would have been no exhibition at all. In view of the bad terms they had been on* it is difficult to believe that Fox really spoke like this, and the good relations which now prevailed between Cobden and Albert, as well as Cobden's well-known inability to flatter, make it still more unlikely that Cobden really said 'I always say that the Exhibition is the work of you and the Prince – I put you first.' Another story of Cole's is that Playfair (one of the Commissioners) had the audacity to ask Albert outright what rewards he had in mind for the man who had worked with him; this too seems improbable, for Albert says nothing about it.

As Victoria and Albert had no doubt always intended, honours were conferred shortly after the exhibition closed. On 1 November 1851 the Commissioners were invited to Windsor, and after an excellent luncheon the Queen was about to knight them all when it was suddenly discovered that there was no sword handy.† Amid much

---

* See p. 203 above.
 † This gave rise to the erroneous report that the honours were only conferred on the spur of the moment.

laughter Albert sent to the barracks for one, and twenty minutes later the ambitions of Henry Cole and his colleagues were satisfied at last. Cobden alone stuck to his principles and refused.

The story of the Great Exhibition is a lesson in leadership and determination. Nothing like it had been attempted in England before, so there were no precedents to guide or warn the 'supreme manager', and the responsibility upon his shoulders was all the greater. Despite the sceptics and the many obstacles, Albert bore everything with equanimity and resourcefulness, and worked with a cheerful confidence which ensured success. Only once did he hesitate: the sudden shock of Peel's death nearly caused him to lose his nerve, but he quickly mastered his private grief and regained his energy. He surprised everyone, except the few who knew him well, by his capacity for leadership and his aptitude for management, and buried for ever Greville's gibe that he had 'a slouching hesitant air'. He confounded those detractors who declared that he deliberated too long about everything he did, for it was surely instinct which made him choose exactly the right moment – the first real signs of calm after the revolutions of 1848.

As the business-manager of a vast enterprise with a horde of employees, Albert was seen and known by thousands who would never have come into contact with him otherwise. All were drawn to him by the magnetism of his personality, his lively mind and broad vision, the honesty which prevented him from pretending to skills which he did not possess and his instant appreciation of the work of others. Not for a long time had a royal prince been so widely known, so wholeheartedly liked or so completely trusted. Relying unhesitatingly on Albert as their guarantee, Fox and Henderson gladly did £80,000 worth of work even before a contract for it was signed; not a brick would have been laid for George IV or William IV until the money was in the bank, but by 1850 Albert had acquired a deserved reputation for paying his bills and for being a man of his word. It was not his rank which had achieved this transformation but his personal integrity and the capacity for business which he was now manifesting daily before the eyes of half London. The success of the Great Exhibition was a mark of the nation's confidence in the man who had designed it and showed beyond doubt the place which he held in its affections.

14

'The duke
had to be content'

BOTH Victoria and Albert were thankful to escape to Scotland as
soon as the Great Exhibition closed, for Albert always complained
that he could not breathe in hot and dirty London. Scotland was
just as hot in that year's Indian summer, but the pure air combined
with exhilaration at the success of the exhibition made everything
seem more beautiful than ever at Balmoral. They had hardly been
there an hour before they were happily planning an expedition to
Allt-na-Giuthasach, their hideaway near Loch Muich, from which
they hoped to climb to Loch-na-Gar. Two days later they set out
in sweltering heat, but as soon as they reached Allt-na-Giuthasach
the temperature suddenly dropped and it became very cold. Grant,
the head ghillie, built a huge log fire and the little bothy was soon
'snug and warm', so that the Queen could lie happily on her sofa
and listen to Albert playing Chopin Nocturnes on the piano which
had been carried up the hillside for him the previous year. Who could
blame her if she wished they might be marooned there for days, so
that Albert would not be able to spoil her holiday by burying his
head in state papers (which happened too often nowadays), but at
any rate this year a long sermon from Stockmar on the necessity
of resting the brain and conserving energy had made him promise
to 'retreat into my shell'. His insistence on working, even on holiday,
had increasingly become the cause of dispute between them, for
their roles had become almost completely reversed in ten years.
('I don't think the Queen thinks of reading a despatch or of doing
anything in the way of business further than scribbling her name
where it is required,' one of her ladies-in-waiting had written of
their stay at Osborne in 1848.) She now demanded more of his time

than ever – time he had once longed to give: but in order to share the work which he had now almost completely taken over himself, not to spend in relaxation – and he had to remind her sharply of their joint duty and to tell her that she would be much happier if she took a greater interest in public affairs. For once he had proved his point just a year earlier. They had each opened a new railway bridge on the east-coast route, she over the Tyne and he over the Tweed, and she had been fascinated with the glimpse this gave her of the world of science and technology which so absorbed her husband.

On occasions like this the Press now reported his speeches in full, although the newspapers did not always give him the credit he deserved: in 1850, for instance, the *Morning Chronicle* thought the speech he delivered when laying the foundation-stone of the Scottish National Gallery in Edinburgh, 'too good for a prince, and cannot be his own', although the *Spectator* saw 'an individuality about them that stamps the real authorship'. For no reason that he knew of, the *Spectator* had suddenly become very pro-Albert, giving lavish coverage to the Great Exhibition and talking of the man who had inspired it as 'one of the least obtrusive but most useful of our public men', praise which Albert accepted a little grudgingly; for he did not care for its partisan tone. He had always deprecated the habit, usual among ministers of the crown, of using the Press as a mouthpiece for their views, and considered it deplorable that ministers should seek to gain control of newspapers solely in order to influence public opinion: for instance, Lord John Russell *The Globe*, and Palmerston *The Morning Chronicle*, while Clarendon was believed to make a point of seeing or writing to Delane, the editor of *The Times*, every day. It seemed to Albert very proper when Lord John Russell gave Clarendon's connexion with *The Times* as one of his reasons for not wishing him to be in charge of the Foreign Office, but his desire to see Clarendon excluded made him deliberately overlook the fact that it was a case of the pot calling the kettle black. Looking back over the past, he felt that Melbourne had been the only minister to show the right attitude to the Press – he always held himself aloof, yet did so with such skill that he never gave offence – but he unfortunately forgot that much had changed in the ten years since Melbourne's resignation.

His own attitude towards the Press was much too simple, quite unrealistic and thoroughly unreasonable. He thought that events should be reported dispassionately and no attempt made to sway opinion about them, and he was far too quick to condemn journalists for seeking sensation, exaggerating and not verifying their facts but trusting to luck that their hunches would turn out to be right. He showed no gratitude for the part journalists had played in making the Great Exhibition a success by attracting great numbers of visitors through the publicity they gave it, failed to see how much he was therefore in their debt, and seems never to have appreciated that it is not enough to do something extremely well if no one knows about it. Newspapers were cheap, good, and widely read in 1851, and their almost daily articles about the Great Exhibition not only praised it generously but also gave it an enormous amount of advertisement absolutely free, but Albert's prejudice against the Press seems to have prevented him from admitting this. He expected infallibility and never forgot a mistake, like that of *The Times* in prematurely leaking the news that the Corn Laws were to be repealed and thus causing havoc in the City; he attributed the disclosure to the sinister influence of Peel's enemies. The power that *The Times* wielded made him liken it to Russia – to be in its clutches was to be 'ruled by a rod of iron; there is not much between selling one's soul to *The Times* and selling it to the Devil.' Yet paradoxically he considered it to be the best paper and in 1855 ordered it to be sent regularly to Ernest in Coburg 'so that you may know what is going on here!'. However, the old distrust was still there, for he warned Ernest not 'to believe everything as gospel, although in the long run the lies neutralise each other.' He was fond of quoting the case of Delane, who learned of Russell's imminent resignation in Lady Granville's drawing-room and promptly published the news without considering the harm it might do, and credited all editors with similar irresponsibility.

It is a pity that Albert could never rid himself of prejudices like these. He and Delane had a great deal in common: both were liberal free-traders, both were in favour of factory legislation like Ashley's and eager for social reform of all kinds. How much easier Albert's life would have been if he had let himself take advantage of these common interests to establish friendly relations with Delane (perhaps through Anson, Phipps or Grey) and use him as a kind of public relations officer to the Court and *The Times* as his own mouthpiece. It would have been accepted as right and proper and would have helped him over many a rough patch – such as, for instance, the hostility of the public towards him at the beginning of the Crimean War. To his own great loss, Albert could never look on newspapers as more than necessary evils.

Christmas 1851 was spent at Windsor and was one of the most relaxed that Albert had ever experienced: 'I cannot complain of this last year,' he wrote to Ernest, 'the Great Exhibition, the problems of which often gave me much worry, went through in an unbelievably happy and glorious manner without the slightest contretemps to to complain of.' The royal postbag was still filled with congratulatory letters from people like M. Thiers, who had made a special journey from Paris to visit the Great Exhibition, and Albert's old mathematics professor, Quetelet; and the Continental newspapers which King Leopold sent had not yet tired of singing the praises of the man who had inspired it – admiration which Albert in no way spurned despite his dislike of the Press. Even better was the delightful thought that Palmerston was no longer a minister of the crown.* He had nearly disappeared earlier in the year, when Lord John had brought his own government down by insisting on prematurely introducing a franchise reform bill. Reform was necessary and Albert was in favour of it, but he was right in believing that the bill was fore-doomed to failure if introduced at that moment. Summoned to give advice, the duke of Wellington said that there were only two alternatives – a return of the Russell ministry, or Lord Stanley and protection again, and he did not think the country would stand for that, to which Albert replied that he and the Queen would not stand for the return of Lord Palmerston. But back he came, larger than life, to boost an even weaker Russell government until removed by his own hand and Louis Napoleon. The incident taught Albert that he could only get his own way with Lord John by being very firm, so when it came to choosing a successor to Palmerston he did not hesitate.

He wanted someone pliable who would do what he was told, and during the past twelve months he had picked out the ideal man for the job – the thirty-year-old Lord Granville (known in London society as 'Puss'), who had assisted him to organise the Great Exhibition, was amiable and not too clever, and who openly admired him. Russell did not give in without a struggle, but fought bravely though badly for his own candidate, Lord Clarendon, who was *persona non grata* with the court for intriguing with the Press; he lost point after point against the implacable Albert, who rode rough-shod over the Prime Minister's efforts to hold on to some remnants of authority over the composition of his own Cabinet. Albert used bullying tactics of the worst kind which can hardly be described as constitutional, barracking every proposal of Lord John's until he wore him down. When, for instance, Russell argued that if he offered the post to Granville he would be acting contrary to

* See p. 192 above.

the wishes of the rest of the Cabinet, Albert briskly replied that if the Cabinet had known that the Queen was determined not to accept Clarendon they might have come to a different decision. When Russell finally put his finger on the tender spot by pointing out that it would look as if Granville had been appointed to please the Court, which wanted a subservient Foreign Minister, Albert evaded the issue with 'We do not care a fig for such gossip', and got his way in the end. Granville, appointed on 26 December, was 'overcome' at his good fortune but 'full of courage and goodwill', as Albert noted when the new Foreign Secretary bowed himself out of the audience-chamber after promising to 'set a good example and see that others do the same' and to have nothing to do with the Press. Albert usually despised toadies, but he laughed heartily when Granville related how a friend of his had found the English so unpopular abroad that their only defence was to say 'Civis Romanus NON sum'. Another dig of Granville's at his predecessor was equally welcome; for the three years during which he had served under him at the Foreign Office, he said, Palmerston had never once spoken to him of foreign affairs.

It never seems to have occurred to Albert that by imposing so young and inexperienced a man upon the Prime Minister he was giving the Queen very bad advice and allowing her to make a mockery of one of the most important government posts and of the Cabinet itself. The best interpretation that can be put on what he called 'this happy choice' is to explain it as the result of nervous exhaustion after the endless battles with Palmerston and reaction after the fatigue and responsibility of the Great Exhibition. Ironically, it was Palmerston who saved him from the consequences of his own folly by turning the government out in less than two months.

His public commitments were by now considerably reducing the amount of time Albert could spend with his children, although this did not mean that he ever neglected their welfare. They were growing up too rapidly for his taste, since greater age meant more squabbles and – what was more annoying from the Queen's point of view – made them clamour for more and more of their father's attention. There were now seven in the royal nursery, four girls and three boys, the youngest (Arthur) born on the duke of Wellington's birthday, 1 May 1850. In the autumn of that year their secure existence was shaken by the resignation of their governess, Lady Lyttelton, who had been as much beloved by the parents as by the children and who left royal service to the sound of sobs and lamentations. Despite entreaties not to drive herself too hard, she was too conscientious, too devoted and cast too much in the mould of her royal master not to have almost worn herself out in charge of so many children. Deprived of her kindly guidance, they were now often apt to get out of hand. Vicky had learned to ride her pony bare-back, and taunted Bertie because he could not manage without a saddle, so he screamed and hit his sister, who hit him back. She could climb trees better than he could, run faster, ride better, indeed was more talented in every way. Affie, the second son, was so mischievous and daring that Albert lived in constant fear that he might do himself a real injury – at five he slid down the banisters but could not control his speed, fell off, would try again, and concussed himself. Even a child as placid as Alice was developing a will of her own and teaching her two little sisters Helena and Louise to develop theirs.

But not one of the children gave as much trouble as the heir to the throne. Bertie was a difficult child, subject to bouts of bad temper and sudden, frightening rages which were as impossible to control as they were trying to witness. While in one of these 'fits' (Albert sometimes used this word when describing them in confidential letters to Stockmar) he had to be watched with the greatest vigilance in case he did some mischief to himself or harm to others: for he would tear at his hair, bite his clothes, stamp his feet, bang his head against the wall and belabour the other children unmercifully, screaming at the top of his voice the whole time. It was most exhausting for all who had to deal with him. Even in his rare sunny moods he could not be trusted alone with the younger ones for a moment lest his mood change, for although small for his age he was so strong that it took two footmen to restrain him. These attacks left him white and prostrate for hours, irritable and stammering if spoken to but otherwise quiet, 'as though he were asleep with his eyes open' as Albert told Stockmar in some concern. Lady Lyttelton, as worried as his parents, confirms this, saying that in these moods he took in nothing, however clearly and calmly she spoke to him. This aggressiveness made the normal relations she enjoyed with the other children impossible in the case of the prince of Wales, but she took the optimistic view that he would grow out of these attacks in time. But even she had to admit that she could not interest him in the simplest lessons until after he was four years old: he ran all over the room, throwing his books about or crawling under the table to tear them to pieces, until his long-suffering governess was quite worn out. Punishment was ineffective, since it only resulted in yet another tantrum. In her conscientious way Lady Lyttelton tried to explain the difference between right and wrong so that he should understand why he was confined to his room or deprived of some treat, but to her dismay he did not comprehend at all; there seemed to be nothing in him to which she could appeal. At five his speech was inarticulate and still babyish, and this, combined with his stammer, made him difficult to understand; this was another cause of tears and tantrums, so that he often went uncorrected. Yet if he were not taught to speak properly, how was he ever going to be understood? More trying than his backwardness in speaking was his compulsive chattering, and when he was in this mood he demanded constant attention. If Vicky was happily employed he would tug at her sleeve, pull at her hair, snatch her books and pencils, all the while talking rapidly and nonsensically in a high-pitched voice; then there would be a fight, both of them shrieking as loud as they could. In yet another mood he would make sudden overwhelming demands for affection, and no amount of caressing or petting would satisfy him. Albert took it for a good sign when an affectionate mood followed a bout of bad temper, trying to believe that he was penitent and wished to make amends, but a few simple questions usually showed that he was not in the least sorry.

It was all very disturbing, but his anxiety did not prevent Albert from drawing up a scheme, with Stockmar's help, for the boy's education. It came to be known as 'The Plan', and was designed with one eye on his special difficulties and another on his future position, an impossible combination which doomed it to failure. Albert was not unaware of the pitfalls, but he was hopeful of success, for the plan was not to be put into operation until Bertie was seven years old and ready to be handed over to the care of a tutor. Until that time no real pressure was to be put on the child, and he was to be taught nothing more onerous than reading and writing and how to sit still long enough to take in a few elementary lessons. It was disconcerting to find that he had made almost no progress by the age of six: he did not understand that he was the Queen's heir and his curiosity had not been aroused by his title, although he had been constantly in the company of his parents. A tour of Cornwall in the royal yacht in 1847 gave Albert a chance to explain that one day he would be king: but when the cheering crowds cried 'The duke of Cornwall for ever' and Bertie asked 'Why do they call me that' he made the great mistake of embarking on an elaborate explanation about the Black Prince and ended by making the child more confused than ever.

It was difficult for Albert to face the fact that his eldest son was below average. How was he to be brought up if he was really incapable of learning? What would become of him and of the succession to the throne? 'The Plan' catered for this as far as possible, for instance by providing that half an hour of arithmetic should be followed by half an hour's drawing, to keep interest alive; by way of contrast, at the same age Vicky had been working the whole morning without the slightest sign of strain, and Albert could not help noticing the difference. Bertie's programme of work was not too much for a child of average intelligence; it imposed lighter burdens than a modern preparatory school and was far less exacting than the course arranged by Florschütz for the young Ernest and Albert.

Yet Albert has been criticised for excessive severity, even cruelty, on very inadequate grounds and at the cost of distorting the evidence. Nothing was known then, of course, about the special needs of backward children, and Bertie's inability to learn was therefore bound to seem like deliberately obstinate defiance to his father and his tutors, but nevertheless Albert ensured that the programme of study made allowance for his son's shortcomings. A day's work of only five hours was diversified by a succession of contrasting subjects; there was to be an hour's rest after lunch, during which Bertie was encouraged to read story books; no religious instruction was to be given, nor was he to be compelled to attend church until he was eight. Again, it has been asserted that Bertie never had a holiday from lessons; yet Lady Lyttelton and Stockmar were always deploring the frequency with which the children were taken away from their work to enjoy 'a semi-gypsy life' for a day or two aboard the royal yacht. Few children were so free, for they were encouraged to bathe in the sea, play on the sands at Osborne, or enjoy pony expeditions and picnics in Scotland: 'an outdoor life is best for children', Albert once told a friend. Again, the separation of Affie and Bertie in 1857 has been charged against Albert as an example of his cruelty to his eldest son, but only by misunderstanding the reasons for it. Affie admired his elder brother and copied him in everything, but when this extended to disobedience and refusal to work it was necessary to separate them in the interests of the younger boy; Bertie indeed suffered the loss of his chosen companion, but his sacrifice was essential to the preservation of his brother's character.

In moments of gloom Albert racked his brains over the problem of educating the queen of England's difficult heir and wondered where he had gone wrong. He sometimes quailed at the responsibilities which Bertie's future position laid upon them both, and dwelt on the misfortune that Vicky was not a boy. If only he knew what was best in the awkward circumstances! For he longed passionately to do the best for all his children; he loved them devotedly, was affectionate and dependable in dealing with them and never sarcastic at their expense.*

Albert's love for his children, and particularly for the prince of Wales, has often been denied; most recently, for instance, Mrs Woodham-Smith has written that Bertie would have bloomed had he been reared in 'an atmosphere of affection, warmth and admiration.' There is, however, a very large amount of reliable evidence that he was brought up in just such an atmosphere: Lady Lyttelton, Lady Bloomfield, Eleanor Stanley, Baron Bunsen, Mr Gladstone and Lord Broughton all testify to the love which both the royal parents bore their children and to the children's close rapport with them.

In March 1849, a year later than hoped, Bertie was put in the charge of a tutor, Henry Birch, who had been a master at Eton, Albert told his stepmother that Birch was 'a young, good-looking, amiable man with great teaching ability.' On the surface this was true; as a scholar of King's College, Cambridge, Henry Birch had won four university prizes, but he was not a pedant and had been very popular at Eton, so that his very normality was an asset. It was Birch's normality even more than his learning which attracted Albert, whose object it was to put his excitable child in calm hands. A second Florschütz, calm and learned at the same time, would have been ideal; but Albert had long ago reconciled himself to the impossibility of finding one in England, where the existence of public schools diverted suitable young men away from the career of a tutor after the Continental fashion. It should be noted, too, that he persuaded Birch to postpone taking Holy Orders on the grounds that a cleric was likely to want Sunday to be a day of far more gloom than was the custom at Windsor, might feel an obligation not to take part in the amateur theatricals which the royal family so much enjoyed (although Birch had acted a good deal at Cambridge), might frown on shooting and dancing and generally feel bound to behave as something of a spoil-sport. When Henry Birch turned out not to be the unqualified success for which Albert had hoped, it was therefore a bitter disappointment, but the blame cannot be laid entirely at Birch's door; at Eton he had been used to dealing with normal boys, and he was baffled by the prince of Wales's excitability, unpredictable rages and total lack of a sense of humour, and was at a loss to know what to do. He began to apply 'The Plan', but

---

* He was far more understanding than Bertie was later towards his own children – after watching him tease them unkindly one day, Asquith wrote 'This is not my idea of family fun.'

although he thought it too severe* he made no attempt to suggest revisions, for he was a little lazy. ('The Plan' itself, of course, had been designed expressly to prevent undue severity resulting from an excess of zeal in a tutor – that is to say, for a purpose exactly the opposite of that with which Albert has been credited!) In these circumstances, it is not surprising that the boy made little progress during the two years of Birch's tutorship, nor that Birch eventually had to go. Hitherto Bertie had shown no sign of affection towards his tutor, but now he suddenly changed, giving Birch so many notes and parting presents that Birch began to feel that perhaps he had had some good effect on his pupil after all.

Both parents were open to suggestion about what to do next, and probably asked too many people and received too much contradictory advice: Dr Varsin, the exponent of freedom and fresh air, was all for Bertie running wild for a time (Albert drily remarked that he could guess what the country would say to that!); Dr Combe, the fashionable phrenologist, examined his head (which Gladstone described as 'small and not well shaped'), diagnosed nervous excitability, extreme obstinacy and a passionate nature, and suggested using his self-esteem to correct these faults – upon which Albert remarked that he knew all this without the expense of calling in Dr Combe. Finally, it was decided to find another tutor. Sir James Stephen, Regius Professor of History at Cambridge, suggested Frederick Weymouth Gibbs, a twenty-nine-year-old don of whom it was said that to have been taught by him was to be sure of success. Unfortunately Gibbs was a dry, prematurely aged young man with a distressing family history – his mother was insane; Albert knew this, but it weighed with him less than Gibbs' Cambridge reputation. Carried away by his good fortune in securing such a prize, Albert forgot that there was a world of difference between instructing clever young men and teaching a boy so backward that, as Gibbs soon discovered, he was 'like a person half silly. . . . He was very rude this afternoon, throwing stones in my face. . . . Running first in one place, then in another, he made faces and spat, and used a great many bad words'. Nevertheless, Gibbs seems to have brought about some improvement, for by the time they were all in Scotland after the Great Exhibition Albert began to find his eldest son quite companionable, and enjoyed taking him

---

* Stockmar also thought it too severe for a boy like Bertie. Further, when Birch suggested that he should meet more children of his own age, Stockmar advised against it on the ground that it was unsafe without constant supervision, and this might appear strange. It is questionable whether Albert paid any more attention to these opinions than he did to Stockmar's constant hints of incipient madness in the Queen.

deer-stalking; this was enough to satisfy him that the change of tutor had been beneficial, and he began at last to see some hope for the future of the heir to the throne.

The years between 1848 and 1851, the first a turning-point in the history of Europe and the second in Albert's career in England, had also seen the disappearance of several of the leading figures of the last generation. As the mid-century passed, a new age was dawning.

Lord Melbourne had died on 24 November 1848; his death had hit Albert even more keenly than the Queen, in spite of the jealousy he had once felt for his wife's former mentor, and he sincerely acknowledged the debt they both owed to him. The Queen wept, and the entry in her Journal – 'a most kind, disinterested friend of mine' – seems a feeble tribute to all the warmth and happiness which this remarkable man had brought into her life, but to such it had sunk, affected by the passage of time and Albert.

A few months later it was Queen Adelaide's coffin which Albert was following to the grave. Although she was only fifty-six, he and the Queen had long looked on her as an old lady and although they grieved they did not feel she had gone before her time.

Nor was he unmoved by the tragic death of Lord George Bentinck, who did not return from a walk and was later found dead in a wood, for he could always rise above personal feelings and forget how hostile to him Bentinck had been.

But the sudden death of George Anson on 9 October 1849 was a terrible shock. Never very robust – small illnesses frequently pros- trated him – he was suffering from a slight cold when he collapsed and died without warning. 'A very hard and painful loss for me' was a typical understatement to cover the depth of Albert's feelings and was as far as he dared to go in revealing his completely shattered state at this unexpected blow.

Next year Louis Philippe himself died at Claremont. Victoria and Albert had been frustrated and angered by his spineless attitude in exile – once he realised that never again would he be *le roi* his decline set in rapidly. But they wiped the slate clean on 26 August 1850, getting up at dawn to make the long drive to Esher in a stuffy carriage on a hot day to comfort the bereaved Queen Amélie, whose resignation in adversity they assured each other was admirable.

Within a few months Louis Philippe was followed to the grave by his daughter Louise, queen of the Belgians, who died in October from tuberculosis aggravated by whooping-cough. A few weeks before her death Albert had taken Victoria and the three eldest children on a short trip to Belgium, ostensibly to show them the haunts he had loved so much as a young man, but behind an elaborate charade he hid his real purpose of giving the Queen a last chance of seeing the aunt to whom she was so devoted. A few months before, Louise had been too ill to come to Osborne with Leopold, so the alarmed Victoria had smartly packed Sir James Clark off to Laeken to report on her condition; he returned to say, as she had hoped, that there was no cause for alarm and that Louise only needed rest and a taste of Alpine air. Doubly deceived, Queen Victoria was catapulted by the shock of her aunt's death into a state of prostration and depression. Albert had to bear the brunt of her lamentations and tears, but he could not see that he had helped to bring it on himself by the absurd way in which he had shielded her from reality. Stockmar's unexpected arrival, bearing Louise's last letter to her husband, did nothing to alleviate the Queen's distress: 'it is the letter of an angel,' Albert told Ernest, 'the expressions of a soul angelic in its purity.'

The reduction in the ranks of the old royals, who were disappearing at a great rate, meant that, left unsupported, the duchess of Cambridge had become almost subdued. The duke's death on 8 July 1850 had passed nearly unnoticed, overshadowed by the tragedy of Peel's accident a fortnight before. Albert could not help remembering what an obstacle he had been to the introduction of modern methods in the army, refusing to countenance anything that smacked of innovation.

A telegram announcing the duke of Wellington's death on 14 September 1852 was brought to Albert on the banks of Loch Dhu, and in that wild and remote spot they both felt deeply moved by the insignificance of man and the timelessness of nature, 'mortality, eternity and the Creator that is behind it all'. As they hurried back to Balmoral, the Queen wondered tearfully how they could manage without his wise advice, but Albert knew Wellington's days of usefulness had long been over, for he was eighty-three and had had several strokes. Only that spring he had brushed aside all Albert's suggestions for modernising the army, and it had been a shock to discover that the victor of Waterloo was still living in the past; it was as though a clock had slowed down, its springs worn out, although it could still tell the time after a fashion.

Instead of being a solemn farewell to a national hero, the duke of Wellington's funeral was, as Albert said, a fiasco. The jostling crowds at the lying-in-state robbed the spectacle of all dignity, and the funeral car stuck fast in the mud by Temple Bar; but the car's preposterous design was not, as many have said, of Albert's doing. A sketch was prepared by Professor Gottfried Semper and submitted to Albert, who must bear some responsibility because he approved it; but the drawing may well have looked better than the finished article, and Albert certainly took no part in overseeing its construction.

Was Albert right when he said a few years earlier that there could be no reform in the army during Wellington's lifetime? He seems to have been one of the few who realised that by now the duke was too old to change or to realise that the thirty years since Waterloo had seen improvements in military methods and equipment abroad. The public, including many MPs, had become so accustomed to trusting Wellington to defend them that there was no demand for the modernisation of defence, and most were inclined to accuse Albert of being too big for his boots when he called attention to the dangers of complacency.

Two years before he died Wellington had come to Windsor with a proposal that Albert should eventually succeed him as Commander-in-Chief of the army. Albert was dismayed. Never having had any military training or any experience of battle, he felt himself quite unfitted for the position; besides, how could he undertake a job of such magnitude and do it properly as well as his other duties for the Queen: 'I should not like to undertake what I could not carry through,' he told Stockmar. Wellington dismissed these objections with a wave of his hand, saying that subordinates would attend to all details and Albert need not spend much time on them, and revealed his real reason for making the proposal – to ensure that effective command of the army remained in the hands of the sovereign and did not fall into those of the House of Commons. Adamant that 'the name and the responsibility cannot be separated', Albert went on to make a decisive point: Suppose there were to be serious rioting, as there so nearly had been in 1848, it would be the Commander-in-Chief's duty to quell it – but how could the Queen's husband shed the blood of the Queen's subjects without imperilling her throne? And he cited the case of the prince of Prussia, who had been forced to flee on the mere suspicion of having commanded troops used for repressive measures. Although he had made his mind up immediately, Albert now prevaricated for a month, letting the duke think he might accept the proposal while actually considering how best to decline it politely. Eventually, on 6 April, he wrote that it was impossible for the Queen to carry out her multifarious duties without the help of her husband, who was her only private secretary: 'I am afraid, therefore, that I must discard the tempting idea of being placed in command of the British army.'

On the whole, Albert handled this affair badly. He came quickly and instinctively to the right decision, yet did not say so at once and have done with it, partly out of kindness of heart and partly through distrust of instinctive decisions, and he tacitly encouraged Wellington to think he would agree by allowing him to compose a long memorandum for the instruction of his successor in the duties of Commander-in-Chief. He got his deserts when Wellington accepted with soldierly promptitude an invitation to explain further details and kept Albert from his boxes and his letters so long that he had to work far into the night to catch up. In the course of the discussions he expounded the duties of the husband of a Queen Regnant with greater clarity than he had managed in an earlier draft of December 1843:

'This position is a most peculiar and delicate one. Whilst a female sovereign has a great many disadvantages in comparison with a king, yet, if she is married, and her husband understands and does his duty, her position, on the other hand, has many compensating advantages, and, in the long run, will be found even to be stronger than that of a male sovereign. But this requires that the husband should entirely sink his own individual existence in that of his wife – that he should aim at no power by himself or for himself – should shun all contention – assume no separate responsibility before the public, but make his position entirely a part of hers – fill up every gap which, as a woman, she would naturally leave in the exercise of her regal functions – continually and anxiously watch every part of the public business, in order to be able to advise and assist her at any moment in any of the multifarious and difficult questions or duties brought before her, some-times international, sometimes political, or social, or personal. As the natural head of her family, superintendent of her household, manager of her private affairs, sole confidential adviser in politics, and only assistant in her communications with the officers of the Government, he is, besides, the husband of the Queen, the tutor of the royal children, the private secretary of the sovereign, and her permanent minister.'*

His decision to refuse to become Commander-in-Chief was a right and wise one, for all the hard work he had been doing for the monarchy would have been imperilled, if not completely ruined, had he been held personally responsible for the early disasters of the Crimean War and thus come into open conflict with public and Press. Even as things were, he went through a period of great unpopularity

---

* This memorandum had a special poignancy for Albert, because it was the last he ever sent to Peel for comment. The reply from Whitehall Gardens was exactly what he had hoped for; Peel wrote that it was 'an admirable document' to which he could not add a word.

and suffered a series of sharp attacks in the newspapers. How much more devastating they would have been, had it been possible to blame him for the army's misfortunes! Moreover, he was coming to believe that the post of Commander-in-Chief was out-of-date and ought to be abolished, along with many other anachronisms which had no place in the modern army. But the papers which the duke sent him had awakened his interest in military affairs much more keenly than before, and at a very opportune moment, only two years before the outbreak of war.

As soon as he heard that Wellington was dead, Albert compared notes with the Prime Minister about men suitable to succeed to his many appointments, and found that they agreed in every particular. No one, of course, could entirely replace Wellington, but Albert took the line that what was lost in authority must be made up in efficiency, and that therefore Lord Hardinge was the best choice as Commander-in-Chief. George of Cambridge was briefly considered but immediately dismissed as too young to carry enough weight and to withstand the many attacks on the army which were certain to be made now that Wellington was gone.

15

'Deaf to the calls of
honour and duty'

RUSSELL'S government did not last long after the dismissal of Palmerston at Christmas 1851; it fell in February 1852 over a Militia Bill which was Russell's hasty answer to public anger that nothing was being done to counter French military preparations. Russell proposed that militiamen should be trained on a county basis, but Palmerston successfully introduced an amendment calling for central control, and brought the government down. Albert entirely shared Palmerston's view, holding with him that a series of separate local organisations would be ineffective against an invasion, but since Palmerston went about glorying in his 'tit-for-tat' he was unable to believe that he had suddenly become a man of principle or that the Queen should commission him to form a new ministry. But although he and Victoria were both glad to be rid of Lord John, who had often been rude and discourteous, the only possible alternative to Palmerston was the earl of Derby (formerly Lord Stanley), who was almost equally unacceptable because he was the leader of the Protectionists. However, there was nothing for it but to send for Derby, who arrived at Osborne on 22 February determined not to be dictated to. He met his match at once in a preliminary interview with Albert, who immediately made it clear that the Queen would not accept Palmerston as Foreign Secretary. Thus headed off from his original intention, Derby suggested that Palmerston should be Chancellor of the Exchequer and Leader of the House of Commons, only to be faced with the devastating rejoinder 'If Palmerston is Leader of the House, how long do you think you will remain Prime Minister?' Worse was to come when the Queen joined them. Primed by Stockmar, whose political wisdom was sadly

227

declining in old age, Victoria announced that although she knew that Derby had never supported liberal principles she expected him to do so now out of respect for her, 'otherwise people will say that I have changed my opinions with the change of ministry'. Reddening with anger, Derby stiffly replied that constitutionally the government was answerable to the House of Commons, so that Albert had to cover for her hastily by saying that the Queen had only wished him to bear her personal views in mind. The Queen's remark may have slipped out unintentionally. She had come straight from a conversation with Stockmar, but she should have remembered the lessons of the past – particularly the Bedchamber affair – more carefully and kept a closer guard on her tongue. Albert did his best to repair her mistake, but was hardly guiltless himself, for he justified his browbeating of Derby on the ground that he was entitled to go to any lengths to save the country from the menace of Palmerston. He conceded ruefully, however, that Palmerston 'fitted the Foreign Office like a glove' and that it certainly suited no one else as well, for every time the question of filling it came up there was controversy. Even so by the end of the interview they had established an ascendancy over Derby, which was doubtless all they had ever intended.

The list of ministers which Derby submitted a few days later consisted largely of 'dandies and roués of London and the turf' and included a considerable number of men (among them his own son) who had no political experience; it was well known that Derby was wax in the hands of relatives and friends. The name of the notorious womaniser and gambler, the earl of Wilton, appeared on the Household list against the position of Master of the Horse, and this gave Albert the opportunity to deliver Derby a severe lecture about the harm that had been done to the crown by careless appointments in the past, and to emphasise his and Victoria's determination to stick to what Melbourne had called the 'damned morality' which had done so much to raise the standing of the monarchy; in future, the Queen would insist that no one should be a member of her Household who was likely to become bankrupt or whose moral character was not above reproach.

With great good sense, Derby at once realised that if he wanted the Government to run smoothly it would be wise to get on the right side of Albert, and he made a shrewd move in that direction when he surrendered his own beliefs by declaring that Protection was no longer a live issue and that he proposed to drop it. Delighted, Albert greeted this as a great step forward which would settle the commercial policy of the country on 'sound and fixed principles' and be warmly welcomed by the working classes, who had become convinced free-traders during the last six years and now understood that a fall in the price of food did not mean a reduction in wages. With tact and charm, Derby soon won the palace over; he consulted them at every turn, let them see that he was keeping a close watch over every department, and got Disraeli to write entertaining and informative accounts of proceedings in the House (Albert thought them as highly-coloured as his novels). Nevertheless, Derby felt his position to be precarious, and said of his government that it should be called 'the Derby militia, fresh from the plough and ready to be disbanded immediately.' The general election in July did not bring much improvement, although his majority was increased, because the prevalence of smaller groupings reduced the cohesion of the main parties – the Peelites, for instance, refused to serve with Disraeli, who had brought their leader down. Albert longed for the halcyon days of Peel, when party loyalty had meant something; now 'Lord John Russell has lost all power over his party. Lord Palmerston is independent and will probably make common cause with the Protectionists. The Peelites have divided, as Sir James Graham has moved considerably to the left and Mr Gladstone pursues bigotry.' 'What a lot!,' Albert wrote to Stockmar shortly before the Dissolution, 'the sooner this session of Parliament is over, the better.'

Although not a soldier, Albert had always taken a keen interest in military affairs since, as a sixteen-year-old boy, he had watched his uncle Leopold conducting the Belgian manoeuvres, but he had been unable to pursue it since coming to England because his political education had had to take priority.

As early as 1842 he had heard Lord Hardinge express concern over the country's depleted stocks of arms, and when Lord Haddington in January 1843 called attention to serious undermanning in the navy, Albert questioned him closely about the effects of steam on navigation and especially on naval strategy in home waters: did not the closeness of Ireland to France constitute a danger? Since the French had more steamships than Britain, did this not mean that they could invade easily? Two years later Wellington told Albert that he was worried about this very question, and said in a public speech that England could not defend herself if war broke out; but he took no action, although it was one of his dreams to raise an army of 100,000 men. Nothing could convince him that the need was for better and more modern equipment rather than for men and, shaking his head over Albert's ignorance, he muttered 'Men, we need more men.' It was therefore all the more galling for

Albert to hear from his Continental relations that Prussia and Austria had modern equipment as well as plenty of men. A visit to the fleet in the Solent in 1845 had given him fresh cause for alarm, for he learned quite by chance that the navy could hardly carry out its ordinary peace-time duties for lack of the proper equipment and funds.

In 1846 Albert asked Peel to consider a programme of rearmament, but was surprised to find him more inflexible on this than on any other subject. A hypothetical war did not disturb him as much as the state of the national finances, which, he said, ruled such a programme out completely, while the country would not stand for an increase in taxation to make it possible. And Peel went on to lecture Albert on the diplomatic reasons why rearmament was such a tricky question: it would not do to appear to threaten other nations, but on the other hand England must not seem so defenceless as to invite attack. That the country was thoroughly defenceless at that very moment did not seem to bother Peel in the very least. Peel positively refused to act, but other ministers had been summoned to the palace, made glib promises, and still done nothing. Among the most supine was Palmerston, in spite of his sabre-rattling, yet the moment he found himself in opposition he began shouting loudly for more arms and improved coastal defences, comparing strong military forces to an umbrella – to have one was to ensure that it was not needed. Anyone might think that rearmament was entirely his own idea, Albert cynically remarked, for he knew that Palmerston was well aware not only that he had been urging it for years but also that recently he had been prominent among those calling for a national militia.

Shortly after Wellington's death, Albert asked his successor whether any progress had been made with a revision of the national defences, and followed this up by urging the Prime Minister to plan for greatly increased expenditure on defence in order to keep England out of war: 'The country is fully alive to its dangers and Parliament has perhaps never been in a more likely state to grant what is necessary, provided a comprehensive and efficient plan is laid before it.' On taking office, Derby had grandly assured the Queen that he at least meant to make preparation for defence and that his plan for a militia was exactly the same as Albert's, but nevertheless after a few weeks it became clear that he had other fish to fry. However, in November, to keep the palace quiet, Disraeli wrote a soothing letter to say that he had budgeted for enough expenditure on defence to meet the Queen's wishes. This was nothing but words, Albert told the Queen angrily, and he had no more faith in a 'very full' conversation which he had with Malmesbury, the new Foreign Secretary. It hurt their pride that even a little country like Belgium was putting its defences in order; Paris was too close to take risks, said King Leopold, likening his position to that of a man in bed with a snake.

By contrast, the British Parliament was obsessed with economy – false economy, said Albert, who had been fighting it for years and complained that because of it British agriculture was not paying, British bloodstock was not thriving and houses for the British working classes were not being built. Economy spelt disaster: no up-to-date guns, and not enough soldiers to man the defences, because economy said that they could not be afforded. There were moments when Albert felt that he was dealing with a flock of sheep, not statesmen, for true statesmen would make it their business to know the shocking facts, facts which it had taken Albert all his time to prise out of Lord John Russell.

However, by the end of October a committee was looking into possible improvements in artillery, and in order 'to save time' (in reality, no doubt, to ensure that the committee did not overlook it altogether) he took the unusual step of short-circuiting official procedures and asking Ernest to get him a sample of the new Prussian needle-gun direct from the factory at Erfurt. A naval review at Portsmouth the following summer showed him that the obsession with economy had left the navy in no better case; the ships were old-fashioned and cumbersome, unsuitable for modern warfare, so that the pageantry of the review was no more than a veneer hiding the rotten wood underneath. Afterwards some of the ships' officers told Albert of rumours that Louis Napoleon was building highly manoeuvrable light craft armed with the latest types of gun. Albert promptly warned Derby that unless something was done to counteract this danger at once, Britannia would not rule the waves much longer; the sight of once-fine warships limping awkwardly through their evolutions at Spithead convinced Albert that at all costs the shipbuilding programme must be speeded up.

Before anything effective could be done about defence preparations, the Derby government fell on 17 December 1852 after Gladstone had slaughtered Disraeli's Budget, which had attempted to increase income-tax. But it was the manner, not the fact, of the fall which chiefly disturbed Albert, for Whigs, Peelites, Radicals and Irish had combined just to bring the government down, not because they were united on principles. Impatiently brushing aside Derby's advice (given unasked, and so unconstitutional) to send for Lord Lansdowne, Albert and Victoria decided that although Lansdowne could not well be passed over, they would consult him and Aberdeen together. But they regarded it as 'Heaven-sent' when illness prevented Lansdowne from making the journey to Osborne, and Aberdeen came alone, because Lansdowne was really too old to take on the premiership, having been Chancellor of the Exchequer half a century before. Although they knew that Aberdeen was not as many-sided as 'good Sir Robert', he was utterly dependable and could play the father-figure which they were always unconsciously searching for in their prime ministers, and was further recommended as a critic of Palmerston, who in revenge had once called him 'that antiquated imbecility'. Aberdeen reacted just as they had hoped, calling himself 'unworthy' and saying that he cared nothing for the spoils of office but was willing to 'save Her Majesty if no one else could be found'. His best stroke, however, was the admirable way he kept his self-control when Albert handed him a list of suitable names for inclusion in the Cabinet which he had drawn up 'as a help' and murmured something about 'these valuable suggestions'.

Whatever may have been the case with the rest of the list, Aberdeen's own wishes certainly coincided with Albert's over the Foreign Office, and he shared Albert's objections to handing it over to Palmerston once more. For several days the delicate business of forming a government hung in the balance, because Russell thought he should have been offered the premiership and for a time refused any lower position, but half of the problem was happily resolved when Palmerston announced that he would accept the Home Office. Aberdeen reported that Palmerston had been exceedingly cordial, reminding him that 'they were great friends (!!!) of sixty years standing, having been at school together', but when Aberdeen had gone Albert and Victoria 'could not help laughing heartily at the Harrow Boys and their friendship'. Palmerston was now safely out of harm's way, for 'if he is in a department where he has to work like a horse,' Albert wrote to the new Prime Minister, 'he cannot do any mischief.' Two days later, meeting Palmerston walking with two sticks because of a severe attack of gout, Albert even thought that his political life was over.

The ministerial crisis had taken so much out of them both that Albert would have liked to break with tradition and spend Christmas at Osborne, but since politics pursued them right up to Christmas Eve a change of plan was impossible. Albert's letters for this period show that he was worn out by long months of anxiety about defence and a week of intense irritation at the indecent jockeying for position by politicians after Derby's fall, and badly in need of a holiday. There had only been a few bright patches that autumn, and none had stood out more than a visit of inspection in October to Stephenson's astonishing tubular bridge over the Menai Straits, built to carry the new railway to Holyhead. Excitedly Albert walked with officials along the top of the tube, asking questions and stopping every now and then to examine some unusual feature that caught his attention, while the Queen, a plump sugar-fairy in pink, was exclaiming with surprise over the freshness of the air as she drove 'at a spanking pace' through it. Albert seldom wrote up his journal, but between several blank pages there is the one word 'splendid' against the date of this visit.

Their rare public appearances together were becoming very precious to the Queen, who was seeing far too little of her husband as he took over more and more of her duties. She was pleased when he was asked to succeed Wellington as Master of Trinity House, but wondered whether the office need be more than titular, so as to protect his scanty free time from further inroads. Of course he would not hear of it, but must familiarise himself with every detail of the history of Trinity House in order to judge the wisdom of proposed changes in its constitution and preside at every meeting – indeed, it was at a Trinity House banquet on 4 June 1853 that in one of his most pungent speeches he used his new position to give timely warning of his most persistent fears by expressing the hope that the English were not becoming so enervated by prosperity 'that from a miserable eagerness to cling to mere wealth and comfort we shall become deaf to the cause of honour and duty.' By October 1853 the Queen was complaining that he never had time for her now, but spent every moment he could spare from state business at meetings of one or other of his multitude of committees. For everyone now clamoured for his attention and it seemed that nothing could be done without him; in this same month, for instance, he had to study the lengthy and controversial report of the Royal Commission on the University of Cambridge, keep an eye on the progress of the building of the Kensington museum nearly every day, and give Lord Raglan his opinion on a new type of shrapnel sent him by Woolwich Arsenal. In spite of these calls on his time, he tried not to let his huge correspondence with friends and relations abroad fall into arrears, although since he never allowed this to encroach on his public work it decreased his leisure time. A disconsolate Queen Victoria can hardly be blamed for lamenting to Stockmar that Albert looked pale and fagged and that she could not persuade him to slow down, but she was quite mistaken; Albert was full of vigour, happy to be so busily occupied, and she deluded herself into thinking otherwise simply because she was lonely and jealous. For his part, he could not understand what she was complaining of, for she had always wanted him to be in demand. She, on the other hand, could now do nothing to hold him back. Even her observance of the traditional birthday rituals – a military band playing his favourite tunes in the morning, fireworks at night – did not prevent him from working on this hitherto sacred day, and she was shocked to notice a look of abstraction come over his face during the concert which the children always performed in his honour, a look which conveyed the clear message 'How soon can I creep away?' She scolded him when she got the chance, but his excuse was always the same – it was all for her.

Ernest's affairs were beginning to take a turn for the worse, and this added to Albert's cares. Here was one kind of work which he did not relish, and although he was devoted to his rascally brother he was often so exasperated with him that he did not trust himself to answer his letters until his temper had cooled. With incredible stupidity, Ernest had fallen into the habit of accompanying each request for a loan with an expensive present to soften the blow, like the beautifully embossed hunting book he sent in January 1853, which was (for once) something Albert really wanted. Time and again Albert paid his brother's debts, but always secretly and never without personal sacrifice. Ernest, who treated the matter as of no consequence between brothers, refused to understand that Albert's pride would not allow him to tell the Queen (particularly after she received a bequest of £250,000 in 1852) and use her money as his own. Only Anson knew the trying subterfuges his master had to adopt and how difficult it was to send even an occasional hundred pounds. 'You think I only need to wave a wand,' he wearily told Ernest in 1851, after paying that year's instalment of debts, 'and hey presto, there it is,' and he reminded him that since he had a thrifty wife, no children and few expenses he ought to be one of the better-off rulers of small states and not to look on himself as a poor relation entitled to ask for money.

Despite the Queen's complaints that she was lonely and neglected, she and Albert often went to the opera or the theatre together during the French actress Rachel's season in London in the spring of 1853. They had seen her in her first big part in Racine's *Phèdre* in 1841, but were astonished to discover that she had now quite changed her style, discarding the fashionable overdramatisation and exaggerated gestures in favour of more restrained movements and a carefully modulated tone which conveyed the moods of the characters she was portraying far more effectively; they were enchanted. It struck

Albert that acting of this kind opened up new and exciting possibilities for the theatre and that the stage might be used to present
social problems. Having heard about it quite by chance, they decided on the spur of the moment to attend the farewell performance
of the famous Shakespearian actor Macready on 21 February 1853,
arriving unannounced and so unexpectedly that Macready fluffed
his lines for the first time in his career when he looked up and
suddenly saw them in the royal box. In those days the number of
new plays each season was very limited, but Albert and Victoria
never minded seeing the same piece several times – it added to their
enjoyment, they said, to be as word-perfect as the actors; they saw
Bulwer's *Not so Bad as we Seem* three times, for instance, and
noticed something new at each performance. Partly no doubt because of his own keen interest in amateur theatricals, Albert was in
fact very assiduous in observing points of detail; it was not a talent
appreciated by everybody – for example, when he at once noticed
something wrong with the cut of Don Giovanni's coat the first time
he saw the opera performed some years before. The royal family
were a familiar sight at the huge theatre in which Albert had persuaded Astley to settle down in 1852, for he had taken care to pass
on his passionate interest in the circus to his children. Although he
had no time to show them how to work the marionette theatre
which he had sent from Germany for them that same winter, they
continued to produce *tableaux vivants* and short plays as he had
taught them to do from an early age. Following in Papa's footsteps,
the children unanimously voted Jenny Lind their favourite singer
and were allowed to stay up late one night in May 1854 when she was
to perform a song he had composed. ('How much better it sounds
when sung by the famous soprano,' Albert told Ernest.)

In spite of his preoccupation with public affairs during and after the
Crimean War, Albert still strove to spend some time each day with
all the family together, reading aloud from some book they could
all enjoy like Alexander Dumas' *Count of Monte Cristo*, George
Eliot's *Adam Bede* or one of Wilkie Collins's stories. Sometimes he
would slip away by himself to catch up with books that he felt were
important: perhaps Pepys' *Diary*, Strauss's *Life of Jesus* (which he
carefully compared with the Gospels), Roebuck's *History of the
Whigs* or – more rarely, because he felt he ought not to waste his
time on them – modern novels like those of Charles Kingsley. All
this sort of thing, however, was pretty well brought to an end by the
outbreak of the Crimean War.

He had been spending more time lately in the company of
scientists, and this too the Queen disliked, because it was a taste

she could not share and because it took him away from her side. He had long been experimenting in photography with Sir John Herschel, the astronomer, who was also keenly interested in this new science, but in 1852, through the British Association, he widened his circle to include Faraday and Lyell (he had read Lyell's *Principles of Geology* in English as a teenager in Brussels), and he thought nothing of travelling to York when the Association met there in 1854 in order to hear these famous men lecture. He even managed to convince the Queen that he was killing two birds with one stone by arguing that he could also discuss university business with Professor Sedgwick, who was bound to be there too, and thus save a visit to Cambridge.

There were many murmurings when it became known that Albert's host for the 1854 British Association meeting was George Hudson, the railway king, who was also a member. Nearly ten years before, when Albert had first become friendly with Hudson, who was then coming into prominence, there had been many otherwise sensible people who could not understand how the Queen's husband could 'lower himself' by consorting on equal terms with such a man, but Albert did not care a fig for class distinctions: it was enough that a man had been able to raise himself by his own efforts and had achieved something worth while – and what was more worth while than the railway? Moreover, he really liked Hudson, who was a man of tact and charm, who could, for instance, settle a bitter dispute between people so different from himself as the Dean of York and Professor Sedgwick by adroitly turning their quarrel into a joke, so that they saw the ridiculous side of their own behaviour; this was just the kind of peacemaking role that Albert admired in others and tried to emulate himself. But probably Albert's main reason for accepting Hudson's invitation in 1854 was to help him rehabilitate himself after the scandals of 1849, when his shady financial dealings had been uncovered. To go to scientific meetings as an ordinary member was a form of freedom which Albert greatly valued, particularly the way he was treated not as royalty but as a gifted amateur who had no hesitation in questioning the professional scientists about anything he did not understand; questioning was the best road to scientific progress, and he once told Dr Whewell that there was no room for obstinacy in science although he had noticed that dons were much given to it. He always took the line that every new theory was bound to be controversial at first, so it was foolish to dismiss what seemed startling simply because it was difficult to understand, and was one of the few to defend *Vestiges of the Natural History of Creation* against its many detractors when it was published anonymously in 1844.* It was unfair and childish of Sedgwick to criticise it so viciously in the *Edinburgh Review*, he thought, and cowardly of Croker to refuse to review it in the *Quarterly*, and he welcomed its enormous success. By the time the seventh edition was published in 1872 Albert was dead, but he would have been glad to know that Darwin had cast the mantle of respectability over it by writing a preface.

Science had entered their family life for the first time at the birth of their eighth child, Leopold, on 7 April 1853, when the Queen's labour was wonderfully eased by the newly-discovered chloroform. But despite his pain-free entry into the world the baby did not thrive. Sir James Clark came rapidly (too rapidly) to the conclusion that he was one of those children who are born with a weak digestion and that the remedy was a change of wet nurse. Albert's own diagnosis was not more successful; he thought the reason the baby was thin and could not eat was shock to the Queen after a fire in the dining-room at Windsor only three weeks before Leopold's birth. In fact the trouble was haemophilia, but this was not realised for several months, and the baby was a constant source of anxiety to both his parents.

The invitation to Princess Augusta to be godmother to Leopold was a symbol of an increased interest in Prussia on Albert's part, while Augusta's eager acceptance showed that she reciprocated it. She had been much impressed during her visit to the Great Exhibition by the many signs of Albert's personal power, and was anxious to cultivate him because he might prove a valuable ally to help Prussia assert herself as leader of the movement towards German unification. It is quite clear from her later behaviour, however, that this strange woman did not care in the least for either Albert or Victoria themselves, but that she was simply anxious to use them as instruments for the achievement of her life's ambitions. At the christening she put herself out to be pleasant to everyone, even Ernest, whom she usually could not stand at any price. Stockmar noticed this, and allowed himself a fleeting moment of alarm, but came (quite wrongly) to the conclusion that she could do little harm. So successfully did she ingratiate herself that she soon became not only 'a dearest friend' but an honorary cousin as well, for whom Albert and Victoria could not do enough. It was a dangerous relationship, into which they plunged with eyes closed but hearts warm at the thought of the growing affection between the two

* *Vestiges* was rumoured to be Albert's own work, but was later known to be by the author and publisher Robert Chambers.

families, and it was one which at first was to have consequences they would hail with delight. Augusta returned home, however, with a strong feeling that Albert was losing interest in German affairs. For the time being, she was quite right; he had seen the storm clouds over Turkey, and all his thoughts were concentrated on the war he feared was coming.

As part of his anxiety about the country's lack of preparedness, he had long been urging the government to purchase a piece of land large enough for the training of a considerable body of soldiers. The existence of possible threats from Ireland and France seemed to him sufficient justification in themselves, but the response from Parliament was at first slow and suspicious: some members accused him of wanting a large army 'for his own ends' and were set on discouraging his 'army mania'. Fortunately Albert's skin had thickened over the years, and he continued his pressure undaunted; eventually land was bought at Chobham in Surrey to serve as a training area. Wellington had shown a marked lack of interest when he first mentioned the idea to him in 1849, and Albert would probably never have got his way had not the menacing posture of Louis Napoleon caused an invasion scare in 1852. As soon as Chobham had been secured, Albert entreated Hardinge to use it to bring the army up to the standards of the Continent 'in peace as well as in war'.

The British army had fallen below the standards of the Continent, he well knew, because it had been starved of money by successive governments and because its ageing and hide-bound commanders had not had the wit to keep themselves abreast of recent inventions. The Prussian needle-gun which he had asked Ernest to procure for him* had arrived at last, and he showed it to Hardinge early in June; to his utter consternation Hardinge handed it back after only a cursory look, murmuring something about 'expense', and it was all Albert could do to control his fury enough to say coldly that he would have thought that at least it was worth thorough examination. 'All this talk of waste of money makes me sick,' he wrote to Stockmar, 'no one mentions the waste of life.'

It was the same story with Chobham. The camp was so much to the liking of army and Press that to Albert's horror it induced a state of euphoria almost at once; on the very day that the sappers first went in to level the ground, newsvendors were already crying 'If Boney comes to Chobham camp, we'll show him English power.'

* See p. 231 above.

Ministers too began to talk as if the army was already fully trained, and Albert had to bring them to their senses sharply. In brilliant sunshine, he and the Queen watched the first manoeuvres at Chobham on 21 June. Everything went off well, but Albert was gloomy because he could see beneath the surface to the reality below. However well a few soldiers might perform on a special occasion he knew that far more would be required if trouble flared up suddenly in the eastern Mediterranean. Still worse was to follow when he went back three days later for a private and more exacting inspection; he cross-questioned the officers and walked over the site, noticing that the tents were badly designed, poorly ventilated and too few in number, that washing facilities were inadequate and the men's food badly cooked and wretchedly served. A heavy storm in the night blew many of the tents down and turned the whole area into a sea of mud, and he was so dejected at the sorry sight that he was tempted to abandon the whole project, but he nerved himself enough to take command of his own brigade of Guards during the afternoon. Again, the troops 'looked smart', but was this enough? How much time was spent on spit-and-polish which would have been better spent in training? How versatile were the men? How quickly could they be taught to use more complicated guns with a quicker rate of fire? How great was their stamina, and how flexible their minds? All these questions and many more worried him profoundly as he journeyed home, ill and feverish with a racking cough. Long before he knew the answers, it was already too late: the men he had seen on Chobham Heath were en route for the Crimea, to defend a cause for which they cared nothing and to die in a war they did not understand.

Two days after leaving Chobham, Albert was lying in a darkened bedroom with a high temperature: like the rest of the family, he had caught measles from the prince of Wales. Soon he was delirious, and it was all his valet Kurt could do to hold him down. For twenty-four hours he recognised no one, and for ten more days he was gravely ill; things might have gone badly with him had Kurt not nursed him devotedly, staying by his bedside day and night and only snatching a little sleep when Albert fell into a restless doze. Only Kurt seems to have realised how ill Albert was (he twice thought him near death), for the Queen was barely convalescent herself and Sir James Clark took his usual blindly optimistic line that the disease was taking its normal course 'a little more severe in the Prince's case, perhaps, because of overwork of the brain, but there is no cause for alarm.' After ten days Albert's temperature dropped and he was able to sit up and take a little nourishment, but was pitifully weak, his hair had fallen out and he had lost interest in everything. The Queen fancifully attributed his slow recovery to the bad weather which kept him indoors and denied him fresh air, and his recovery was without doubt abnormally slow if he had only been suffering from measles.* When he was up and about again in August the Queen noticed with a pang that he was not himself, for he walked with a stick, rested in the afternoons – things he had never done before – and looked dejected. He and Vicky convalesced together. She was recovering the more rapidly and read to him one day from a newly-published life of Wellington; he showed his first signs of returning health when he told her to note the duke's remark 'You cannot have a little war.' It was autumn before he was doing a full day's work again, but he was still not properly fit, for although he ate better and had more colour, his usual lively interest in everything around him was missing and he was often silent and withdrawn; at thirty-three his resilience was still great, but he had been so ill that he needed more time and peace than those around him allowed for or could understand – if he flagged, the Queen tormented him with anxious questions and Sir James Clark feebly said he needed 'bracing'.

Things had not been quite well between husband and wife since the birth of Leopold in the spring. The baby had been slow to thrive, and Victoria's suppressed anxiety had made her edgy and difficult to live with. One evening when they were compiling a register of prints together a quarrel suddenly flared up; Albert rebuked her for not keeping her mind on her work and misleading him by turning over several pages at once, whereupon she suddenly exploded, then burst into a storm of crying, heaping insults upon him between sobs. It was all so sudden, and its cause so trivial, that he was stunned. Instead of shaking some sense into her, as he should have done – which would have ended the quarrel as soon as it had begun – he turned on his heel, stalked out and shut himself up in his room. She had of course been anxious about the baby and about him, but he was quite unable even to perceive that the root cause of her nervous state was the way he had built up an absorbing life for himself in which she had little part, and that the fact that he was doing it for her only made it harder for her to bear. He made the mistake of looking for tangible reasons for her distress and, was genuinely bewildered when he could find none. 'I am often astonished at the

* The severity of his symptoms suggests that Albert was suffering from encephalitis, which can be a complication of measles.

effect which a hasty word of mine has produced,' he wrote to Stockmar in complete sincerity. The Queen did not understand her own conduct any better: although she knew that deep down inside her there was a nagging unhappiness which came to the surface every now and again, she put it down only to anxiety about the baby, the other children or Albert's health. It may seem facile to say simply that she was jealous, but she did deeply resent the way in which Albert's work for her had come between them, and no other explanation of her behaviour is as convincing. Vicky was beginning to take this 'adored being' away from her too; soon after the Great Exhibition, Albert had started giving the child occasional lessons in the evening (Victoria said he would never have spared the time to do it for her), and both had found the experience so enjoyable that the lessons slipped naturally into a nightly routine which nothing was allowed to interrupt. Vicky was eager to learn, Albert eager to teach this quick, responsive and intelligent girl who worshipped her father and rushed to the lessons with a single-minded desire to learn which Albert welcomed but which cut her mother out completely. It was only human of Victoria to find fault with Vicky, and Albert to scold Victoria for being unfair; another cause of tears and recriminations. Tears frightened Albert, especially if he was the cause of them; unnerved and fearful that he might lose his temper, he took refuge in a deplorable practice which Stockmar had taught him – the little note. Devised as a means of cooling tempers, Albert's little notes probably did nothing but prolong their quarrels. In the role of father-figure which the notes necessarily emphasised, Albert could not fail to appear patronising, however well-intentioned he was; nor was Victoria the kind of unemotional woman who could be content to sit back meekly while her husband analysed her reasons for being angry with him. What she needed, what she longed for, were strong words answering strong words, followed by reassurances that he still loved her – not chilling little notes that said so. Above all, she craved for more attention: it was not enough to know that her husband spent his whole life devoted to her service if she saw so little of him.

Too much should not be made of quarrels like this. They were no worse than in most happy marriages, and there is not the slightest evidence that they 'embittered the life of the Queen and the Prince' once they were over. All the disagreements, the hasty words, the tears, the hurt silences had no other cause than the deep love which each bore the other, which nothing could change.

It was unfortunate that Albert never quite grasped this fundamental truth, but the fault was far more Stockmar's than his own.

In their voluminous correspondence Albert unburdened himself to Stockmar as freely about his marital affairs as about everything else, and a father-confessor was of enormous value to a man so given to suppressing his feelings; but Stockmar was not the best person to advise Albert on how to deal with his wife, for he invariably took too severe a line over the Queen's outbursts, reverting with tedious repetition to his old bogey, incipient madness. This was why he always stressed that tempers must be kept in as low a key as possible and a face-to-face battle avoided at all costs. Queen Victoria was too intelligent not to know that Albert's censures on her conduct in his 'little notes' did not come so much from his own heart as from Stockmar's imagined insight into her character, and she realised that Stockmar knew far less about her than he thought he did. In any case, the old man was getting out of touch; after 1850 he spent most of his time in Coburg, and his knowledge of what was happening in England – and particularly of what was happening at Buckingham Palace – was derived entirely from Albert's letters, which were bound to be biased however much he liked to convince himself that he was being commendably impartial. The baron was under the same delusion himself when he advised Albert to 'weigh up both sides carefully' in a particular case and then went on to tip the scales decisively on one side.

There were other ways too in which Stockmar was beginning to show that he was out of touch with England and particularly with Albert. After Wellington's death he wrote a letter which might have had serious repercussions if Albert had paid any attention to it: now was the time, he said, to step into the old duke's shoes and become 'the idol of the people', replacing Wellington in the eyes of the country and the world. There had always been occasions when Stockmar's ideas of the British Constitution were wide of the mark, but he had never before given Albert downright foolish advice. He knew very well that Albert was working for Queen and country to the limit of his endurance, and no one understood better the difficulties he had to contend with, so that it is almost incredible that he could so completely misconstrue the situation and the man. He had observed the strain which mediation during ministerial crises imposed upon Albert, had noted his constant efforts to get the country's defences improved as well as the risk that Louis Napoleon might strike first. He knew how hard Albert had tried to induce the government to re-think their eastern policy and clarify their undefined commitment to defend Turkey, and how much he feared that Stratford de Redcliffe's behaviour and the Czar's aggression might lead to war with Russia. Moreover, Stockmar was well aware that all these pressures had been building up before Albert had recovered from the fatigue of the Great Exhibition, had been at their worst while Albert was in bed with measles, and that an unkind fate had added Coburg family worries to his burden at the same moment. In deep financial trouble, Ernest wrote to ask for a large sum of money to keep the bailiffs out (Stockmar himself had to help Albert raise it and keep it secret from the Queen) and to demand that Albert come over and solve problems that had arisen over the working of the new Coburg constitution. What a time to urge Albert to become the 'idol of the people' and a second Wellington! Stockmar had evidently forgotten that what he was proposing was in flat contradiction not only of the vow Albert had taken (with his approval) to sink his personality in that of his wife, but also of his own merciless criticism of Victoria's suggestion to make Albert King Consort: the prince, he had said on that occasion, did not need a defined position. His mind must have gone back into the past, to his old idea that Albert had a feeling of inferiority, so that he could be demonstrating his own confidence in him by giving him impossible heights to scale.

Albert's reply to Stockmar was reasonable and kind:

'Your appeal to me to take the place of the duke for the country and the world shall stimulate me to fresh zeal in the fulfilment of my duties. The position of being merely the wife's husband is, in the eyes of the public, naturally an unfavourable one, inasmuch as it presupposes inferiority, and makes it necessary to demonstrate, which can only be done by deeds, that no such inferiority exists. Now silent influence is precisely that which operates the greatest and widest good, and therefore much time must elapse before the value of that influence is recognised by those who can take cognisance of it, while by the mass of mankind it can scarcely be understood at all. I must content myself with the fact that constitutional monarchy marches unassailably on its beneficent course, and that the country prospers and makes progress.'

But was he really content? Vicky for one was shrewd enough to guess that her father's occasional bouts of 'lowness' did not come from overwork but from dissatisfaction with the anomaly of his position. The harsh reality hidden in her little brother Arthur's question was not lost on Vicky: 'If Mama is Queen, why is not Papa King?'

16

'Killed by their
own people'

THE new Parliament met on 10 February 1853. The Cabinet was
brilliant and strong, filled with illustrious names, among them the
duke of Newcastle, Sidney Herbert and William Ewart Gladstone,
all of whom had been staunch supporters of Peel over the Corn Laws.
The Queen and Albert expected great things of this new government: how could they fail? Sir James Graham, a parliamentarian
of many years' standing, cooled their ardour somewhat by pointing
out drily that such a Cabinet would, like a team of high-mettled
horses, need a great deal of careful handling; was Aberdeen the
best coachman, he wondered. However, Lord Lansdowne, to whom
Albert turned for comfort, silenced their alarm: with such a calm
and judicious Prime Minister all would be well! It was a team Albert
had long wished to see working together. 'The realisation of our
own ... most ardent wishes' was indeed very true, but from the
opinions in the Press it seemed that there was some doubt whether
the country had as much faith in the ministry of All-the-Talents
as the sovereign and her husband. To their delight Palmerston was
not given the Foreign Office; during the time that the Cabinet was
being formed his voice had not been heard in the negotiations, and
they had not had to endure ultimatums like those he had thrown
with such impudence at Derby, refusing office unless eight of his
friends were included as well. But Palmerston's place as a trouble-
maker was at once taken by Lord John Russell, who accepted the
Foreign Office on the condition that he could hand over to Clarendon as soon as the government was firmly established – and then
resigned within two months, to the momentary alarm of Albert,
who feared that Palmerston's unwonted quietness meant that he

was plotting to oust Clarendon and seize the Foreign Office again.

Aberdeen turned out to be a Prime Minister after their own hearts, a statesman of the fast-disappearing Stockmar breed. From the very first he was meticulous in letting the palace know everything that went on in Cabinet and in submitting the text of despatches abroad in good time, accepting suggested alterations and even on occasion offering a revised version for scrutiny (a courtesy unheard of even in Peel's day). What is more, Aberdeen was as much a stickler for memoranda as Albert, and this without it once being suggested to him. His relations with the palace were so warm that Albert could frequently save time by writing direct to the Prime Minister, just as he used to write to Peel – when the Queen was in bed with measles in July 1853, for instance, the two men settled a problem over Turkey between them without troubling her. He never made the mistake of forcing Queen Victoria to do something against her will; a month later he advised her to prorogue Parliament in person because this would have a calming effect on the public after Russia's recent invasion of Moldavia and Wallachia, but raised no objection when she refused on the ground that, with Albert now ill, she was reluctant to make a special journey from Osborne alone and wanted to reserve her strength for a state visit to Ireland in the autumn. His tact brought its reward, for when he did take a firm line the Queen and Albert meekly gave way. It was the custom for one minister at a time to be in attendance at Balmoral; when it came to Palmerston's turn in the autumn of 1853 they wanted to refuse, but yielded when the Prime Minister pointed out that to give Palmerston a private grievance would increase the fierceness of his disagreement over Turkey in Cabinet and might decide him to bring the government down. As it turned out, Palmerston behaved so well at Balmoral that they were sorry to see him leave.

The late summer was hardly a propitious moment for the Queen to leave the country – the Russians had occupied Moldavia and Wallachia in June, and the war-clouds showed no signs of lifting – but Albert had some time ago promised to visit the Dublin Exhibition of Art and Industry and Aberdeen advised against cancellation lest it seem that the government was about to declare war. They received a tumultuous welcome in the streets of Dublin on 30 August, and it was therefore disappointing to find the exhibition itself poorly attended although the quality of the exhibits was surprisingly high. Albert was taken with a novel method of hatching salmon and with the strange grey-tinted glass – designed to protect pictures and tapestries from damage by sunlight – which had been used in the gallery windows ('every museum in England must know about it,' he said). They were whirled round Dublin by the Irish railway king, William Dargan, on his miniature railway, and were struck by an enterprise which was attracting tourists to the city; a still more vivid impression was created when Dargan refused the offer of a baronetcy, and Albert ruefully contrasted this with the way his own assistants had clamoured for honours in 1851. Unfortunately their few days' stay in Ireland gave them the quite false conception that the Irish had a healthy respect for the British monarchy and could be an industrial nation if shown how to make the best use of their natural resources.

They reached Balmoral on 6 September, intending to stay only for about ten days but in fact remaining for nearly six weeks. Although outwardly restored to health, Albert was still listless and depressed after measles, and in this mood was easily distracted from preoccupation with the threat of war by the lure of field-sports. In spite of bad weather he shot twenty-six stags during their stay at Balmoral and felt his energy gradually returning. To prolong their holiday thus, even for so good a reason, was a bad mistake, for it meant that Albert became more and more out of touch at a time when the situation was continually worsening, allowing authority to slip out of his hands, and was in consequence able to exercise less influence than he otherwise would have done over the final steps which led to the Crimean War.

An urgent message from Aberdeen recalled them to Windsor on 14 October, to find a Cabinet divided against itself and out of the Prime Minister's control – a situation, in fact, where Albert's moderating influence had never been more urgently needed. Uncharacteristically, Albert now leaned too much on Aberdeen's advice, a strange reversal of roles after the strenuous efforts he had made over so many years to dominate successive Prime Ministers, and quite failed to see that the quality he most admired in Aberdeen, his love of peace, dangerously unsuited him to deal with the current situation because it was rooted in a positive horror of using force. Furthermore, he was unable to believe that a Cabinet containing such a distinguished combination of intellect and experience, which he had to all intents and purposes chosen himself, could possibly go wrong or that divisions within it could be more than superficial. The Cabinet seemed none the less to be losing its grip of affairs, and the public, egged on by Palmerston, was loudly demanding that some means be found to halt Russian aggression.

In these circumstances Albert began to regret bitterly that he had urged the reappointment of Stratford de Redcliffe as Ambassador to Constantinople in the previous January, for it seemed to him, as

to many others in London, that de Redcliffe was provoking a conflict which might otherwise have been avoided. Albert was not alone
in making this mistake – Clarendon and *The Times* shared it, for
instance; de Redcliffe's well-founded reputation for arrogance
concealed, both at the time and for long afterwards, his many
contributions towards the maintenance of peace, like his solution
of the dispute over the Holy Places in April, his damping-down of
the Moldavia–Wallachia crisis in July, and his repeated efforts to
persuade the Turks to a compromise. Just before he left Balmoral in
October, Albert had seen clearly enough that the encouragement
England and France had already given to Turkey had effectively
taken the choice between peace and war out of their hands and
placed it in Turkey's; but now, under Aberdeen's influence, he
joined the anti-Palmerston faction and precipitately demanded de
Redcliffe's recall without weighing up the issue in his usual cautious
way: de Redcliffe's despatches, he said in a letter he drafted for the
Queen to send to Aberdeen, 'exhibit clearly on his part a desire for
war and to drag us into it.' Public opinion, dissatisfied that Aberdeen and Clarendon were not taking strong action against Russia,
soon began to demand their resignation, and it was not long before
Albert and Victoria were very much of the same mind themselves;
but since to desert Aberdeen would be to play into Palmerston's
hands, they could do nothing. A hint that he might take a stronger
line produced the gentle rejoinder from Aberdeen that 'if he had
known Her Majesty's opinion earlier he might have been more
firm' – a reference to their delay at Balmoral.

By Christmas there were new dissensions in the Cabinet: Lord
John Russell was insisting on introducing a Parliamentary reform
bill, in the knowledge that Aberdeen disliked it and would probably
resign, thus giving him a chance to regain the premiership. Albert
was in favour of reform but condemned Lord John's timing until it
became known that Palmerston too was threatening resignation;
upon receiving this unexpected good news, he promptly changed his
mind, in the hope that Palmerston would resign on this unpopular
measure and so cook his own goose. By allowing his old antipathy to
Palmerston to direct his actions in this way, Albert was diverting
his own attention from the main issues and allowing his view of the
country's interests to be distorted by prejudice. The Aberdeen correspondence contains several letters from Albert about the collection
of evidence which might be used against Palmerston in order to speed
up his resignation, perhaps in the hope that, as he wrote to Ernest,
Palmerston would 'outwit himself, as clever men sometimes do.'
So uncharacteristic a concentration upon side-issues is difficult to

explain, and the only possible conclusions seem to be either that his recovery from the attack of measles in July was unusually slow or that he had in fact been suffering from something far more serious, such as encephalitis, the effects of which would have lasted much longer.*

On 16 December, to the great surprise of the palace, Palmerston was as good as his word. His resignation coincided with the arrival in London of news of the Russian attack on the Turkish fleet at Sinope which had taken place three weeks before, and the popular Press soon managed to persuade itself that the 'shame' of Sinope had forced him out of office and that Aberdeen deserved censure for not lifting a finger to protect the Turks. The first results were that Palmerston had to be brought back into the government within a week and that a fleet was despatched to the Black Sea. Albert, of course, took Palmerston's return very much to heart:

'Now Palmerston is again in his seat and all is quiet. The best of the joke is that, because he went out, the Opposition journals extolled him to the skies, in order to damage the Ministry, and now the Ministerial journals have to do so, in order to justify the reconciliation(?) . . . I fear the whole affair will damage the Ministry seriously. Palmerston gulps down, it is true, all his objections to the Reform Bill (which is to be altered in none of its essentials), but he will lead the world to believe that it is to *him* concessions have been made.'

Popular outcry demanded another victim, however, and fastened upon Albert: he had been behind Palmerston's resignation, it was rumoured, just as he had been responsible for hounding him out of the Foreign Office the previous year. So long as it was only the gutter press which accused him Albert was disposed to ignore the attacks, but he could no longer do so when a responsible paper like the *Daily News* called him 'a male Mary Ann Clark',† and asserted that he took his orders from Prussia and was intriguing against England with his foreign relations. 'The Emperor of Russia now reigns in England', Albert wrote in his New Year letter to Ernest. 'It is said that he telegraphs to Gotha, you to Brussels, and Uncle Leopold to me. And I influence Victoria. She presses on old Aberdeen and the voice of the only *English* minister, Palmerston, is not heard. On the contrary, *at* court and *from* the court everybody intrigues against him.'

* See note on p. 240 above.
† Mary Ann Clark, one-time mistress of the duke of York, who carried on a brisk and profitable trade in army commissions.

Early in January 1854 there were new attacks, pamphleteers got busy; it was rumoured in the clubs that Palmerston had steamed open the Prince's letters and found them full of treason, and when 'Puss' Granville chose this unfortunate moment to propose a statue on the site of the Great Exhibition it was claimed that Albert was demanding one in order to aggrandise himself. London seemed to go mad; a *Punch* cartoon showed a nervous Albert on skates narrowly avoiding a hole in the ice marked 'Foreign Affairs, very dangerous', and a crowd actually gathered to watch the 'German lad' being led in chains to the Tower with his wife and children. Albert lost his sleep and his appetite, and the Queen her temper. She was angry with everyone, especially with Albert for not being angry enough, and both of them began to look pinched and ill. Finally, about the middle of the month, came the most serious attacks of all, for this time the silly lies had a basis of truth. A leading article in the *Herald* attacked Albert for being present at audiences between the Queen and her ministers and for taking part in their deliberations; 'it is too bad that one man, and he not an Englishman by birth, should be at once Foreign Secretary, Commander-in-Chief and Prime Minister under all administrations.' The article was signed by 'An M.P.', but Albert understood that it came from the virulent pen of Lord Maidstone, whose wife was a daughter of that Lord Uxbridge whom Albert had unceremoniously thrown out of his comfortable rooms in Buckingham Palace as long ago as 1840. The past had caught up with him.

What capital the newspapers would have made out of the truth! They did not know that Albert not only saw ministers with the Queen, but frequently on his own, that it had become the practice for the Prime Minister and the Foreign Secretary to communicate with him direct, and that he sometimes wrote to them without consulting her.

A second article in the *Herald* demanded the dismissal of foreigners like Stockmar* and the employment in future only of 'honest Englishmen' at court. When she read this, the Queen broke down. 'The country is as loyal as ever, only a little mad,' she wrote to Stockmar, but Albert put it more forcefully 'We might fancy we were living in a madhouse.' Madhouse indeed it seemed when even Leopold set current in London a story that Palmerston and Louis Napoleon were seeking revenge on Albert because he had refused to

---

* Stockmar had never held any official position in England. He once described himself as Victoria and Albert's 'second father', however, and it was common knowledge that they confided in him freely. But by 1854 he was coming to England less often than formerly, and for shorter periods.

allow the marriage they had planned between Prince Jerome and Princess Mary of Cambridge; for all Albert had done, as he said, was to protect an innocent girl from 'one of the greatest scamps in all France'.

The next point of attack was Albert's connexion with the army. Lord Raglan's friends had never forgiven him for promoting Hardinge over Raglan's head, accused the new Commander-in-Chief of being no more than a tool of the Prince, and blamed Albert for things which he knew nothing about, like the quarrel between Hardinge and Sir George Brown over the weight of the soldiers' knapsacks which resulted in Brown's resignation. All this was such manifest nonsense that Albert did not think it worth contradicting, but Palmerston and Hardinge felt that it should be publicly refuted and urged him to publish his correspondence with Wellington and reveal that he had declined the post of Commander-in-Chief, together with the reasons which had led him to do so. Obstinately Albert refused to defend himself by using private letters, but his refusal contained also an element of bitterness that his wife's subjects could think so ill of him, and he was surely justified in calling them 'cold and unfeeling, with hearts of stone'. Only a short month earlier, up to the moment of Palmerston's resignation, he had still been on the crest of a wave of popularity, acclaimed by all, the details of his dress imitated on every side (the invention of the sewing machine made off-the-peg clothes possible for the first time, and copies of Albert's suits, with their high-buttoned jackets, small lapels and narrow trousers were made by the thousand), but now he was suddenly 'a foreigner' again, with an imagined connexion with the new national enemy, Russia, and therefore next door to a traitor.

While the attacks were at their height Albert sought advice from the Lord Chancellor (who was 'forced to leave his court and hasten to Windsor', according to Macaulay) about the advisability of taking legal action against the *Morning Advertiser*, which had printed the most scurrilous articles. The Lord Chancellor was abrupt and unsympathetic but wisely discouraged him from any such step. Albert was forgetting the sound rule he had made for the Queen long ago – never to descend to the level of one of her own subjects – and this is a measure of the distracted state to which unhappiness had reduced him, so that for a moment he discarded all his principles and gave way to a natural and human desire to retaliate. When this mood had passed, he wondered whether he were not being blackmailed (rather as Melbourne had been in 1837) to get rid of Aberdeen or do lasting damage to the monarchy. It was a bad moment to receive an eight-page essay from Stockmar which began with the unfeeling remark 'I cannot wish, hard as you may have been hit by it, that you should have been spared this experience' and went on to use twenty-year-old evidence to show how the corrupt British party system was undermining the Throne and to make the grotesque claim that the Crown had 'supreme authority' over its ministers (an implied rebuke to Victoria for not asserting herself).

The bitterness of Albert's feelings can be judged from the reply he wrote to this hurtful and almost entirely irrelevant discourse on 24 January. It included the following passage:

'A very considerable section of the nation had never given itself the trouble to consider what really is the position of the husband of a Queen Regnant. When I first came over here, I was met by this want of knowledge and unwillingness to give a thought to the position of this luckless personage. Peel cut down my income, Wellington refused me my rank, the Royal Family cried out against the Foreign interloper, the Whigs in office were only inclined to concede to me just as much space as I could stand upon. The Constitution is silent as to the Consort of the Queen; – even Blackstone ignores him, and yet there he was, and not to be done without. As I have kept quiet and caused no scandal, and all went well, no one has troubled himself about me and my doings; and any one who wished to pay me a compliment at a public dinner or meeting, extolled my "wise abstinence from interfering in political matters". Now when the present journalistic controversies have brought to light the fact, that I have for years taken an active interest in all political matters, the public, instead of feeling surprise at my reserve, and the tact with which I have avoided thrusting myself forward, fancied itself betrayed, because it felt it had been self-deceived.'

The tide began to turn in the third week of January. Delane struck a blow for fair play with a leading article in *The Times* which said that the insults had gone beyond the bounds of decency and must cease. (Dasent's biography indeed likens Delane to Albert for their joint desire to awaken the country to its danger, and condemns Delane's earlier attacks as disgraceful.) The *Spectator* wanted all the newspapers which had slandered Albert to publish an apology, beginning with the *Morning Advertiser* which (the *Spectator* had discovered) had been printing outrageous stories simply to boost its falling sales. As soon as the Queen had opened Parliament on 30 January, Lord John Russell vindicated Albert completely in a short but telling speech: 'When the people of this country, always just in the end, have reflected on these matters, I think the result of these calumnies, base as they are, and of these delusions, blind as

251

they have been, will be to attach the crown still more strongly to the realm and to give a firmer and stronger foundation to the throne.' Resounding cheers broke out from all sides of the House as he sat down, and Albert was deeply moved by the warmth with which Lord John had defended him, for they had recently been more at loggerheads than ever; but as an honourable man Lord John could not stand aside and allow the slanders to continue unchecked. 'Nothing could have been more clear, complete and dignified' than his words, Albert wrote to King Leopold.

After Lord John's speech not one voice was raised against Albert again, and the whole affair was soon forgotten by everyone except the victim, upon whom the strain of coping with attacks from within the home as well as from outside it at one and the same time had left its mark. For the Queen's fury and anguish at the unfairness of the slanders had made her accuse him of timidity and cowardice during those terrible three weeks. Of course she now wanted to make amends for her unkindness, and revived once more her proposal to make him King Consort. Although Aberdeen was in favour of this, and although he was himself certain the trouble would never have arisen if his position had been less anomalous, Albert felt a sudden distaste for the whole idea. Angrily, he told the Queen to put it out of her mind.

Surprisingly, the western powers made no move against Russia during the winter of 1853/4, and an Anglo-French ultimatum to Russia was not delivered until the end of February, three months after the destruction of the Turkish fleet at Sinope. The inevitability of an eventual war between England and Russia had been one of Albert's first conclusions after his marriage – 'From what I have been able to learn of English policy by reading despatches and studying secret reports, it is absolutely certain that there will be war between England and Russia within five or six years,' he had written to Ernest in August 1840 – but his greatest fear had long been that war was coming before the country was ready to wage it. For the first time he now found that he did not see eye to eye with Aberdeen; Aberdeen wanted to avoid war altogether, but Albert sought merely to delay the inevitable until the necessary guns and rifles were ready.

Another worry which preyed on his mind was a growing uncertainty whether the Prussian participation upon which he had counted would actually materialise. Quite forgetting that the influence of William's sister, Nicholas I's wife, to whom he was deeply attached, might easily incline the king to the Russian side, Albert had for several years been courting the Prussian royal family, partly in the hope that he might thereby have a hand in the future unification of Germany, but partly also to ensure Prussian support in a possible future war with Russia or France: hence the invitations to stand godparent to his children, the lavish entertainment of Prince William when he was a refugee in 1848 and when he visited the Great Exhibition three years later, the warm welcomes to Princess Augusta and the fêting of Prince Adalbert and the Prussian navy at Portsmouth in 1853. But Albert's greatest mistake was to carry on for several years a clandestine correspondence with King Frederick William in which he freely criticised British policy and British ministers, thus of course giving Frederick William the impression that he had a special relationship with Albert and inadvertently encouraging him to think that he might secure special terms if he joined a coalition against Russia. When Frederick William began to demand such terms (a free hand in Germany, and guaranteed protection against French or Austrian attack) during the summer of 1853, Albert felt he was being blackmailed, and he criticised Frederick William's behaviour as 'unworthy' when Prussia finally declared her neutrality in March 1854; in both cases he seems not to have realised that the fault was largely his own for deluding himself that England and Prussia had extensive common interests. It was small consolation to reflect that Frederick William could not sleep at night for thinking about the lines of Russian troops menacing his frontier.

The impressive appearance of the British force as it cheerfully embarked for the east in April deceived everyone but Albert, who knew that there were very few soldiers left at home who could be sent out as reinforcements if casualties were heavy. 'This is the consequence of those institutions which demand that a ridiculously small peacetime army should suddenly embark on great wars,' he wrote to Ernest, and continued with a reference to 'fine-looking men, marching superbly, but whose coming ordeal makes me shudder to think of.' The offer of double pay in the army, and the prospect of prize money in the navy, were bringing plenty of recruits to both services, and the Queen was no doubt right when she wrote that the war was 'popular beyond belief'; but in spite of this Albert was a solitary pessimist, scolded at home for prophesying heavy losses by his wife and daughters who were busily knitting comforters for the troops and excitedly talking of how they would celebrate victory. All Albert could think of was the terrible waste of life. Gazing down one grey and gusty evening at the cheering crowds in the Mall, he was filled with incredulous wonder that the nation had suddenly thrown off its habitual reserve and abandoned itself to the 'terrible cry to arms'. Only a chance opportunity to hit back at the Czar cheered him up at all: the British ambassador, Sir Hamilton Seymour, recalled from Berlin, told him of a rumour that Nicholas intended to publish Albert's letters in order to compromise him 'to a very high degree', and it was with wry amusement that he told Seymour that the Czar was welcome to publish letters 'as uninteresting as they are innocent' which merely contained announcements of the birth of their children.

Scarcely a day passed but a friend or relation left for the front. Among them was George, the duke of Cambridge, who was to command an infantry division; he looked in poor shape, overweight and pasty, and a good deal more inclined to sing the praises of his French chef than to think about the well-being of his men, Albert thought; they might as well throw in the sponge at once if all the generals were like him. George's facile pen was quick to send the dismal news from Vienna that the Austrian Emperor Francis Joseph intended to keep his country out of the war and that there was 'no hope' of his joining the alliance. A month later Ernest called on the Emperor and reported that it would not be long before Austrian troops were fighting alongside the English and French! Both were unreliable, neither was to be believed, said Albert gloomily, throwing the letters into the fire. George did not like Constantinople when he reached it, finding the city unhealthy, but alarmed Albert by discovering that the Sultan was a poor specimen and Turkish morale low; 'the "sick-man" ', he wrote, 'is excessively sick indeed, dying as fast as possible.' (Reeve of *The Times* had recently been in Constantinople and had reported that 'the whole state of Turkey is rotten to the core.') The letter showed clearly enough that the heart had gone out of George, and it took the heart out of Albert too to learn that George had no idea how well equipped his division was and that he thought at least ten thousand more troops were necessary (preferably four or five times as many) because of the strength of the Russians and the grandiose plans of the French. For Albert knew only too well that there were no trained reinforcements available yet, and that even when they were ready they would not be up to the standard of the veterans.

What most shook Albert, however, was the continuing complacency of the country in spite of mounting difficulties. *The Times* was almost alone when it loudly demanded an increase in armaments; Delane's arguments were the weightier because he had just returned from a month in Paris and had plenty of solid evidence to show that the French were far better prepared, for he and several others had visited every naval and military arsenal in France. Another leading article attacked ministers for slackness and for not recreating Wellington's waggon-train to supply the expeditionary force, and caused *The Times* to be quite undeservedly accused of spreading gloom and despondency. In the circumstances Albert, who disliked it as a rule, thought that publicity of this sort was a necessary evil, and as time passed he came more and more to rely on William Russell's excellent reports from the front line, which were to establish *The Times* as the foremost national newspaper. Delane had sent Russell out with the British army, and within a day or two of landing at Gallipoli he was sending home stories which were to shock and horrify the whole country. His despatches corroborated all that Albert had been saying for years – that men were suffering, as he had foreseen that they would, from the results of neglect, indifference and complacency: the commissariat was inadequate, medical supplies insufficient, hospitals badly run and pest-ridden. Russell's fearless exposure of mismanagement helped to bring about the fall of the Aberdeen coalition, which was responsible for it, and to hasten the departure of Florence Nightingale and a small band of nurses for Scutari, where she found conditions in the hospitals every bit as badly in need of improvement as Russell had said.

War fever did not leave the palace untouched. The Queen's enthusiasm – in a marked contrast to her husband's gloom – was so great that nothing was too much trouble for her if it would encourage the troops; she willingly rose before dawn and stood shivering in the half-light on the balcony to wave them on their way, and travelled down to Spithead with Albert and the four eldest children to watch the fleet set sail for the Baltic. The sight of the ships brought out the martial feelings of everyone but Albert, who had inspected the twenty screw-driven men-of-war two days earlier and knew that, fine as they were, they represented the navy's whole battle-strength and that there was nothing to reinforce or replace them. Even Albert could not help being a little stirred by a ship as magnificent as the *Duke of Wellington*, with her 130 guns and her speed of eight knots, but all his love of mechanical innovation could not prevent him from reflecting that there was risk as well as ad-vantage in the introduction of steam, for the enemy could use it too: steam had put a completely different complexion on international disagreements. The Admiral commanding the Baltic fleet, Sir Charles Napier, had invited Albert to his cabin after the inspection and spoken very frankly about the limited range of his fleet; Albert was not surprised at this, for he had not believed Napier's boastful speech at the Reform Club just beforehand – after dining rather too well he had promised to be 'in Kronstadt or in Hell' within a month. Even when Napier failed to take Kronstadt, the Russian naval base in the Baltic, at all that year, however, Albert was inclined to defend him to the Queen, who was horrified that he had shown off like a Frenchman; it would be a sorry day, he told her, when a man could not make a light-hearted speech at a relaxed club dinner without fear of a wrong interpretation in the Press next day; the fault lay in the reporting, not in the speech.

The prospect of war had already begun to make life uncomfortable for everyone that winter, and spring was late and chilly. As an example to the country, the Queen quickly began to practise economies. Always impervious to cold, she barely noticed the effect of smaller fires, but Albert suffered dreadfully. Regularly at six every morning he could be found dealing with the Queen's boxes, wrapped in a rug and vainly trying to warm his hands over his reading-lamp; one morning he shivered so much that he could not work so, greatly daring, he rolled up newspapers and made a fire in the embers of the old one, but of course he was soon found out and accused of weakness by the Queen. If he sometimes ran along the corridors, swinging his arms to work up a circulation, the Queen unkindly made out that he did it to save precious time, so little did she understand his sufferings. At the depth of the cold in February, he took to wearing a fur-lined coat indoors, removing it only for meals or a brisk skating session with the children; even so he developed a cold in the head and could not throw it off for six weeks. Leisure became a thing of the past for him. A welcome break from an indoor life was provided by a happy day he spent with Lord Hardinge and General Sir John Burgoyne riding on Aldershot Common to see whether it was suitable for a permanent army camp. Almost overnight, Albert had become an enthusiastic army man: one wall of his study was covered with maps of the Black Sea and the Crimea – which, alas, were copies of an unreliable and misleading Russian map dated 1837 – and he scrutinised them until he knew the whole area like the back of his hand. In consequence he was among the first to suggest that the armies should move from the region of Constantinople to Varna (in what is now Bulgaria) as a stepping-stone towards a landing in the Crimea, and that the capture of Sebastopol, the fortress which dominated the Black Sea, should be the prime objective of the allied generals.

The war, Albert was beginning to find, altered his relationships with people profoundly. He had always got on well with his Russophile stepmother, so he wrote her a kindly letter soon after war was declared; 'I feel for you, for I can understand and forgive your heart for being Russian. All I ask in return is that you will grant me your forgiveness.' But all he got by way of reply was a chilly assurance that she would continue to pray for him. The new but growing disharmony between him and Aberdeen was more serious. Aberdeen's suggestion of a day of national humiliation and prayer 'for the success of our army by land and sea' seemed to Albert singularly inept, calculated to do no good at home and infinite harm abroad and to suggest that England was uncertain of the rightness of her cause. A third and more surprising change was that of his attitude towards Napoleon III, which was brought about by a visit to the latter's camp at St Omer in early September. Hitherto he he had never had a good word to say for the French Emperor, but now he was completely conquered by the charm with which Napoleon deliberately set out to change the adverse opinion which he knew his guest held of him. He made a point of receiving Albert like a reigning monarch, and with tears in his eyes confessed his emotion at the sight of French troops forming a guard of honour for an English prince while their bands played 'God Save the Queen'. The two men conversed in French, and Albert was quick to notice that Napoleon spoke it with a German accent (perhaps deliberately exaggerated for Albert's benefit), which he put down to his education in Augsburg, and that quotations from German literature came trippingly off his tongue. Napoleon was at pains to let it be seen that he kept a strict court and that he was eager to listen and learn, never pretending to knowledge he did not possess. Their conversations ranged over a variety of topics, but it was on politics that their *rapport* was most marked: 'We discussed foreign and domestic affairs,' Albert wrote to Ernest on his return to London, 'and I must admit that his views on most things are very moderate and reasonable.' Napoleon warmed Albert's heart by showing no ill-will towards Prussia, whose disinclination to join the alliance he said he could well understand. No two men could have been more different, for Napoleon was everything which Albert usually despised – a womaniser, a braggart, and a man uninterested in culture and the arts – yet before long there was a strange affinity between them and Albert was reflecting that he had far more in common with this *parvenu* emperor than he had ever had with Louis Philippe, despite his royal blood. Indeed had it been proposed now and not in 1852, Albert might even have consented to the emperor's marriage to Victoria's stepniece, Adelaide of Hohenlohe, instead of refusing on the ground that she must not throw herself away on an upstart. Napoleon had asked for her hand two years too soon, but perhaps he was better suited by the sparkling Eugénie de Montijo than by the mouselike Adelaide.

Behind this new and curious friendship lay, of course, the hard fact that England and France needed each other: as Clarendon pointed out, French military assistance was indispensable if the war was to be brought to a successful end, while Napoleon needed the prestige of an alliance with an established power and the military glory his soldiers might win in the Crimea.

When, after six months of apparently aimless preliminaries in Constantinople and along the western shores of the Black Sea, the allied armies eventually landed in the Crimea in September 1854, a suitable point at which to attack and beat the Russians seemed at last to have been found, and the public clamoured for the fighting to begin. Victories on the Alma and at Balaclava during the next few weeks, even the mad but glorious Charge of the Light Brigade, only whetted their appetite for news that Sebastopol was under siege, for the capture of the great Russian base was now the declared objective of the whole campaign. But the armies' approach-march was slow, and by winter everyone was becoming impatient, even the Queen. Albert was almost alone in warning against hasty action, because it might lead to a repulse, and in recommending careful preparation before the mounting of a heavy and deliberate assault. Mingled with the vociferous demands for something dramatic to be done at once, however, was a paralysing lethargy and an almost total lack of ideas, even on the part of the Cabinet, about the practical steps which would be necessary before victory could be won. In contrast, ingenious suggestions poured from Albert's fertile mind. Among the best was his proposal that reconnaissance parties of naval officers should be landed on the coast in the neighbourhood of Sebastopol to cut communications and prevent supplies from being brought up to the garrison, and that they should begin by seizing a suitable base for their operations. He was fully aware of the dangers of armchair generalship but was not always able to avoid them because the maps were so inaccurate, and he later admitted that the location he had suggested for this base was quite unsuitable because the maps did not show the rockiness of the terrain. When cholera appeared in the army in January 1855 and he discovered that those who survived it were being sent back into the front line while still unfit, he was quick to propose the establishment of a convalescent camp on the island of Corfu. He had foreseen the need for large quantities of medical supplies and for warm clothing long before others thought them necessary; he sent fur-lined coats to the officers of his own Brigade of Guards at his own expense during the first terrible winter, but as a rule he could do no more than bombard the War Office with urgent requests which they were usually unable to fulfil. Incompetence on the massive scale which was apparent everywhere nearly drove him frantic. The difficulty of ensuring quick reinforcements to the front without an intermediate base between England and the Crimea became evident at an early stage, and Albert's letter to the Secretary of State for War of 28 November 1854 was the basis upon which the Cabinet decided two days later to establish a reserve army of 26,000 men in Malta. By far his largest scheme, and the one he had to fight hardest for, was his Foreign Legion. Although thoroughly aware of the pressing need for recruits, ministers froze at the word 'foreign' and declared that it would be unpopular (Albert, out to win the war not popularity, brushed this aside) and would show 'ingratitude to our brave armies in the Crimea.'* Nevertheless, from behind the scenes Albert steered the Foreign Enlistment Bill through Parliament before Christmas with the energetic help of Palmerston, who had become one of his staunchest supporters in calling for the urgent prosecution of the war. Albert's purpose was to persuade young Germans just released from military service to enlist in the British army rather than emigrate to America; large numbers were recruited, and Albert found it 'a strange bit of home' to review row upon row of German faces staring out of English uniforms at Shorncliffe early in the New Year. A committee of three did the preparatory work for the railway which was built between Balaclava and the siege-works outside Sebastopol (the other members were Newcastle, Secretary of State for War and Hardinge, Commander-in-Chief of the army). They met at Buckingham Palace, and the Cabinet accepted their proposals at once; work began in February, and the railway was in use before the end of March 1855 – here was a rare case where things were done with the speed and efficiency Albert liked to see. Finally, the idea of the Victoria Cross originated with Albert, and he was particularly insistent that it must be an award for bravery open equally to all ranks and that there should be no limit to the number of holders; his first sketch of the cross itself was made while commuting in an unheated train between Windsor and London during the freezing winter of 1854–5.

As William Russell's highly critical reports from the Crimea began to come in regularly, public opinion found it impossible to believe that so much could be wrong with the British army and was inclined to accuse him of exaggeration. Even Albert shared this tendency,

---

* Derby called the Foreign Enlistment Bill 'unconstitutional, impolite and degrading'; Cobden denounced it as 'immoral' and urged every patriot to fight it!

particularly because he feared that the new breed of journalists might give away valuable information to the enemy, and he agreed with the British general who said that the Russians had no need of espionage because they could get all they wanted for fivepence by buying a London paper. But he was immediately sceptical of the rumour that Sebastopol had fallen directly after the battle of the Alma on 30 September which seemed to discredit Russell, reminded the Queen that Austerlitz had at first been reported as a French defeat, and refused to join her in celebrating round a victory bonfire. She taxed him then with needless pessimism, but within a few days he was completely justified. The last remaining doubts about the accuracy of Russell's reporting and the extent of the mismanagement in the Crimea were banished in the summer of 1855, when *The Times* bought up and published a number of soldiers' letters home. These made it clear that the bulk of the army had perished not from Russian sword and musket but from English muddle and incompetence, 'killed by their own people' as the *Morning Chronicle* put it.

The vicissitudes of the autumn's fighting lowered the coalition's credit, and in January it was wavering towards its fall. As soon as Parliament reassembled on 23 January after the Christmas recess a decisive blow was struck by John Roebuck, the Radical MP for Sheffield, who moved for the appointment of a select committee to inquire into the conduct of the campaign, and hinted that 'a person in a high place' ought to be impeached. When Albert later learned that it was he himself that was meant, he realised with a sense of shock that the stupid accusations of 1853 were not dead and buried, as he had supposed, but were still lively enough to be trotted out again. Newcastle was able to refute Roebuck's charges point by point: he, not Albert, had appointed Raglan to command the troops in the Crimea; Hardinge had agreed to the appointment, and was not being kept at home against his will so that Albert could influence him; Albert's income was barely sufficient, even with strict economy, to cover the necessary expense of his household, and he had bought no land for himself next to the museums in South Kensington; he had drawers full of letters from Albert, all containing valuable suggestions for the better conduct of the war, which was his sole and consuming interest. It was a thankless task, Newcastle observed, to work behind the scenes for the good of the nation, as the Prince was continually doing. In the end, however, Albert was vindicated; the Roebuck Committee found no evidence against him and his popularity did not suffer as it had done the previous year.

The coalition's fate was sealed when it was heavily defeated on Roebuck's motion of 29 January, but Aberdeen had already put his

own head on the block by making a speech in which he found something to praise in the Czar, the most hated man in England. Albert
gave him the rebuke he deserved, but all the same it was painful to
see Aberdeen go. However, an essential feature of a coalition is that
its members should hold together, and this one was hopelessly
divided over Roebuck's motion. Moreover, Albert had noticed that
the difference between his views and Aberdeen's had grown greater
as the war progressed: both were men of peace, but Aberdeen could
not give his heart to the prosecution of war, whereas Albert worked
for victory with might and main. Palmerston's popularity had risen
so much of late that he was the obvious successor to Aberdeen;
Albert regarded this as inevitable, although it seemed like putting
the clock back, but Victoria would not give in without a struggle.
Twisting and turning in her efforts to avoid a man she so distrusted,
and without consulting Albert, she sent in turn for Derby, Lansdowne and Russell, who each refused the premiership. It was all
very well for her ministers to resign, she complained, but *she* could
not resign – she sometimes wished she could. By 4 February she was
so distracted that she was ready to give way, but Albert had almost
lost patience with her. Pale and silent, they were both working at
their desks when she suddenly exclaimed that to have Palmerston as
Prime Minister was objectionable in many respects 'and personally
not agreeable to me, but I think of nothing but the country'. It was
capitulation; overjoyed, Albert jumped to his feet and embraced
her tenderly. 'Precious time has been wasted,' he told Stockmar
that night, 'but with God's help we shall make it up.' Palmerston
kissed hands as Prime Minister two days later.

The appointment was immensely popular; the newspapers and
the clubs went mad with joy at the prospect of having 'the man of
the day' at the head of the government. Despite his dyed hair, false
teeth, short sight and deafness, which in anyone else would have been
crippling signs of old age, the vigour of the man was astonishing, and
it struck Albert with amazement that at seventy-one Palmerston
could hurry through a heavy snowstorm late at night to answer his
sovereign's call; he showed not a trace of fatigue and although his
coat was wet he made light of it. To his surprise, Albert himself felt
the magnetism of the man and was soon positively welcoming
Palmerston's energy in place of Aberdeen's indecisiveness, as the
statesman emerged from the ashes of the Foreign Secretary and
everything about him became less repugnant. Once the tension
between them had been eased after Palmerston's dismissal in December 1851 Albert could appreciate his old enemy's good qualities and
observe (what he had never noticed before) that they were now

united by a remarkable similarity of views. Nor could he forget that Palmerston's had been the decisive support in the debate over the Foreign Legion. Clothed with full responsibility at last, the new Palmerston began to show the qualities which the Queen and Albert considered essential in a Prime Minister. In the midst of all the popular excitement that victory was 'now a foregone conclusion' (as the newspapers were saying) his was the calm and moderating voice, and his list of Cabinet appointments was instantly acceptable. The new Secretary of State for War,* 'Bison' Panmure, had for five years been pressing as hard as Albert for a unified command of the army; 'I concur in His Royal Highness's remarks,' he had commented on a memorandum of Albert's,

> 'that our army is a "mere aggregate of battalions" – each of these perfect in themselves . . . but only pieces in the entire structure of an army. . . . The system by which an army should be provisioned, moved and brought to action . . . is non-existent. . . . We have no means of making general officers or of forming an efficient staff. . . . For great operations we are inadequate, as the result has proved.'

All the same, Panmure soon found that he was not his own master, for Albert oversaw every detail, determined to root out every vestige of past inefficiency. One day, when the two of them had solved a tricky problem together, Albert hinted that perhaps he had been foolish to refuse appointment as Commander-in-Chief on Wellington's death; the civilian at heart had become a soldier by necessity.

Raglan's meagre reports did nothing to counterbalance Russell's alarming accounts of the privations suffered by the soldiers, and in consequence still more disturbing rumours were current. Right at the beginning of the war, when he had foreseen that lack of information might lead to public disquiet, Albert had devised a printed postcard which a wounded or even illiterate soldier could have completed for him and sent home to his family. His suggestion had not been taken up at the time, but now Albert managed to get Panmure to put it into operation. Alongside this, he secured the adoption of a system of regular returns from the front of the number and condition of the men, horses, guns and stores available, something which had never been done in such detail hitherto. No doubt Raglan was to blame for this and other past omissions and failures, but Albert and Victoria stood by him throughout and knew, for instance, that he did not deserve the reviling to which the public subjected

---

* With whose office that of Secretary at War was now amalgamated.

him when he failed to take Sebastopol. He had clamoured for reinforcements since the battle of Balaclava, although it had taken
Albert's sense of urgency to push the Foreign Enlistment Bill
through Parliament. Though it was almost *lèse majesté* even to think
it, Albert believed that the real culprit was Wellington, who had
held the post of Commander-in-Chief for too long and let the army
run down in the decades after Waterloo.*

Gradually, almost imperceptibly, Albert's had become the
decisive voice, and it was therefore natural that he should be
chairman of a committee to consider the two most urgent requirements – recruits and reorganisation. The winter's experience had
shown that military organisation was woefully defective, and it
seemed that the army in the field grew no larger however many
reinforcements were sent, for cholera and the climate constantly
depleted it. By the time the committee began its work in June 1855,
Albert had ceased to feel astonished that he could wield so much
influence under the dreaded Pilgerstein, but the relief was tremendous. The committee worked swiftly; among other things, it recommended the creation of new battalions, the allocation of some of them
to training and reserve at the Malta base, and the drafting of
militiamen to garrisons abroad so that experienced soldiers could
be sent to the Crimea. After this, Albert said that at last he could
feel safe.

In February 1855, Napoleon III had set the English dovecotes
wildly fluttering by proposing to go to the Crimea, take command
of his troops and capture Sebastopol. He was already 'one up' on
Albert in his conduct of the campaign, and a visit to the field of
battle would incidentally bring a further advantage through all the
military and diplomatic benefits a great French success in the Crimea
would confer. He had been telegraphing orders daily, even hourly,
to General Canrobert, and had heard that Albert had never thought
of doing anything of the kind – although he might have been less
pleased with himself if he had known that his interference had nearly
broken Canrobert's nerve. As soon as Napoleon's proposal was
known, Clarendon was sent post-haste to catch him training his
troops at Boulogne and try to cool his ardour for military glory.
When Clarendon completely failed to change Napoleon's conviction
that his destiny lay with his soldiers in the Crimea, there was
nothing for it but to invite him to Windsor in the hope that the

* 'In his extreme desire to keep the military subordinate to the civil power, he
treated the army as a machine to be taken to pieces and packed away in small fractions
until it should be needed.' Hamley, 107.

Queen might be able to deflect him from his troublesome purpose.

The prospect of a long and stuffy drive with two people whom he scarcely knew made Albert's heart sink as he travelled down to Dover to meet the Emperor and Empress on 16 April; but to his surprise the time passed pleasantly as Napoleon once more, as at St Omer, played the part of an eager pupil and Eugénie listened with just that touch of intelligent deference that is so flattering to clever men. Eugénie and Albert had never met, and the French couple were both strangers to Victoria, but they had not been many hours at Windsor before they captivated them both. Victoria shrewdly noticed that Eugénie was not really beautiful but made everyone think she was by her personality and her unaffected manner. In her simple plaid silk travelling-dress and black velvet shawl, without jewellery, she looked young and appealing; the Queen and Albert instantly took her to their hearts, and found it difficult to understand how the stories of her wildness had originated. Napoleon's bizarre appearance – large head, short legs, and huge waxed moustaches above a curiously delicate mouth – was soon forgotten as Victoria fell under the spell of the immense charm which he turned upon every woman he met; she was so flattered to be told how wonderful she had looked as she drove to Westminster Abbey for her coronation eighteen years earlier that she even discerned 'a great deal of German and nothing French' in his character. A programme of activities was arranged by Albert to fill every moment of the state visit: a grand review of the Household troops, the Garter ceremony, a State ball and (at Napoleon's special request) a hilarious climb to the top of the Round Tower. Throughout, the Emperor was easy, calm and dignified, as though he had been born a king's son and brought up to his high position.

A Council of War was held on 18 April, at which Albert took the chair. Napoleon withstood all attempts to dissuade him from going to the Crimea, but Albert divined, with some amusement, that he enjoyed being the centre of attention and was prepared to yield in the end. More business was done during an afternoon stroll the two men took together. Albert explained that the professed French object of securing the independence of Moldavia and Wallachia would play directly into Russian hands (because a new and weak state would be an easy prey for Russian aggression) and inquired whether France still stood by the joint declaration in favour of the integrity of Turkey. Evidently unused to such plain speaking, the Emperor looked shaken and said he would answer in the morning. Next day he thanked Albert for opening his eyes to the devious ways of the Russians and undertook to abide by the joint declaration.

At a second Council of War, a plan of future operations was drawn up, and Albert was sincere when he remarked later on that it had been a pleasure to do business with Napoleon. But it was not until the French were on the point of leaving that Victoria boldly asked Napoleon 'not to risk his neck in the Crimea, for his life was much too precious', got the answer she wanted, and in return promised that they would visit Paris as soon as it could be arranged.

The dust had hardly settled after the imperial pair's departure before King Leopold hurried over, crusty, suspicious and full of warnings against the French impostor, demanding an account of everything that had happened and trying to dissuade them from paying a return visit. His children, who had accompanied him, almost succeeded where he failed; they infected their cousins with scarlet fever, so that for a time the trip to Paris was in jeopardy – it was only at the last minute that Sir James Clark pronounced them all out of quarantine.

For his part, Napoleon had also wondered whether Albert might after all be reluctant to leave London during the war, and therefore took pains to dangle in front of him the most tantalising bait he could devise – an annotated list of the French manufactures which would be on display at the Paris exhibition, which was to be the ostensible reason for the visit. There was indeed some hesitation on Albert's side, which this list may have helped to overcome, and for two main reasons. Admiral Lyons's foray into the Sea of Azov had not compensated for the failure of the assault on the Redan at the end of May, in which he had lost three friends 'all three irreplaceable, who have given their lives for nothing'; and Ernest had not lightened his consequent depression by stupidly proposing to join them in Paris. As the years wore on, Albert was finding that hints were no use where Ernest was concerned and that nothing but plain speaking would do: 'I consider it my duty not to leave you in any doubt,' he wrote bluntly, 'that you will not do us a favour by being present. Our visit is to be a strictly English visit to the Emperor and the French people, not an assembly of the Coburg family at the Bonaparte court. Your presence would only harm us.'

The journey to Paris on 18 August was slow and fatiguing – first fog, and then the train's frequent stops for speeches of welcome delayed them, but Victoria was enchanted by her first sight of Paris: 'I never saw anything gayer or more beautiful,' she wrote to King Leopold. They were to stay at St Cloud, the only French royal palace which had appealed to Albert when he was in France eighteen years earlier; but the long journey and the rich but unappetising food had upset his digestion, and even the sight of Salon de Diane, one of the most perfectly proportioned galleries in the world, could not raise his spirits when it was crowded with people and hot with the hundreds of wax candles that illuminated it.

Next morning Napoleon led Albert to his room directly after breakfast for a businesslike discussion of the war. He was exultant at the news of the French victory on the Tchernaya a day or two before, and deduced from the poor quality of the prisoners taken that the Russians were at the end of their tether; this success, he told Albert confidentially, would stop the cries for a premature peace because French troops were 'playing the game for England'.

The changes in Paris, all accomplished by the Emperor in the space of a very few years, astonished Albert. A cramped and still largely medieval city had been transformed into an imperial metropolis; no one could appreciate better than Albert, who had once suffered from claustrophobia in its narrow streets, how Napoleon had opened Paris up with his boulevards and squares, letting in much-needed light and giving a remarkable sense of spaciousness. Nevertheless, Albert had a strange feeling that he was being cleverly steered away from everything which was less creditable to the new régime than the beautification of its capital city.

In order to ensure that Napoleon was in no doubt about their attitude towards Louis Philippe's widow, Amélie, who was still living in England, Albert arranged for Victoria to have a frank talk with him on the subject, but with great tact Napoleon stopped her as she started to speak. He quite understood, he said, but went on to make the excuse that he had only confiscated the Orleanist family's private property to prevent it from being used to finance intrigues against his government, adding, however, that he felt no animosity towards the family and would be delighted if Amélie passed through France on her way to Spain. Without the least embarrassment, he arranged a tour of places associated with Louis Philippe, because he knew that this would give Victoria pleasure. Neuilly, the summer palace, which had been burned down in the revolution of 1848, was a place Albert remembered well from his youth, when Louis Philippe's three daughters had been gay unmarried girls and their brothers schoolboys home for the holidays. A visit to the Chapel of St Ferdinand, built over the spot where Louis' heir had been killed in a carriage-accident a dozen years before, led him to muse over the fate of the luckless Orleans family, already become mere spectres, ghosts that belonged to a past now dim and distant, so successfully had Napoleon supplanted them. 'You may well imagine what a strange impression so many changes produced',

Albert wrote to his stepmother in Coburg, 'all this is vanished before the wind.'

The exhibits at the *Exposition Universelle* were evidently of high quality, but Victoria attracted so much attention when she appeared on the Emperor's arm that Albert preferred to slip in quietly later on with Lord Clarendon. In other ways too Napoleon went to endless pains to entertain his guests. The *déjeuner champêtre* at Versailles was among the highlights for Albert, although he usually did not like pseudo-rustic expeditions, because it was simple yet grand and graced by the presence of the Empress Eugénie, who was not allowed to appear at every function because she was expecting a child and had to take care of herself after several miscarriages. Eugénie strolled up and down with Albert, looking ravishing in a flowered dress, her auburn hair drawn back from her face the better to show off her large blue eyes, daringly outlined in black pencil. They talked of Spain, Eugénie painting a vivid first-hand picture of the Spanish marriage crisis which, Albert reflected, would have helped him enormously at the time of his cousin's candidature for the young Queen's hand, and Albert in return telling her of the special difficulties he had encountered in 1845. Victoria thought Albert was attracted to Eugénie because she was gentle and good, but in fact it was her enormous strength of character which appealed to him. In a curious way, he sensed that she understood him better than he did himself; ridiculous as it may sound, she represented the mother-figure he so badly needed, someone he could lean on to ease a burden which he was dimly beginning to realise was too heavy for him to bear and which Victoria could not lighten because of her complete dependence on him. There was a rapport between Albert and Eugénie which had nothing to do with love or even flirtation, though it did include mutual attraction as well as understanding and respect in the very highest sense. There is no doubt that Eugénie was drawn to Albert's dependability and trustworthiness, his quick mind and genuine care for humanity; above all, she envied the Queen her faithful husband.

Eugénie could not accompany them to the opera, but her softening influence remained, enabling Albert to bear cheerfully the long tedium of the presentations which followed what to his mind was bad music and a still worse ballet. As they drove back to St Cloud in the moonlight, Napoleon suddenly burst into a German song. Albert instantly took it up, and the two of them sang duets all the way home, much to Victoria's amusement. Despite Leopold's warnings against this very thing, Queen Victoria – who never did anything by halves – had now gone over unreservedly to the

Bonapartist side and could find no faults at all in the new régime. Everything was done so much better and so much more royally than in Louis Philippe's day, she thought – the roll of drums for Albert's birthday showed Napoleon's imagination and desire to please, while the state ball at Versailles was indescribably grand. Among the distinguished guests presented during that ball was the Prussian minister at Frankfort, Count Otto Bismarck, whose malevolent influence was to overshadow the lives of his host and hostess, Queen Victoria and her children. On that glittering evening nothing foretold that fifteen years hence Napoleon would be a humiliated exile and that Bismarck would proclaim the German Empire in that same Galerie des Glaces.

It did not take Napoleon long to see that the way to Victoria's heart was to sing her husband's praises, so he laid on the flattery as thickly as he dared, but there is no doubt that he was genuinely impressed by Albert's talents and amazed by the enormous power he wielded. Here was a man to be cultivated. Nor was Albert unaffected by the Emperor's charm, although it was not his nature to share his wife's uncritical enthusiasm for the French alliance. 'I have frequently talked with Albert, who is naturally much calmer and particularly much less taken by people, much less under their influence than I am,' the Queen wrote to Leopold soon after her return to England. 'He quite admits that it is extraordinary how very much attached one becomes to him when one lives with the Emperor at one's ease and intimately as we have done during the last ten days.' Aberdeen was wrong when he said that the impression on Victoria of the 1843 visit to the Chateau d'Eu would be indelible. But next to the disappearance of Louis Philippe, the most tremendous change since those days was in the position of Albert, who was now England's diplomat-in-chief. It was entirely owing to his skilful handling of Napoleon that the Anglo-French alliance during the Crimean War went so smoothly, for no one could tell at first in which direction Napoleon would look for friends – to England, to Germany or to Russia. At the time of his second *coup d'état* Lord Derby had deprecated the tone taken by the Press, especially *The Times*, which he considered imprudent enough to drive France into the arms of the Russians, and the scales had been tipped in England's favour only by Albert's visit to St Omer, after which Napoleon declared that 'the union of England and France is necessary to resist Russia and America'. Albert never spoke a truer word than when he said that it was 'a piece of extraordinarily good luck that such a man as Napoleon turned up when he was most needed.'

Sebastopol fell at last on 9 September 1855. Albert could scarcely believe General Simpson's telegram when it reached him at Balmoral;

'God be praised,' he said as he handed it to the Queen, for on their return from Paris a fortnight before he had not expected the fortress to fall until the spring. 'Our bonfire on Craig Gowan blazed out magnificently,' he told Stockmar. 'It illuminated all the peaks round about; and the whole scattered population of the valleys understood the sign and made for the mountain, where we performed towards midnight a veritable Witches' dance, supported by whisky.' Victory was soured for the Queen and the rest of the country by the fact that it was the French who had made the decisive assault on the Malakoff redoubt while the English were being repulsed at the Redan. Patiently Albert explained to her what an alliance meant and scolded her for dressing up pride as patriotism. For himself, he rejoiced that the fighting was surely over now. There is a legend that Albert lacked imagination, and his ability to hide his feelings lends it some support; but the war had been a nightmare to him from the start, and he had mentally shared the sufferings and the privations which the soldiers had undergone. He would lie awake at night and try to work how far they were due to the generals in the field and how far to the politicians at home. One deep regret remained – that Lord Raglan had not lived to see Sebastopol taken: 'He bore his many trials like a true hero and Christian,' Albert wrote to Stockmar. 'How dreadfully misunderstood! Every action criticised by those sitting safely at home without the faintest understanding of his insurmountable difficulties, so terrible that they could not be imagined except by those on the spot'; and he shared the admiration for the common soldier which shone through Raglan's despatches, however terse. At St Omer he had prophesied that 'when the fog that envelops everything in the Crimea has cleared away, the men who have endured so much so uncomplainingly will be looked on in future with respect because they have earned it.'

As Stockmar had always foreseen, the chief difficulty about the Anglo-French alliance was holding it together long enough to secure results. Cracks opened in it as soon as peace talks began, as the French took a far softer line towards Russia than Albert and the British government; but in the event it was Prussia which proved the greatest hindrance to the work of the peace conference. Prussia had maintained an armed and rather pro-Russian neutrality throughout the war, and now demanded a seat at the conference table. To admit her would create a dangerous precedent, said Albert, for 'no one who has not taken part in the conflict has a right to interfere,' but he weakened his case when he explained his view at length 'for the sake of friendship' to the prince of Prussia. As soon as Napoleon heard rumours that a marriage between the

Princess Royal and Prince Frederick William of Prussia was in contemplation, he took it for granted that England would side with Prussia, until Clarendon disabused him with the remark that 'my sovereign and her husband put the interests of the country before their personal feelings' and saw to it that Prussia was only admitted when all the important business had been done.

The peace settlement was greeted with disapproval, for the whole country wanted to go on fighting until England had won a victory. Even in Parliament the Foreign Secretary had to face a barrage of abuse; paradoxically it was Disraeli who defended him best with the cynical remark that the war had been conducted so ineffectively that he could welcome any peace which was not disgraceful. Lord Cowley said that England would have obtained better terms if the talks had not been held in Paris but in some dull little German town; with no distractions, the delegates would have applied themselves vigorously to the job in hand in order to get away as quickly as possible.

Palmerston came out of the war more popular than ever. It was with Albert's full approval that he was given the Garter in April 1856: 'Less we could not have done.'

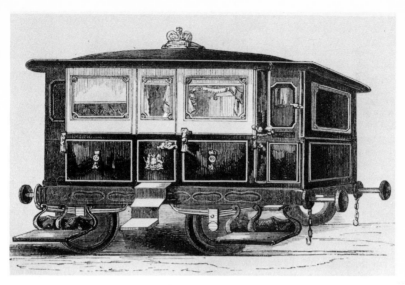

The first Royal Railway Carriage, 1843

Colonel Phipps, Mr Gibbs, Prince of Wales, Prince Albert, Baron Stockmar, Dr Decker, Baron Ernest Stockmar, April 1857

Albert in Highland dress

Building Balmoral, June 1854, drainage pipes in left foreground

The opening of the Great Exhibition

Osborne, Isle of Wight. Terrace and Pavilion

Royal party at the Crystal Palace, 17 June 1857: Queen
Victoria, Prince Consort, Princess Royal, Princess Alice,
Prince Frederick William of Prussia, and Archduke Maximilian
of Austria

17

'Friendship cannot
go much higher'

It was not surprising that Albert suffered a reaction when the war was over. After being stretched to the utmost for so long, he felt jaded and at odds with himself when suddenly there was nothing of the greatest urgency to occupy his mind. He was not ill, as the Queen thought, but he longed to get away from public affairs for a little so that he could forget about the destruction and death of the past two years. But first the price had to be paid for a friendship which had been useful to England during the war: Victor Emmanuel, the king of Sardinia, took it for granted that the English queen would wish to reward his alliance by inviting him to pay a state visit to London. Albert had nothing in common with this fat, eccentric roué save a love of constitutional government (and even that they interpreted differently), but there was no escape. Dutifully Albert showed him round London at the end of January 1856, suppressing his own boredom and restraining his guest from some folly a dozen times a day; after this, he was only too glad to get up at five on a bitterly cold morning to escort him to Dover on his way home. It was a poor reward for his efforts to be told by George of Cambridge that Victor Emmanuel had tried to make mischief in Paris on his way to London. Although trivial in itself, this incident showed Albert clearly that it was in the interests of most European countries to keep England and France apart, and he decided to be on his guard in future.

The sour taste of the Sardinian king's visit was removed on the day of his departure by the pleasure of presenting colours to the Royal German Legion, his own creation, in which he felt justifiable pride. By the time he reached the parade ground at Shorncliffe, snow was falling fast, but a huge crowd had gathered to see these strange foreign soldiers whom they had heard so much about. To his delight the Legion went through its movements with steadiness and precision, but when the moment for presenting the colours came Albert was suddenly overcome with emotion at addressing German troops in their own language on English soil. Could it be a foretaste of better relations between the two countries? An observer in the crowd that day has left a curious account of Albert's demeanour as he saw it: 'the Prince,' he complained, 'showed none of that benign kindliness manifested by the duke of Cambridge when it was his turn to review a batch of foreign legion troops. The Prince's manner was stiff and disdainful; he stared straight ahead of him as though he was ashamed of his kinship with this foreign rabble and wanted to get the business over as quickly as possible.' We know from Albert himself, however, that he was deeply moved, and the explanation of the discrepancy is perhaps to be found in a recurrence of that suppression of his true feelings which had been such a feature of his childhood.

As a sign of his return to normality, Albert took up again his old habit of riding about London on his horse 'Little David' to visit art galleries and artists' studios. The Pre-Raphaelites were just beginning to exhibit when war broke out, but the critics handled them roughly, in particular Millais' 'Christ in the house of his parents' on the ground that it was 'blasphemous'. Albert had watched Millais at work on the canvas and had found it genuinely religious, and he strongly resented the critics' attacks. Directly he could find the time after the war, he began trying to stimulate a revival of patronage by art dealers, who had formerly been willing to help new and struggling artists by bringing their work before the public but now allowed the critics to dictate standards of taste and only bought what was popular. Albert could not afford to be a patron on as large a scale as he would have liked, but he discovered and launched John Martin, for instance, by commissioning him to paint the Deluge trilogy (the idea was inspired by Turner's 'Deluge'), having persuaded the duke of Sutherland to promise that he would buy two of the canvases. By arranging that several early Italian paintings should be purchased for the Crystal Palace collection at Sydenham he was able, in Lady Eastlake's words, to 'raise the whole standard of art education' in England. He persuaded the Queen to employ young artists to make copies of the family portraits by Winterhalter, Landseer, Ross and Thorburn to send to relations abroad; it was dull and uninspiring work, no doubt, but it provided them with a regular income until they could establish themselves in their own right. In the spring of 1855, when the news from the Crimea was at its most dismal, Albert gained relief from worry by going to inspect the famous Bernel art collection, which was then up for sale. Exasperated by what he called the 'expensive mistakes' of piecemeal purchases in the past, he urged the Government to buy the whole collection for the nation at once, only to be met by a flat 'No' from Gladstone.* The government took the same intransigent attitude over the Soulages collection, which was auctioned in Toulouse the next autumn, and which Albert was so anxious to acquire for South Kensington that he guaranteed £1,000 himself. After dithering about in a way that set his teeth on edge, the Government half promised to secure it, then suddenly changed their minds at the last minute, so that Albert had to send a frantic appeal to his friends among the Manchester Art-Treasures Commissioners; they instantly responded, bought the whole collection, and generously allowed South Kensington to buy it from them item by item over the years at purchase price. In Albert's words to Stockmar, 'Friendship cannot go much higher.'

Well before the Crimean War was over, Albert was thoroughly disillusioned with Prussia, and particularly with her wavering and unreliable king, who had first insisted on remaining neutral and then demanded a share in the peace-making. The fundamental reason, he was coming to realise, was that Russia had progressively enslaved Prussia since Waterloo, so that now 'the fetters are not easy to break', as he told Ernest, even forbidding him to mention the name of Prussia again.

His understanding of Prussia was dangerously coloured by three misconceptions of which he and Victoria could never rid themselves. Since they were unable to think of their own interests separate from England's, they assumed that this was also true of the Prussian royal family and imagined that when the latter wrote warmly to them, for instance, it meant that Prussia was favourably disposed towards England; they quite failed to comprehend that the King might well be writing what was for the moment expedient and was in no way expressing his policy as ruler of Prussia. The difference between the constitutional systems of the two countries invited a second misconception, well though Albert of course knew that the difference existed. When he criticised British ministers to Frederick

---

* About the same time, Albert discovered that Gladstone had been against the scheme for the South Kensington museums from the start, on the ground that they were a waste of money. This may explain Henry Cole's remark, not long before the opening of the Great Exhibition, that he was worn out by Gladstone's discouragement.

William*, he was no doubt unwise, but he was writing privately and 'off the record', and was therefore both bewildered and furious when in December 1854, General Usedom arrived in London to negotiate on political matters with strict instructions from the King to deal only with Albert and on no account with the Foreign Office. Finally, his emotions about Prussia (whether at any given moment it was friendship or hostility that he felt) were really emotions about the king or his advisers and not about the country as a whole; he could separate them in his own mind, and expected the British Press to do the same – which of course they could not, so that he became unreasonably angry when in January 1856 some of the newspapers were talking threateningly of war with Prussia.

The harmful consequences of all this were compounded by his wilful blindness to the defects of the Prussian royal family, particularly to those of Prince William – whom, since he was out of favour with his brother the King, Albert exonerated from all blame for Prussia's recent misdemeanours. Anxious to strengthen his friendship with William, heir-presumptive to the Prussian throne, with whom he had kept up a desultory correspondence throughout the war, Albert and Victoria invited his son Fritz to Balmoral in September 1855. Fritz was the unhappy son of totally incompatible parents who had quarrelled since the day of their marriage and lived apart as much as possible. Albert had known about their dislike of each other ever since William and Augusta stayed at Buckingham Palace for the Great Exhibition, and he knew too that they were both equally to blame for the rift, but he had long ago concluded that to face up to these uncomfortable truths created too many problems and had decided to ignore them altogether. Moreover, the idea of a romantic love-match between Vicky and Fritz had by now taken root in his mind as a contribution towards healing the breach with Prussia and as a step on the long road to German unity, politically the more acceptable because, as he had noted with pleasure in 1851, Fritz appeared to have inherited all his mother's liberalism. Thus there were plenty of reasons for him to ignore the Prussian royal family's shortcomings, but he stored up trouble for the future by pretending that they did not exist.

Fritz of Prussia reached Balmoral on 14 September, the day after the Sebastopol bonfire. With the suitor actually in the house Albert behaved rather strangely, almost as if at the last moment he could not face the consequences of what he had done. He made no attempt to bring Vicky and Fritz together, but monopolised Fritz himself

* See p. 253 above.

from morning till night. The good weather was an excuse for the men to go deer-stalking, and every evening he took Fritz off to his study to discuss Prussia's 'deplorable politics'. On a family expedition to picnic in Glen Derry, Albert beckoned Fritz to sit beside him so that they could continue their discussion, and even prevented Fritz from riding with Vicky on the way down by persuading him to dismount and walk with him. After nearly a week of this, and with the end of his visit fast approaching, Fritz at last summoned up enough courage to blurt out his longing to 'become one of our family'; he was, of course, instantly accepted. But naturally there had to be conditions, since Vicky was only fourteen; Fritz (who was ten years older) was made to understand that the marriage could not take place for at least two years, but was allowed to speak to her himself and find out her feelings.

Vicky was well suited to become queen of Prussia one day; she was highly intelligent, had a charming personality and great strength of character and was already astonishingly well versed in politics and in her father's liberal principles. Fritz was not so well educated as his future wife, but Albert was quick to excuse this because he had been forced to spend so much time 'playing at soldiers, one of the diseases from which Prussia is suffering' and was happy to notice that he was willing to learn; above all, he was 'innocent' – which in Albert's language meant that he had not sown any wild oats.

Except for Stockmar, a handful of close relations and one or two members of both governments, all pledged to secrecy, no one was to be told of the engagement yet; but Albert's excitement was so great that he did not know where to draw the line and eventually the news leaked out. The papers got hold of the story and used it to stoke the fires of their abuse of Prussia for her behaviour over the Crimea; Albert and Victoria came in for their share of blame for allowing their daughter to contemplate marrying into so contemptible a country.

The moment the engagement was settled, Albert took to his bed with an acute attack of rheumatism in his left shoulder, and was soon so ill that he could scarcely eat; for a day or two he was in a state of collapse. Jealousy perhaps, or more likely a sudden realisation of how lonely he would be without this adored child, hit him hard and suddenly; here was one unpleasantness which he could not push to the back of his mind. A rare entry in his diary 'I have endured frightful torture' did not refer only to physical pain. What did he really know of Fritz? Of Fritz's family? Of Prussia? This mood was to pass (though never completely), and was soon replaced by the pleasure of instructing Vicky for her position as Fritz's wife and Prussia's future queen.

As soon as he had reached this happier frame of mind, Albert was seized by an uncharacteristic urge to tell Stockmar all about his hopes and plans for Vicky and Fritz and about their – in his own words – 'ardent love' for each other. Victoria began reliving her own romance with Albert, and in her letters to Fritz unconsciously put into Vicky's mouth words of affection which the child did not yet know how to use: 'What joy it will be for Vicky just to look into your dear eyes.' 'Vicky has never been so happy before, as when you kissed her.' A wonderful romantic novelist was lost when Victoria became a queen! Albert carried on where she left off: 'From the moment you declared your love and embraced her, the child in her vanished; I hope the long period of waiting will not make you impatient.' Astoundingly enough, they both handed these letters to Vicky to read before they posted them, as samples of what was now expected of her; an imaginative girl, she learned quickly, and 'Dear Fritz' at once became 'My precious, madly-loved Fritz . . . whom I think of day and night.' The emotions of all three were at fever pitch, presenting a picture of romance as lush as that portrayed in the shilling novelettes which Bertie was later to buy in secret at railway-stations. 'The intended is more and more in love every day,' Albert wrote to Ernest, which made that cynic roar with laughter.

The hint dropped by Albert early in 1856, that Fritz would do well to broaden his mind by travel, looked like turning sour when he was sent to represent his uncle the king at the coronation of Czar Alexander II at St Petersburg. Fritz little guessed the consternation this news caused at Windsor, for the Crimean War was scarcely over and his future parents-in-law were afraid that he was too un-sophisticated to escape corruption in the licentious atmosphere of the Russian court. Unable to forbid the visit, Albert had to content himself with warning Fritz that the new Czar would like nothing better than to make him 'an appendage of Russia', but Victoria did not beat about the bush: Alexander, she wrote, wanted to 'snap up' Fritz for one of his sisters. A hasty reassurance from Fritz that he was not to be lured away did not do half as much to set their minds at rest as his keen observation of the shadier side of Russian life; even educated people were ignorant, he wrote, 'and the lower classes look on the Czar as some kind of demi-god.' 'Deplorable,' they told each other, and Albert pressed his advantage home ruthlessly: 'with your sound and sensible Teutonic background you are bound to have more in common with England than with Russia. With the new element in your life, you will be able to find your proper level.'

But the fear that Fritz might be 'trapped by Russia' persisted, and Albert let himself go indignantly to Ernest (who was always hovering on the brink of friendship with Alexander): 'the Russians are getting all the principal families of Germany into their net.'

Fritz's visit to Russia rekindled the hostility of the Press towards the engagement; let the Princess Royal marry whom she will, the papers argued that autumn, as long as he is not a member of a paltry German dynasty which kow-tows to the Russians. Albert began to feel that the attacks were indirectly aimed at himself and were simply a renewal of the pre-war insinuations that he was a Russophile. Did not the idiots realise that he had planned the marriage for the express purpose of disrupting and scattering the pro-Russian ultra-conservative influences in Berlin (the party which had tried to hinder the peace-talks) and to encourage the liberals? He almost succeeded in convincing himself that opposition came only from the 'fashionables', who did not count, although Arthur Dasent, Delane's biographer, made it plain that almost the whole country was anti-Prussian and agreed with Robert Lovell's recent articles in *The Times* listing Prussia's sins against Britain.

Albert has been praised for his courage in making the first move towards the reconciliation with Prussia when the prestige of that country was at its lowest ebb in England. But need he have been so precipitate? He had always laid so much stress on proper timing that it seems extraordinary he should have forgotten it now. Why, at a moment when he knew that the final assault on Sebastopol was being mounted, did he invite to Balmoral the nephew of the man who had refused to help Britain against Russia? It would have been so easy to wait a few months. On the other hand, the war had shown Albert how tenuous were the links between England and France and how desirable it was to cultivate a closer relationship with Prussia instead. But he overlooked the fact that the man in the street was not interested in the finer points of politics and only remembered that Prussia had shown the white feather. It was just the kind of situation which brought out Albert's worst qualities. If he wanted something badly enough, he would always go for it ruthlessly and without hesitation or delay, not stopping to wonder whether a more patient and tactful respect for the opinions of others might not smooth his path and enable him to gain his end more speedily. This trait was inherited by Kaiser William II, but with far worse consequences, because he entirely lacked the unselfish desire to do good which redeemed it in Albert.

Although they feigned indifference, the tremendous public outcry against the Prussian marriage triggered off an acute anxiety-state in both Albert and Victoria – 'Distasteful articles are part of our daily bread,' said Albert, striving to be philosophical – not because they feared that there might be some truth in the accusations, but because they dreaded that the Prussian royal family might take offence and call the marriage off. As for the charge that Prussia was a despotism, Albert wished that he could make it known publicly that Augusta was anxious for her son to meet the liberal Prince William of Löwenstein at the Prussian legation when he (Fritz) next came to England; but it was strange that Albert saw nothing ominous in her refusal to let them meet in Berlin. He wrote to Augusta excusing with uncalled-for humility the insults to her country in the English Press, but at the same time he made it abundantly clear that he would not have contemplated the marriage had he not been certain that when Fritz became king, Vicky would have the opportunity to practise the constitutional principles in which she had been reared.

It was with a heavy heart that Albert set about preparing for Vicky's confirmation. It was not the solemn act of her being received into the Church that weighed him down, but the decision that must follow it – the date of her marriage would have to be fixed. This was something he would willingly have postponed, although on the other hand preparing his child to be queen of Prussia was a wonderfully exhilarating experience, a sacred task which he could not entrust to anyone else. He had even taken a major share in her religious instruction, so that it was not surprising if her views were an exact copy of his own. Very sound they were too; a broad middle way so as to hurt no one was the proper course for a queen whose husband's domains would embrace Protestants of every shade, Roman Catholics, Jews and non-believers. Most important of all, she had been taught to be tolerant, free from bigotry and prejudice, while fortunately, the Prince of Prussia had brought Fritz up (less from conviction than to thwart his High Church wife) on much the same Lutheran lines as Albert himself. This similarity of views strengthened their hands against the Prussian nobility who were for the most part either High Church, intolerant or indifferent.

Vicky's confirmation brought out an unsuspected mawkishness in her parents. Their knowledge of the adolescent mind, so sure when they dealt with other people's children, often went astray when they came to deal with their own. It was eighteen months before they told Alice, who was Vicky's constant companion, a single word about her sister's engagement, and then they sprang it on her the day before Vicky's confirmation, with the result that she was so prostrated by shock that she sobbed throughout the ceremony and was too ill to attend the reception which followed it. The sisters shared a bedroom and most of each other's secrets, yet this important piece of information had been needlessly kept from the sensitive thirteen-year-old, whose heartbreak at the thought of the coming separation was absolute. She was too young to notice 'signs' for herself when Fritz was at Balmoral, and so it was her parents' duty to prepare her for something which they should have known she was bound to regard as a major calamity. Short-sightedly, they took the view that so young a girl could not possibly understand the true nature of marriage, and that therefore there was little point in telling her.

Albert had by now become so English that nothing would induce him to fall in with Prussian demands for what he had so keenly wanted for himself in 1839 – a formal announcement of the engagement, at a special ceremony conducted for that purpose. The only concession he would make was for the relations to be told by letter – 'It is enough,' he said. The Prussian court followed this up by an even more outrageous demand: to have the marriage in Berlin. Without a second's delay, Queen Victoria dealt with this in the way it deserved; she did not wait for Albert to draft one of his judicious letters, but dashed off a masterly rejoinder: of course the marriage must take place in England for 'whatever may be the usual practice of Prussian princes, it is not every day that one marries the eldest daughter of the Queen of England.' Neither Victoria nor Albert could see that they had brought this piece of impertinence on themselves; humble at one moment, imperious the next, they had confused the Prussians completely, and Princess Augusta was quite justified when she complained that Queen Victoria was unpredictable. All through the engagement, in fact, they were most unwise in the plainness of their language in letters to the Prussian royal family; Victoria went too far in admitting that Vicky was not perfect, for instance, and Albert should have known better than to tear Manteuffel and his policy of neutrality to pieces and to tell Fritz that in consequence of it Prussia had 'renounced her position as a great power'.

Ill-considered remarks like these trickled back to Coburg and alarmed Stockmar so much that he begged Albert to be careful of what he said to Princess Augusta, since she was inclined to be indiscreet, but he also warned Albert not to be too compliant. The Prince paid at least some heed to both points, and certainly took a strong line when he demanded that Vicky's household should include two girls of her own age and should all come to Windsor to be inspected, together with the personal physician whom

Augusta had chosen for her, and he insisted that Stockmar's son should be appointed as her secretary. On top of all this, the duchess of Kent, to whom Albert was devoted, did not like the marriage one bit; Fritz was agreeable enough, but she could never forgive the Prussians for not lifting a finger to help Coburg during the Napoleonic occupation of her youth. She and Albert were both upset by the situation – she because she sensed that Albert was determined on the marriage, he because concern for Vicky's happiness was the cause of their first disagreement – but Albert nevertheless viewed it philosophically, remarking 'She will be reconciled in time.' Indirectly, Fritz had something to do with this calmer mood, for the maturer tone of his letters showed that he was already beginning to benefit from his future father-in-law's advice.

As the marriage drew nearer, Albert turned his mind more seriously than ever towards the education of the young couple for their future task. He told Fritz repeatedly that he ought to spend less time soldiering and more in familiarising himself with politics and government, and the fact that these letters were not addressed to Fritz's father perhaps indicates an awareness on Albert's part that he was trying to interfere without proper justification – though of course with the best of motives – in the affairs of a foreign country and that William was beginning to resent it.* As for Vicky, she was subjected to a daily routine of essays on history, literature and politics, to be corrected by her father and taken later on to Prussia to guide her when far away from the fountain-head of all wisdom. On scientific subjects, Albert felt that others would do the job better than he, so her governess, Miss Hildyard, took Vicky twice a week to South Kensington to hear lectures by Faraday and Hofmann and to receive private tuition from them. It delighted Albert to know that the fruits of the Great Exhibition were being of use to his daughter. What fun they had together, going over Vicky's notes!

But the fun, and all the planning which led up to it, were only parts of a gigantic piece of self-deception which enabled Albert to push to the back of his mind the awful truth that before long he would lose his favourite daughter for ever and which allowed him to concentrate instead simply upon the pleasurable preparations for the marriage and upon the benefits it would confer on Prussia. A minor example of the same thing can be seen, strangely enough, in his renovation of the Buckingham Palace ballroom which had been hastily decorated in 1840 and not touched since. The colour scheme was Victoria's, and Albert had not had the heart to tell her what an

* *Cf Vicky*, p. 103.

atrocious effect it created, but had put up with it in silence for more than fifteen years. Now, soon after Vicky's secret engagement, he began suddenly to redesign and redecorate it completely, perhaps to create a worthy setting for Vicky's first public appearance but partly – and perhaps unconsciously – so that by burying himself in work for her present pleasure he could build up a new stock of memories to console him in the years without her that lay ahead. Most of the guests at the grand ball which inaugurated the new ballroom were astonished at the magnificence of Albert's taste, and Charles Eastlake had a perfect opportunity to snub one of the few who criticised it by calling the wall-paintings second-rate: 'Very true. It is a great pity that the designs are only Raphaels.'*

The approval of Vicky's marriage threw a new light on the way Albert had raised the standing of the monarchy. Whereas eighteen years earlier there had been rancorous debate in Parliament about his own allowance, as a result of which it had been fixed at an inconveniently low figure, there was now no dispute at all about Vicky's dowry either in Parliament or in the Press – and this in spite of the fact that Prussia was in great disfavour at the time. 'I had to read all the speeches that were made in the House of Commons about Vicky's dowry,' Albert wrote to Ernest when it was all settled. 'There was nothing disagreeable, on the contrary, all the best opinions were confirmed, and I am glad of it, because our credit on the continent is closely connected with it.' Albert was quite right. The foreign newspapers said quite openly that France and Prussia were watching to see how the British Parliament handled the dowry question, in order to assess the respect in which the royal family was held in England. They got an unmistakeable answer: the abuse of Albert at the beginning of the Crimean War had long ago dissipated itself, and on the eve of his daughter's marriage the monarchy had never stood higher in the regard of the English people.

---

* The excellent taste which Albert showed when designing a building or planning a room went sadly astray when he advised the women of his household about what they should wear. At Vicky's special request he designed her dress for the reopening of the ballroom, her first formal occasion. Because it was the result of several sketches, it had everything – lace flounces, ribbons, streamers and embroidery, all topped with a wreath of convolvulus and jewels entwined in her hair – and only her youth enabled her to carry off the overpowering effect. Similarly, the strong colours Albert used so well in the home looked out of place when translated into terms of female apparel and were most unbecoming on his wife's and daughter's tiny figures. For the Tuileries ball of August 1855, for instance, he enveloped Victoria in a white silk dress embroidered with huge red geraniums. This was intended as a foil for the Koh-i-Noor, which he thought suited her to perfection, but there are several contemporary accounts which say that she was far too small for it and that the jewel weighed her down. Yet all three recognised perfect taste when Eugénie appeared at Windsor in a simple green silk dress with a plain white bonnet.

18

'To fit a gentleman with a gentleman's education'

ONE of Albert's chief anxieties, as soon as the Crimean War was over, was that the government might allow the army to fall back once more into a condition of ineffectiveness. It had begun the war small, ill-equipped and with its commanders in the grip of out-of-date ideas, but by 1856 it had become a large and powerful force. 'In appearance, arrangement and marching the British soldier is admitted to be superior not only to the French but to the Russians as well,' Albert wrote to Ernest in the autumn of that year. 'They (i.e. French and Russians) even said as much, and were full of praise for the British artillery, admitting that they had nothing like it.'

Even before the ink was dry on the peace treaty, however, the Cabinet was considering what economies could be made in the army and navy – intent, like so many of its predecessors and successors, on dismantling the armed forces as soon as the immediate need for them was over; Hardinge himself took the view that another army could always be got together again in case of need. It amazed Albert that politicians and generals alike should have learned so little from the experiences of the past two years and should be so unwilling or so unable to face the possibility of future emergencies. Aldershot had not been created, he told Hardinge, simply for a handful of toy soldiers, and he hoped that through Fritz he could draw on Prussia's long experience of military organisation and learn some useful lessons about the maintenance of larger forces in peace-time. Three chief changes in the traditional system were essential, to his mind. First, the divisions of the army should be organised into two corps under a unified command. Next, in order to ensure a continuous supply of properly-trained young officers, the purchase of commissions should be abolished and promotion by merit instituted. But this brought him up against an old foe, the ignorance and lack of education among the officer-class, and necessitated a third change. The only acceptable recommendation for command in the army should be merit based on proper training; it was not enough to be born a gentleman, as the complacent traditional view had it, but for an effective fighting force it was, in Albert's words, necessary 'to fit a gentleman with a gentleman's education'.

Several years earlier, Albert had become convinced that the existing military schools were obsolete; there were embryo officers in them who could scarcely write their own names or perform the simplest calculation, had hardly read a book in their lives and cared for nothing but handling a gun and mindlessly maintaining a brutalising discipline. In a memo which he drew up in 1850 Albert suggested that those who could do no better than this must be weeded out (for ignorant men made bad officers), the educationally or temperamentally unsuitable directed into other careers, and commissions granted only after examination. Not until this stage should successful candidates pass onwards for specifically military training, for he was convinced that boys should not be brought up to be soldiers and nothing else – as he showed, for instance, in his advice to Fritz to learn more and soldier less.

Improvements in the education of young officers-to-be were not Albert's chief concern at this time, however, nor were his main preoccupations military. The search for an ideal pattern of education suitable for the modern world had already been exercising his mind for some time when he wrote the memorandum mentioned above in order to apply some part of his thoughts to army purposes. His own education under Florschütz and at Bonn had been very different from the almost entirely classical studies at English public schools, and the contrast had struck him forcibly as he gradually discovered it in the course of conversation with Anson and Phipps (an Etonian and a Harrovian respectively) and other members of his household. Notably, he had learned more of history, philosophy and scientific subjects than his English contémporaries, and felt that they suffered greatly from the comparison. His contact with Cambridge had further whetted his appetite for science, which was expressed in the Mansion House speech before the Great Exhibition, for instance. But additional impetus to his thinking about the proper contents of an educational syllabus seems to have been given by the peculiar situation of his second son Alfred who was to inherit Coburg if Ernest had no heir, yet who would become King of England should

Bertie die young – and so must be educated in a manner suitable for both countries. A letter to Ernest in 1849 shows him reflecting on the shortcomings of public schools for this purpose.

Decisions about the schooling of the two eldest children were even more pressing, however. Albert and Stockmar had exchanged memoranda about it almost as soon as they were born; two years of discussion preceded the selection of a tutor for Bertie in the spring of 1849, and Vicky was, under Albert's own direction, by then already showing early signs of what she later became – the perfect product of what might almost be termed the Florschütz-Albert educational system. The necessity for taking practical decisions about his own children, therefore, as well as many years of deliberate reflection, lay behind his remark to Stockmar in 1850 'only through education can a human being learn to know himself and thus become fulfilled.' The essential thing was the widest possible preparation for life, an outlook a good deal broader, particularly in the scope of the subjects to be studied, than that of perhaps all but the very best products of the classical education of a gentleman which, under the influence of Arnold of Rugby, was taking deep root in contemporary England.

An opportunity to put his ideas into practice seemed to present itself in 1851, though only fleetingly. Albert proposed the foundation of an annual scholarship in memory of Peel, but Lord John Russell was too timid to put the proposal before the Cabinet in the merely outline form in which Albert had so far presented it, and the project petered out. The lesson was not lost on Albert, particularly as it was one Stockmar had often tried to teach him – that complete and careful preparation of every detail in advance was essential to the success of any scheme.

It seems almost certain, although exact and positive proof is lacking, that the foundation of Wellington College came about because Albert took this lesson to heart. The Prime Minister, Lord Derby, was staying with Victoria and Albert at Balmoral when the news of the duke of Wellington's death on 14 September 1852 was received. The three of them at once began discussing a project to establish a school as a memorial to him; Derby put a proposal before the Cabinet as soon as he returned to London, and by 5 November he was reading to the Queen the draft of a public appeal for funds which was issued the same month. Thus the plan for a school was ready within a very short time from the moment at which it was first mooted; it was ripe for discussion by the Cabinet within a few days and for public scrutiny in seven weeks. Derby had scholarly tastes as well as a great love for the turf, but there is nothing about him to suggest that he would have originated the idea of a school. Albert, on the other hand, had been pondering plans of education for several years; and the speed with which the Wellington College scheme got off the ground, and in so complete a form, is most convincingly explained by the supposition that it already existed in outline form in Albert's mind before Wellington's death suddenly offered the chance of putting it into practice. Indeed it might not be too much to say that the idea was born on the day that Albert wrote to Ernest about the complexities of Affie's education in 1849. Although the purpose of Wellington College was 'the education of orphan children of indigent and meritorious officers of the army,' its curriculum was to be as broad as possible, with the emphasis shifted away from classics, and with history, modern languages and scientific subjects prominently included; thus Wellington was neither to be a military school nor to conform to the conventional pattern of the English public school. 'It would have been hardly worth while to establish another public school, in competition with those already existing,' Sir Charles Phipps wrote on Albert's behalf to the Headmaster, Benson, on 8 September 1860, 'unless advantage were taken of the absence of old customs and prestige to establish a system more in accordance with the requirements of the present day,' and he passed on some comments upon recent examination papers, which Albert thought of too low a standard in mathematics. Phipps went on to stress the importance of history and geography for success in life 'in these utilitarian days', to admit that Harrow had taught him little about either, and to wonder whether his own sons were learning enough at Wellington about 'the events of the reign of George III, with their effect upon the other countries of the world, and the consequent alterations in the geography of Asia, Africa and America.' A year earlier Charles Kingsley, newly appointed royal chaplain and a man whom Albert greatly admired, explained to the Dean of Windsor why he was sending his son Maurice to Wellington. 'I want my boy to go into life knowing how to use his faculties somewhat better than the majority of the lads I meet, and knowing a little more of the universe, both physical and spiritual, than they do'; the Crimean War had shown what 'noble and brave gentlemen' the public school system turned out, but had also revealed that most of them were 'practically imbecile when they were thrown into any unexpected circumstances.' Both writers are evidently very close indeed to Albert's thinking, and Kingsley's has been called his 'educational testament'.

The close supervision which Albert exercised over Wellington in its early years is shown, for instance, by another letter from Phipps to Benson dated 28 February 1860, which records that Albert had noticed with disapproval that a 'system of fagging and flogging was creeping in', contrary to his intentions. (Although he had been Albert's own choice as headmaster, Benson had in fact already begun to move away from Albert's ideas and to transform Wellington into a second Rugby.)* Another point upon which Albert had laid great emphasis was that Sundays should not be made too gloomy by an excess of chapel services or religious instruction: 'His Royal Highness has the strongest feeling upon the inexpediency of thus making the services of the Church and the study of the Bible irksome to boys.' To encourage the habit of reading, which he thought most desirable, as well as to interest the younger boys – who formed the majority in the early days – Albert presented a large number of books to found a library.

Albert's supervision was by no means confined to educational matters pure and simple. He was easily persuaded that the Sandhurst area offered a better site for the school than Banstead, his first choice, partly because it reminded him of Beverloo,† partly because building materials were available close at hand, thus saving expense – and partly, perhaps, because its proximity to Windsor would enable him to ride over and keep an eye on the place as often as he felt inclined. He chose the architect, John Shaw, who had built the naval school at New Cross which he had opened in 1843, but evidently brought his own influence to bear upon him: the entrance courtyard is very reminiscent of the Schloss at Homburg (with which he was familiar through his father's visits to take the waters), and he insisted on having the main gateway moved into a symmetrical central position. He took a close interest in the placing of the statues of Wellington's generals in the alcoves along the façade, and selected William Theed, who had worked for him at Osborne, to sculpture them.

Wellington College was Albert's both in conception and in execution; but in the last half-dozen busy years of his life he obviously could not maintain close day-to-day control over it, and the first headmaster departed widely from his ideas in consequence.

It was so evident that, with the end of the Crimean War, the government would once again let the army run down that Albert

* E. W. Benson had been an assistant master at Rugby for seven years before becoming the first Master of Wellington College. He was later Bishop of Truro and, from 1882–1896, Archbishop of Canterbury.

† The exercise area of the Belgian army, which he had visited in August 1836; see p. 21 above.

deliberately created two eye-catching opportunities to draw attention to the army during 1856, in the hope that public opinion might help him to prevent it from being reduced to a dangerously small size once more. Quite apart from defence needs, he felt it a poor reward for returning soldiers to be told at once that their services were no longer required, and believed that the public might agree with him, so he arranged for the new training-camp at Aldershot to be formally inaugurated by a large-scale review in April, at which the Queen, in full uniform and wearing the star and ribbon of the Garter, rode down the lines on her chestnut, Leopold, to the sound of massed bands and the flash of steel as the men presented arms in the royal salute. Even more spectacular was a march through London on 9 July by the last contingents to return home, still in the uniforms in which they charged the breach at Sebastopol. It taxed Albert's ingenuity to the full to choose a route which would show them off to the greatest possible number of people and so have the maximum effect, and he eventually settled for them to march from Nine Elms Station, across Vauxhall Bridge and St James's Park, past Buckingham Palace – where the Queen waved a welcome home from the same balcony where she had stood to watch them depart three years before – and up Constitution Hill into Hyde Park. There he waited for them to join him and a battalion of the Guards in a parade which was to be, in his own words, 'the closing act of the war' and proved 'a moving review . . . veterans of battle, many of them still quite young although prematurely aged by their experiences, bent but not bowed, cheerful and proud because victorious.'

Two days later he took Victoria to naval manoeuvres at Spithead in perfect summer weather which gave them a panoramic view of the whole fleet. He was less anxious than he had been in Hyde Park, for he was fairly confident that the navy would be kept in good shape, since every British politician was a sailor at heart and 'believed that he needed nothing else to guard his island home'. The vast crowds which greeted them at Portsmouth bore witness, he felt, not only to the pull of naval events but also to the popularity of the Crown, and he longed to be at the helm of the *Fairy* amid the hundreds of small craft rather than surrounded by formality on the deck of the *Royal George* – although he did enjoy watching a mock attack on Southsea castle by swiftly manoeuvring gun-boats.

In September 1856 the Queen and Albert met Florence Nightingale at last, when Sir James Clark brought her to Balmoral. She and Albert immediately recognised similar qualities in each other: complete confidence in their own ability to overcome obstacles which to others seemed insurmountable, and an inner force which drove them forward no matter how discouraging the omens. Her account of what she had done at Scutari, and her clear analysis of reforms still needed in the army medical service, so invigorated Albert that when she had gone he exclaimed 'What a head! I only wish I had her to help me.' This is the more remarkable because Florence Nightingale possessed many of the characteristics which he usually disliked in females – aggressiveness, self-assertiveness, toughness and an ability to beat down an opponent in argument. Apart from a natural curiosity to hear at first-hand all about her work in the Crimea, Albert had had a particular reason for wanting to talk to her ever since he had laid the foundation-stone of her hospital at Netley the previous May. He had thought the plans for the interior lay-out deplorable, and was delighted when she confirmed his opinion that it was old-fashioned and inconvenient, allowing for too little ventilation and for the beds to be close together, thus encouraging the spread of disease. With incredible folly, Panmure and the War Department had not consulted Florence Nightingale about the design, but neither she nor Albert yet knew that building was already too far advanced for improvements to be incorporated into it, although she enlisted the support of Palmerston, who attributed all the trouble to the vanity of the architect, who had sacrificed utility in order to design a building 'which should cut a dash when looked at from Southampton river.'

The Anglo-French alliance had begun to wear a little thin during the negotiations leading up to the Treaty of Paris, and became still more attenuated when Napoleon III began a flirtation with Russia early in 1857. In an attempt to preserve the alliance, Albert wrote a diplomatically-phrased letter to Napoleon in April 1857, in which he dwelt on the common Western civilisation which linked France and England but divided both from barbarous Russia. More remarkable than the terms of the letter, however, were the circumstances of its despatch. Only a few years ago, the Foreign Secretary would have dealt with business of this sort without consulting the palace; now, the same man, as Prime Minister, accepted Albert's draft without changing a word and agreed to his taking a major foreign-policy initiative. Relieved as he was, Albert found this total change of heart difficult to get used to! The letter brought quick results; the Emperor was all humility, played the penitent for all he was worth, and asked whether he could come to Osborne to explain his policy and to prevent the misunderstandings which were apt to arise when 'a revival of communications between two monarchs is too long delayed'.

Osborne had always been simply a holiday home, and Albert had vowed never to do business there; but the opportunity was too good to be missed and he promptly invited Napoleon to stay. In the past, there would have been another reason as well for him to hesitate: he had recently discovered Napoleon's marital infidelities; but instead of allowing his private disapproval to stand in the way of a meeting (as he would once have done), he was now statesman enough to know that someone as important as the French Emperor could not be slighted for sexual licence alone. He suggested that the Imperial pair should come for four days, as though casually and as part of the yachting season, and (as he put it to Ernest) 'so as not to arouse Czar Alexander from his slumbers – a Russian imperial visit on top of the other would be too much.' At the last moment the visit was almost wrecked by a gate-crasher. A day or two before it was due to begin, Napoleon's cousin 'Plon-Plon' arrived unexpectedly, sent by Fritz to try to eradicate the bad impression his rudeness had made on Victoria and Albert in Paris in 1855; they would have got rid of him at once, but were warned by Lord Cowley, the British Ambassador in Paris, that in an unsettled country like France 'Plon-Plon' might become ruler overnight and that it would therefore be unwise to alienate him.

'Plon-Plon' had scarcely gone before Napoleon and Eugénie arrived on 6 August. The Emperor may have asked to come, but the style in which he was received was dictated by Albert: to emphasise that state visits never took place at Osborne there were no ministers present and Victoria and Albert, surrounded only by their children, were waiting quite informally on the beach. Eugénie had sensed the informality in advance and nothing could have been less ostentatious than her white muslin dress and lace parasol; the Emperor, too, was in a holiday mood, suave and affable as ever. Even so they were both completely astonished by the simplicity of life at Osborne – an almost total absence of guards and ceremony, children running in and out and joining them at meals, the whole party taking shelter from the rain in the model dairy during a walk in the plantation and watching the Queen and Vicky give a demonstration of butter-making. In consequence they looked a little out of place, Albert told Ernest, 'and I have to rub my eyes to be sure that I am not dreaming when I come upon Napoleon and Eugénie standing together in the drawing-room of our simple little home.' Serious business began with the arrival of ministers from London and Paris, who promptly shut themselves up with Albert and the Emperor in the former's study to try to settle the Balkan disputes which were threatening the Anglo-French alliance. Most of the serious differences were ironed out by Albert and the Emperor as they walked to the beach and back before breakfast. By some plain speaking during these conversations, Albert persuaded Napoleon to reaffirm his loyalty to the Anglo-French alliance and to the preservation of the integrity of the Turkish empire, while Napoleon in the end did no more than grumble that he was accused of being false to the alliance just because he sometimes showed that he had a mind of his own.

In almost sole charge of the negotiations and continually immersed in the details of business, Albert was hugely enjoying himself, and as soon as he began to realise that he was achieving valuable results he saw how right he had been to break his rule about keeping state affairs away from Osborne. It was gratifying to know that his efforts were appreciated in the right quarters: Cowley said that the strain of audiences with Napoleon would be greatly eased; Clarendon was almost fulsome in his praise of the way the French alliance had been reinvigorated; and Palmerston magnanimously recognised the part Albert had played when he told the Queen 'The Prince can say many things that we cannot.'

Always sensitive to the moods of others, Albert was quick to notice that the personalities of Napoleon and Eugénie had undergone a subtle change during the two years since they had last met. The Emperor seemed more withdrawn than before, his gaiety almost forced, so that Albert wondered if he was well. But the biggest change was in Eugénie, who was emerging, he could see, as an important figure in her own right. She had not wasted her time, but had taken her own education in hand, read widely, studied politics and started to become a more mature and confident woman. At their first meeting Albert had sensed that she possessed great strength of character, but it was evident that she was now developing an intellect to match it. If only Donna Maria had done the same thing, he reflected, the history of Portugal might have been much happier.

Anti-climax followed the imperial visit, despite the arrival of George of Cambridge who (mercifully!) came just too late to interrupt the talks and lower the tone of conversation. None of them could settle to anything, and as the weather was perfect for sailing Albert suggested a short cruise in the royal yacht. They sailed close to the French coast and suddenly found themselves confronted by Napoleon's new harbour at Cherbourg. It was a terrible shock. They had no idea that the fortifications were so massive nor that they covered such a vast area; the breakwater was three times the size of that at Plymouth, and the dockyards were enormous, as large as

those Albert had dreamed of one day persuading the British government to construct. Clearly, the French had created, and in a very
short time, a nightmare for their neighbours and a threat to peace:
the steam-propelled warships riding at anchor in the bay looked far
from innocent, and the shore-batteries behind them were evidently
capable of resisting a heavy attack. Dismayed, they asked themselves whether they could ever sleep easily again. How much longer,
Albert wondered, would Britannia rule the waves?

In August the following year an invitation came from the Emperor
to inspect the new fortifications – no doubt bigger than ever by now,
they told each other dolefully. They hurried across the Channel in
low spirits, which were not lightened by overcast skies and a heavy
sea-mist; in an effort to calm their taut nerves, Albert took Victoria
below and read *Jane Eyre* to her; but it was pure pretence, and
neither of them took in a word. As they neared the French coast
they both became so agitated that they had to rush on deck again,
to be faced by a daunting line of battleships at anchor along the
whole line of the breakwater. The sight so upset him that Albert felt
ashamed he had castigated the Press for the anti-French articles
which had demanded to be told whom France was preparing to
invade. 'Cannons, cannons, cannons,' *The Times* had written in a
leading article which had particularly annoyed him, 'they pour
upon you from every corner, they command everything.' Indeed
they did! A sudden deafening salute from the guns (how terrifying
the blast would be in other circumstances!) shook them out of their
painful reverie.

The meeting with Napoleon and Eugénie was constrained. The
Emperor looked cross, the Empress ill, while consternation showed
plainly on their own faces, in spite of all their efforts to appear
smiling and unconcerned. Matters did not improve even during an
excellent luncheon; glum and silent, Napoleon ate nothing, and
though Eugénie tried to keep the conversation going she was not
as tactful as usual in her constant references to the harm done by the
British papers. Albert explained that he quite understood, but that
they were powerless to interfere with a free Press. That afternoon Napoleon made his point still clearer by taking his guests up
a steep and winding road, not without danger from falling stones,
to give them a good view of all his fortifications. Albert spoke the
truth when he said they were 'truly magnificent' and that England
had nothing like them. On the way the Emperor did not make him
and Victoria feel any better by reminding them that it was a
hundred years to the day since the British fleet under Admiral Howe
had bombarded Cherbourg during the Seven Years War. That

evening Albert suffered an attack of nerves at the thought of making a speech to seventy guests after dinner the next day on board the *Bretagne*; he knew only too well that 'the eyes of all Europe were on everything that was taking place at Cherbourg', and the thought that every word he uttered was certain to be scrutinised for hidden meanings undermined his confidence. However, some hard work in his cabin alone with the Queen produced a thin but not unsatisfactory text; keeping to safe ground, it briefly sketched the friendship between the two nations which was the root of the prosperity of both. Albert read it over to the anxious Queen, and was surprised how sincere it sounded. When he delivered it, he found that providentially he had struck the right note, echoing Napoleon's assurance of France's 'unalterable devotion to the English alliance'.

After this nerve-racking experience the fireworks came as a welcome relief. It was a beautiful summer evening, warm and without a breath of wind, and Albert thought he had never seen anything to match the way the fiery cascades of colour from the rockets flashed across the background of stars – but unfortunately illuminating row upon row of warships, each one a silent warning. Not far away, the *Victoria and Albert* floated solitary at anchor, dwarfed into insignificance by the French fleet. But the crew ingeniously did their best to redress the balance when Napoleon escorted his guests back after the fireworks: a powerful electric beam picked out the Emperor's barge and followed it all the way back to the shore, making it a solitary point of light surrounded by darkness.*

The following morning they parted from their hosts on friendly, even affectionate, terms, but the extra warmth which had been a feature of the Windsor and Osborne visits was missing. All the way home, Albert was silent and preoccupied, complaining of a headache and general malaise. His feelings spilled over when he wrote next day to the duchess of Kent from peaceful Osborne: 'the war preparations in the French marine are immense! Ours despicable! Our ministers use fine phrases but they do nothing. My blood boils within me.' More than ever, he was convinced that England must do something about her defences. If ministers did not look sharp, they would wake one morning to find the French on their doorstep, and it would not be a friendly visit.

The moment they returned to London, Albert attacked Lord Malmesbury (now Foreign Secretary) about the peril presented by the Cherbourg defences. The reply was meant to be reassuring – it

* Electric arc-lamps and generators powerful enough to work them had recently been the subject of successful experiments. Trinity House sponsored some in 1857 and held a trial at the South Foreland lighthouse in 1858.

was the Cabinet's opinion that the Emperor had built his vast fortifications not to menace England but to impress his own subjects – but Albert was not satisfied. Would they never learn? The past two years told a sorry story. In 1856 the clamour for a reduction in income tax had been so great that it had been necessary to meet it by cutting military expenditure, with the result that by now the army had sunk to a mere eighteen battalions, despite Albert's pleas to Palmerston, who, he knew, did not support this short-sighted policy. The steam-fleet, once Albert's pride and joy, had after all been broken up at the end of the Crimean War, the docks reduced in size and men dismissed, just because the ships needed repairs and the gun-boat flotilla new equipment. To bring the navy up to standard again would require far more money than the country could afford. There were times, Albert told the Queen, when he felt that he was fighting a lone battle.

A little more than a year before the Cherbourg visit, the anomaly of Albert's position had been brought to an end at last, when the Queen created him Prince Consort by letters patent on 25 June 1857. The change in his style was long overdue, and the old opposition was crumbling when Palmerston advised the Queen to get it over and done with. The new title was generally approved, *The Times* remarking that the British people had adopted it quite naturally many years before.* 'Of course it ought to have been done long ago,' Ernest said in his letter of congratulation, and probably spoke for many; but as Albert reasonably pointed out, it had been difficult to make up for an opportunity once missed. The relief to Queen Victoria was enormous, for now they could go abroad without the awkwardness of the Queen of England's husband claiming a higher position than his German rank warranted: 'an English prince has rights as such, and they cannot be denied him anywhere in Europe'; no longer would she have to be for ever on the look-out to ensure that her husband's rightful place was not usurped by some pushing Grand Duke.

The timing of the announcement had depended upon the death of the duchess of Gloucester two months earlier and upon the fact that at sixteen the prince of Wales was fast growing up. With the disappearance of the last of the 'old royals', the one obstacle remaining from the past was removed. But the chief consideration was, as Albert said, that so long as he remained merely prince of Coburg, 'mischief-makers could easily have stirred up the prince of Wales

* Many of the letters in the Whewell collection about Albert's candidature as Chancellor of Cambridge in 1847 refer to him as Prince Consort, for example.

not to allow a foreign prince to take precedence before him, or he might have given his father precedence as a matter of grace.' 'Permission given by courtesy of the prince of Wales' would have been intolerable. Mischief-makers or no, for a week or two there were plenty of stories of Albert's wilful self-aggrandisement current in the London clubs. Perhaps the silliest was to the effect that Lord Granville (whom everyone knew to be sycophantic where royalty was concerned) was supposed to have asked Stockmar (whom in reality he hardly knew) to use his influence to prevent the grant of the new title.

Vicky's last summer at home passed too quickly for Albert. Fritz came again, and so did the Archduke Constantine of Russia, to try to interest British financiers in railway construction. Vicky's 'good fortune' had given her parents a reputation as match-makers – King Pedro of Portugal, Ferdinand's son, for instance said he would not dream of marrying without his uncle Albert's advice, and willingly accepted Stephanie of Hohenzollern, the 'perfect girl' whom Albert selected for him. Stephanie was a Catholic, but in Albert's opinion not a bigoted one, and he hoped that her marriage would be 'the beginning of a new era for thousands of poor retarded people for whom Ferdinand has accomplished so little. He was too much under his wife's thumb.' His Continental family now looked on Albert much as the English had once looked on the duke of Wellington – as the man without whom nothing could be settled. He played an important part in arranging the marriage of Archduke Maximilian of Austria to King Leopold's only daughter Charlotte. When Max came to England for the christening of Princess Beatrice in the spring of 1857, Albert decided as soon as he set eyes on him that he was just the man to bring out the best in the shy and intro-spective Charlotte. It was fortunate that Max took an equal liking to Albert and soon developed a great respect for his political wisdom, for along with his desire to bring about a happy marriage, Albert (who always translated family relationships into political terms) had conceived the idea of using Max to lure Austria back into the German fold and thus to promote the unification of his country.*

Albert attended Charlotte's marriage (strangely, he does not seem to have been shocked that she was to be married by proxy) in Brussels cathedral on 27 July 1857, mainly because he regarded it as a kind of dress rehearsal for Vicky's wedding and wanted to see

* Ironically, Albert predicted a long and successful life for this tragic young man, who was shot in 1867 after Napoleon III had proclaimed him Emperor of Mexico and then withdrawn his support. The shock drove Charlotte out of her mind.

how Leopold managed things, for the marriage of a king's daughter did not happen every day. But he missed the far greater opportunities which the occasion offered him. Since almost every European royal house was represented, here was a Heaven-sent chance for him to talk to and assess all those with whom Vicky would be mixing in the near future. The Prussians in particular were eager to meet the new-made Prince Consort, who was rumoured to rule his wife and her country with a rod of iron, whom even the French Emperor was said to fear and to whom Russia kow-towed, for they suspected that if they did not look out they would soon find themselves ruled by him through his daughter the Princess Royal. When Albert kept aloof from them, the Prussians put it down to pride and began to tear him to pieces as they talked to the other wedding-guests, until they almost came to believe the fictions they made up about him. But the real reason for his strange behaviour was no more than sheer fatigue. In order to try to forget the ache in his heart at the thought of losing Vicky, he had worked himself to the bone through a sultry spring and summer, and was now too worn out to make conversation. The ceremony, too, made him sad, and he found his uncle's unhappiness at the loss of a daughter infectious. His only compensation was that, as Prince Consort, he signed the register immediately after the bride's grandmother Queen Amélie and before an Austrian archduke, who gave way to him without a murmur; it made a pleasant contrast to the unseemly scrambles at previous ceremonies.

19

'A future disappearing into the past'

Even the customary field-sports could not rouse Albert from his lethargy when they went to Balmoral early in the autumn of 1857. For three weeks he did not go out stalking at all, and then one night five stags appeared suddenly outside the house; the whole family rushed out to see the unusual sight, the servants shone torches, and Albert instinctively reached for his gun, but they looked so beautiful that he let them go.

The Crimean War came at a critical stage in the construction of the new house, so that Albert had been forced to deny himself the pleasure of supervising the work and had handed it over to the architect, William Smyth of Aberdeen. Other set-backs followed. A fire destroyed the workmen's huts and all their possessions, and although he and the Queen at once made up the whole loss out of their own pockets, there were then strikes for shorter hours and higher wages caused by the discontent of the migrant labourers, whom it had been hard to replace because of the lure of gold in California and Australia. But the new building was finished at last and the only trace of the old house left was a print the Queen bought in Aberdeen and some sketches in her Journal; it gave Albert an eerie feeling to walk over the spot where it had once stood. The new house, planned as a home not a palace, combined features of the Scottish baronial style with those of the Rhineland castles Albert was so fond of, and had a tall tower and flagstaff which he could see from the hillsides while out stalking.

In both construction and interior decoration Albert had made every effort to use local products. Behind his lavish use of tartan lay the purpose of encouraging an industry which had been depressed for several years, although the result was 'not very *flatteur* to the eye', as Lady Augusta Bruce wrote in her Journal. When Landseer painted the Queen in a dress made of it, tartan cloth became the fashion and trade boomed. Everything Albert did was news nowadays, and even before the building was completed the *Morning Chronicle* (once so hostile) published a long and admiring article about the castle and its grounds. Once started, the river of journalism flowed steadily on, as other newspapers described the model farm, the unusual trees and the shrubs which he had planted and the roses chosen to flower during their autumn holidays.

Albert looked on the welfare of the royal tenants as a sacred trust. Because Balmoral was in such a remote spot, he designed comfortable cottages for them and invited tradesmen to settle in the neighbourhood to cater for their needs, his object being to create a self-sufficient estate which could depend upon its own resources. Planning the year's work with the farm manager and trying out new implements as soon as they were invented, publicising them if they prove successful, provided a welcome relief from the burden of state affairs and gave him the right to say, 'We agriculturalists of England . . .'. Farming, he once remarked, was the only enterprise open to royalty, because in practising it they could not be accused of taking the bread out of the mouths of the needy.

He was still in a heavy mood when at Balmoral that autumn he began to compile a list of guests for Vicky's wedding, and his spirits were not raised by the realisation that there would be many gaps in it. Charles of Leiningen, whose motto was 'Life is for enjoyment,' had died of a stroke in November 1856 not long after the Queen and Albert paid off all his debts. Donna Maria's death, and the necessity of taking second place to his son Pedro, had so broken Ferdinand of Portugal that he would never face the journey. But the gap which saddened Albert most of all was that left by his childhood playmate Lynette Reuss-Ebersdorf, who had died at thirty-four of a fever contracted while working among the poor of Vienna; 'all the best are being taken,' he said when he heard the news, 'it is most mysterious,' and this peculiar use of the word 'mysterious' was taken over and constantly repeated by Victoria whenever she referred later on to his own or his contemporaries' deaths. Albert had always thought of Lynette as belonging specially to his Coburg days. How small that world had now become! It had nearly become smaller still when Ernest had lain at death's door for a week in March 1855, and Albert now reminded him that the family ranks were sadly depleted 'as in a line facing the enemy whose bullets

strike to carry off first one and then another . . . one has the feeling
. . . of holding closer together.'

His responsibility for allowing Vicky to marry so young had been
weighing heavily upon him for several months. The newspaper
warnings against the Prussian connections, hitherto disregarded,
came back to disturb his dreams and drive away sleep as – for
the first time, and too late – he wondered whether after all Prussia
was perhaps not the bed of roses he had imagined it. It was some
consolation to remember that the young people were in love and
quite prepared to shoulder the heavy responsibilities which were to
be their lot. These responsibilities might fall to them sooner than
expected, since the king of Prussia had recently had another stroke
and his brother the Regent appeared to be failing. Victoria was
apprehensive too, and worry made her irritable and quarrelsome,
complaining that her husband was so immersed in his own affairs
that he could not spare the time to keep her spirits up. Overwhelmed with the same guilt that oppressed him, she was distracted
by thoughts of Vicky marrying so young and going so far away,
and unfairly inclined in her heart to blame Albert for allowing it,
quite forgetting her own frenzy of joy at the time of the engagement.
It made matters worse that Vicky was far more with Papa than
with Mama – or, for that matter, than Mama was with Papa.
Her deep and sincere love for her child did not stretch as far as
sharing her husband with her, and although not consciously jealous
she did feel pushed to one side and neglected. For Albert had
intensified his instruction of Vicky, spending long hours endlessly
discussing Prussian politics (which bored Victoria) with her and
keeping her up late at night correcting an essay or going over a
memorandum, so that he was quite washed out. It was then that
Victoria's moans about Prussia being so far away would burst out,
and she would attack him for leaving her so much alone. Recriminations flowed as fast as her tears, and it was difficult for Albert,
unhappy himself, to be patient and not lose his temper. In calmer
moods, she tried piteously to explain her feelings to him, although
it was not easy since she barely understood them herself. Nor did it
help matters that heartache and preoccupation with wedding arrangements combined to make Albert fear a confrontation so much that
he reverted once more, as he had done a few years earlier,* to the
Stockmarian 'little notes', addressing her as 'Dear Child' in his
role of father-figure and yet fondly imagining that he was being
tender and understanding. After years of the closest union with an

* See p. 241.

emotional women he was still unable to realise that what she wanted was more attention and less talk about the struggles she had with her difficult temperament. Albert could not see that cold analysis (cold because of his superhuman efforts not to lose his temper) was the worst possible way to tackle any question that touched the heart. It was unfair of him to hurt her deliberately by saying that she was 'too severe with the children' and that she 'wanted to get rid of Vicky.' These notes prolonged the Queen's sense of injustice and did nothing to assuage her feelings. Albert should have realised how humiliated she felt at finding herself in the position she had so often ridiculed in other women – pregnant, and with a marriageable daughter. Even after the birth of Princess Beatrice in April 1857, her feelings were still ambivalent though calmer, for the tension remained agonising.

The tension was broken by tragedy. The news that Victoire de Nemours had died suddenly at Claremont on 10 November* reached them directly after a bad quarrel. They had returned from Scotland only the night before, and the Queen had come downstairs next morning to find Albert dressed ready for a shoot at Bagshot. At Balmoral, she had lost him to Vicky and stags; here at Windsor, it would be Vicky and pheasants. It made little difference that she knew very well that Albert had no intention of staying with the guns all day and that he only went shooting at all because they had guests who needed to be entertained. There were some 'low and hasty exchanges' between them before the Queen flounced off without the usual kiss and Albert stalked out in suppressed fury. It seemed like a judgement on them both when late that morning they received the tragic message from Claremont that Victoire had dropped dead without warning. They came to their senses in a flash. Albert acted as he should have done long before – he took her in his arms and told her tenderly through her tears how terrible it would be if he were to lose her.

Victoire's death opened up a new source of anxiety for Albert. Suppose Vicky too died in childbirth? Might she not be several months pregnant by this time next year, and still only seventeen? In particular, neither he nor the Queen trusted foreign doctors' treatment of women in childbirth; they called it 'that dreadful coddling' and believed that it was weakening to a constitution which needed rather to be braced after its ordeal, and this distrust was

---

* 'Claremont has claimed another victim from our family,' Albert wrote to Ernest next day, for Victoire died only four days after the fortieth anniversary of Princess Charlotte's death, in the room above hers, and also after childbirth.

behind Albert's constant preaching, during Vicky's first two preg-
nancies, of the need for fresh air and exercise, cold sponges and sea-
bathing – all regarded as scandalous modern indecencies in Prussia.

The holiday period was not as cheerful as usual because everyone
from the Queen down would keep referring to 'Vicky's last Christmas
at home', and even Vicky brought tears to her father's eyes by
whispering the same thing to him during morning service in St
George's Chapel. Albert could hardly make a pretence of gaiety –
even baby Beatrice's engaging ways did not raise a smile – but comforted himself with the hope that Vicky would not guess the misery
in his heart. 'I do not, however, let any hint of this be seen,' he
wrote bravely to his stepmother in Coburg, yet his pale, set face
did give him away and the Queen became anxious and Vicky
distressed.

The streak of masochism in Albert was never more in evidence
than during the preparation for Vicky's marriage. There was no need
for him to supervise everything personally, but the pain he suffered
when he insisted on doing so made the enterprise all the more worth
while. The revival in January 1858 of his old argument with Fritz
about the desirability of appointing young Ernest Stockmar as
Vicky's private secretary was another worry that was almost
enjoyable. In the end, Fritz was made to understand that there were
two reasons for the choice – that Ernest Stockmar had inherited an
understanding of the Coburg family, and that he knew both the
English and the Prussian courts – and that ill-disposed persons who
called him a secret political agent of England were to be ignored. To
masochism there was now added a new measure of self-deception.
Although he really knew that Prussian critics of the marriage could
not be dismissed so lightly he told Fritz 'the people to whom you
belong, and to whom Vicky is to dedicate herself, do not fear and
hate English influence but will rather be pleased that your future
wife is an English princess.' His only authority for so manifestly a
false statement was Fritz himself, who in his anxiety to please had
gone a little too far in glossing over the truth that Berlin was
almost wholly opposed to the marriage. He allowed himself to be
misled like this by going back to his old prejudice against the Press:
all criticism of the marriage was manufactured by the Prussian
newspapers, which wrote 'trash' and 'do not reflect the mood of the
people', and he tried to protect himself from unpleasantness by
refusing to read them.

One of the first things which began to stir up doubts in his mind
about the accuracy of his picture of Prussia was an unfamiliar
glimpse of the character of his new friend, Princess Augusta, which

was given him in the autumn of 1857. With charming ingenuousness, Vicky showed him some passages in Fritz's letters which referred to 'Mama's fluctuating moods, which sway her to such an extent that sometimes, when opinions differ, it is wiser to pretend to agree so as not to irritate her still further. . . . She is too autocratic a character to put up for any length of time with not having a say in everything.' This opened up awful prospects in front of Vicky, and to smooth her path it seemed best to write to Augusta's husband the Regent in terms which assumed the greatest intimacy between the two families: Vicky looked on him as her protector and guide, her 'second father', and on Augusta as her 'second mother' (this conveniently overlooked their failure to get on with their own children, and shows how far Albert had strayed from reality). At the same time the Queen wrote to Fritz on similar lines; her carefully-worded letter was meant for other eyes as well, and begged him to think of herself and Albert as 'Mama and Papa'.

Albert's letters to the Regent at this period are a far cry from the stern lectures he had sent to Prussia in the years before the engagement, and the sudden change of tone that autumn betrays the extent to which he had deceived himself. For several months he had behaved like a man in the grip of an experience which deprived him of the power of reason, and as he now slowly began to recover, it was the distance of Prussia from England and the uncertainty of the family situation Vicky would find there which caused him apprehension, rather than the fact that he was handing her over to another man. His state of mind was an unenviable one, and it was a blessing that he and Victoria were able at any rate now and then to display some vestiges of commonsense and to think how they could best ensure their daughter's comfort and convenience – when they insisted, for example, that Vicky's new household should come to England so that she could get to know them in advance.

Finding room for the hordes of foreign royalties, and their enormous suites, who were expected for the wedding was a gigantic task: 'we will manage it somehow . . . but you will not have to mind being packed pretty tightly,' he told Ernest at Christmas. Many of them coolly announced that they would be arriving early, which meant that extra entertainments would have to be arranged. Precedence was very tricky, for an international incident could almost be sparked off by an error in a seating-plan, and checking to see that there were no mistakes quite wore Albert out. The day before the court moved to Buckingham Palace he organised a shooting-party, but the Germans turned it into a shocking *battue* and made themselves very unpopular. A letter from Coburg spelled trouble. Ernest blandly stated that he was bringing a large suite (although his brother had warned him not to do so), since his position as a reigning duke demanded proper style. Hastily Albert sent a special messenger to stop him from doing any such thing. 'For Alexandrine one maid, one lady-in-waiting; for you, one valet only. Otherwise you will have to find lodgings for them yourself. Our little house is full to overflowing.' For once, this was no exaggeration. Not the least of his difficulties was the thoughtless behaviour of the guests, who expected their host to know the hour of their arrival as if by magic, a lack of consideration which gave a bad impression and was increased by the strange appearance and uncouth manners of many of the younger princes, whose military swagger and brash conversation set Albert's teeth on edge. Some of them actually defended duelling in his presence, and he was thankful to notice that Fritz showed up splendidly beside men like these.

Busy as he was, Albert still had uneasy moments. Of course he knew that it was an arranged marriage, but it was an arranged marriage of the best kind; there was love on both sides, and a serious purpose behind it which Vicky understood very well. Yet there was something ominous in the way the Prince of Prussia had to be forced into attending the wedding. An offhand letter from him had explained that now he was Regent he could not spare the time, and there was an effrontery about the tone of it which Albert did not care for. Albert's reply was polite but very firm: 'I should be neglecting my duty if I hesitated any longer in pressing you not to deny us your presence. . . . No great harm can come to your business by an absence of so few days.' Appearances apart, there was another reason why he wanted Prince William to come. Somehow or other he had got it into his head that William would be a support to him in the difficult business of parting from Vicky: but it did not go down well with him that William dwelt so much on his sacrifice in making the journey, since he was about to make a far greater sacrifice himself by handing his favourite daughter over to William's son. The strange contradictions of Albert's character were never more apparent than in his relations with the Prussian court. Shrewd and sophisticated in his handling of British ministers, he was astonishingly naive and trustful in his dealing with the Prussians, and they were quick to recognise this and turn it to their own advantage. The Prussians had a paralysing effect on the Queen too; in her correspondence with Augusta she dwelt on none of Vicky's best points and undoubted talents, but instead put all the emphasis upon her good fortune in marrying into the Prussian royal family and upon her own hopes that she would be worthy of the high position

Prince Albert 1854

Prince Alfred, Mr Gibbs
and Albert Edward,
Prince of Wales, February
1854

Prince Albert's Birthday Table, Osborne 1859

Albert's brother—Ernest II, Duke of Saxe-Coburg-Gotha

The Royal Family at Osborne, 24 May 1854: Prince of Wales, Princess Royal, Prince Arthur, Princess Alice, Prince Albert, Queen Victoria, Princess Louise, Duchess of Kent, Princess Helena, Prince Alfred

Lord John Russell, by Watts, *c* 1852

Sir Robert Peel, by Linnell, 1838

Viscount Palmerston, by Cruikshank, *c* 1

which was to be hers. Although they had moments of clearer vision, neither Albert nor Victoria really took in the fact that it was they, and not the Prussians, who were conferring the greater honour. What was Prussia in the 1850s beside rich and powerful Britain? Or the heir to only part of a still disunited Germany in comparison with the eldest daughter of the ruler of a world-wide empire?

On the wedding-day Albert effaced himself as far as possible, for he feared that his feelings might betray him. But when the three of them were daguerreotyped together just before they left for the Chapel Royal it was the Queen who trembled so much that her figure came out blurred and Albert who looked calm and composed. He succeeded in hiding his emotion from all but those closest to him, for that night the Queen wrote feelingly that 'Dearest Albert took her [Vicky] by the hand and gave her away – my beloved Albert, whom I saw felt so strongly.' As he and Leopold walked to the chapel, Albert had reflected how, tense and anxious, he had followed the same path with his father and Ernest eighteen years before. Yet how much more of an ordeal it was this time! Then, he had felt eager and confident at the thought of his future with Victoria; now, hard as it was to believe, a precious part of that future was already disappearing into the past.

At the time of his own marriage, Albert had protested at only being allowed two days' honeymoon, but now he thought it quite enough for Vicky and Fritz. He stage-managed the festivities splendidly so that there was no time to sit and brood in the intervals between them. There was a banquet every night, a Garter ceremony for Fritz, a state ball in the Waterloo Room, and a reception next day at which so many new people had to be talked to that even the indefatigable Princess Augusta was quite worn out. The young German princes seemed if anything more distasteful than ever, with their sabre-slashed cheeks and their heel-clicking, their risqué conversation and their inability to hold their drink. He did not trust himself to think of Tuesday when Vicky and Fritz were to leave for Prussia, and was almost glad when it dawned too grey and foggy to lift the heavy atmosphere of bereavement that hung like a pall over Buckingham Palace. When he joined the Queen and Vicky after breakfast he noticed at once that they had been crying, although in front of him they made a brave attempt to talk brightly of other things. He himself was beyond tears. They all three walked to the Audience Room, where the duchess of Kent was waiting, surrounded by her sobbing grandchildren, who all rushed to their sister and showered her with kisses. At the head of the great staircase the Queen faltered and nearly broke down. Distressed beyond words,

Albert took her hand and whispered that he hated to leave her at this moment, even to see their child safely on her way. Vicky was too overcome to take proper leave of the servants standing to bid her farewell at the foot of the stairs, and scarcely knew what was happening as her father led her out into the icy courtyard and watched Fritz wrap her tenderly in a shawl and lift her half fainting into the carriage. The band struck up a rousing march as the procession moved into the Mall on the first stage of the journey to Berlin.

When he returned at four from Gravesend, where Vicky embarked on the royal yacht, Albert tried to comfort the sorrowing Queen by giving her an account of the cheering in the streets and of the young girls throwing flowers for the bride and bridegroom to walk on. In his anxiety to wring some consolation out of this wretched day, he did not see that all this was only the excitement of the moment, came (like that on the wedding day) from the romantic heart of the British people, and would not last; he forgot that it did not by any means prove that the Prussian marriage was popular after all or that they had been right to ignore the criticisms of the press.

The letter Albert wrote his daughter that night reveals his true feelings in a way that he had never done before or would again:

'My heart was very full when yesterday in the saloon you laid your head on my breast to give free vent to your tears. I am not of a demonstrative nature, and therefore you can hardly know how dear you have always been to me, and what a void you have left behind in my heart; yet not in my heart, for there assuredly you will abide henceforth, as till now you have done, but in my daily life, which is evermore reminding my heart of your absence.'

20

'It is the government, and not the Commons, who hold back'

THE lively interest which Albert had always shown in the lands outside Europe was much quickened by the events of the mid-fifties. America in particular fascinated him; the self-sufficiency which he tried to establish on the Osborne and Balmoral estates was in some ways his equivalent of the self-sufficiency which conditions forced upon the pioneers who were opening up the prairies, and he was one of the few who did not share the haughty attitude which most Englishmen of his time affected towards what they called the brash and uncultivated manners of Americans. For all her newness, he was inclined to think that America was sometimes ahead of England in politics – for instance, unhampered by tradition, the United States had already adopted the secret ballot without fuss. He took every opportunity of finding out more about the country and its appeal to immigrants from Europe. When, after the Crimean War, the British government offered the Germans in his Foreign Legion the chance of enlistment in the regular army, he questioned many of them about their intentions and discovered that only a handful were prepared to accept the offer and that most preferred to stick to their original purpose of emigrating to America and welcomed the challenge of freedom in a new society.

American neutrality during the Crimean War did not annoy him as much as Prussian, since it did not mean American indifference; many American doctors volunteered for service with the troops and were prominent during the cholera epidemic. But there was one awful week during the winter of 1855–6 when a break with the United States seemed likely. It was alleged that the British Minister in Washington was infringing international law by recruiting volunteers

305

in the United States, and his recall was requested. In retaliation, Palmerston prepared to demand the withdrawal of Buchanan, the American minister in London, and a serious incident was in the making. Hearing of this by chance, Albert at once sent for Palmerston and headed him off from his hasty action by telling him that he had private information that Buchanan was in any case about to leave London in order to run for President. Calm was restored, but it was as well Albert remained alert to the possibility that Palmerston's blindness to anything outside Europe might lead him to tread unwarily again, for it was only at the last moment that he was able to prevent Palmerston from expelling Buchanan's successor, George Dallas, as soon as he set foot in England. When summoned to the palace and lectured on the impropriety of his and the government's attitude, Palmerston was genuinely taken aback at Albert's indignation. Dallas's frank manner and cultivated tastes soon made him a welcome guest at Windsor, and Albert said that a few more men like him would do London society a great deal of good. It was not many months, moreover, before Albert was able to show Palmerston how well a friendlier policy paid, for it was Dallas's favourable reports which led Congress in December 1856 to present the Queen with the *Resolute,* in which the last English Arctic expedition had sailed, which had been found abandoned by a party of American explorers and refitted at American government expense.

Albert's other special extra-European concern was India. He had been fortunate in urging that the temptation to deplete the British garrisons in India to reinforce the army in the Crimea should be resisted at all costs (not to resist it would be 'most irresponsible,' he told Stockmar), but he had spoken to empty air so long as the war lasted; when it was over he returned to the charge, recommending the immediate restoration of all the regiments which had been transferred and a considerable increase in the number of troops stationed in India. It alarmed him that there was a serious outcry about the level of income-tax in Parliament in February 1857, for he had long regarded income-tax as an unavoidable part of national life, and saw that the controversy over proposals to reduce or abolish it was certain to obscure more important issues and lead to compensating proposals for cuts in the army; and he was disgusted when one of the first actions of Palmerston's new government after the election of March 1857* was to propose just such a reduction.

* Two old faces were missing from the new House of Commons, those of Cobden and Bright. No one regretted their absence more than Albert, who believed that 'fiery elements' like them were necessary for a strong Parliament.

The news of the outbreak of the Indian Mutiny in May 1857 was no surprise to Albert. Some years earlier he had wanted the establishment of a Royal Commission on India with wide terms of reference, because he feared there might be trouble brewing (particularly over the way in which the British disregarded Indian religious feelings), but the government had refused to set it up. Both he and Victoria had long been critical of the conventional Anglo-Indian habit of referring to Indians as niggers or barbarians; above all, the Governor-Generals had done far too little for the country – 'the place is so high it turns people's heads,' Victoria wrote.

The immediate cause of the Mutiny derived from this attitude of lofty disdain, which led to a clumsy disregard for Indian religious susceptibilities when cartridges for the new Lee Enfield rifle were issued. The grease on the cartridges contained tallow made from the fat of pigs and cows, although the pig is unclean to Muslims and the cow sacred to Hindus, and the majority of the native troops (who belonged to one or other of these religions) were therefore outraged at having to bite the cartridges open before use. This, coming on top of the Enlistment Act of 1856, which compelled new recruits to swear to serve overseas if required (a Hindu who crossed the sea incurred ritual pollution) created the atmosphere in which the garrison of Meerut mutinied on 10 May 1857, shot their officers and took possession of the nearby capital, Delhi, by force.* The massacre of two hundred European women and children at Cawnpore in July, and other similar atrocities, shocked British opinion both in India and at home. 'It is impossible to speak of the horrors which are taking place,' Albert wrote to Ernest early in September, 'but the heroism of the English and the calmness, the confidence and the endurance being shown are remarkable and uplifting to see.' Both he and Victoria felt their helplessness keenly. What should they do? Palmerston wanted them to order a day of national prayer and humiliation, the sort of thing they had been scornful about when Aberdeen suggested it during the Crimean War. Let the government

* The affair of the cartridges provoked a sudden reaction among the native troops stationed in Delhi and an area extending some two hundred miles eastwards. It was unpremeditated and unorganised, and it only found just enough support outside the army to make the title of 'rebellion' as appropriate as 'mutiny'. There were nevertheless causes which lay deeper than the affair of the cartridges: the growing economic monopoly of the small British ruling class (particularly after the recent large-scale annexations of native states), for instance, and the ill-judged propagation of Christianity which, by seeming to equate the advance of western-style education with compulsory conversion, suggested an intention to root out Indian religions. 'More than a purely military rising . . . but less than a national rebellion' (R. Hyam: *Britain's Imperial Century*, 221), the Mutiny was the outcome of social dislocation and the clash of old and new.

rather fall on its knees and humble itself, was Albert's grim comment, for Palmerston had turned down Napoleon III's offer to speed the passage of troops to India by transporting them across France by train, and had refused help from Belgium and Prussia. Above all, the Cabinet had taken too casual an attitude from the start and had rejected Albert's plea during the spring that the garrison of India should be strengthened in case an emergency arose. His diary bears witness to his frustration at their dilatoriness: 'the Cabinet must look the question boldly in the face.' Long years in England had taught him that 'it is the Government, not the Commons, who hold back.'

By autumn the worst of the danger had passed, the British position was being restored, and the question of punishment for the mutineers attracted increasing attention. Press and public cried out bloodthirstily for speedy vengeance, and were incensed at the proclamation of the Governor-General, Canning, against indiscriminate executions. Albert sided unhesitatingly with 'Clemency' Canning, insisting that the severest punishments ought not to be imposed except on conclusive evidence, and endeavouring to ensure that the Cabinet kept a sense of proportion. It was therefore all the more infuriating when George of Cambridge made a speech at Sheffield identifying himself with the party of retribution; his speeches were usually incoherent, but this time he made his meaning clear as daylight: 'I trust that no undue leniency will be adopted,' he thundered. 'I am sure that the country will support all who have the manliness to inflict the punishment'.* The widespread cries for vengeance and the almost unanimous approval of the savagery with which the rebellion was put down, though understandable directly after the massacres, were shocking when passions had had time to cool, and they throw the more tolerant attitude which Albert maintained throughout into still higher relief. He was one of the very few who were disgusted by the bloodthirstiness of the victors and did their best to stop it.

The Mutiny showed beyond doubt the impossibility of ruling what was now a vast empire through the East India Company.† The Queen assumed sovereignty in 1858. Malmesbury, the new

---

* Provoked by this, and remembering with indignation George's craven malingering during the Crimean War, Albert drily remarked that George was the best armchair general he had ever met.

† The East India Company, founded in 1600 for the purpose of trade, had gradually acquired extensive territories in India. Strong as was the backing which the British government gave to the Company, it was not the government but the Company alone which had the right to, and responsibility for, these territories until the transfer of sovereignty in 1858.

Foreign Secretary, drafted a proclamation setting out the principles upon which the government of India would in future be conducted, but the Queen and Albert rejected the draft because it was too impersonal and narrow-minded and because it gave no hint of the warmth of their feelings; in particular, they took exception to a passage which mentioned the Queen's power of 'undermining native religions and customs'. They had already rebuked Ellenborough, a former Governor-General, some time before for talking in this way. It was wrong even to think of westernising India, they had told him: how would he and his friends like to see themselves Indianised? Rather than speak of 'undermining', Albert preferred to emphasise that the sincerity of the Queen's own religious beliefs prevented her from wishing to disturb those of her new subjects.

Albert had quite a different document in mind, one that breathed 'generosity, benevolence and religious toleration'. He wanted to point out clearly, and not in ambiguous language that frightened because it was not understood, 'the privileges which the Indians would receive in being placed on an equality with the subjects of the British crown, and the prosperity following in the train of civilisation.' Furthermore he believed that it was useless, when speaking of the future, to use such abstract phrases as 'to reduce poverty,' which would sound empty to the starving who had never known anything else. Something to catch their imagination and bring them hope was needed, and an indication of how they were to be helped: 'a direct mention of railways, canals and telegraphs should be made, with an assurance that these . . . will be the causes of their general and individual well-being.' The text of the Proclamation was remodelled accordingly, and they added a personal touch in the form of a short prayer: 'May the God of all power grant to us, and those in authority under us, strength to carry out our wishes for the good of our people.' Composed by Albert, the Proclamation was nevertheless the voice of a female sovereign speaking to her more than a hundred million eastern peoples. It was done, and Albert was satisfied that it was well done.

Shortly before his death it gave him great pleasure to play a leading part in founding the Order of the Star of India, with the Queen as Grand Master. Of the twenty-five knights, half were to be Indians, and when the first investitures took place at Windsor in November 1861 Albert had the 'quiet satisfaction' of watching Victoria bestow the Order first on the Maharajah Duleep Singh, who had been deprived by the East India Company of the lands which he had ruled with humanity and justice.

A first-hand account of Felix Orsini's attempt to assassinate Napoleon III on 14 January 1858 reached Albert the next day. Ernest was staying at the Tuileries on his way to London for Vicky's wedding ten days afterwards, and had been in the opera house when the bomb exploded in the street outside. He was able to give graphic details of the blood-stained scene and was full of praise for the calm and courageous conduct of the Emperor and Empress; their first thought, as they picked themselves out of the débris of their carriage, was for the passers-by who had been hurt, and as for themselves – 'Danger is our business', said Eugénie. It was soon discovered that Orsini's plot had been hatched in London, and Albert at once predicted that this was the beginning of the end for the French alliance, for the French Press immediately accused the British government of complicity. Although he knew that this was absurd, Albert warned the Cabinet that the French government might use the bomb as an excuse for war and reminded them of the threat presented by the Cherbourg fortifications. He entirely agreed with Palmerston's prudent attempt to take the heat out of the situation by introducing the Conspiracy to Murder Bill, and was profoundly disturbed when the Commons threw it out. The news was brought to him in the middle of a meeting of the Royal Horticultural Society, and his first thought was that this would mean the fall of the government and all that would be entailed in the way of extra trouble at a time when he had hoped to be free to guide Vicky by correspondence through her first difficult weeks in Berlin. Palmerston resigned directly after he was defeated on the second reading of the bill on 19 February in a debate during which he was attacked, for the first time in his life, for being too mild – ironically enough, when for once he was in the right. When he came to Buckingham Palace a few days later Palmerston found Albert full of sympathy. As they walked in the garden, he told a sorry tale of stupidity and war-fever which had made even great friends like Russell and Grey desert him. He was gloomy about the choice of a successor; of the two possible candidates, one had no party and one – Derby – could only doubtfully command a majority. They agreed that there was nothing for it but for Albert to advise the Queen to send for Derby, but only on condition that before taking office he submitted the names of the Foreign Secretary and War Secretary for approval. Derby proposed Malmesbury and Panmure respectively; the former was acceptable, the latter not (because he had not fulfilled the promise he had shown when, as War Minister during the Crimean War, he had seemed the only man energetic enough to get things done) and when Derby suggested General Peel (Sir Robert's brother) instead Albert immediately agreed, for the name conjured up the happy past. It was a load off Albert's mind to have the War Office settled, for Ellenborough 'was demanding(!!) either it or the new India Office,' and he knew that Derby was as weak as water when it came to resisting pressure from his friends. Albert also urged upon Derby the necessity of pressing on at once with the last government's two pieces of urgent unfinished business – the Conspiracy to Murder Bill and the change in the constitution of India.

Disgusted with Derby's weakness and the jockeying for position in his government, Albert was anxious to get away for Easter. This sort of thing always horrified him; he had no sympathy with ambition for its own sake, and was even a little hard on politicians who wanted to better themselves by becoming ministers if he suspected that they did so for material gain. He could not understand that his own lofty sentiments were beyond the reach of ordinary men, and when he said of young Stockmar 'he has no ambition' he meant it as the highest praise. It was partly because he suspected that Palmerston was tainted in this way that he never quite trusted him; men of his rank and position, he said, should be above such things.

Martin says in his *Life* that Albert needed to get away because he was fatigued, but Albert's letters to Ernest and to Stockmar show that the real reason was that he wanted to keep up with events in Berlin, which it had been impossible to do in the hurried life in London. From the moment of Vicky's departure for Prussia the newspapers which he had once scorned became meat and drink to him. He scanned every account of her reception and treasured every word of praise; fortunately for his peace of mind the reports were far better than he dared hope, and his spirits rose when he read that she was 'winning golden opinions everywhere'. She had bravely taken to heart a lesson he had tried to instil into her from childhood (and into the Queen too, but with rather less satisfactory results) – never to think of herself, but always of others: 'You have kept down and overcome, your own little personal troubles,' he wrote, proud of her achievement, 'perhaps also many feelings of sorrow not yet healed. This is the way to success, and the only way. If you have succeeded in winning people's hearts by friendliness, simplicity and courtesy, the secret lay in this: that you were not thinking of yourself.' Fritz had helped to lead Albert into this fool's paradise by a charmingly naïve telegram 'The whole family is delighted with my wife,' which was in reality very far from the case.

Although Vicky had been gone only a few weeks, it seemed an eternity to her father, and yet she was so ever-present that he told

Ernest if he shut his eyes he could still believe her amongst them, so like was her voice to her mother's. Secretly he devised a plan which kept up his spirits wonderfully – to go to Prussia quite soon to see how she was settling down. He excused this early intrusion into her married life to himself by pretending that he needed to consult the Regent about Prussian affairs, for he reckoned that he now had the right to a voice in them and that, should Frederick William die soon, his brother would not be able to cope with the situation alone. Vicky knew nothing of the plan, but the trust she placed in her father increased his self-confidence without yet burdening him with responsibility. For the moment he believed that it was right and proper that she should correspond more with her mother than with him, and she poured out all the Berlin gossip, details about her household and much else besides every day (and sometimes even twice a day) to the Queen, who replied at equal length in a unique long-distance conversation. Albert was at pains to explain to Stockmar that he had 'arranged' for Vicky to do this. For him, the serious side. Before she left, Vicky had promised faithfully to impart the progress of her 'inner life' to her father, and he looked on this as a 'sacred trust'. Thus he prolonged into another generation the relationship between himself and Stockmar, but this time it was he who held the position of mentor: 'that outside of and in close proximity to your true and tranquillising happiness with dear Fritz your path of life is not wholly smooth, I regard as a most fortunate circumstance for you, inasmuch as it forces you to exercise and to strengthen the prowess of your mind.' The tortuous and seemingly heartless reasoning is astonishingly like that of Stockmar's letter to Albert when he was cast down by attacks in the Press at the beginning of the Crimean War,* but the intention in each case was kindly, to brace and fortify the recipient.

It seemed that there was nothing Vicky experienced which he had not gone through himself. Homesickness, 'that painful yearning', was the worst and – surprisingly – was often strongest at moments of great happiness. But there was also the fickleness of friends, the

* See p. 251 above. Stockmar's letter reads: 'Still I cannot wish, hard as you may have been hit by it, that you should have been spared this experience. You could not marry the Queen of England without meaning, and without being bound, to become a political soldier. A mere garrison life, however, never makes a soldier, and, some household disagreeables apart, you have led hitherto nothing but a peaceful, comfortable, pampering, and enervating garrison life, in which a pedantic overestimate of material and personal matters may no doubt flourish, but never the manly thinking, the vigorous feeling, which alone will stand the test, when brought into conflict with the actual perils of life. It is only in war, under its threatened or real wounds and bruises, that a real soldier is formed.' Compare also Stockmar's attitude over the Lehzen affair, p. 93 above.

312

ups and downs of popularity, the fatigue which came from the exacting demands of rank, sudden bewildering depressions that re-kindled the longing for home, the lassitude and sadness which would creep up without warning. Much can be learned about Albert's feelings during his early years in England from his letters to his daughter, as he relived through her experiences the bitter-sweet memories of those days. Because Stockmar's steadying influence had reassured him then, Albert understood that it was of the utmost importance for Vicky to know that the strange feelings which some-times threatened to overwhelm her were nothing to be afraid of but absolutely natural.

Yet unwittingly this loving father made serious mistakes and complicated his daughter's life. The first and most disastrous was that, in trying to prevent her from suffering as he had done through lack of an assured status, he insisted that she should be known among the proud Prussians as 'the English Princess' – a piece of folly which he should have avoided, for it gave her stiff-necked new relations the impression that her husband's title was not good enough. Again, he was quite right to value her good sense, but it was unwise to use her as a go-between to convey messages of a political nature to her father-in-law, who held strongly to the German belief that a woman's place is in the home and only in the home – for it made him seem to be interfering in Prussian domestic affairs. Like Victoria* he made another mistake, a case where good inten-tions were marred by stupidity, in writing too freely about Vicky's faults to Princess Augusta, so that she could help the young bride to overcome them. Augusta did nothing but magnify the faults and use them against Vicky, and so the consequences lasted for years. Finally, it was unfortunate that Albert could not resist the tempta-tion to interfere in Fritz's life, badgering his father to give him suitable training in government and to allow soldiering to drop into the background for a change.

The plan was that Albert should travel to Coburg in the spring. Vicky would meet him there and they would explore the Rosenau and the surrounding country together; it was a treat which he looked forward to excitedly, for it was something he had dreamed about since her birth. He had no doubt what her feelings would be. But the joy of showing Coburg to Vicky had to be postponed, for she fell and sprained her ankle, and Dr Wegner would not allow her to travel because she was pregnant. Instead, it was arranged that

* See p. 302 above.

he should spend two days with Ernest in Coburg before going to Potsdam, where Vicky and Fritz were living temporarily in Schloss Babelsberg. However, it even seemed for a few days that the trip would have to be put off altogether, for Albert caught a severe chill while reviewing troops at Woolwich in a bitter east wind. Like Dr Wegner, Sir James Clark tried to lay down the law, but with less success – travelling while not fully recovered might be dangerous, he warned. For years Albert had regularly disregarded Clark's advice, and he was not going to have his pleasure spoiled by listening to him now. Apart from everything else, he knew that Ernest had gone to a great deal of trouble and expense in making preparations to receive him in proper style, and would be upset if they all went for nothing.

Relations between the brothers had been strained for some time and this was a chance to patch things up. Although Ernest was no angel, Albert must take his share of the blame for the misunderstandings which had arisen lately. His commands to Ernest were becoming more frequent and more overbearing, for the older he became the quicker he was to show his displeasure when he did not get his own way; not unnaturally Ernest resented being treated like a schoolboy by his younger brother, particularly when Albert did not bother to hide his distrust of Ernest's ability to make the proper arrangements for his visit. Letters had passed back and forth between them, Albert's precise down to the last detail but showing no consideration for anyone's feelings except his own. Not once had he asked if a particular suggestion was convenient, although it is just possible, by reading between the lines, to see that this is implied, though in a rather lordly fashion. It was one thing to ask Ernest to keep people away ('Please keep my visit a secret and refuse other visitors. The few days are for us alone' was reasonable enough) but to tell him to get rid at short notice of relations already staying at Coburg – or to make them alter their plans for his convenience – was behaving in an unpleasantly dictatorial fashion. 'Leopold Brabant has promised to arrange his visit so that he will have left before I arrive' does sound selfish of Albert, and it is impossible not to feel some sympathy for Ernest on this occasion at least. Apart from Albert's testiness, however, there was another cause of disagreement; ever since Vicky's marriage the brothers had been crossing swords fiercely about German politics – Ernest accused Albert of truckling to Prussia – and in their disputes Ernest was always the more clear-headed because he was the less involved.

At last, on the afternoon of 27 May, Albert started on his journey, travelling incognito with a suite of only seven, which was considered a very small party indeed. Crossing the North Sea the *Vivid* rolled horribly in a storm and Albert was sick; consequently he looked pale and drooping when he was met on the quay at Antwerp by his cousin Philippe of Flanders, who promptly took his woebegone appearance for confirmation of the rumours that Vicky's marriage was unhappy and that Albert's journey was to bring her home.* As the train passed through Mainz, memories of visits to his uncle Mensdorff came flooding back. How carefree he was then! His father and grandmother were alive, he and Ernest were still close, he was half promised to Victoire, and Victoria had not yet come to the throne. How much had happened since then, and how old he was becoming, to derive pleasure from reminiscence!

In Coburg, Ernest and Alexandrine had made discreet but sumptuous preparations in his honour and laid themselves out to please him. It was not so much the return of the native as a private visit by a reigning monarch. Everyone was subdued in his presence; there was a difference in the way people behaved towards him which he would have noticed and not liked a few years ago, but now he took it for granted. All the old haunts were revisited: the Hofgarten, with its brand-new mausoleum (not yet quite finished) where Ernest and Alexandrine would be buried but where Albert's bones would never lie; the Veste, which seemed more than ever, in that quiet world, to breathe of the Middle Ages, and where he knew and loved every stone; the Ernst-Albrecht Museum, where he hailed with delight the stuffed birds, pinioned butterflies, stones and shells they had collected as boys long ago. Once he had known exactly where they had found every one, but now he had quite forgotten. The face of Coburg was changing too – there was a new barracks and a huge new brewery. The smart new station caught his eye, and it gave him pleasure to reflect that he had been instrumental in bringing the railway to Coburg – what a valuable link with the rest of Germany and Europe it would become. They called on Stockmar in his tall yellow house in the centre of the town. As Albert clasped the old man's withered hand he was almost overcome to realise that this trusted friend might not be with them much longer. But Stockmar was cheerful and in the best of health although as thin as a skeleton, walked as briskly as ever, and talked about politics in his usual lively fashion. One evening they went to a performance of *La Sonnambula*, but Albert had heard Jenny Lind sing the title-role at Covent Garden and found Coburg's best only second-rate by comparison. He was recognised and given a standing ovation, followed by 'God Save the Queen'. The next night he had to sit through

---

* The rumours were groundless but widespread: *cf Vicky*, pp. 73–4.

a play put on specially for his benefit, *Graf von Schwerin* by Ernest's secretary von Meyern, a drama full of allusions to German politics; the audience loved it, cheered and stamped their feet, but Albert did not care for it and told Ernest regretfully that 'it would not go down well in London.'

The Rosenau had never looked lovelier, the trees so green, the air like wine; Albert felt intoxicated, but found it strange that he could not recapture the past and wondered if he was becoming blasé. The truth hit him hard – the Rosenau was no longer home. 'Home' had for many years meant England, Victoria and his children, and with a sudden longing for them he gathered pansies he found growing on the terrace beneath the window of the room where they had slept in 1845 and sent them to her, carefully wrapped in wet moss, together with a single forget-me-not, picked from his grandmother's grave.

The heat in the train carrying him to Prussia was almost unbearable, and before they reached Grossbeeren, where Fritz was to meet him, he had developed a racking headache. Strung up and nervous, he became more certain with every mile that all was not well with Vicky. No one had said a word, but it was what they had left unsaid that upset him – Princess Augusta, Prince Hohenzollern, Ernest and Alexandrine, both the Stockmars. The younger Stockmar had travelled to Coburg on purpose to bring a doleful letter from Vicky, who had not yet heard the good news that her father was coming to Babelsberg, and he had looked so cast down that Albert was afraid to question him – and of course regretted it a moment after he left. It was a wonderful relief to reach Potsdam at last and to find that all was well. 'The relationship between the young couple is all that can be desired,' he wrote to the Queen that night. So great was his joy at discovering that his fears were only imaginary, that he was blind to many things he should have noticed. He saw nothing strange in the Regent's stiff manner, nor absurd in the King's silly antics (although their meeting was private, Frederick William received him in full-dress uniform, complete with helmet and sword), nor unfriendly in Queen Elizabeth's cold welcome. Enveloped in a warm glow of happiness, he found it easy to be affable to everyone, even to the notoriously licentious Prince Fritz Karl, whom in the normal way he would have cold-shouldered. It was more difficult to ignore the primitive conditions in the Prussian palaces, but in his cheerful mood even this seemed more amusing than shocking, so that he made only a passing comment on the fact that the Queen of England's daughter was marooned in Schloss Babelsberg without either bathroom or water-closet and that her parents-in-law did not seem to think this strange.

At the end of July Albert was able to keep his promise to 'bring Mama next time'. But they had got no farther than Düsseldorf when they received news that Albert's valet Kurt was dead. The relationship between Albert and Kurt had long been far more than the usual relationship of master and servant; he had entered Albert's service almost thirty years before, when Albert was seven years old, so that he had been his friend from childhood. Twice Kurt had saved his life – once from fire at Kallenberg in 1835, and again when he nursed him devotedly through his serious attack of measles eighteen years later. Kurt's death meant more than just the breaking of the last link with boyhood in Coburg, for this faithful Swiss had been the rock on which he had always leaned most heavily when things were not going right. His value lay in his knowledge of Albert's temperament, which he had watched over for so long, and he understood his anxieties and fears without a word being said; there were no restraints with Kurt, but a freedom between them that was unique. The Queen gave some of the reasons for this in her Journal; Kurt was 'invaluable; well-educated, thoroughly trustworthy, devoted to the Prince, the best of nurses, superior in every sense of the word. . . . I cannot think of my dear husband without Kurt. . . . We had to choke our grief down all day.' The loss of Kurt was serious. Without him, and without Vicky, Albert was to suppress his feelings more than ever for the remainder of his life – there could be no substitute, the confidence that had been built up over thirty years could not simply be transferred to another. Still more, the Queen's praise for Kurt's nursing skill was no exaggeration, and if Albert were to have a serious illness now there would be no one to care for him with the same skill and devotion.

It was cruel that Albert's first carefree holiday since the Crimean War should be marred in this way. He had almost recovered his equanimity, however, by the time they reached Berlin and found Vicky 'quite the old Vicky still'. But the visit was, at Albert's own suggestion, to be that queer hybrid 'semi-incognito', and this caused difficulties from the start. Calculated to please no one because of its ambiguities, it placed Vicky in a most awkward position: she could only invite a few of Fritz's relations to meet England's queen and her consort, and so the rest sulked and took it out of the innocent cause of their loss of face – yet the favoured few were appalled by the lack of ceremony, since they placed a very high value on the outward trappings of royalty and immediately began wondering whether England was really as powerful as they had been led to believe.

The many problems which Albert had intended to thrash out with the prince of Prussia were never once touched on, since the wily

William took good care never to be alone with him for a moment. Albert had no idea that William was harbouring the grudge that he was turning Fritz against him – during one of their quarrels Augusta had shouted that Albert thought Fritz was afraid of his father ('Fear stands in the way of love,' Albert had unwisely written to her). The thought that Albert was discussing his son with her behind his back infuriated this proud and stubborn man. As a penniless refugee in England in 1848 he had been forced to swallow unwelcome advice, because it is the lot of outcasts to put up with humiliation, but the boot was on the other foot now that his brother's failing health meant that he would soon be king and hold a higher position than could ever be Albert's. On the other hand, the blame for their failure to communicate did not all rest on William's shoulders. Not long before he left England, Albert had written somewhat heavy-handedly to the Regent, telling him that the coming autumn's elections in Prussia ought to be free, adding 'the eyes of Europe are upon you.' (William, of course, took this to mean Albert's eyes.) He went on: 'Everyone . . . in Europe is waiting anxiously to hear what line you will follow. I imagine that you have thought out your plans and are taking counsel with your friends as to the measures that you will adopt.' William did not reply. Many years of quarrelling with his wife had taught him that silence is golden, and he observed that rule to the letter during the whole of Albert's stay in Berlin.

In spite of these drawbacks, the rest of the holiday passed off better than might have been expected. To his great surprise, Albert sailed effortlessly through a series of reviews and excursions – steamer-trips on the Havelsee, picnics on the Pfaueninsel and so on – all in blazing heat, without any of the fatigue which had marred the holiday in Paris in 1855. Ernest, now ageing fast, turned up unexpectedly on Albert's birthday, 26 August, and the brothers mourned the loss of Kurt together. The last day of all was terrible: 'Parting was very painful,' Albert wrote laconically in his diary. To leave Vicky again so soon was heart-breaking, and the Queen could not stop crying as she got into the carriage which was to take them to the Wildpark station.

The journey back to England matched their feelings – it rained incessantly and the train was oppressively hot. Irritably, Albert tried to make notes for a speech he was to deliver to a working-men's club in Islington, but he could not concentrate. Instead, his mind would keep running on worries about Vicky. Everything that he had dismissed so lightly in Berlin earlier in the summer now hit him twice as hard. Social conditions there, he had just learned, were even further below those in England than he had ever imagined – and, what was worse, no one seemed to mind. Would they take proper care of Vicky when her baby was born? Were medical standards in Prussia high enough? What of Napoleon and France? If war came, which side would Prussia be on? In any case, Vicky would be cut off from home and family. With a sickening jolt he realised that this marriage, from which he had expected such happiness, had so far done nothing but make him vulnerable.

London was sweltering in a heat-wave when they arrived there three days later, the air dry and fetid after weeks of drought, and a thick coating of dust lay over everything. The heat made the Thames smell worse than usual as Albert set off with his equerry, Colonel Ponsonby, to inspect the cleansing work which had been going on in the river since May. For several years he had hammered away fruitlessly at successive governments to 'clean up the insalubriousness of England's finest river that in its present condition is a disgrace to all London,' and had been surprised when work suddenly started that spring. From the moment when he had first seen the rat-infested river-banks, where human beings lived in filth and squalor, he had been haunted by the sight, but knew that he would never be able to do much to improve things alone. He had failed to interest a single MP or to secure the appointment of a Royal Commission, and nothing happened even after the cholera epidemic of 1853–4, for those who could afford it simply fled to their country houses and stayed there until the all-clear. The stinking river threatened every Londoner with typhoid fever and diphtheria; 'A little smell never killed anyone' was simply not true, for thousands died every year. (Albert's cynical comment that perhaps the government thought them better dead was repeated everywhere.) It was all the more strange that Parliament was so inert, since it was not unusual for members to faint from the dreadful Thames stench during the heat of the summer, and sore throats and swollen glands were accepted hazards of the London season. The Buckingham Palace windows were never opened between June and September, and Albert and Stockmar often had to break off their games of skittles on the lawn because of the clouds of flies that bred in the slime along the river. But that spring Derby had suddenly told him that after the annual strong letter from the palace the government was going to set to work on a comprehensive scheme of drains and sewers for the whole city in order to clean the river up, and that there was 'a plan afoot to rehouse(!!!) the poor wretches living under the embankment.' Albert was amazed to find that the citadel had fallen just as the assault had slackened, for this year his private secretary had merely sent the letter as a routine measure, and he could not help 'dwelling on the many lives which would have been saved if it had been done years ago.' At first he was inclined to give the credit for the sudden change to Lord Shaftesbury (the former Lord Ashley), but it was he himself who had worked the miracle.

It had come about in a curious way. As soon as he took office as Prime Minister, Derby had been surprised to discover how powerful Albert had become. Six years ago, he had found it useful in a vague sort of way to have Albert on his side, but now it was clear that without the support of the Prince Consort it was impossible to govern successfully. Unlike his predecessor, Derby feared responsibility, a weakness which to his credit he recognised and tried to overcome; 'he had, to his surprise, reached the position of prime minister of England without in the least wanting it.' By contrast, Albert enjoyed responsibility and seemed to thrive on it; his shoulders were broad, Derby sensed that he could lean on him, and in moments of difficulty it would be a greater comfort to talk things over with the Prince Consort than with a member of his own Cabinet, for he would be more likely to receive constructive help and guidance. With a view to understanding him better, Derby read Albert's accumulated memoranda on a variety of topics, and was convinced by what he had repeatedly written about the pollution of the Thames and conditions along its banks. The drainage scheme was the result.*

* A comprehensive system of drains and sewers, more than 100 miles long, was designed by Sir Joseph Bazalgette and constructed during the next 15 years. For the first time, it prevented the discharge of sewage into the Thames in London by conveying it further downstream. The Embankment was built over part of the reclaimed and formerly foul-smelling mud-flats.

21

'Sentimentality is a plant that cannot grow in England'

PREPARING his eldest daughter to be the future queen of Prussia had so absorbed Albert that he neglected to supervise the education of his eldest son, and this slackening of the reins had lamentable results. The prince of Wales had fallen alarmingly behind, not only in his studies but in his behaviour, and after Vicky's marriage Albert dejectedly forced himself to return to his duty; he had Vicky's cleverness before him as the goal at which Bertie must aim, although he tried to steel himself to recognise that his son would never attain it. He had been glad to be rid of Bertie while he was giving Vicky special coaching, and had despatched him on a walking-tour of the Lake District with four boys of his own age, one the ponderous William Gladstone, the statesman's eldest son. The result of this holiday was a frail little essay on 'Friends and Flatterers'; 'the nature of a friend', the prince wrote, 'is to tell you of your faults, and that of a flatterer to lead you into any unimaginable vice.' One of his tutors, the Reverend Charles Tarver, defended him by saying that at least the sentiments expressed in the essay were 'right-minded', but one cannot help sympathising with Albert's despair, so feeble were its contents. Bertie's attempts at letter-writing were no better – bad enough, indeed, to make Albert think he was behaving childishly on purpose. He could not be, he must not be, as stupid as that. A trip to Königswinter on the Rhine near Bonn followed, with the same four companions and 'for the purpose of study'. At a similar age, sixteen, Albert had longed to join a reading party in that jolly little town. What happiness it would have been to sit undisturbed in the warm sunshine, a pile of uncut books by his side waiting to be devoured. Instead, he had been made to accompany his selfish old

321

father on a tour of the fashionable watering-places, where he knew no one and had nothing to do but kick his heels day after day in silent humiliation as he watched duke Ernest and his friends making fools of themselves. His own feelings about books and reading were so different from his eldest son's that he cannot be blamed for thinking that he was giving the boy a treat by sending him to Königswinter, and envying him his good fortune.

According to young William Gladstone, it was at Königswinter that Bertie kissed a pretty girl for the first time (an occupation at which he was to become a past master), but although William retailed the incident at length in a letter home of the kind which Albert longed to receive, no word of it reached Buckingham Palace. Bertie was just the age for hero-worship, and he made Fritz the object of his adoration, with the result that he wanted to be a soldier and wear a splendid uniform. It became his burning ambition to join the army, although he had little idea what this meant, but he was so persistent that Albert had to remind him of the other duties of the heir to the throne. Perhaps it could be considered later on, for an army training could be very useful; the thing to do was to get on with his studies now, and keep the army before him as something to aim for in the future. There were times when Albert was irritated beyond endurance by a boy who was making so wretchedly little use of chances which he would have jumped at himself when he was the same age. 'He is idle and weak,' he wrote to Vicky in a fit of depression, and confided to her in another sad letter that he never knew whether Bertie understood or not when he explained things, because all he ever said was 'Yes, yes, yes'. It was to be hoped that his confirmation might make him more serious-minded, and indeed while he was being prepared he did seem 'quiet and gentle, and properly impressed'.

Confirmation marked the end of childhood, and directly afterwards he was sent to live at White Lodge, Richmond Park, which had been vacant since the death of the duchess of Gloucester in 1857, accompanied by Frederick Gibbs and Charles Tarver as tutors. Faced with his son's persistent pleading, Albert had given way to his wish to enter the army, but he was to be kept 'away from the world' while he prepared for it, Albert told Stockmar in a long letter about his progress. Unfortunately, Bertie did not understand that the army meant more than merely a smart uniform. The shock of realisation was profound, and he took his bad temper out on his new equerries, two of whom were young veterans of the Crimea with Victoria Crosses. The military atmosphere these appointments created was designed with a purpose, for Albert wanted Bertie to have some idea of what a soldier's life was like before he plunged into it too far to be got out again with dignity; but militarism was balanced by the softening influence of Lord Valletort, who had spent his youth in attendance on an invalid father. From all these young men, Albert hoped, his son would learn deportment and proper behaviour by example – how not to loll in armchairs, stand about in unbecoming attitudes, talk to his elders with his hands in his pockets, and so on, for Bertie slouched badly, dragged his feet, paid scant attention when spoken to, and talked too fast and too indistinctly, all defects which would be great handicaps for a king. Albert put a high price on good manners, scrupulous politeness and consideration for others, and the avoidance of thoughtless or bantering words, and he knew that although Bertie could not stand chaffing himself there was no greater tease in all England than the heir to the throne.

Members of the young prince's household were encouraged to introduce him to cultural pursuits – music, drawing, poetry and play-readings. Albert had no objection to light and amusing books so long as these were kept for leisure hours; on the other hand, he did not want his son to waste his time on billiards and cards until he began to show some improvement in his work – then, perhaps, they might be allowed as a reward for effort. The rules Albert was laying down for Bertie's education were much the same as those he had devised for the Queen fifteen years ago, when he took her 'improvement' in hand: then, they had brought satisfaction to both teacher and pupil, but now they did no good at all. Mother and son were too different in temperament and intelligence for the repetition to be a success. It was not long before the Queen's moans to Vicky in Berlin were worse than Albert's. 'I am in despair,' ran one letter. 'The systematic idleness, laziness, disregard for everything, is enough to break one's heart, and fills me with indignation.' In the circumstances, it was hardly wise to urge Bertie to think for himself and not follow others, and it was particularly unfortunate that he should choose to do so over a matter on which both his parents held strong views which they felt should be shared by the whole family in order to present a united front to the world. Bertie wrote to ask whether he could take the Sacrament every Sunday with his equerries at Mortlake Parish Church. Albert was against this, for he and the Queen took Communion only three times a year themselves, and he did not want it to seem that he and his son thought differently on so important a matter; but if Bertie had 'a real yearning of the heart', he should certainly go as often as he wished. The argument lasted so long that Bertie lost interest before it was over, leaving

Albert with the feeling that his son was unable to sustain his interest in anything for any length of time; for if he had had a really serious desire in the first place he would have fought harder to get his way.

Frederick Gibbs resigned in November 1858 and Colonel Bruce was appointed Bertie's governor on his seventeenth birthday. This was the occasion for a solemn letter from Albert: he was now answerable directly to his parents and he must try to become 'a good man and thorough gentleman. ... Life is not given to be frittered away but is composed of duties, and a man establishes himself by the way he carried out these duties.' If this letter seems heavy and humourless, it must be remembered that it was written to a youth who would one day be king of England and who up to now had shown little conception of what the position would demand, even though he had lived close to his parents all his life. Bertie burst into tears on receiving this letter, and when Albert heard of this unusual display of emotion he dared to hope that perhaps the heir to the throne was beginning to understand his responsibilities at last.

A few weeks with Vicky in Potsdam followed, and there was a certain amount of guile about Albert's plan – some of Vicky's cleverness and sparkle might rub off on her brother. 'Do not miss any opportunity of urging him to work hard,' Albert wrote to her beforehand.

'Unfortunately, he takes no interest in anything but clothes, and again clothes. Even when out shooting, he is more occupied with the cut of his trousers than with the game. I am particularly anxious that he should have mental occupation in Berlin. Perhaps you could let him share in some of your lectures, etc. An elder sister's influence can often be effective.'

Another reason for the trip was not mentioned in the letter – to take a look at a certain princess of Saxe-Meiningen, for Albert had the idea that 'harnessed to a good wife the awful anxiety for the future which has so oppressed us both might abate to some degree.' An early marriage, with its attendant responsibilities, was now regarded by his parents as the solution to the problem of the prince of Wales. Marriage had certainly calmed the Queen and set her feet on the right path; but what they both forgot was that the personalities of mother and son were totally different. On his return all Bertie could talk about was balls, reviews, the success of his investiture with the Order of the Golden Eagle by the Regent, and what a good fellow Fritz was for getting him made an honorary colonel in the Prussian Guards so that he could wear the uniform at a parade. Albert thought he had never seen the boy so animated as when describing this uniform, and the Queen admitted that it had the advantage of not showing his knock knees. Questioned in more detail, Bertie was astonishingly vague about everything: he had met so many people that he could not possibly remember the colour of the Meiningen princess's hair, nor could he tell them anything else they wanted to know. After this, Vicky's glowing letter describing his success with her difficult new relations and all that they had done to amuse him did not go down well. Bertie had not been sent to Berlin to be amused, and it was not his social graces that needed cultivating (he was too keen on them already), but his brains. And as for the vagueness: since Albert well knew that his son could be quick and sharp enough when his mind was set on something – which was seldom – he was very inclined to think that Bertie was feigning stupidity on purpose to irritate. Early in December, in yet another complaining letter to Vicky, he said that Bertie's intellect was 'of no more use than a pistol packed at the bottom of a trunk if one were attacked in the robber-infested Appennines.'

Nevertheless it gladdened Bertie's parents' hearts to discover that Vicky's influence had done a little good – and after all, it must mean something that Vicky had evidently enjoyed talking to her brother, even though the Queen still found him 'very dull; his three other brothers are all so amusing and communicative.' Although there was still a long way to go, his manners were visibly better, but on the other hand he showed an independence in dress which alarmed them. The flowing Byronic curls, so beloved of his mother, had all been cut off, and he sported the latest Prussian hair-style instead – very short, with a centre-parting – which the Queen said made him look 'all head and no face'. Alas, even the slight improvement in manners was only skin-deep, as his father discovered to his chagrin. While he was charming Berlin society, behind the scenes he was tormenting his new valet, pouring wax on his livery, throwing water over his clothes, tearing his ties and striking him in the face. 'To play such tricks on a servant,' Albert told Vicky angrily, 'is unforgivable.'

But they must battle on, for Albert believed that no one was irredeemable, not even his difficult eldest son. In the belief that the best school was 'the eternal stress of life' – from which, oddly enough, his own plans had hitherto protected Bertie – Albert now sent him to Rome. Like his father before him, he had an audience with the pope, but told his parents nothing about it. It might never have happened, for all the impact it made. Could Bertie not make his letters 'a little less factual', Albert wrote in despair, 'we would like to receive arguments, reflections, and a conversational style.' Next, Scotland. As 'the nation's child', Bertie was to be given a taste of the principal educational establishments in the British Isles, beginning with Edinburgh. The gloom of Holyrood was quite a shock after the gaiety of Rome. On the rare occasions when they stayed at Holyrood Palace, the Queen and Albert were always made melancholy by the desolate atmosphere; even a single night under its roof was a penance, and they always referred to it as 'sombre Holyrood'. But the gloom does not seem to have prevented Bertie from enjoying at any rate Dr Lyon Playfair's lectures on the composition of iron, which for some reason amused him. Bertie had already left Edinburgh when Albert held what he called an 'educational conference' of Bertie's tutors there on his way to Balmoral at the end of August. It astonished him that they spoke well of their pupil, although it was noticeable that all praised his personality and charm but had not a word to say about his intellect.

He was to go to Oxford in the autumn. Henry Liddell, the Dean of Christ Church, refused Albert's request that he should not be attached to a college, insisting that he be admitted to Christ Church in the normal way, since to do otherwise was against University regulations, and these could not be set aside. He was to live in Frewin Hall with his governor and his household: there, one October evening, Bertie tried on his cap with its gold tuft and found that it went particularly well with his new hair-style. Once more he took his studies lightly (Albert wished that he could take his own work with the same easy nonchalance), but quickly picked up a new vice – smoking. Colonel Bruce was made to pay for his charge's idleness and levity, being subjected to a lecture on Albert's anxiety that precious time should not be wasted through social demands. Bertie too received a dose of fatherly admonition – it was impossible to exaggerate the importance of doing well, but he might give a few dinner-parties for distinguished dons. At the same time, his mother scolded him for eating too much, said that he was getting fat, and put down the sick headaches of which he complained not to overwork but to 'imprudence'. To prefer good food to mental effort was an attitude Albert could not understand; something of a masochist himself, he was angered and bewildered by the sybaritic inclinations of his son. He wanted to be fair – 'I must not censure him', he told Vicky – but found it hard to live up to his good intentions, and before long was writing angrily 'I have never in my life met such a thorough cunning lazy-bones.' Vicky saw further than her parents, for she sensed the truth that Bertie was incapable of learning. She therefore took the sensible line – it was indeed the only possible line – that he should be encouraged to do the few things that he could do well and enjoyed doing, even if it were merely swaggering about in new clothes and 'being on show' in public – which, to his father's amazement, he seemed to like very much. Albert rightly pointed out that an easy solution of this sort could not be adopted with the heir to the throne. If only Vicky had been the boy!

When Vicky came to London with Fritz in November she was pained to hear her mother dwell so frequently on Bertie's shortcomings. If she defended her brother she was quickly slapped down – she would soon see things in a different light if she lived at home, the Queen said tartly. Forced to give an opinion, she had to admit that at the moment Bertie was certainly not fit to inherit the Throne which was now to all intents and purposes occupied with such credit by dearest papa. Something of the same sort must have been in Albert's mind when he wrote to Vicky in the New Year 1860: 'When one considers that he might be called upon at any moment to take over the reins of government in an empire where the sun never sets and where progress is identified with the civilisation of mankind, one's mind becomes confused by the very idea.' The Queen had put it more bluntly: 'The greatest improvement, I fear, will never make him fit for his position. His only safety, and the country's, is in his implicit reliance in everything on dearest papa.' Bertie's inability to learn caused the Queen to become obsessed with imagining the catastrophe of her own death; if this happened, Bertie would only be able to carry on if papa did all the work. But Albert himself knew very well that he would be relegated to a back seat the moment Bertie became king.

Oxford was more fun than the prince of Wales expected. There was plenty of scope for hunting, tennis and rackets, but he treated the young men selected as his companions so rudely that they soon slunk away in distaste. This did not mean that he was in the least lonely, however, for there were plenty of adults only too ready to toady to the heir to the throne. The results of his first examinations were awaited with anxiety, and great was the relief when Dr Liddell wrote that his performance had been satisfactory. To show how pleased they were, his parents decided to give him a holiday in Coburg. It was a huge success from everybody's point of view. Stockmar hurried across the square to the Ehrenburg Palace to catechise Bertie, and then wrote a letter of congratulations on 'the improvement in your son' – the first encouraging words he had earned for years. Albert's reply revealed more about his own relationship with his son than he realised: 'that you see so many signs of improvement in the young man is a great joy to us; for parents who watch their son with anxiety and set their hopes for him high are in some measure incapable of forming a clear estimate, and are at the same time apt to be impatient if their wishes are not fulfilled.'

During the Long Vacation of 1860 the prince of Wales went to Canada to open a railway bridge over the St Lawrence River at Montreal and to lay the foundation-stone of the federal Parliament building at Ottawa, with a short trip to New York and Washington thrown in. Albert's eyes had been turned with longing on the New World for so many years that the fact that he sent his son instead of going himself is a certain sign that he really did love this difficult boy. The tour was meant to make up for all the scoldings he had been given and to say, better than words ever could, that his parents were gaining confidence in him at last. All the details were arranged beforehand, and Albert took much vicarious pleasure in the pain-staking care with which he prepared notes about the main features of each town his son would visit and made drafts of all the speeches he would have to deliver. That he was able to do this at long range with such skill is a tribute to the intensity with which he had applied himself to the study of the North American mind for a decade or more, and it enabled him to draw attention delicately to the services which the British monarchy had rendered to those 'distant rising countries who recognise in the British crown and their allegiance to it their supreme bond of union with the mother country and each other' without ruffling anyone's susceptibilities. The tour could not have gone off better. The Canadians thought he looked 'every inch a prince' and took him to their hearts, and at the opera in New York the audience rose to a man as he entered and sang 'God Save the Queen'; but the style of Bertie's success bore out the truth of Albert's assessment of his son's character: 'He has a strange nature, no interest in things, only in people.' Notwithstanding this, Vicky had never read such an enthusiastic letter about him as the one she received from her father while Bertie was on his way back. 'Is that not remarkable for the most republican city in republican America,' Albert wrote ecstatically, after Bertie had been warmly received in New York. 'He was immensely popular everywhere and really deserves the highest praise, which should be given him all the more, as he was not spared any reproof.'

Welcome confirmation of this came in a letter from President Buchanan, who judged the visit 'a triumph from beginning to end'. Here at last, evidently, was something Bertie could do well: 'As Ambassador Extraordinary he might do the throne some good.' Dare they look on the future with more hope?

As a reward, Bertie was given permission to smoke, so long as he promised never to do so in public; there were a great many things that Albert was forced to accept nowadays, even if he did not approve, and smoking was one of them. Philosophically, he came to the conclusion that now and again he must not be too rigid, but should give way, especially in comparatively innocent matters. The world was changing, and one must bow to it whether one liked it or not. 'It is sad, for it cannot be regarded as progress.'

Cambridge, where the prince of Wales went in January 1861, welcomed him with as much enthusiasm as America had done. The Queen put this down to Albert's prestige as Chancellor, confident that it could have nothing to do with Bertie himself. Cheering crowds greeted him at the station, in the streets and at the entrance to Madingley Hall (where he was to live) as the Reverend Tennyson Turner poured out endless verses of welcome – his brother-in-law the Poet Laureate having flatly refused to compose an ode for so trifling an occasion. His parents were annoyed at so much fuss over 'a mere student prince', lest it should go to his head, but they received no co-operation from the Master of Trinity, who arranged a special ceremony of matriculation, or from the people of Cambridge whose local paper (which Albert had ordered to be sent to him regularly) was soon printing daily reports of Bertie's social doings – his frequent dinner-parties, the crowds that mobbed him when he attended the University Church ('as if he was the man in the moon come down to earth,' said Albert wryly), his parades round the town in the phaeton which had been bought simply to bring him in the four miles from Madingley for lectures. Albert would never have recognised his son in the glowing accounts Lady Affleck (second wife of the Master of Trinity) gave her sister of the heir to the throne at tea in the Master's Lodge, but inevitably there was some criticism amid all the fulsomeness. Victoria and Albert were inclined to welcome this, because it was more natural; but when the *Cambridge Daily News* said that Bertie was 'small, insignificant, and quite ordinary', Albert commented that royalty was not expected to be human: what did the public want – four legs, two heads and two faces?

Things got worse during the Easter Term, in May and June. Albert began to dread opening the local paper and reading yet another account of Bertie watching cricket at Fenners dressed in the latest fashion or attending one of the almost nightly dinner-parties which university society vied in giving for him. Had things like this been only occasional recreations, Albert would have been well satisfied, but he could not rid himself of the fear that his son was spending his time in idleness and dissipation, and he looked in vain for any evidence of study. In fact, although Bertie got on well with his private tutor, Charles Kingsley, and other dons, not even

Kingsley could improve his essays, which remained those of a prep school boy to the last.

The company which the prince kept at Cambridge has brought him much sympathy in subsequent years, and it has been suggested, for instance, that dinners at which all the men were over thirty and no ladies were present except Lady Affleck and Mrs Bruce must have been very tedious for a young man. The truth is the exact opposite. He derived great satisfaction from the deference of distinguished men who were older than he, particularly since they considered it an honour to entertain him, listened to his lightest word with grave attention and laughed at his every joke; the childless Lady Affleck, who doted on him, never implies by a single word that he was either lonely or unhappy. To suggest that he was bored is to misunderstand the immaturity of his character, which fed on admiration and grew fat on it. If 'photographs show the prince of Wales looking small, crushed and miserable, in yet another circle of imposing learned dons', the fault lies in the photography and in Bertie's un-photogenic face. There is abundant evidence of his enjoyment of life at Cambridge, and none whatever of any unhappiness – but of course also none that he had the remotest idea what his father had sent him there to learn. All his life he was to prefer the company of his seniors, especially older women, and he never felt the lack of the young companions for whose company he is reputed to have been pining.

The education and training of the prince of Wales was taking up so much of his time and energy that Albert had to remind himself that his other children needed attention too. The little girls were no trouble, and in Miss Hildyard, their principal governess, the Queen and Albert had chosen a conscientious and well-educated woman who was not only an excellent teacher but well able to keep order and discipline among the temperamental foreign governesses. Of the boys, Arthur, with his passion for soldiers, gave no trouble and only Leopold caused them any real anxiety. Daring, strong-willed and full of high spirits, he was determined to behave like other boys in spite of the haemophilia which was such a handicap to him – the slightest fall or bruise might spell disaster.

The most difficult problem was to decide about the career of their second son, Alfred. He was growing up rapidly, and although three years younger than the prince of Wales, was already a foot taller by the time he was fifteen. 'Affie', as he was called in the family, was fearless and imperturbable, a cheerful extrovert who exuded self-confidence and dash and was always being ticked off roundly for taking undue risks. As children, Bertie and Affie did everything together; but their abilities were very different, and the backwardness of the elder soon began to have a harmful effect on the development of his younger brother. By May 1856 Albert was forced to recognise that 'the difference in their ages and abilities disturbs them both' and reluctantly decided to separate them – reluctantly because he did not want to hurt either of them and because he remembered the pain of his own parting from Ernest. From an early age, Affie had shown a strong desire to enter the navy; but since he could not do so until he was fourteen, a young engineer officer was engaged as his tutor meanwhile and he was sent off to Geneva to spend the next few months learning French. Albert explained his attitude at length in a letter to his brother which shows clearly how anxious he was not to thwart his children's own inclinations but simply to mould them as little as possible consistent with their inherited responsibilities.

'First, as regards his wish to enter the navy: this is a *passion* which we, as his parents, believe we have no right to oppose, because it never does any good to withstand the spontaneous desires of youthful spirit. We have done what we can not to encourage it, and since it goes along with a strong inclination for science, particularly mechanics, we have assigned a young engineer to him, hoping that he will be able to interest him in this branch of the service. But his love for the blue jacket has always shown through and, given the remarkable perseverance of the child, it is not to be expected that he will give the idea up. An example of his perseverance is his violin, which he learned to play secretly, in his spare time, as a surprise for us; he cannot be parted from it. Another example is his mechanical models, to which he devotes every spare moment. . . . The service will make him acquainted with all parts of the world and he will have become more generally capable than he would by staying here or in Germany. The service, with its strict discipline and the early responsibility it gives young officers, is a marvellous training for life.'

The passage in which Albert explains why he chose Geneva suggests that even as late as 1857 he still felt his German origin was held against him.

'But there are also two other considerations – first that the small German courts are not unjustifiably accused of illiberality here, and my connection with them is always held against me as a crime, so that the experiment of sending one of our sons to be educated abroad would have met with the greatest opposition and have had the worst construction put upon it in the public mind. There is actually something attractive to the English in the experiment itself. The choice of republican Switzerland and of traditionally Protestant Geneva has been received well, granted that an experiment of this kind was to be made at all.'

Affie's wish for a naval career raised a tricky problem, however: it had long been accepted that, if Ernest remained childless, Affie should inherit the duchy of Coburg and Gotha – but the navy might make him disinclined for this. Ernest had to be propitiated, therefore, by the suggestion that Affie should spend a couple of weeks with him on the way home from Geneva, but also reminded him that in any case only one life stood between Affie and the English throne. Affie came back from Coburg full of enthusiasm for his father's old home, and his account of all he had done with Ernest made Albert quite homesick. What had happened to the twenty years since his own boyhood at the Rosenau? They had gone in a flash, and in moments of depression he felt they had left little mark behind. 'It needed the pressure of the many troublesome and worrying affairs, of which every day brings me plenty, to bring me out of that mood and back to reality,' he told Ernest. 'Sentimentality is a plant which cannot grow in England, and when an Englishman finds himself becoming sentimental he gets as frightened as if he were having a dangerous illness, and blows out his brains.'

22

'He is king in all but name'

So wholeheartedly had Albert thrown himself into the task of educating the Queen, and so thoroughly had he carried it out, that by the mid-'fifties he had transformed the way she exercised her royal powers and had made their partnership a remarkably powerful one. The single most important instrument in this transformation was the memorandum, the legacy of Stockmar's training. By showing her how to make correct records of her conversations with ministers, and the like, Albert taught her to be exact and disciplined in thought and writing, and increased the confidence with which she expressed her views by giving her the means to support them with precise evidence. Albert himself recorded everything in this way, from minute details about the family estates at Coburg to British politics at the highest level, in order that he should have a note of what he thought or had said on any subject. These memoranda had always stood him in good stead, and as soon as Victoria learned his methods, politicians who had known her in early days began to be surprised by the exactness of her knowledge. She now demanded detailed information from them and would not be put off with vague and inconclusive answers. A good example is the letter of 4 August 1857 in which she drew Palmerston's attention to the way the new steam navy had been run down after the Crimean War and called for a statement

> 'as to the force of screw-ships of the Line and of other classes which can be got ready at the different dockyards, and the time required to get them to sea for actual service and also the time required to launch and get ready the gunboats. She does not wish for a mere general answer from the Lords of the Admiralty, but for detailed reports from

the Admirals commanding at the different ports, and particularly the Captains in command of the Steam Reserve. She would only add that she wishes no unnecessary time to be lost in the preparation of these reports.'

Queen Victoria had come a long way from the casual Melbourne days! All her ministers recognised that the change was due to Albert's teaching, and the recognition increased their respect for him. Greville noted a conversation he had with Clarendon on this very point; he was not so much surprised that she should ask for detailed information as astonished that she could refer knowledgeably to the answers many months later. None of her predecessors had ever been able to do this, and she caught out many an unwary minister with her penetrating questions. Clarendon liked to boast that he encouraged the methods her husband had taught her so well, but even he sometimes fell into her trap. It was about this time, too, that he told Greville that Albert was 'King in all but name, although he acts through her and never alone. All his views and notions are those of a constitutional sovereign, and he fulfils the duties of one and at the same time makes the crown an entity and discharges the functions that properly belong to a sovereign.' It was Greville who reported some gossip told him by Granville to the effect that Albert had on many occasions rendered the most important services to the government and prevented them from getting into 'scrapes' of various sorts. Greville repeated this without any of his usual sarcastic comments, because he found it easy to believe, Clarendon having told him that Albert had written some of the best papers on political questions he had ever read. Albert too had come a long way!

The journey had left its mark on him, however. As he became more powerful, more respected and more sought after, he took opposition less kindly. 'An angel', he had been called as a child by his doting grandmother, but even then he was an angel with a temper. Now, the Prince Consort's frown was feared, and knees would tremble at his displeasure. But sometimes he took this and his own authority so much for granted that he acted hastily and without preparing the ground properly, and suffered unexpected set-backs. For many years he had wanted to move the National Gallery out of its decaying buildings in Trafalgar Square to new premises at South Kensington, but during the spring of 1857, in a hurry to get down to Osborne, he behaved as though the move was settled before it was even discussed, and was outvoted at a meeting of the Trustees. Furious at the rebuff, but recognising that he had only himself to blame for not proceeding with more tact and caution, he determined not to make the same mistake a second time. A month later, as chairman of a conference on national education, he acted very differently; his first speech was so carefully prepared, so well founded on statistical evidence, and so persuasive, that he got his way at once and did not even need to use all the information he had collected. His public speeches, indeed, were now always eloquent, and were delivered with such confidence that he seldom referred to the notes in his hand – unlike some prominent politicians, whom experience had rendered careless, diffuse and rambling, like Sir James Graham and Lord Malmesbury.

There were some drawbacks to Albert's increasing power and authority, however. Ministers consulted him regularly – sometimes they did not even see the Queen at all – and nothing was done without his consent; but the resultant pressures on his time were very great, and it was a defect in him that, like Peel, he could not or would not delegate a part of his work to others. Some said, in consequence, that he had a power-complex – which made the Queen furious, for she knew that it was only conscience and a sense of duty which made him take on so much, and she saw the energy he put into everything he did. Others argued that he did not use his power impartially, showed undue favour to the middle and lower classes, and complained that no one was giving that dreadful thing, democracy, a bigger boost than England's uncrowned king with his talk of the right of every man and woman in the land to be given an equal chance.

Amid all these criticisms, pressures and temptations, however, Albert stuck firmly to his vow of self-abnegation, although it was becoming more difficult to do so and although the Queen did not realise the great strength of mind it required. He was powerful, but he never overstepped the line, although it was finely drawn; he never usurped the Queen's position, never allowed power to go his head. It would have been easy to assume the functions of an absolute monarch, but he always resisted the temptation. Visitors from abroad noticed this more clearly than most Englishmen. The American minister, Buchanan, for instance, told his successor that 'the Prince Consort exhibits great discretion in a very trying position.'

The amount of travelling he did was enormous, most of it by train. To Manchester, to open an exhibition of art treasures; to Liverpool, to launch a ship, open a shipyard, or inspect the docks; to Portsmouth, to visit the navy; to Aldershot, to inspect the army; to several towns in Yorkshire, to visit factories; to Oxford, to Cambridge; from Windsor to London and back almost daily at certain seasons, until the discomfort of the old horse-drawn carriage journeys became a dim memory . . . all over England, Scotland and Wales, in fact, wherever a railway-line was laid, so that the royal train grew shabby in his service. Boxes of papers and a shelf-load of books accompanied him everywhere, and when work was done he would reach for Gibbon's *Decline and Fall*, de Tocqueville's *Ancien Régime* or one of Kingsley's novels. He was anxious not to overlook anything of interest that was published, and reading in the train afforded a golden opportunity, for 'if only I had more time' was his continual cry. His private secretaries had to be strong men to keep up with him. When his wife, anxiously watching for signs of the lassitude that Stockmar had warned her against, saw that he was pale and tired at the end of the day, she put this down to exhaustion and overwork. The truth was far simpler – his was the type of skin that soon grew pale without fresh air and exercise, and his tiredness was only the natural consequence of a day's work well done. He never visited a town for one purpose alone, but always to fulfil a long programme which started early and finished late. In July 1857, after a day spent at various functions in Manchester and ending with a walk round the art exhibition and conversations with numerous strangers, he refused to return to Worsley Hall with the Queen but insisted on touring an india-rubber factory and other works, and paid for his rashness with an upset stomach which he obstinately attributed simply to the heat. 'Albert very tired and not quite well,' the Queen wrote in her Journal that night, her own pleasure diminished by concern for him. Albert never fully understood the extent of that concern, nor the reasons for it. Next day, barely half an hour after returning to London, and still not quite recovered, he was at the station to greet King Leopold and his sons, who were coming for a short holiday (Leopold noticed how enthusiastically they were cheered), and then had to rush off to chair a meeting of the Fine Arts Commission for which he was already late. There was a large dinner in honour of the Belgian king that night, but even so Albert refused to cancel Alice's lesson or allow her prep. to go unmarked. (He could never make the Queen understand that teaching was for him a form of relaxation which restored his good humour after a tiring day – she would only believe that this was just an argument put forward to stop her from worrying.) He was courteous and attentive to everyone at the concert following dinner, but she wrote in her Journal that he looked 'fagged and pale'.

Towards the end of the 'fifties Albert's preoccupation with work was becoming a major bone of contention between husband and wife. If she had been less demanding, he might have dropped his stubborness, relaxed more and spent more time in her company, but as

336

things were he was away so much that in the summer of 1858 it took him two months to finish reading *Jane Eyre* to her. Never very good at communicating his feelings to anyone (only after many months of daily contact did Charles Eastlake appreciate 'the true niceness and charm of Prince Albert's nature'), he was now often so busy that he did not have time to let even his wife know how he felt. Yet his whole life was dedicated to her service. He made the mistake of thinking that because she knew this, and because she was sure of his eternal devotion, she could not possibly be jealous or angry that so much of his work took him away from her; he believed, too, that it was unfair of her to turn and rend him for spending too much time talking science with Faraday or politics with ministers. None of this was new, of course – it had tended to come between them ever since Albert began to acquire power and influence – but it all took a turn for the worse in the last few years of his life.

Marlborough House was to become the London home of the prince of Wales, and his parents hoped that he would be living there by the autumn of 1859. It meant a great deal of reorganisation to turn the place from a picture-gallery and museum (which it had been for years) into a private house, since one of the greatest problems was to find another building of the right size and shape to rehouse the exhibits and display them to the best advantage. The solution was to build additional galleries at South Kensington, and this work renewed Albert's partnership with Henry Cole, who told him that there was a feeling at home and abroad that there should be a second Great Exhibition, and that he had only to say the word to set the wheels in motion. Albert's feelings were ambivalent: Was it wise to try to repeat a success? The old magic could never be recaptured, and his was an essentially progressive nature. Besides, his position was very different from what it had been in 1851: then, he could be spared, but now he could not. On the other hand, the educational value of an exhibition would be as great as ever, and so would the encouragement to industry and invention. In the end and under pressure from Cole, he allowed a second exhibition to be planned for 1862, but on a smaller scale; perhaps, suitably revised, it might become an annual event. But on one thing he did insist: this time he must remain more or less in the background, as 'adviser'.

Indeed, Albert saw himself in this capacity more and more. Was he not already adviser to the Queen, to Vicky and Fritz, to the Prince Regent of Prussia, the Coburg family, Don Pedro of Portugal, the king of Saxony and even King Leopold, who had lately written for guidance about the education of the count of Flanders. He was in demand outside royal circles as well; Cambridge dons and prominent international figures in the world of art and of books all clamoured for his opinion on their problems, and he gave them as much attention as he could spare. It sometimes made him feel sad that everyone had confidence in him except his own eldest son, that everyone looked to him for advice except the prince of Wales. Vicky listened to him in everything, and so did his other children, but the heir to the throne resisted all his father's efforts to prepare him for it, and gave him a profound feeling of failure. This would not have mattered so much if there had been 'compensations' like great ability or a personality as strong and vigorous in Bertie as in little Leopold, whose intelligence and adventurous nature enabled him to overcome his crippling handicaps. It was impossible, too, not to be aware of the talk that went on behind their backs about the hereditary antipathy between a reigning sovereign and the heir to the throne. No one except Albert understood how hard it was for the Queen to face the certainty that she would be succeeded by a son who might destroy all that his parents had laboured and hoped for together.

Derby's government was in difficulties during the early months of 1859, and gave long notice that it would soon fall. Defeated on a reform bill in the spring, it won a reprieve by means of a general election, but was outvoted almost as soon as it met the new House of Commons and resigned on 11 June. Palmerston was the likely head of a Liberal administration, but although he had behaved faultlessly towards them when Prime Minister between 1855 and 1858, the Queen and Albert had already determined to do their best to cheat him out of a second term of office. Against his better judgement, Albert gave way to the Queen's wish to send for Granville instead, and his action was as foolish as it was naïve; yet it cannot have been wholly abhorrent to him, since he was now quite strong enough to overrule her if he wished – perhaps the temptation to have at the head of the Queen's government a man who would bow to his every wish was too great to resist. But Granville could not form a Cabinet, and declined the Premiership, which left the Queen with a choice between Russell and Palmerston. When they were ruthlessly cross-questioned, the choice resolved itself: Lord John was willing but full of conditions, Palmerston behaved most sensibly. So Palmerston it was.

The first six months of 1859, during which the Derby government was tottering to its fall, were also months of mounting tension abroad, and Albert was throughout anxious to have a stable government in office as soon as possible in order to devote his whole attention to European affairs. The secret agreement between Napoleon III and Cavour at Plombières in June 1858 had already made it certain that there would soon be a war to liberate Italy from the Austrian yoke, but it was Napoleon's New Year remarks to the Austrian ambassador about the bad relations between the two countries and Victor Emmanuel's speech about Italy's 'cry of pain' ten days later which told Europe that war would come soon.

Albert's first thoughts were for Vicky, who was just about to have her first child, the future Kaiser William II. She would be in danger if Prussia became involved in a European war on the side of Austria against the Franco-Piedmontese alliance. At first he tried to play down the danger, reassuring her that Napoleon was only a 'paper ogre' at whose court 'they play, make love, enjoy themselves and dream', but when her letters showed her becoming increasingly distracted at the prospect of Fritz having to go to war he dropped the pretence and admitted that war was indeed likely. Anxiety about their daughter made Victoria and Albert work each other up into a state of panic as the situation worsened during the spring, and they could not understand why public opinion in England was so unperturbed, so convinced, as one newspaper put it, that 'the French emperor is not fixing his eyes on us'. After all the references, at the time of Vicky's marriage only a short year earlier, to 'England's child', whose fortunes would be felt by everyone as if she were their own, it was disappointing to find now that the rapport with the people of which Queen Victoria liked to boast was fast disappearing; and for the English to overlook the danger to Prussia seemed to Albert 'cold, unfeeling and hard', as he wrote unjustly to Ernest in a letter in which anxiety overcame commonsense. Indeed, Albert was in these months only able to see things from one angle – how they might affect Vicky – and he lacked his usual good judgement in foreign affairs throughout the war of 1859, even after Prussia declared her neutrality in March.

In spite of Prussian neutrality, however, Albert was still concerned when war began in April, but the rapidity of the French and Piedmontese victories over the Austrian armies in June soon relieved him of anxiety: 'Thank God Vicky is safe'. He shed no tears at Austria's defeat, for he had long since abandoned her in favour of Prussia as the chosen leader of the movement towards German unity – 'The boasting of the Austrians and the miserable impotence of their enormous army has only brought contempt upon the Austrian power . . . they are of no use for anything except to create trouble for the whole of Europe.'

French military activity in the summer of 1859 made Parliament and people see that the Cherbourg arsenal was no pretty toy but sheltered a fleet which could be used to invade England, and in response to public clamour the new government hurried through an Act of Parliament setting up a Volunteer Defence Force. This was in fact an old idea of Albert's – he had suggested it during the Crimean War – and it brought Palmerston back into royal favour. Men flocked to the recruiting offices until there were more than could be coped with, but there were difficulties. Gladstone, as Chancellor of the Exchequer, felt bound to preach economy, taking the line that money spent in peace-time on preparation for war was money thrown away; but Albert felt that he was being consistent with the Chancellor's principle of economy when he advocated taxation at war-time rates to pay for defence. In the end Gladstone was forced to unlock his money-box, although he only brought the pennies out very slowly, one by one, to equip the volunteers. Public imagination was 'captured by the sight of lawyer, statesman, shopkeeper, teacher and labourer all drilling together in perfect harmony, marching in step as never before in England's first truly democratic army.' The Queen was wholeheartedly behind the movement: 'Fritz would have been surprised to see 18,000 volunteers marching at Aldershot like the finest troops,' she wrote proudly to Vicky, 'many of the best-educated people, peers, gentry, artists* in the ranks.' Albert agreed about their appearance but thought them 'rather awkward from a military point of view' though still different from the peasant recruit or the militiaman. On the other hand, it was a change for him to praise the fairness of the descriptions in the Press 'which in some papers could be called glowing', and to see – even if a little late – that there was a positive value in publicity: and it was almost unprecedented for journalists to be invited to a royal reception, as they were to Osborne during the spring of 1860 when the Queen and Albert entertained the Volunteers. In Hyde Park on 23 June 1860 there was a splendid review of the Volunteers, parading for the first time their new badge, with the motto 'Defence not Defiance' which Albert had given them. The Queen vied with *The Times* in exclaiming over the spectacle ('the appearance, drilling, marching superb . . . no one could anticipate such perfection in so short a time'), and in a speech at Trinity House that night Albert drove home the truth that 'the more educated the men, the quicker they

* Her inclusion of artists among the 'best-educated people' reflects the success of Albert's effort to raise their status.

learn'. Two days later a rifle competition was held on Wimbledon Common. The Queen, in a smart military outfit of navy blue, opened the proceedings by firing the first shots, 'the best spirit prevails among them', she told Vicky in a letter sprinkled with military expressions. Who was playing at soldiers now?

The autumn holiday at Balmoral in 1859 was marked by two things – their first all-night journey by sleeping-car from London to Edinburgh, and the first signs of what proved to be Albert's final illness. The saving of time through night travel, as well as a new demonstration of the enormous advances in railway technology over the last twenty years, appealed greatly to Albert and justified to him the expense of constructing the sleeping-car. He found the swift transition from the heat of Osborne to the chill of the Highlands astonishing, but the mountain air quickly restored him to health after the stomach disorder from which he had suffered in August; he called it 'cholerina' and it may really have been some form of gastro-enteritis. For several days he could swallow nothing but a little milk and water, and once he fainted away while trying to dress. His valet Lohlein was alarmed, but Albert forbade him to tell the Queen, insisting that he was only suffering from 'weakness'; however, he lay white and panting for several hours, unable to move or eat. A fit of acute depression followed, from which he had not fully recovered when they set out for Scotland. Soon feeling fit again at Balmoral, he enjoyed acting as President at the meeting of the British Association for the Advancement of Science in Aberdeen in mid-September and gave a successful presidential address on the theme of the difference between the English and the German schools of scientific thought. The preparation of this address had caused him much trouble: 'I read thick volumes, write, perspire and tear what I have written into shreds,' he told Vicky in mock despair a month before he delivered it, nerves getting the better of him at the prospect of speaking in front of 2,500 leading scientists; he was determined to maintain the high standard he had always set himself and dreaded failure when there was little chance of it. Of course the address went down well, and so did the visit of the British Association to Balmoral. 'They tumbled out of four wagonnettes like trippers eager to enjoy their first sight of Highland games. I had to restrain them,' Albert wrote, 'out of respect for their grey hairs, and to persuade them that they were not expected to take part.' After the meeting he relaxed in the hills, stalking deer with Grant his head ghillie, but he had little luck this year – his gamebook only recorded three stags, and only one was of any size. On the way south he opened the new Glasgow waterworks at Loch Katrine and toured a slate-quarry, but it rained all day and he was soaked to the skin. The consequence was a recurrence of gastric trouble, a sinister feature of which was 'violent cramp at the pit of the stomach, which lasted very sharply for two hours at noon, several days running' during the second half of October. As soon as he heard about it, Stockmar wrote in great alarm. He was troubled on two grounds – lack of proper nursing since Kurt's death, and the repetition of similar attacks: 'All round you there is a want of thoughtful care for the repose, the tending and the nursing which are so necessary for the sick and convalescent. I feel this more seriously now than ever, because the recent attack seems to have been more violent than its predecessors.' It was a severe indictment of conditions in the royal household, but it was unhappily prophetic; lack of proper attention was to prove disastrous in two years' time when he was again struck down by the same sort of trouble.

Vicky came home on a flying visit in May 1860. Her education had not ceased when she became a mother; if anything, Albert stepped up the pace, and the essays on constitutional law which she sent back from Berlin for comment became longer and more erudite. She had a genuine flair for politics, and her father once jestingly remarked that he could do with her as his foreign minister. Now that she was a married woman, her parents talked quite openly in front of her, and she was allowed to say anything she liked. Making use of this freedom, she began to try to soften their attitude towards her brother, pointing out that Bertie's faults did not seem so bad when compared with those of Prussian princes and that, since he did not like reading, other talents might be developed in him which would be useful when he became king. But Albert was not impressed by even a favourable comparison with 'some of the most profligate young men in Europe' and scolded her for suggesting it.

She was more successful in opening her father's eyes to the disturbing state of the 'Black Horse Inn' and the iniquities of the 'innkeeper' – this was the way he now always sarcastically referred to the Prussian regent and his court. With a shock, he had just learned from Vicky that Princess Augusta had become a confirmed Francophile, and so it was small comfort to receive, while Vicky was still in England, a memorandum from the Regent which revealed a vacillating and uncertain attitude towards France. Albert described this memorandum as 'muddled, contradictory and dangerous for the future', and could not help being relieved to think that William was ageing fast and that there might soon be a younger and more far-sighted ruler upon the Prussian throne. He was glad of the chance of letting off steam to Vicky about Napoleon III as well, and in their conversations wondered whether his change of heart after the battle of Solferino (the slaughter made him suddenly seek for peace, thus letting the Italians down) did not suggest that Napoleon's luck might be running out at last.

On Vicky's marriage, the fifteen-year-old Alice had taken her place as the daughter of the house and as her father's pupil, but her calmer nature meant that Albert's concentration on her caused the Queen none of those pangs of jealousy from which she had suffered over Vicky. Both Victoria and Albert were now suddenly against early marriage, but the Queen changed her mind again as soon as Alice was confirmed in 1859 and began to wonder whether the girl might not be too plain to catch a husband. Albert implored her in vain not to write here, there and everywhere in search of one, but his calm confidence infuriated her, and they exchanged sharp words. Suitors came and went; Alice lost her heart when Louis of Hesse (whom the Queen had privately earmarked for her years ago) arrived in the summer of 1860, but Louis' slowness in coming to the point sent the Queen into a frenzy and made her accuse Albert of 'not caring what happens to our children' when he remained unperturbed. He could never realise that behind her indecent haste to marry her daughters off lay memories of the insecurity which had afflicted her before he came on the scene. Albert's reaction was decisive; he sent Louis away, telling him to return in three months if he wished, for he saw how undignified it was for Alice to wait on his pleasure. Louis returned in the autumn, proposed and was accepted. It is difficult to understand how a girl as charming and intelligent as Alice could be so taken with a red-faced bucolic young man who was in no way good enough for her, but she accepted him at her parents' valuation (Albert could see no fault at all in Louis once he had declared himself). A bolder request for a parliamentary grant than had been made for Vicky was accompanied by reminders that the Queen had never asked the country for a penny for herself in the twenty-four years of her reign and that, while during that time eight members of the royal family had died and nine been born, the yearly allowance from Parliament had diminished by £189,000. It was also suggested that provision should now be made in advance for all the Queen's children.

Another of their children was turning out even more satisfactorily. Alfred wrote cheerful letters from on board the ship on which he was serving in the Atlantic and Mediterranean during 1858 and 1859, and passed his midshipman's examination on the voyage home in

February 1860. The Queen's wish for his return to be greeted at Portsmouth by a royal salute gave rise to a piece of naval ingenuity. So great an honour could plainly not be paid to one so young, so the admiral neatly extricated himself from the necessity of disobeying a royal command by suggesting that Albert (who did not know of the Queen's order) should join the ship and accompany his son. His presence justified the salute. Alfred was posted to the School of Navigation at Alverbank in the Isle of Wight, where he passed all his examinations with such high marks that his father, when shown his papers, had no fault to find. Intelligent without being intellectual, Alfred was never idle ('the contrast with *someone else* is very sad', the Queen told Vicky) and gladly joined in the evening lessons along with Alice whenever he was at Osborne. The favourable comparison with the prince of Wales came out again at Alfred's confirmation in April, if in a somewhat back-handed way. He was more nervous than his brother had been, and mumbled the responses, but Albert did not scold him, as he would have done his elder brother. By way of contrast, Bertie's appearance at the service irritated his mother beyond endurance. She thought his clothes 'quite frightful' (they were in the latest fashion) and that his mouth and nose 'looked enormous' – the big Hanoverian nose was a great handicap, in her opinion. The criticisms were justified, but neither of his parents made proper allowance for Bertie's natural teenage desire to assert his independence.

Welcome as was Alfred's success in the navy, it complicated the question of his eventual inheritance of Coburg and Gotha. An even greater complication was Ernest's mismanagement, which Albert now set about remedying – so far as he could at long range – in order that his son should inherit a well-governed state unencumbered by debt. For many years he had been urging Ernest to put his house in order (particularly by improving the prosperity of the family estates from which they both derived income), though with little effect, but he redoubled his efforts after Alfred's confirmation. He was particularly anxious that Ernest should unite the governments of Coburg and Gotha in order to increase the likelihood that they could maintain a degree of independence when the unification of Germany eventually came about; Stockmar had been warning him for twenty years that the small states would have to lose their individuality in a united Germany, but Albert, with his intense local patriotism, seems never to have accepted this wise advice. Among other things, he urged on Ernest the desirability of allowing a free Press, to encourage the growth of mutual trust between ruler and people, of introducing trial by jury and of choosing his officials wisely, for the time had come to move from personal to constitutional government and this could only be done with the help of trustworthy ministers. Above all, he pressed Ernest to husband the state's resources, for he had noticed that Alfred, like his uncle, was inclined to be casual about money and would be unlikely to initiate a programme of economy when he became duke. The letters exchanged between them show that Ernest began to listen to his brother's advice during the last two years of Albert's life, and to modernise the states of Coburg and Gotha in the directions Albert had indicated.

23

'Like the hawk, I must not sleep, but be for ever on the watch'

A PLAN to visit Coburg in September was almost frustrated by another attack of stomach cramps, this time accompanied by shivering and aching limbs. Sir James Clark diagnosed exhaustion from overwork and too much sea-bathing, but said there was no cause for alarm. Although by that time he had barely recovered, Albert insisted that they should start on the date arranged, 23 September; the sight of his old home would do him good, he said. King Leopold met the royal party at Antwerp with news that the king of Prussia was failing and could not live much longer, and that the Regent was in scarcely better shape – a hint that 'our Prussian children' might be on the throne sooner than either Vicky or her father had expected. At Aachen, where the train stopped to pick up the Prince Regent, Albert saw that Leopold had not exaggerated and that William was indeed ageing fast: his complexion was yellow, he coughed continuously, and he seemed breathless. It was lucky that Albert could not read Prince William's thoughts, for they matched his own; William was struck by the deterioration in Albert's appearance, thought he looked suddenly twenty years older, was pale, stooping and overweight, and far less talkative than of old.

News had been brought to Albert in the train of the death of his stepmother, the dowager duchess Marie; it was therefore in no very cheerful mood that they reached Coburg, to be greeted by Vicky and the others in full mourning. Even baby Willie's white dress was decorated with black bows, but the first sight of his grandson raised Albert's spirits a little, and he was struck by the child's good looks and by his likeness to Ernest; 'surely he is meant for great things'.

346

It was a relief, too, to see Vicky looking so well after the birth of her second child Charlotte the previous July, for Albert had had an uncontrollable fear that she would die in childbirth this time.

Stockmar seemed hardly changed when they saw him next day, but the old man himself was shocked at Albert's wan looks, for which he was quite unprepared by the sketchy and almost casual accounts of his various attacks of illness which Albert had given him. That afternoon they all drove in two carriages to the Rosenau, Albert in the second with Vicky. As they approached the house, Albert stopped the carriage so that they could walk the rest of the way by a short cut he had used as a boy. They had not gone far when, to Vicky's consternation, he suddenly turned pale, stumbled and murmured in a low voice that he did not feel strong enough to revive childhood memories, and made as if to turn back. By a great effort he composed himself enough to struggle on with her holding his arm tightly, and before long was able to begin pointing out to her the features of his beloved Rosenau, a pleasure he had promised himself since the day she was born – the hall where the Christmas tree always stood, the steps down to the yellow drawing-room with its star-spangled ceiling, where he had been christened, the huge semi-circular alcove on the landing where he used to sit and read for hours. But revisiting old haunts was tinged with melancholy. Only that morning the startling realisation had struck him like a blow: nobody knew him now. Even as they were walking up, not half an hour before, they had passed a group of peasants, natives of the place, who had greeted him politely but as a stranger. It was the same in Coburg itself, no one recognised him unless he was with the queen of England, not even the custodian of the family mausoleum in the Hofgarten. He began to feel an alien, a man whose roots were not here, and a sense of desolation seized him.

Another day, on an expedition to Schloss Kallenberg to try out some new guns of Ernest's, his spirits rose again for a moment when he found that he was quite a match for Fritz, who prided himself on his marksmanship. A few hours later, he was called back to Coburg on business. As a young man, he had always driven himself about the countryside alone, and it seemed natural to do so again now, even though the only carriage available was a four-in-hand, a difficult vehicle to manage, which he would have to drive from the box like a coachman. As the horses were being harnessed up, he remarked jokingly to his old tutor Florschütz that he hoped that he would get back in one piece. He had only gone three miles, and was nearing a level-crossing, when the horses took fright at the sound of a train's whistle and bolted. Fortunately Albert was able to jump clear, but only seconds before the carriage overturned as the crazed horses dragged it headlong into the train of trucks. Although scratched and badly shaken, Albert was not really hurt, and when the Queen and Vicky hurried in to see him he was lying on his valet's bed with lint compresses on his face, fussed over by Stockmar. He made light of what had happened, but Vicky knew of the unreasonable dread of carriage accidents which he had never been able to conquer since suffering nightmares after the duke of Orleans and the king of Saxony had been killed in this way within a year of each other. The Queen had become used to hearing Albert complain that he was accident-prone, and it was Stockmar's opinion that the reason his accidents turned out worse than other people's was because he lost his nerve at critical moments. Both men were wrong, but in differing measure; Albert had indeed had several serious accidents,* but although full of courage at the time his highly-charged imagination dwelt on the danger afterwards until he became tense and strained. Stockmar completely misjudged the way his nerves affected Albert. At dinner that night Albert seemed better, but talked incessantly in the febrile way of a man whose nervous system had undergone a severe shock. Watching him, Stockmar reflected that if anything more serious should ever happen to him, he might succumb at once without a struggle. His medical training should have made him suspect instead that Albert's unnatural excitability might be the outward symptom of something deeper which the accident had brought to the surface. He did not know, however, of Albert's sinister confession to Vicky that as the horses bolted the thought flashed through his mind that his last moment had come, and that he found himself positively welcoming it.

On the last day of all, Ernest and Albert went for a walk alone. It was a kind of farewell to all the scenes to which both were so passionately attached. Suddenly Albert stopped and covered his face with his hands. At first Ernest thought something had got into his brother's eye; then, looking closer, he saw that Albert was weeping: a premonition that he would never see Coburg again had just come over him.

Albert and Victoria returned to England only a week before the historic meeting of Victor Emmanuel and Garibaldi on the banks of the Volturno and the consummation of fifteen months of drama in the foundation of the Kingdom of Italy as Garibaldi handed over the Naples he had freed to the king whom Cavour had made great. The

* For some of which he cannot be blamed in any way: cf. pp. 94–5.

annexation of the central Italian principalities, the cession of Savoy and Nice to France as the price of Napoleon III's help, and the expedition of Garibaldi and the Thousand which liberated Sicily – all these had filled Albert with mixed feelings during the spring and summer of 1860. While naturally pleased to observe the liberation of Italy from oppression and the spread of constitutional monarchy to almost the whole peninsula, he disapproved of the methods by which Cavour had achieved these things and was bound to deplore both the scant regard which he paid to international treaties and the summary removal of ruling princes against their will. His chief reaction to events in Italy seems, however, to have been a mixture of envy and regret that Piedmont-Sardinia was managing to unite Italy while Prussia still passively acquiesced in the ancient dismemberment of Germany. Insuperable obstacles stood in the Prussian monarchy's way at this moment – the illness of both the king and the regent before the former died and William succeeded in January 1861 alone prevented any activity, but still more serious was the obstinate refusal of Prince William to espouse the cause of unity or to make progress along the road to constitutionalism, a refusal which had lately forced itself upon Albert's consciousness. Thus it was not so much what Italy was securing, but what Germany was being denied, which most prominently held his attention.

Palmerston's frequent changes of attitude during the tense months which saw the making of the Italian kingdom irritated Albert so much that they almost led to a renewal of their old hostility. But Palmerston was becoming more anti-French as Napoleon III's actions threatened both English security and European peace, and from the winter of 1859–60, with the cession of Savoy and Nice, he was committed to a programme of rearmament similar to that which Albert had been advocating. It was a notable event when the two men were in firm alliance over the Fortifications Bill in July 1860, and Albert helped to ensure the passage of the measure through the House of Commons by letting it be known that the Prime Minister had his full support.

Rearmament was not proceeding nearly fast enough to allay the profound fears Albert harboured about French intentions, however, particularly as far as the navy was concerned, and the question preyed on his mind in the weeks after their return from Coburg. By the middle of November he was writing to Stockmar 'England's life-blood lies in the sea, yet how much longer will she be able to look on the ocean as her own? The complacency displayed by ministers never ceases to amaze as much as to irritate me. . . . They refuse to believe that there is a mighty fleet equipped with every modern invention that can make short work of a few miles of water at anchor in French ports'. The extent of the threat presented by the French navy was underlined a few days later by a letter from King Leopold, which dwelt upon the enormous number of ironclad steamships of the same class as the mighty *Gloire* which the French were building – each among the largest men-of-war afloat, mounting thirty-two guns and capable of firing broadsides which could 'smash the British navy to atoms '– in order to fulfil their boast of possessing a navy twice as strong as Britain's. Since he received no reply, beyond a formal acknowledgement, to his many requests for information, Albert eventually wrote a heated letter to Lord John Russell on 8 December: 'It is a perfect disgrace to our country, and particularly to our Admiralty, that we can do no more than hobble after the French, turning up our noses proudly at their experiments and improvements, and, when they are established as sound, getting horribly frightened and trying by wasting money to catch up lost time, and all the while running serious risk of our security.' The reply showed that at last something was being done to make good France's twelve-months' start in the race to build a new generation of battleships, and Albert pressed home his advantage by pointing out that mere numerical equality with France was not enough, since Britain had to defend Gibraltar and Malta against attack from the sea as well as being prepared to resist any fleet France could concentrate in the Channel.

At the end of November the Empress Eugénie arrived in England unexpectedly, on her way to the Highlands (which Albert had recommended to her) to recover from a period of ill-health. She was invited to Windsor, and there on 4 December Albert was delighted to learn that she did not agree with her husband's schemes for the aggrandisement of France – 'The best way to govern the French is to keep on surprising them,' she said, excusing his behaviour. Next day Albert himself went down with another attack of nausea and shivering, which compelled him to take to his bed with internal pains so violent that for a moment he thought his end was near. 'I was too miserable yesterday to be able to hold my pen,' he told Vicky when he was beginning to recover forty-eight hours later. He was not quite himself again until just before Christmas, a holiday of unclouded happiness spent as usual at Windsor. The weather was cold enough for skating, and Albert pushed the Queen in her ice-chair as swiftly and skilfully as he had ever done and helped the younger children build a snowman. Once again there were happy evenings alone together, with music or with reading from George Eliot's *Mill on the Floss*, Wilkie Collins's *Woman in White* and Charles Kingsley's *Hypatia*. Albert engaged a theatrical company to entertain his guests, and laughed uproariously at a performance of *My Wife's Mother* in St George's Hall. Nothing marred the Christmas happiness save Vicky's absence; the Queen felt that everything was just as it had been in the early days of their marriage, but Albert's cheerful mood had dissolved by the time he added, as a postscript to his greetings to Ernest for the New Year, 'though I don't expect much good of it.' The spell was finally broken when they went to Osborne for a week's sea air in January and Albert was lured away to inspect the construction of the new coastal defences at Portsmouth and Gosport.

Prussian affairs were becoming an increasing source of anxiety. The death of King Frederick William IV on 2 January 1861 placed his brother William on the throne, but William's first actions confirmed that he was nothing like the man Albert had once supposed him to be. He was ready to accept Frederick William's instruction not to take the oath to uphold the constitution and acted as if the Divine Right of Kings was reality not myth; he proposed to incorporate an act of homage in the coronation service once more and issued a manifesto in menacingly harsh terms. Albert was alarmed and disgusted, for a few years of this sort of thing would make the succession very difficult for Vicky and Fritz by endangering the throne and placing obstacles in the way of the liberal programme they wanted to institute. In order to forestall this as far as possible, and in the misguided belief that his action would help Vicky and Fritz, Albert now began to bombard the new king with advice in a series of long and detailed letters instructing him how to behave in foreign and domestic affairs. This interference was made worse by the form in which it was conveyed. Albert knew that William was not very clever, but he went too far in oversimplifying what he wrote, almost giving William the impression that he was being treated like a child who needed guidance in everything. This only made William more obstinate; tact, a delicate touch and a great deal of cunning were called for if any result was to be achieved and if the door of Prussia was not to be slammed in his face for William's lifetime. A deep anxiety about the future well-being of Vicky and her husband was the primary cause of this uncharacteristic behaviour on Albert's part, but the ill-health from which he was now almost continually suffering sharpened his imagination, darkened its colours and took away his sureness of touch. So he hectored William instead of giving him hints gentle enough to make him think that

351

KING WITHOUT A CROWN

the ideas were his own, and achieved nothing. William threw most of his letters straight into the fire, but when he did answer – as in the case of a long lecture on European affairs which accompanied the Garter in February 1861 – he did so at fulsome length but without one word that was relevant. William could be cunning as well as obstinate, and with these tactics he soon had the upper hand. Albert's methods were clumsy and ill-chosen, particularly in view of the extreme importance to him personally of the end he was trying to attain. But during a short visit she paid to Osborne in July 1861, Vicky had given him a hair-raising account of how things stood in Berlin, and he now saw more clearly that William was determined to follow the road to autocracy, and trembled for his daughter and for Germany. He was even prepared to regard an attempt to assassinate William as 'a bad deed, but in a good cause' because the student who made it claimed that his object was to put Fritz on the throne and so further the prospect of German unity; and one of the last letters he wrote about Prussian affairs was grimly prophetic: 'Pray Heaven not to make us a present of Herr von Bismarck to end the ministerial crisis.'

During the winter and spring of 1860–61 Albert's health took another turn for the worse. For some time past his hair had first grown thinner and then begun to fall out, and although he now ate less and less, his weight continually increased, with the result that he became more easily tired and took longer and longer to go through the Queen's boxes making corrections and comments upon despatches. For the first time he began to feel a distaste for work. Since the amount he undertook had grown steadily year by year, he was now in real danger of falling behind, which meant that he had little time to relax, so that reading and the piano became things of the past; only his letters to Vicky were never neglected, for this tie with his child must be maintained at all costs. Worst of all, the pressure of routine business was becoming so great that in his weaker state he found no time to think and to reflect; a danger arose that his vision would be foreshortened and his judgement impaired.

Physical symptoms of ill health multiplied, although he seldom paid proper attention to them. In the New Year he often complained of feeling bloated and sick, frequently suffered from dizzy spells and sometimes ran a temperature. These attacks of sickness, accompanied by great pain, had begun to be serious two years earlier, when 'spasms' and 'shivering' are mentioned for the first time.*

* See pp. 314–5, 341–2 above.

Reassured by Sir James Clark, the Queen did not take these warning signs seriously enough, for Clark pointed out that they often occurred directly after something had happened to depress him – a bad report on Bertie, a disquieting letter from Vicky about Prussian affairs, a storm while Affie was at sea – and put them all down to 'nerves'. No doubt the attacks did have a nervous background, but their violence stemmed from a deeper cause: this might have been looked into had not Dr Baly, the extremely skilful young doctor who was being groomed to replace the incompetent Clark, been killed in a railway accident in January 1861. Although the spring was a mild one, Albert never felt really warm, and irritably blamed the Queen for open windows and damped-down fires; when she resented his scoldings, he retorted sharply that her phobia about overheated rooms prevented her from considering anyone's feelings but her own. His always poor circulation was giving him more trouble than ever, and his habit of rubbing his hands together to work some warmth into them became correspondingly more marked. Rheumatism in the right shoulder plagued him too, and the pain kept him awake at night. The Queen tartly reminded him that he had complained about his shoulder for twenty years,* but she forgot that this did not make present pain any easier to bear.

One night when they were touring the Midlands early in 1861 and had a heavy programme of engagements, the Queen was awakened by groans. Albert had been sick and was lying across the bed doubled up in agony, sweat pouring down his face. Terrified, she wanted to call for help, but Albert stopped her, saying that it would pass. By dawn he was a little better, and with the Queen's help was able to crawl back into bed, where he dozed until morning. He carried out the next day's engagements just as planned, and only Victoria could guess how weak and ill he felt. Consulted as soon as they got back to London, Clark told the Queen exactly what she wanted to hear – that the Prince needed rest and must reduce his commitments or risk a nervous breakdown; Albert, however, laughed at his doctor's advice and his wife's fears, insisting that rest only bored him and made him feel more tired than ever. 'It is all the fault of my weak stomach,' he wrote to Stockmar, who had responded to an urgent appeal of the Queen's to beg him to take more care of himself.

About the same time an old torment returned – toothache. Although his teeth were excellent, he had had trouble with his

---

* Ever since being thrown against a tree by the vicious horse Tom Bowlby in 1840; there is no mention of pain in the shoulder before this accident. A bone may have been broken or displaced, the damage going undetected.

gums since he was a young man. An abscess had kept him in bed for several days during his Italian tour in 1839, and for years afterwards he complained intermittently of dental pain, although nothing wrong could be discovered. By 1860 the pattern had changed and the discomfort could no longer be disregarded; occasional engagements had to be cancelled, something which he would never have allowed to happen before. This latest attack was the worst for many years. On the night of 14 February he did not sleep a wink, but this time he obstinately insisted on keeping his promise to preside at a meeting of the Fine Arts Commission next day. There was a special reason for this; funds were short, the success of the 1862 Exhibition was in jeopardy, there was a risk that money already spent would be wasted if more were not provided, and Albert felt that no one but himself could persuade the government to loosen its purse-strings. At the meeting he sat in a draught and woke up next day with his cheek red and swollen and the nerves in his teeth throbbing painfully: 'My sufferings are frightful,' he wrote in his diary. The royal dentist, Mr Saunders, lanced an abscess but without bringing immediate relief, and it was not for nearly another week that Albert was well enough to go out again. The worried Queen called Saunders in for a second consultation. Saunders had not observed Sir James Clark in action for nothing, and reassured the Queen with airy words so successfully that she began to feel Albert was making a fuss about nothing and dismissed the matter from her mind. Albert, however, was not taken in; from his puzzled expression he deduced that Saunders did not know the cause of the trouble and began to wonder whether there was something seriously amiss.

For nearly two years he had been keeping to himself the secret that in Sir James Clark's opinion a tumour on the duchess of Kent's arm was cancer, and would prove fatal. He could not help wondering now whether the abscess on his gum had a similar origin. But with mistaken kindness and because he could not bring himself to tell Victoria that her mother was dying, he passed the duchess's tumour off as erysipelas and allowed Victoria to go on living in a fool's paradise – which was not difficult after the duchess's lively manner at a garden-party to celebrate her seventy-fourth birthday in August 1860. The household had helped him to keep up the pretence, as if the Queen were not mature enough to cope with the realities of life, a piece of unfairness for which Albert was to pay heavily later on. With his mind thus burdened by a new fear, and with a cough to add to the remains of toothache, Albert set off with the Queen for a rest at Osborne on 26 February, in accordance with Mr Saunders's advice. They had scarcely settled in when news came of the sudden death of Sir George Couper, the duchess of Kent's Comptroller, who had 'gone out like a light'. This immediately reminded him of his new worry and, still plagued by the cough which kept him awake at night, Albert found for the first time that Osborne no longer cheered and relaxed him and failed to get his usual pleasure from discussions with the farm manager. In desperation, he tried a little manual labour, but only gave himself lumbago when he helped to plant out young trees in the nursery. Through all this, he told the Queen nothing of what he was suffering in mind and body, but kept his feelings to himself as usual and made light of everything – for instance blaming the sharp contrast in climate between Windsor and the Isle of Wight for his failure to respond to the change. In view of this, the Queen can hardly be blamed for not noticing how really ill he was a few months later.

Politics pursued him even in his sick state. The French occupation of Syria filled him with grave misgivings for the peace of Europe, but in his unhappy frame of mind it is not surprising that no solution to the problem concluded the memorandum he wrote before they returned to London. Yet Osborne had done him some good, for he had more energy and slept better. Their short ten days away had brought a great deterioration in the duchess of Kent's health, however, and it was no longer possible to prevent the Queen from becoming alarmed. A few days later they were called away from inspecting the Royal Horticultural Society's new gardens in South Kensington by the news that her condition was desperate, and Albert at last had to break the truth to the Queen. They hurried at once to Frogmore, where the duchess died next morning, her hand in her daughter's.

It was of course partly because she had been given so little time to become used to the idea that her mother was critically ill that the Queen now completely collapsed in a nervous breakdown that soon became the talk of Europe. In a curious way, Albert looked upon her excessive grief as right and natural, and did nothing to stem it; indeed, he fed it with his tenderness and love. On the other hand, it is difficult not to blame the Queen for self-indulgence on a most extravagant scale which added to the burdens of a sick and overworked husband. Yet she did not collapse without reason: deep remorse for her behaviour towards her mother during Lehzen's reign must have played a part, and in some obscure way her violent expressions of grief atoned for what she had said and done then. Her guilt-feelings had not been assuaged by time, as Albert had hoped, and this may account for what would otherwise seem extraordinary behaviour. The demands this made on his time and patience stretched Albert to the limit, but the devotion he showed in trying circumstances must surely destroy for ever the last vestiges of the absurd legend that he had never loved the Queen, for nothing but love could have given him the energy to cope with her violent bouts of weeping, granted the precarious state of his own health. Yet paradoxically it was very likely unconscious worry about this very thing which made her behave with such abandon, thereby actually hastening the decline of the one being she loved best in the world.

Without Sir George Couper to explain things, Albert's task as sole executor for the duchess of Kent was a stupendous one, for he refused to employ professional help to assist him in sorting out his aunt's tangled affairs and regarded it as a sacred trust for himself alone because of the mass of private papers she had left. The duchess had thrown nothing away – she had preserved every letter from the Queen, every curl cut from her head, and there was even a book recording every detail of her childhood; Albert had to work far into the night, cutting vital rest to a minimum, and soon began to look very worn. The news of her mother's breakdown brought Vicky flying post-haste from Berlin, but it was her father's altered appearance that frightened her, and she was appalled both by the amount of work he was doing and by the Queen's total refusal to attend to State business or to take any interest in her brothers' and sisters' welfare. Berlin had for some time been full of gossip about Victoria's 'madness', and Queen Augusta had been at pains to dwell on the 'many peculiarities' she claimed to have often noticed, but Vicky found the truth in some ways even more disquieting. She felt bound to tell her father what she had heard, however much it might distress him and although all he could do was to deny the 'vile rumours' in a letter to Ernest. What she could not tell him, however, was her alarming discovery that her mother positively enjoyed her sorrow and did not wish to be shaken out of it, for her visit was confirming the truth of what the Queen had written earlier: 'I love to dwell on Mama and to be quiet and not roused out of my grief.' Vicky found this destructively self-indulgent, and Princess Hohenlohe scolded her half-sister for it, reminding her of their mother's own stoical behaviour when left among strangers as a destitute widow with a small baby.*

* The duchess of Kent, mother of Princess Hohenlohe and Queen Victoria by her two marriages, had been left destitute and friendless when her second husband, the duke of Kent (Queen Victoria's father) died in 1819. For the source of her unhappiness during the next few years, see p. 88 above.

While Victoria was still in this state, the younger children went down with measles – an extra burden for Albert, particularly as little Leopold was for a time dangerously ill. Bertie came home, and he too thought that his mother was over-dramatising her sorrow, but good-naturedly accompanied her to the mausoleum* at Frogmore in which the duchess of Kent was buried, a visit which seemed to do her good.

The question of Bertie's marriage was becoming pressing. The duchess of Kent had said that it would be his salvation; Albert was too cynical to agree, and wondered whether any girl would take him, since if she possessed all the virtues required in the wife of a future king, together with beauty and the capacity not to be 'knocked under', she was not likely to look twice at an insignificant young man who was not in the least clever, even with the prospect of a crown thrown in. Photographs taken at the time in fact bear out these strictures, for they show Bertie with a small head, receding chin and vacant expression, and one of the Queen's ladies (Eleanor Stanley) said he looked 'comic' when he wore the Garter. So it was no easy task to set about finding a wife for him. 'Unfortunately, princesses do not spring up like mushrooms out of the earth or grow upon trees', Vicky had said. But Albert had come to believe that the country wanted to see Bertie married, and told Vicky that he could almost hear the public saying 'You must marry the Prince of Wales off. Unless you do so, he is lost.'

Vicky was set to look over the few suitable Protestants, but Bertie turned up his nose at them all as too plain until she heard of Alexandra, the sixteen-year-old daughter of King Christian of Denmark, who was said to be both beautiful and intelligent. With a dispute over Schleswig-Holstein still on her hands, Prussia was bound to be unhappy at the prospect of a marriage alliance between Denmark and England, although Vicky made light of his. A more serious obstacle (until Vicky discovered that there was not a grain of truth in it) was the 'very bad reputation' which the Queen of Denmark's family was said to have – the duchess of Kent had been brought up on terrible stories about the goings-on at Hesse-Cassel family gatherings in Schloss Rumpenheim outside Frankfort. Bertie still obstinately refused to be 'rushed' into a meeting with Alexandra much to his parents' surprise when they considered 'how little he has to offer except England', and even when Vicky engineered one

* This was a dual-purpose building designed by Albert. The duchess of Kent had used it as a summer-house for many years, but it was always intended that she should be buried there. This throws some light on the Victorians' uncomplicated view of death.

in the cathedral at Speyer, Albert had to tell his son to show a little enthusiasm unless he wanted to be beaten in the marriage stakes by the son of the Czar of Russia, and unkindly upbraided him for being as cautious as he was himself. 'I don't think he is capable of enthusiasm about anything in the world,' was his sour comment. A year earlier, when Bertie was on the point of visiting Coburg, he had warned Ernest that his eldest son had 'a strange nature, real Brunswick – little interest in things but an incredible interest in people. This characteristic made the old royal family very popular here.' Now even this interest seemed to have gone, for all Bertie would do was ask whether they could 'keep Alexandra for him' while he looked round at other princesses, confidently proclaiming that she would attach importance to getting him and would wait because he was the best match! It would not be fair, Albert thought, to bind Bertie against his will, and he certainly could not be made to fall in love to order, but by June Vicky was convinced that her brother was beginning to be attracted to Alexandra.

24

'Everything
but health'

SUMMER was late that year, with cold and damp weather well into May; Albert several times ran a temperature and complained that he 'could not breathe' more often than for several years.. But he refused to pay any attention to the Queen's plea to cancel the levées and Drawing-Rooms in May and June which he was to hold in her place, saying that to do so would cause disappointment and expense. His temperature rose again after the first levée and was accompanied by 'heaviness of the limbs' and depression, but although very unwell he could not go to bed because next day there was to be an important meeting of the 1862 Exhibition committee, which he particularly wanted to attend. The result was that the 'attack' (as he now called these mysterious indispositions) took longer than usual to clear up; he was beginning to notice, too, that the attacks were becoming steadily more frequent and that each left him a little more spent than the last.

For her birthday, 24 May, which was spent at Osborne, Victoria emerged from the solitude into which she had withdrawn since her mother's death, but would not discard her mourning nor allow the household to do so, and there was a family dinner instead of the usual public celebration. At first Albert had begun to feel a little better in the fresh air of the Isle of Wight, but he ran another temperature on the 27th. Once more he refused to put off the arrangement he had made – to take Bertie and Louis of Hesse to watch the manoeuvres at Aldershot – since he was expected, he said, and must not let people down; the success of Aldershot had become a matter of personal pride with him as it went from strength to strength and became a show-place for foreign visitors. Directly after this, and without warning, he announced that they must go back to London at once, several days earlier than planned, overriding the Queen's objections that they had no official engagements there and that she was not well enough. The explanation may be that he already knew that he was a sick man and that he saw the danger of her self-indulgence in grief and wanted to shake her out of it; for were she to carry on in her present fashion it might be months before she was really fit to transact state business, and if during that time he became seriously ill she would be unable to stand on her own feet. She fought hard to stay at Osborne, and when she knew that she was beaten gave way to an extravagant paroxysm of grief, unburdening herself to Vicky (who had troubles enough of her own) with the words 'Men have not the sympathy and anxiety of women. Oh no!'

Remarks were passed about his dejected appearance when Albert opened the Royal Horticultural Society's new gardens on 5 June surrounded by the whole family except the Queen, and her break-down was the generally accepted explanation. It was a dark showery day, but the gay dresses and magnificent blooms made such a contrast that he became quite cheerful as he walked round inspecting the exhibits and marvelling at the ingenuity of modern science which could produce a blue carnation. Heavy traffic delayed his return, and he had to bolt his dinner in order to be in time to preside at a meeting of the Society of Arts which was to hear a paper about the 1862 Exhibition. He was involved in so many things nowadays that he could not give sufficient time to any of them, yet he could not drop any because he felt that his reputation was at stake and that things would not go right without him. Life had become 'a treadmill' and he was often heard to say only half jokingly that he would have to cut himself in two. Later in June, King Leopold came over to dis-cover for himself just how ill Victoria was. He found her looking well although still in low spirits, but was shocked at the change in Albert, so shocked that he prolonged his stay and wrote a worried letter to Stockmar asking for advice. The reply came by return; it begged Leopold to persuade the Queen to put an end to the morbid and unnecessary court mourning, which was inducing the Coburg melancholy in Albert and undermining his health. When Leopold brought the subject up, however, Albert refused to agree, saying that wearing black suited his mood and that Victoria would in any case certainly not even go into half-mourning before the duchess's birthday on 17 August.

Albert's appearance was not the only shock Leopold received. He noticed with horror something he had never seen before – signs of tension between husband and wife. They had become apparent only lately, when Albert told her that if she did not leave Osborne and go back to London she would be neglecting her duty and adding to his burdens, and when in return she complained to Vicky of his heartlessness. Now she took Leopold aside and criticised Albert sharply for planning to visit Bertie in Cambridge and leaving her alone while she was too unwell to fend for herself. Later, Albert defended his conduct with the plea that it was not a private visit but an obligation, since he was going as Chancellor to inspect the museum of anatomy and attend a lunch in Trinity and a lecture in the Senate House. It did not take Leopold long to realise that neither of them was telling the whole truth, and that the root of the trouble was to be found in the mass of business which made it impossible for Albert to spare a moment for her alone. Every day, after his official engagements were over, there were letters to write or despatches to read and comment on for the guidance of ministers. It was late before he could finish, but only because he was doing the Queen's work for her.

The deaths during the summer of Cavour and Sidney Herbert, in each case largely from overwork, seem to have directed Albert's eyes to the seriousness of his own condition. Although they had only met for half an hour, Albert had been much struck by Cavour's personality and took a morbid interest in the details of his last illness, the way wrong treatment had hastened his end and the extent to which years of strain had weakened his resistance; and he began to wonder whether there was not some similarity between Cavour's case and his own – perhaps they were both the victims of some undiagnosed disease. Sidney Herbert, too, had 'stayed at his post too long for his health', and there were others, like Sir James Graham, who had once been strong and vigorous but was now so 'used up physically and politically that he has nothing left to live for.' All around there seemed to be warning signs, but his illness had eroded his strength too much for him to pay proper heed to them. Hardly a letter to Stockmar at this period but contains the phrase 'I am far from well.'

Vicky, the one person capable of helping him, came to Osborne in July, but to convalesce after influenza, and she was so taken up with her own sufferings that she did not realise how close to disaster her father was. Since the spring he had started to show signs of something like a persecution complex, treating every article in *The Times* which criticised England's foreign policy as if it were an indirect attack upon himself; for instance he insisted on reading an article of 12 April attacking the government's alleged anti-Indian attitude as an implied criticism of his own views, although there was nothing in it to show that the Prince Consort was its target and although it was far milder than many he had dismissed with scorn in the past. In consequence he went about looking wronged and aggrieved. He even upbraided Ernest for supposing that he was behind Austria's determination to hold on to her Venetian province although Ernest had never suggested anything of the kind and was taken aback by the accusation. Finally, the English papers' eulogies of Cavour's services to Italian unity brought painfully to mind how much worse off Germany was by comparison and how she was drifting away from friendship with England.

The complications, real and imaginary, of the Danish marriage preyed on Albert's mind. Prussian designs on Holstein could not be reconciled with the British government's current view that both Schleswig and Holstein should be guaranteed to the Danish Crown by all Europe, but some progress had been made towards the marriage itself. Recently Bertie had paid a flying visit to Coburg, where his uncle had warned him that because of Prussian objections Princess Alexandra was the one girl he must *not* marry, quite forgetting that to a young man forbidden fruits are sweeter. Bertie's ardour was quickened, and he immediately saw her in a new light, the more readily because everyone was telling him that she was very pretty and a great catch. Suddenly he imagined himself in love. Albert had never expected the marriage to be well received in either England or Prussia, but he hoped that tact and delicate handling would overcome all difficulties. Above all, it must not be allowed to seem a triumph for Denmark over Prussia, and the only way to ensure this was to keep it a secret from the British Cabinet; 'only thus can we keep the game in our own hands', he wrote to Ernest in July, 'only thus can we take the political heart out of it.' If it were presented as a love-match, it might be passed off as a non-political union brought about by 'our Prussian children'. 'If we are to found Bertie's future on a happy family life,' he continued, 'we have no other choice.'

It was a tremendous comfort to have Vicky and Fritz, with their two children, at Osborne again in July, but since Albert did not intend to have this precious time with his eldest daughter spoiled, Bertie had to be got out of the way before they arrived. In Albert's present frame of mind, it was irritating to have him clamouring for Vicky's attention and monopolising Fritz, and in any case he did not want to parade his failure with Bertie in front of Fritz and Louis of Hesse, lest it dimmed his authority with them. It pained him to realise that he could deal with other people's children so much better than with his own eldest son. The case of the Sandhurst cadets shows that he had a high degree of commonsense and insight into the minds of adolescents. The cadets had clashed with authority over discipline, and Albert pointed out that if there was already a scale of punishments there ought also to be a corresponding scale of rewards, in order to encourage them to see a proper connexion between their conduct and their prospects.

The Queen and Albert went to Ireland in August to see Bertie parading with his regiment at the Curragh. To his surprise, Albert found that he looked 'quite military', but the duke of Cambridge blighted even this brief happiness by saying that Bertie was not cut out for a soldier. Albert's forty-second birthday was spent in Dublin. It was not pleasant to remember that it was thirty years since he and Ernest had shot their first stag together, and with the swift passage of time and the overwhelming pressure of work preying on his mind he wrote ominously to Ernest 'I know that I dare not stop for a moment to relax. Like the hawk, I must not sleep, but be for ever on the watch.'

Rising early had always come easily to Albert; the first hours of the day, he always said, were the best and the most productive. Winter and summer, he was in his study as the clock struck seven, reading despatches and preparing his many memoranda. Behind his meticulous care never to allow a day to pass without attending to his papers, was the very real fear that if he fell behind he might never catch up again. This fear had been so much on his mind lately that after each of his 'attacks' he had somehow managed to struggle out of bed even earlier next morning to tackle the pile of papers which had accumulated. His work had by now grown to alarming proportions, but he still insisted that everything must go through his own hands, and it was a matter of pride that all his speeches were his own. The growth had been so gradual that the load had become too heavy before he realised it, but not a despatch or a letter was put on the Queen's desk to which he had not drafted an answer. He went through every newspaper directly after breakfast, marking passages for the Queen, and then saw his secretaries at nine and after them his librarian or one of his equerries. If there were a minister staying in the house, as at Osborne and Balmoral, he would invite him into his study for a consultation, reporting it to the Queen immediately afterwards. He made his own private record of everything, whether it concerned the country or the family, and by 1861 the bulky file he kept on Prussia because of Vicky had a slighter companion on Hesse-Darmstadt, prepared with a view to helping Alice and Louis remedy the neglected affairs of the duchy when they succeeded.

A few hours in the fresh air occasionally were vital to his health, and he tried to ensure that he got them. During the season, he managed an hour or two's shooting right up to the end, but pressure of work had compelled him to give up hunting by 1859. To ride about London informally was still one of his greatest pleasures, for it provided his only means of keeping in touch with what painters and sculptors were doing* and 'nothing dries up creative talent like neglect', but he never dropped the habit of going into the Queen's room before he went out and as soon as he came back, and always wanted to know in precise detail what her plans were for every hour they would be apart.

If it were not for the fact that he never felt well any more, Albert would have been a perfectly happy man. Loved, respected and powerful, doing good and useful work which he enjoyed, his attention sought by all and sundry, he was in his element; but it may be that his unselfishness in listening to everyone's problems, and the repeatedly proven accuracy of his political forecasts to ministers of the crown, had induced a touch of megalomania – it would, after all, have been unnatural if such absolute reliance upon his advice by so many had not generated a feeling in him that he was always right. If voluntary and devoted service to England did become in a sense megalomania during his last years, however, it was but a consequence of the canker that was eating away his life. Until illness began to make itself felt about 1855, he had accomplished more in two short decades than many men in a long lifetime. The key to his success was unquestionably his marriage, for a man of his temperament could never have done so much had his domestic life not been supremely happy. In February 1861 Albert wrote to Stockmar: 'Tomorrow our marriage will be twenty-one years old! How many a storm has swept over it, and still it continues green and fresh and throws out vigorous roots.'

The usual journey to Balmoral at the end of August began in a summer storm – 'a cloudburst with thunder and lightning accompanied us to the station, and as we drew out of St Pancras the night sky was covered with eerie blue light' – but the contrast between London and Deeside had never been greater, and Albert felt better immediately. Deer-stalking began at once, and on two successive days he brought down three large stags. He attributed his good marksmanship to the new breech-loading rifles the Queen had given him on his birthday, and wrote to Palmerston strongly urging the

* See p. 118 above.

364

adoption of the breech-loading principle by the army, since it was 'sure to carry the day eventually'. Several pony expeditions into the hills seemed so much like the old days that the Queen began to recover her spirits at last; fresh air and the sight of new faces did her good, she said, quite forgetting that until lately nothing would induce her to see even old and friendly faces, let alone new ones! All this made for a more relaxed atmosphere, and Albert began to take life more lightly again. He was soon a better colour, smiled more often and did not seem nearly so careworn.

In quite the old brisk style he set about making arrangements for little Leopold to spend the winter in Cannes under the care of Dr Günther of Württemberg, whom Lord John Russell had warmly recommended. 'The birds are leaving the nest,' he wrote to Ernest, and his mood darkened again at the thought that Affie would be serving in American waters for the next twelve months. The navy had proved the 'best school' for him, but they were still searching for the 'best school' for Bertie, Did it exist, they wondered? Had he any real talents, and how could they be most fully utilised? Was he being allowed to get away with too little work at Cambridge and was he spending too much time hunting and beagling? Under cover of watching the Prussian manoeuvres in the Rhineland, Bertie had gone off to take another look at Alexandra, and seemed to be liking what he saw, though it was a pity that they made front-page news every time they appeared together. In view of this, it was a load off his mind to receive from Vicky glowing accounts of the amiability and good sense of Alexandra's parents. If only Louis' uncle, the Grand Duke of Hesse-Darmstadt, would show some good sense too instead of unreasonably refusing to allow Alice and Louis to live with him while a house was being prepared for them.

Albert put the Grand Duke's behaviour down to anti-British feeling, and regarded it as a microcosm of the attitude which prevailed in Germany. A much more important example of this was the news that the king of Prussia was going to meet Napoleon III at his hunting-lodge at Compiègne,* for the Frenchman was certain to run rings round William's simple military mind; not for a moment did Albert believe William's excuse, passed on by Vicky, that it was to be a mere courtesy visit in return for that paid by the Emperor to Baden-Baden the previous autumn. Albert hated situations like this which he was powerless to alter.

* The hunting lodge had a bad reputation for the licentious manners which were said to prevail there. Victoria and Albert had been on tenterhooks for several months because of a rumour that Napoleon was about to invite the prince of Wales to stay with him there.

They both faced the autumn in better health, but unprepared for the blows which lay in store. On 2 November came news that Vicky had caught a cold which was threatening to turn into pneumonia; this caused Albert to send Dr Jenner (Baly's replacement) post-haste to Berlin, and he was on the point of following himself when a telegram announced that she was beginning to recover. Faint with relief, he postponed the trip until the New Year – a tragic decision in view of what was to come.

It was discovered that alterations to the private chapel at Buckingham Palace and to Marlborough House had been badly done during the Balmoral holiday, giving Albert the impression that he dare not take his eyes off anything for a moment and necessitating so many journeys between Windsor and London to supervise the re-doing of the work that he joked that he would have to build a house on Paddington Station to save himself time. More practically he had an office fitted up in the royal train so that he could work during the journey. Nor was this all. What with presiding over the governors of Wellington College, making a speech to the Royal Agricultural Society, keeping an eye on the progress of the 1862 Exhibition building and on the use which the Royal Horticultural Society were making of his suggestions about the arrangements for their spring show, he was soon quite worn out again and all the good that Balmoral had done was being lost. When the Queen begged him not to go to London so often, he replied bleakly 'I must, there are so many things to do.' Scarcely a week after they returned from Scotland, the Queen was writing to Vicky that overwork was making him 'very trying' and was soon reduced to begging Phipps to help her restrain him. But all was in vain, Albert would listen to no one; he was so wound up that he could not stop.

In this state he was ill-prepared to withstand news of the deaths of close relatives. First the king's brother, and then the young king Pedro of Portugal himself succumbed to typhoid at the beginning of November; Albert felt Pedro's death the more particularly because he was everything Bertie ought to have been. He and Victoria tried to draw consolation from picturing the happy reunion of Pedro and his dead wife Stephanie in Heaven, and they gave way completely to melancholy for several days, discussing in morbid detail all those they knew who had been wiped out by this terrible scourge. Only lately, John Brown, the Queen's servant, had explained how he had lost three brothers from typhoid in six weeks, following this up with the hope that there would be no deaths in the Queen's family in the coming year – that was only a month ago, and already there were two.

On top of all this came a letter from Stockmar breaking the news of an amorous escapade of the Prince of Wales at the Curragh Camp, which was already the talk of the Continent.* The thought that it was all up now with a marriage to Princess Alexandra cast Albert down as never before. History was repeating itself, he said dully; it was Ernest and the Dresden servant-girl all over again – except that Ernest was only the heir to a small duchy and Bertie to a great kingdom, much of whose throne's authority and power was owed to the efforts and self-sacrifice of his father. When Lord Granville tried to excuse Bertie by saying that he had done no more than get into a scrape like every young man, Albert reminded him coldly that the Prince of Wales was not every young man. Long experience of Ernest's peccadilloes had not toughened Albert in the least; he was 'stricken to the core' and became at once a prey to serious insomnia. Racked with neuralgia and irritable from lack of sleep, he sat down to write Bertie an imaginative description of the horrors which might follow a liaison with a 'low common woman', and to recommend that he confess everything to General Bruce; it is a letter which shows Albert to have been in an abnormal state of mind before the end of November.

A few days later, on the morning of 21 November, still in a state of shock, Albert drove from Windsor to Sandhurst in pouring rain to inspect the new Staff College, returning pale and soaked to the skin in time for a luncheon he could not eat. Victoria was alarmed at first, but calmed down when she convinced herself that he was not about to have one of his bad attacks, she told Vicky, 'but a cold, with neuralgia and a great depression which has been worse these last three days. The loss of rest at night . . . was caused by a great sorrow which upset us both greatly – but him especially, and it broke him quite down. I never saw him so low.' Vicky's birthday letter from her father was quite in the old style, and ended with a reminder that 'without the basis of health it is impossible to raise anything stable. . . . Therefore see that you spare yourself now, so that at some future time you may be able to do more,' but she knew that he had consistently disregarded his own advice. His last letter to her was written on 29 November and distressed her terribly. For many years he had told her things which he kept hidden from the Queen, because he sensed that in weaker moments he could lean on her strength. Now he confessed to her that he was at a very low ebb: 'Much worry and great sorrow (about which I beg you not to ask

* Some of his brother officers mischievously introduced an actress, Nellie Clifden, into his bedroom one night. Bertie took a fancy to her, and she followed him to Windsor, so that the affair leaked out.

questions) have robbed me of my sleep for the last fortnight. In this shattered state I had a very heavy catarrh, and for the past four days I am suffering from headache and pains in my limbs which may develop into rheumatism.'

A year before, Albert had told the Queen 'I do not cling to life. You do: but I set no store by it. If I knew that those I love were well cared for, I should be quite ready to die tomorrow.' Thinking back over these words some years later, Queen Victoria took them to be a pious submission to God's will, but they have been more often read as Albert's death-wish. It is more likely that they are neither. Long before, Albert had caught the habit of philosophising from Stockmar, and both could speak very sententiously on occasion. The remark just quoted is probably only an example of this habit; he was still in good health when he made it, and the Queen herself admitted that he spoke the words without a trace of sadness.

The Curragh episode could not be allowed to die down but must be thrashed out with Bertie in person. Although sleepless, aching all over, and without appetite, on 22 November Albert travelled to Cambridge, and father and son had a serious talk in the country lanes round Madingley. It was to be their last. There had been many sad passages of arms between them, not all Albert's fault by any means, but this time Albert forgave his son and returned home with an easy mind. But he also returned near collapse. Typically, the prince of Wales had never before been tempted to explore the Cambridgeshire countryside, and was soon completely lost, with the result that he made his sick father walk an unnecessarily long way, again in the rain, thereby draining Albert of his last drop of energy. The 'strange nature' which his father recognised but could not understand was never more apparent than at this last meeting, for Bertie failed to see what was apparent to everyone else – that Albert was very ill indeed. He did not spare his father, but only because he was (and was always to remain) quite incapable of any feeling for the distress of others; there was no malice, but one of the normal human emotions was missing.

Next day Albert found it difficult to get out of bed but then insisted on going out to shoot with Ernst Leiningen in the morning although he looked strange and acted like an automaton. As they set off, Ernst noticed that his uncle had become very thin and was unusually quiet, but paid little attention when he shot as well as ever. The afternoon was spent listening to harrowing accounts of Pedro of Portugal's last illness retailed by Count Lavradio, who brought a despairing letter from Pedro's father 'which touched me to the heart in its sorrow'. At night he had to sit up late considering a successor to Sir Edward Bowater, Leopold's governor at Cannes, news of whose severe illness was brought to him during the evening.

Although full of rheumatic pains and thoroughly unwell ('I have scarcely closed my eyes all night for the last fortnight', ran the final entry in his diary), Albert was able to walk to Frogmore on the morning of Sunday 24 November with the Queen, to show the Leiningens the duchess of Kent's mausoleum, but returned so faint and weak that he had to go to his room and lie down. He insisted on being present at dinner as usual, but could not eat a mouthful and looked pinched and ashen.

The Queen had not yet realised that Albert was very ill. She found it easy to explain away all the warning signs as the consequences of shock and worry about the prince of Wales, and attributed his despondency to male weakness (men, she always maintained, could not bear trouble and anxiety as well as women). Everyone, including her doctors, had always gone out of their way to keep her in ignorance of everything unpleasant. Indeed, the whole of Albert's last illness was bedevilled by this universal fear of upsetting the Queen. Albert was no better than the rest; he had suppressed the vital evidence from which it would have been possible to deduce that for two years he had been moving steadily towards his grave. His recurrent sickness and inability to digest food, his wan appearance, loss of energy, irritability and changed character are all consistent with several different serious internal diseases, but he kept so quiet about all his symptoms that nobody could arrive at a diagnosis which carries much conviction in the light of modern knowledge. Indeed he made superhuman efforts to behave normally – misplaced courage that in the end only added to his miseries.

Although almost lacking the strength to dress, he got up at seven every day as usual and was present at every meal, but ate nothing. On 29 November he went with the Queen to inspect the Eton Volunteers, later watching them devour an immense luncheon in the Orangery; the weather was mild, but in spite of wearing a fur-lined coat he 'felt as if cold water were being poured down his back.'

Already desperately ill, and with just a fortnight to live, he had still to perform his last service to the nation: to preserve the peace between England and the country he had always longed to see, the United States of America. He had been watching with mounting anxiety the civil war between North and South which had broken out in the spring, and on 27 November was at once alarmed by the news of what became known as the 'Trent affair'. Three weeks earlier, a Federal warship had boarded the Trent, a British mail steamer, and arrested two Confederate agents. The Cabinet resolved to demand satisfaction for the insult to the British flag and the breach of international law, and the Press adopted a menacing tone. Lord John Russell's draft despatch to Washington was harsh and unyielding, and when the Queen brought it to Albert as he lay on his sofa he exclaimed, 'This means war.' Although almost too weak to hold a pen, he went to his desk at once and redrafted it in much milder terms which would enable the Federal Government to retreat without loss of face. It is fitting that the last public action of a man of peace was to avert so tragic a conflict.

By 4 December Albert was running down-hill fast. Food nauseated him, and he vomited when he tried to swallow even a little chicken broth. But he still had no temperature and again the doctors reassured the Queen that it was only worry which had upset his delicate stomach, as so often in the past. Sir James Clark, summoned from retirement to give his opinion, found Albert lying fully-dressed on a sofa, an open book in this hand but staring dully out of the window. Clark's smooth 'There is no cause for alarm' was exactly what the Queen wanted to hear, but she ordered her bed to be moved into her dressing-room to give him more chance to rest at night. Next morning he was up as usual, but there was a wild look about him and he was complaining 'How long will I have to endure this?' By midday he felt better, talking quite naturally, and the improvement was sufficiently maintained in the evening for him to laugh at little Beatrice's recitation of a French poem. During the night of the fifth to the sixth, however, he was so restless that he went from room to room in search of repose but without being able to sleep. The bird-songs at dawn, he said, reminded him of his childhood at the Rosenau, and for some reason the Queen took this for a bad sign. He tried to drink a cup of tea, but choked over it.

The most striking thing a day-by-day chronicle of Albert's final illness reveals is the extraordinary absence of proper nursing care. He should never have been allowed to wander about at night in the cold – a pauper in a workhouse would have been better off in this respect – and even Jenner and the Windsor physician, Dr Brown, who volunteered to watch him at night from 9 December (no one had done so until then) were unable to prevent him from padding about in a silk dressing-gown for hours at a time, irritable beyond belief, heavy-eyed, with parched mouth, brown tongue and pallid sweating skin. His greatest need was for the expert nursing which only the dead Kurt had ever given, and it is astonishing that nobody ever tried to provide it, for his dejected air dumbly beseeched those around him to take charge. For the first time in his life he did not wish to be master of the situation.

It was not until 6 December that Dr Jenner steeled himself to tell the Queen that he and Clark suspected a low fever, which would have to take its course and would last about a month from the date of the Sandhurst visit. Alice's sharp eyes told her, however, that the doctors were puzzled and did not really know what was wrong with her father. She was almost certainly right. If it was typhoid – which was the final diagnosis – why was there no temperature and no agonising headache, and why was the patient able to get up and move about with such comparative ease (he was fully dressed every day until 10 December, four days before he died)? Typhoid was given as the formal cause of death; but it has to be remembered that there had been talk of little else except typhoid at Windsor since the news from Portugal, so that the thought was firmly implanted in everyone's mind. The single exception may have been Jenner, the uncertainty of whose diagnosis must be balanced against his lack of authority; he had only succeeded to his post nine months before, on the death in a railway accident of the newly-appointed royal physician, Dr William Baly, and was very much in awe of Sir James Clark (who, Clarendon once said, was 'not fit to treat a sick cat') and consequently under his thumb. In view of Clark's experience and reputation, and of the way the Queen welcomed his anodynes, it would have been very difficult for a young man like Jenner to disagree with his diagnosis. But it seems strange that the man who had isolated the typhus germ should not have been able to recognise the destructive early symptoms of the kindred typhoid fever, if indeed that were really what Albert was suffering from. Moreover, there was not a single case of typhoid at Sandhurst, where Albert was alleged to have caught the disease, and anyhow he neither ate nor drank there; nor was there any typhoid in the vicinity of Windsor at the time, nor was any contact ever identified.

On the other hand, Jenner may perhaps have suspected something else, and in any case, the 'attacks' during the last two years must have been the onset of the disease which was in the end fatal. Cancer of some kind is one possibility, but diagnosis of any except the common visual cancers, like that from which the duchess of Kent died, was unusual in those days. Jenner was the nearest thing to a scientist or a specialist among the royal doctors, the rest of whom were ordinary general practitioners – and not very good ones at that. He may have suspected that Albert was not suffering from typhoid; but in the then state of medical knowledge nothing could anyhow have been done to save him, and Jenner may have realised this and kept silent.*

Because he was no worse on 8 December, the doctors agreed to tell the Queen that there was some improvement in Albert's condition, and their judgement seemed to be confirmed when he asked to hear some music – the first time for several days that he had made such a request. He wanted a chorale, so Alice played *Ein' feste Burg ist unser Gott* quietly in the next room; but he had soon had enough: 'Das reicht hin', he murmured. It was Sunday, and while the Queen listened to Charles Kingsley preaching in St George's Chapel ('But I heard nothing') Alice stayed by her father. Soon he wanted his sofa pushed closer to the window so that he could watch the clouds moving across the sky, and when he called for some more music she played his favourite German songs. Glancing up as she finished, she saw her father lying as though asleep, but as she moved to cover him with a rug he opened his eyes and smiled. 'Were you asleep?' she asked. 'No, but my thoughts were so happy that I did not want to drive them away by moving.' He was still alert enough in the evening to take an interest in Sir Walter Scott's *Peveril of the Peak* when the Queen read to him, and her heart leapt with thankfulness, but later on he showed a sudden strange dislike of his own room, asked for the 'King's Room' to be made ready for him, and insisted on walking to it himself in spite of his weakness.

Next day, 9 December, Lord Methuen and General Francis Seymour (who had been his companion in Florence in 1839), called at the castle on their return from a visit of condolence to Lisbon, and against the doctors' advice Albert insisted on seeing them. The Queen and Alice felt that this was a hopeful sign, but afterwards he was more depressed than ever.

Until now the illness of the Prince Consort had been concealed from the public, and it was only when the cancellation of a shooting-party at Windsor made it necessary to issue an official bulletin about his health that it became widely known that he was unwell. Palmerston, who had been staying at the castle less than a fortnight before, when serious symptoms had first appeared, was gravely disturbed. Crippled with gout himself, he nevertheless travelled to Windsor to urge that a further medical opinion should be sought, but met with fierce resistance from the royal doctors – afraid, as usual, of frightening the Queen. Palmerston persisted until he beat down their opposition, but then found that the Queen would not give her consent for fear of alarming Albert. But when he became

* See Appendix II.

delirious, Clark and Jenner grew frightened and called in Dr Watson and the aged Sir Henry Holland to share their responsibility, but still assured the Queen that his tendency to wander in the mind 'was of no moment, though very distressing'.

On the tenth, the Queen seized on what she thought another hopeful sign. For some reason Albert had been moved back to his own room, and on the way stopped to look at a reproduction of a Raphael Madonna which he had given the Queen some time go, saying 'It helps me through the day'. At his evening visit Dr Watson encouraged her to believe that there had been some improvement, and early next morning she found Albert sitting up in bed drinking beef tea, quite his old affectionate self.

By Thursday 12 December his temperature had risen, he found difficulty in breathing and was constantly delirious; the deterioration was so apparent that the doctors could no longer hide it from one another. How much longer could they hide it from the Queen? In his few lucid moments, Albert seemed consumed with worry – about Leopold's health, Vicky's safety, and the welfare of even distant relations whom he had not seen for years. He asked Alice if Vicky knew of his illness and received the reply 'Yes, I told her you were very ill.' 'You did wrong. You should have told her that I am dying.' Alice knew that it was true. But she noticed that every time he tried to say the same thing to her mother, the Queen burst into such heart-rending sobs that he became silent again. Sensing that there was something of importance which he wanted to say, Alice chose a moment when the Queen was out of the room, drew a chair close to the bed and listened attentively to her father's disjointed mutterings. But she could make little of what were presumably his last instructions.

Friday the thirteenth dawned dark and forbidding, and the invalid was visibly worse. Dr Jenner felt bound to give warning that he feared congestion of the lungs had set in, but Albert was wheeled as usual in his sitting-room. He could no longer look at the Raphael as they passed it, but lay staring fixedly out of the window, his wasted hands tightly clasped. The afternoon brought a shivering fit, but he seemed a little better at night. Nevertheless, on her own initiative, Princess Alice summoned the prince of Wales from Cambridge and Sir Charles Phipps telegraphed Berlin that the Princess Royal should be prepared for her father's death. The Prime Minister, too, was warned to be ready for an event which he found 'too awful to contemplate'.

About six o'clock on the morning of Saturday 14 December Dr Brown came to tell the Queen that the Prince was much better and that there was reason to hope that the crisis was over. In her Journal the Queen gives a vivid picture of the way the sickroom appeared when she went in a little later. There was a sad look of night-watching about it that pierced her to the heart – the candles burnt down to their sockets, the wan faces of the waiting doctors. Yet 'never can I forget how beautiful my darling looked, lying there with his face lit up by the rising sun, his eyes unusually bright, gazing as it were on unseen objects, and not taking notice of me'. Again the doctors tried to reassure her, but this time only half-heartedly; there had been 'a decided rally' but they were 'very, very anxious', and if the Queen wanted to go out she should not be away more than a quarter of an hour and should stay close by. When she came back about midday she found Albert being given sips of brandy, but lying down to prevent fatigue. 'He is not worse,' Dr Watson said, 'the pulse keeps up,' but 'we are very much frightened, but don't and won't give up hope.' It was his rapid breathing which alarmed her, and a darkness about the face and hands which Jenner also noticed.

The next few hours passed much as usual, but Victoria was at last coming to realise what no one had dared tell her – that her husband was dying. He was conscious in the early evening, kissed her when she put her arms round him, but gave a heavy sigh and soon relapsed into delirium. Alice brought in the younger children, but he did not recognise them. With superhuman self-control, Victoria remained calm as the minutes ticked by, noticing with a spurt of hope that Albert was able to get out of bed by himself when his sheets were to be changed, although he was too weak to get back again and had to be lifted. His breathing was still laboured, but the doctors told her that there was plenty of air passing through the lungs and that there was hope so long as this was so, and they even managed to interpret a fit of heavy perspiration as nature's way of throwing off a fever. Soon after ten she was recalled from the adjoining room by Princess Alice, who told her that the end was near. Quite calm, almost beyond feeling, Victoria knelt by his side and clasped his thin cold hand, while the children and members of the household grouped themselves round the bed. As the castle clock chimed the third quarter, Albert's breathing became gentler, he gave a soft sigh, and it was all over.

Epilogue

It is ironical that Albert was given the kind of funeral he most detested, with all the grotesque trappings of royal burials – mourners in long black cloaks and wide-brimmed hats with 'weepers' – which he had told the Queen, after the death of the duchess of Gloucester, were out of place in the modern world and ought to be abandoned. But he had left no instructions about his funeral (although it may well have been these which he was trying to give Alice in his last hours),* and so the Queen cannot altogether be blamed for yielding to her instinct to cover everything with black. So much black crepe was used to drape the rooms and corridors at Windsor that the whole country's supply of it was exhausted, and more had to be dyed in a hurry. The only concession to his wishes was that the funeral on 23 December did not take place at night by torchlight, but at midday.

The coffin was taken from the castle to St George's Chapel in a hearse drawn by six horses, and escorted by a detachment of Life Guards. The Queen could not face the ordeal of watching her husband's body carried out for burial, and left precipitately for Osborne, so that only the solitary figures of the Prince of Wales and his eleven-year-old brother Arthur followed the coffin up the aisle. Contrary to custom, the pall-bearers were not public figures but personal friends like Sir Charles Phipps and Colonel Seymour, and it was Seymour's task, as a friend of twenty years' standing, to place the crown, sword, baton and field-marshal's hat upon the coffin as it rested before the altar. The music for the service fitted Albert's own tastes: the

---

* See p. 373 above.

thirty-ninth psalm to an adaptation of a Beethoven theme which Albert himself had made at Osborne only the year before, Martin Luther's hymn to the tune 'Gotha' and, as the coffin was lowered into the vault, a chorale of Albert's own composition, which filled the chapel with a sound that was almost gay. The burial was only temporary, because the mausoleum was not yet built.* How often they had talked of such a thing, but how young they had felt and how remote death had seemed until just the other day. Now, Victoria hoped that she would soon 'lie beside her husband until the sun set and the moon wanes to rise no more.'

Almost inevitably her grief, her emotional nature and her great love for him led Queen Victoria to distort Albert's image, and she soon began to paint the picture of a man so pure and good that no ordinary mortal could have attained such standards. She tried to comfort herself with the belief that he had died because 'the wickedness of the world was too much for him to bear', and by her own actions began the process of dehumanising him and turning him into a stained-glass-window saint (Tennyson's 'wearing the white flower of a blameless life' seemed to her to strike just the right note) which has lasted almost to the present day. Sir Theodore Martin claimed objectivity in the preface to the biography which she commissioned from him ('I have had no panegyric to write. This would have been as distasteful to Your Majesty as it would be unworthy of the Prince'), but he was only occasionally able to achieve it, so continuous was the interference which she could justify by the assertion 'I understand even every wish of his, better than before.' She began littering the countryside with statues, although she had agreed with Albert when he condemned the duke of Wellington's son for wanting to do the same in memory of his father, and should have remembered that he had then added 'If I should die before you, do not, I beg, raise even a single marble image to my name.' Another example of her almost wilful misrepresentation of him is provided by an account she gave Vicky in 1861 of a conversation between them on the subject of death five years earlier: 'He always said that he would not care if God took him at that moment, he always felt ready.' There is a sententious ring about this which is not quite in character, and it is in sharp contrast with the level and matter-of-fact tone of a letter to Ernest only a few months later: 'My best wishes for your fortieth (!!!!!) birthday. I can hardly believe that you have reached the age which seemed to us, in our

* It was ready enough for the coffin to be placed there in a temporary sarcophagus a year later, but the final interment did not take place until November 1868.

youth, to mean old age!' and with his own reflections when he passed the same milestone himself – that although he knew he was getting old he hoped that he would be spared long enough to do all the things he had in mind.

Albert was of course a man of high though not rigid principles, but this did not make him superhuman or mean that he could not unbend, still less that he carried his principles farther than a reasonable conception of honour and duty required. He explained his attitude in these matters to Ernest in 1851, and was always true to his own doctrine :

> 'I cannot overcome my astonishment that you can conclude that "only the egoist can look back upon his life with satisfaction". I think he is the farthest away from all real feeling of happiness, because he tries to get away from the laws of nature which call for care and hard work. I have never yet seen anyone succeed in overcoming the laws of nature by putting moral duties aside, nor have I seen an egoist who was happy.'

Mr Roger Fulford was the first to reveal, in 1949, something of the man behind the legend the Queen created, the first to use the word 'charm' to describe his personality and to give a glimpse of a family founded on affection and trust whose life revolved round its head. That the legend prevailed for so long was partly because evidence to dispute it was both scarce and hard to interpret. Bolitho's exceedingly inaccurate translations and some of the *Letters of the Prince Consort* (many of which are entirely political and therefore do not come into the present reckoning) were for long almost the only clues to the real man, apart from the documents chosen by the Queen and printed by Martin. Even so, Albert's letters, though factual and robust, do not betray the twinkle in the eye, the half-smile and the tolerance which made him a sympathetic listener and a congenial friend.

What were Albert's services to the monarchy? By the mid-'forties, with Peel's help, he had wiped out the last traces of the bad Regency days and begun to establish the monarchy on a better and more modern foundation by uniting crown and nation and setting the throne above party. Encouraged by Melbourne, Victoria had taken sides like her ancestors, but the 1832 Reform Bill made change essential in this as in so many other respects. Her very mistakes (over the Bedchamber affair, for instance) sometimes helped Albert to accelerate change by offering himself as a soothing influence on the rough places of the constitution. But in order to do this he had first to seek and exercise power. There were occasional exceptions to the wisdom with which he used it – they are chiefly concerned with foreign affairs and with Prussia, towards which his attitude was almost romantic and visionary rather than realistic, and the value of whose alliance to Britain he always overestimated – but the exercise of power was inseparable from the task of service which he had set himself. If he sometimes went too far (his use of 'we' and 'us' in letters to Frederick William invited and inadvertently encouraged the misconception that he and Victoria held views distinctly different from those of the Cabinet), and if he was lacking in the power of self-criticism, he learned his lesson in later years and in 1854 told Frederick William that he was stupid if he supposed that a constitutional monarch could act behind the government's back.

Victoria reigned for forty years after Albert's death, and in spite of occasional aberrations (such as her initial self-imposed seclusion and her open dislike of Gladstone) she never quite forgot what he had taught her: that in Britain it is not the monarch who governs but the Cabinet through Parliament. Above all, he instilled a sense of duty and a respect for principle into a woman who was at first reluctant to observe them but who under his guidance became a model without which it is now impossible to imagine the British monarchy.

Appendix I

The 'Bedchamber Question'

SEVERAL strands were interwoven in the brief crisis of 1839 which goes under the name of the 'Bedchamber Question', and they continued to affect the relations between crown and ministers during the next few years.

One was that Victoria liked Melbourne and disliked Peel, whose cold and reserved manner made it in any case difficult for a young girl to like him. Since Melbourne had been her political mentor in her first years as Queen, she became rather naturally also a partisan of the Whigs – that is to say, dangerously lacking in the impartiality which is required of a constitutional monarch.

Another strand was that during Melbourne's prime ministership an inordinate number of ladies belonging to prominent Whig families (including the wives of several ministers) had been appointed to the royal household. In consequence, a future Tory prime minister might well fear that their informal influence would counteract the formal advice he tendered to the Queen. It was an additional complication that many of these ladies were lax in their morals and that the customs of the Regency still prevailed among them and their lovers.

It was of course for the crown to appoint the members of the royal household. It was also for the crown to appoint the prime minister, and on his advice, the members of the government. But were both functions exercised in the same way and under the same conventions? Or was one private and personal, the other public and political? Should ladies-in-waiting change when ministers did? If not, where was the dividing line between the two kinds of appointment? In 1839 Peel made it a condition for his acceptance of the premiership – which Melbourne had advised the Queen to offer him, because of a shift in the political complexion of the House of Commons – that she show her confidence in him by dismissing the Whig ladies of her household. Feeling this an affront to the crown, to her privacy and to her Whig predilections, Victoria emotionally refused (in later life she admitted that she was wrong). Peel therefore refused office, and Melbourne remained prime minister for two more years. There had been real room for doubt about the precedents governing the appointment of the Queen's ladies (not since Queen Anne's day, over a century before, had they been in a position to exercise so much political influence) but it was really the Whigs, not her ladies, whom the Queen was defending in 1839, and that (as well as Peel's very reasonable demand for a public expression of royal confidence) is why what should have been a trivial matter assumed momentary constitutional importance.

Cooler counsels eventually prevailed in 1841, but there was at one time a danger that the same impasse would be reached.

Victoria revealed that she was still thinking as a partisan in 1841 however, by writing shortly after the Tories won the General Election 'The Queen strongly feels that she made a mistake in allowing the dissolution of 1841; the result has been a majority returned against her of nearly one hundred votes'. Constitutional monarchy requires a crown which does not identify itself with one party in this way, but is prepared to accept the leader of that party which enjoys the country's favour for the time being. This was a new and imperfectly understood idea in the 1830s and for several more decades: 'It is only within the last fifty years', wrote Gladstone in 1878, 'that our constitutional system has settled down.' The Reform Bill of 1832 had in fact marked the watershed between the old and the new, and had put paid to the last remnants of the monarch's former power to govern by his own will – for instance, to his power to dissolve Parliament except upon the advice of his ministers. But it is easier to see this in retrospect than it was during the early years of Queen Victoria's reign, and periods of friction and dispute like the Bedchamber incident were the consequence.

Appendix II

Did Albert die
of typhoid?

THE accepted view that Albert died of typhoid is unconvincing because it does not explain all his symptoms. It therefore seemed worth while to inquire whether any alternative diagnosis was possible. To attempt a diagnosis many years after the patient's death, and on written evidence alone, is notoriously dangerous; it is unlikely that all relevant information was recorded – much may have been forgotten or overlooked, or have seemed in the then state of medical knowledge to be without significance. This said, however, responsible medical opinion which I have consulted is prepared to make the following observations:

The diagnosis of typhoid does not fit all the facts. There is evidence that Albert had been in declining health for some time. There is general evidence from those who knew him that his health was being undermined (supposedly from overwork) and specific evidence that he appeared thin and may have had swelling of the abdomen (and possibly the ankles) before his last illness. This suggests that he may have been suffering from a chronic wasting disease before the final episode. The final acute phase does not sound like a characteristic attack of typhoid. There is no clear report of high fever; nor of the prostration which is so usual; nor of delirium, which is common. Albert was moving about, although weak, almost to the end. There is no evidence of the source of infection, nor was there an epidemic of typhoid at the time – it is necessary to exercise great caution before questioning the diagnosis of the physicians who were present. But diagnosis was less exact in 1861 than it is today, and the royal physicians were under considerable pressure to give a precise cause of death. The surviving evidence gives grounds for thinking that they were mistaken in diagnosing typhoid, and for believing that Albert's final illness may have been a terminal episode following a more chronic but ultimately fatal disease such as cancer, or hepatic or renal failure.

Governments 1835-1865
and some of their leading members

April 1835 – June 1841   WHIG
> Prime Minister: Lord Melbourne
> Home Secretary: Lord John Russell
> Foreign Secretary: Viscount Palmerston

The government resigned in 1839. Peel attempted to form a government but failed because of the 'Bedchamber Question', and Melbourne continued in office.

August 1841 – June 1846   CONSERVATIVE
> Prime Minister: Sir Robert Peel
> Home Secretary: Sir James Graham
> Foreign Secretary: Earl of Aberdeen

June 1846 – February 1852   WHIG, WITH PEELITE SUPPORT
> Prime Minister: Lord John Russell
> Foreign Secretary: Viscount Palmerston

February 1852 – December 1852   CONSERVATIVE
> Prime Minister: Earl of Derby
> Foreign Secretary: Earl of Malmesbury

December 1852 – February 1855   COALITION OF WHIGS AND PEELITES
> Prime Minister: Earl of Aberdeen
> Home Secretary: Viscount Palmerston
> Foreign Secretary: Lord John Russell 1852–3, then Earl of Clarendon
> War and Colonies: Duke of Newcastle

February 1855 – February 1858   LIBERAL
> Prime Minister: Viscount Palmerston
> Foreign Secretary: Earl of Clarendon
> War: Lord Panmure

February 1858 – June 1859   CONSERVATIVE
> Prime Minister: Earl of Derby
> Foreign Secretary: Earl of Malmesbury
> India: Viscount Stanley

June 1859 – October 1865   LIBERAL
> Prime Minister: Viscount Palmerston
> Foreign Secretary: Lord John Russell
> War: Sidney Herbert

Biographical Notes
and Glossary

ABERDEEN 4th Earl of, 1784–1860. Secretary of State for War and Colonies in Peel's Cabinet 1834–5; Foreign Secretary in Peel's Cabinet 1841–6. Prime Minister 1852–5.

ANTI-CORN LAW LEAGUE *See* Corn Law.

ARNOLD Thomas, 1795–1842. Headmaster of Rugby School, 1828–42.

ASHLEY *See* Shaftesbury.

BENTINCK Lord George, 1802–48. Tory MP 1826–48. A leader of the Protectionists against Peel 1846–7.

BRIGHT John, 1811–89. With Richard Cobden led Anti-Corn Law League in the years before 1846. Also with Cobden, opposed Palmerston's foreign policy from 1858. Member of Parliament from 1843.

BROUGHAM Henry Peter, 1st Baron Brougham and Vaux, 1778–1868. Barrister and politician. Lord Chancellor in Melbourne's Cabinet, 1830–4.

CAMBRIDGE George, Duke of, 1819–1904. Grandson of George III. Commanded divisions at the battles of the Alma and Inkerman in the Crimean War. Commander-in-Chief of the Army, 1856–1895.

CARDWELL Edward, 1813–86. Secretary to the Treasury 1845, and a devoted Peelite. As President of the Board of Trade under Aberdeen, reformed the Merchant Marine code. Secretary for Ireland under Palmerston 1859–61. Reorganised the British army while Secretary for War 1868–74.

CAVOUR Count Camillo, 1810–61. Architect of Italian unity as Prime Minister of Piedmont-Sardinia 1852–59 and 1860–1. When English friendship seemed unlikely to be of political assistance, turned to Napoleon III and enlisted French help in war against Austria 1859. On France's sudden withdrawal in July 1859, resigned in despair; but soon returned as Prime Minister and negotiated the adherence of the republican Garibaldi and Naples (which he had occupied) to Victor Emmanuel, thereby uniting Italy.

CHADWICK   Sir Edwin, 1800–90. One of the first great practical reformers who applied Benthamite rationalism and scientific knowledge to the amelioration of social conditions. Secretary to the Poor Law Commissioners, 1834–46. Produced Report on the Sanitary Conditions of the Labouring Poor 1842, and was consequently made one of the three members (Ashley was another) of the General Board of Health.

CHARLES ALBERT   King of Piedmont-Sardinia, 1831–49. Led Italian attack on Austrian domination 1848 and abdicated in favour of his son Victor Emmanuel when defeated by Austria at Custozza and Novara 1848–9.

CHARTIST MOVEMENT   Founded during the economic depression of the late 1830s to meet the needs of skilled workmen not enfranchised by the Parliamentary Reform Act of 1832 and as general protest against social and economic conditions. Produced the People's Charter, which demanded manhood suffrage, voting by ballot, equal electoral districts, abolition of property qualification for MPs, payment of MPs and annual Parliaments. Prominent 1837–42 and 1847–8, when it presented a monster petition to Parliament. Non-violent, and refused to use force to gain its ends, even in 'the year of revolutions', 1848.

CLARENDON   George Villiers, 4th Earl of, 1800–70. Lord Lieutenant of Ireland in Russell's Cabinet, 1847–52. Foreign Secretary under Aberdeen and Palmerston, 1853–58.

COBDEN   Richard, 1804–65. Liberal MP 1841–57 and 1859–65. One of the leaders of the Anti-Corn Law League.

CORN LAW   Customs duty imposed 1815 on foreign corn entering England until home prices rose to a stated level. Thus the Corn Law kept up the cost of living for the benefit of landowners, and hence became a symbol of aristocratic domination. Anti-Corn Law League founded to secure its repeal. As a Conservative, Peel was committed to the Corn Law, but became convinced that repeal was necessary when potato blight struck Ireland in 1845 and the Corn Law prevented relief to the consequent famine. Repealed 1846.

CROKER   John Wilson, 1780–1857. Politician and essayist. Long connected with the Quarterly Review.

DERBY   Edward Stanley, 14th Earl, 1799–1869. Conservative MP 1835–51. Colonial Secretary in Peel's Cabinet 1841–5. Resigned over Corn Law and became one of the Protectionist leaders. Succeeded to earldom 1851. Prime Minister 1852 and 1858–9.

DISRAELI   Benjamin, 1804–81. Conservative MP 1837–76; leading Protectionist 1845–50. Chancellor of the Exchequer in Derby's Cabinet 1858–9 and again 1866–8. Prime Minister 1874–80. Created Earl of Beaconsfield 1876.

EASTLAKE   Sir Charles, 1793–1865. Painter. President of the Royal Academy from 1850 and of the National Gallery from 1855.

FICHTE   Emmanuel, 1797–1879. Son of Johann Gottlieb Fichte (1762–1814, philosopher and inspirer of German resistance to Napoleon). Professor of philosophy at Bonn 1836–42, where his emphasis on moral freedom, the application of science and reason, and on the duty of each individual to strive for self-improvement, greatly influenced Albert.

BIOGRAPHICAL NOTES AND GLOSSARY

GLADSTONE   William Ewart, 1809–98. Under-Secretary for War 1834–5, President of the Board of Trade 1843–4 and Secretary of State for the Colonies 1845–6, in Peel's governments. Chancellor of the Exchequer 1852–5 in Aberdeen's Cabinet and 1859–66 under Palmerston. Later Prime Minister.

GRACE   John, MP 1847–58. Member of the Building Committee for the Great Exhibition.

GRAHAM   Sir James, 1792–1861. Home Secretary in Peel's Cabinet 1841–6, First Lord of the Admiralty under Aberdeen, 1852–5.

GRANVILLE   2nd Earl, 1815–91. Foreign Secretary 1851–2 under Russell, Lord President and Chancellor of the Duchy of Lancaster 1852–8 in Aberdeen's and Palmerston's Cabinets, again Lord President under Palmerston and Russell 1859–66.

GREVILLE   Charles Cavendish Fulke, 1794–1865. Clark of the Council 1821–59. Political diarist.

GREY   Charles, 2nd Earl, 1764–1845. Whig MP 1786–1807, Foreign Secretary 1806–7, Prime Minister 1830–4.

GREY   Lieut-General the Hon. Charles, son of the above. Private Secretary to Prince Albert 1849–61, later Private Secretary to Queen Victoria.

GUIZOT   François, 1787–1874. French historian and statesman. As minister of Louis Philippe restricted freedom of the Press 1833. Briefly ambassador in London 1840. Foreign minister and in effect head of the government 1842–8; his rigidly conservative policy contributed to the fall of Louis Philippe.

KEBLE   John, 1792–1866. *See* Oxford Movement.

LANDSEER   Sir Edward, 1802–73. Best known for his paintings of animals, but also portrait painter to Queen Victoria.

LOUIS NAPOLEON   *See* Napoleon III.

LOUIS PHILIPPE   Son of Louis-Philippe, duke of Orleans (1747–93), who sided with the French Revolution in its early years and was known as 'Egalité'. Related to the royal house of France through both mother and father. Raised to the throne after the July Revolution of 1830 as a bulwark against mob rule, and became known as the 'bourgeois king'. Forced to abdicate by the revolution of 1848, and fled to England.

MACAULAY   Thomas Babington, 1800–59. Historian and statesman. Wrote for *The Edinburgh Review* from 1825. MP 1830, and quickly made his mark by eloquent speeches. As member of Supreme Council for India 1834–8, wrote a famous minute on Indian education and helped to reform the law. Secretary of State for War 1839–41. His *History of England* began to appear in 1848.

MALMESBURY   3rd Earl of, 1807–99. Foreign Secretary under Derby 1852 and 1858–9.

MANNING Henry, 1808–92. Ordained in the Church of England 1833, soon joined Oxford Movement. Received into Roman Catholic Church 1856. Archbishop of Westminster 1865, Cardinal 1877.

MELBOURNE William Lamb, 2nd Viscount, 1779–1848. Whig MP 1806–29, when he succeeded to the viscountcy. Home Secretary in Grey's Cabinet, 1830–4. Prime Minister 1835–41.

NAPOLEON III Louis Napoleon, 1808–73, nephew of Napoleon I. Twice raised revolts against Louis Philippe and attempted to restore the Napoleonic régime, but was unsuccessful. Elected to the Assembly after the 1848 revolution and elected President in December 1848 largely on the strength of his name. Secured the extension of his four-year term of office to ten years by means of a *coup d'état* in December 1851 and became Emperor of the French a year later after an overwhelming popular vote.

NEWMAN John Henry, 1801–90. Fellow of Oriel College, Oxford 1822, and vicar of the University Church from 1828. With Keble and Pusey, founded the Oxford Movement 1833, stressing continuity from the early Church, spirituality and ritual. Their *Tracts for the Times* attracted much attention, and Newman was a leader of Oxford opinion by 1837 although already moving slowly towards Rome. He was received into the Roman Catholic Church in 1845.

O'CONNELL Daniel, 1775–1847. Irish patriot. Leader of the movement for repeal of the 1801 Act of Union with England.

ORSINI Felix, 1819–58. An Italian who began as a young man to conspire against Austrian oppression of Italy. Took part in the 1848 revolutions. Fled to England 1853. Believing France the main obstacle to Italian unity, attempted to assassinate Napoleon III 14 January 1858. He failed, but Napoleon soon began to assist the Italian unification movement.

OXFORD MOVEMENT Founded by Keble, Pusey, Newman and others in 1833 to promote spirituality and ritual, and stress the continuity of the Church of England with the Church of Rome. Consequent weak emphasis on Protestantism and the Reformation led to attacks on them with their *Tracts for the Times* (whence the alternative name Tractarian Movement), particularly Tract 90 (1841), seemed dangerously to narrow the gap between the two Churches. Newman's conversion (1845) reduced the movement's impetus but did not halt a tendency for the English Church to have a more prominent High Church wing than formerly.

PALMERSTON 3rd Viscount (in the Irish peerage) 1784–1865. Whig and Liberal MP 1830–65. Foreign Secretary 1830–41, 1846–51 under Grey, Melbourne and Russell. Home Secretary in Aberdeen's Cabinet 1852–5. Prime Minister 1855–8, 1859–65.

PANMURE Lord, 1801–74. Secretary at War in Russell's government 1846–52, Secretary of State for War under Palmerston 1855–8.

PEEL Sir Robert, 1788–1850. Tory MP 1809–50, Prime Minister 1834, 1841–6. *See also* Corn Law.

PRE-RAPHAELITES A circle of painters including Rossetti, Holman Hunt and Millais who advocated a return to the style and values in painting current before the time of Raphael (1483–1520).

PROTECTIONISM The policy of protecting home production by means of tariffs, i.e. of retaining the Corn Law.

BIOGRAPHICAL NOTES AND GLOSSARY

PUSEY   Edward Bouverie, 1800–82. One of the leaders of the Oxford Movement.

REEVE   Henry, 1813–95. Member of the staff of *The Times* newspaper 1840–55; edited *Edinburgh Review* 1855–95.

ROSS   Sir William, 1794–1860. Miniature-painter, patronised by English and foreign royalty.

RUSSELL   Lord John, 1792–1878. Younger brother of the duke of Bedford; created Earl Russell 1861. Whig MP 1813–61. Prime Minister 1846–52. Foreign Secretary in Aberdeen's Cabinet 1852–3 and again 1859–65 under Palmerston.

SHAFTESBURY   Anthony Ashley Cooper, Lord Shaftesbury, 1801–85. MP from 1826. Succeeded father as 7th Earl of Shaftesbury 1851. Social reformer and philanthropist; Evangelical in religion, Tory in politics. Long active in favour of restricting hours of work in factories (the Ten Hours Movement) and although not in Parliament when the 1847 Act was passed, piloted the 1850 Act through the House of Commons. Founded Ragged Schools Union 1844. Member of the General Board of Health when it was established 1848.

SMITH   The Reverend Sydney, 1771–1845. Journalist and wit. Co-founder and first editor of *The Edinburgh Review*. Soon moved to London, where he supported liberal causes and acquired a great reputation as journalist and preacher.

STANLEY   *See* Derby.

STRATFORD DE REDCLIFFE   Viscount, 1786–1880. Entered Foreign Office 1807. Minister in Constantinople 1810–14, and at once acquired a reputation for independent action. Minister to U.S.A. 1819–23. As ambassador to Constantinople 1842–58 exercised great influence over the Sultan and encouraged reforms; pro-Turkish in negotiations with Russia before Crimean War, but the charge that he was seeking war is ill-founded.

THIERS   Marie-Joseph Louis, 1797–1877. Established a reputation as historian in the 1820s. Promoted Louis Philippe's cause against Charles X in 1830. Chief Minister 1834–6 and 1840–8. Elected to the Constituent Assembly after the 1848 revolution, and supported Louis Napoleon for the Presidency of the Second Republic, but later in disfavour with Napoleon. Head of government of Third Republic after 1871.

THORBURN   Robert, 1818–86. Miniature-painter. Received his first commission from Queen Victoria in 1846.

TRACTARIANS   *See* Oxford Movement.

VICTOR EMMANUEL III   1820–78. King of Piedmont-Sardinia 1849–59, first king of united Italy 1860.

WILBERFORCE   Samuel, 1805–73. Archdeacon of Surrey 1839, chaplain to Prince Albert 1841, Bishop of Oxford 1845–69.

WINTERHALTER   Franz-Xavier, 1806–73. One of the most famous portrait painters of the nineteenth century. Commissioned by most of the royal families of Europe, including that of England.

WISEMAN   Nicholas, 1802–65. Appointed cardinal-archbishop of Westminster 1850, when the Roman Catholic hierarchy was reintroduced into England for the first time since the sixteenth century.

Bibliography

(All books published in London unless otherwise stated. Dates of publication in brackets.)

AGNEW, D.   Royal Collections in England, in *History Today*   3 (1953) 339–352

AIRLIE, Mabel, Countess of   *Lady Palmerston and her Times*   (1922)

ALBERT, Prince Consort   *Principal Speeches and Addresses*   (1862)

AMERY, L. S.   *Thoughts on the Constitution*   (1948)

AMES, Winslow   *Prince Albert and Victorian taste*   (1968)

ANON   *The Progresses of Her Majesty and Prince Albert in France, Belgium and Holland*   (1844)

ANON   *The Private Life of the Queen, by a member of the Royal Household* (1898)

ARGYLL, John, Duke of   *V.R.I., her life and Empire*   (1901)

ARONSON, Theo   *Queen Victoria and the Bonapartes*   (1972)

ASHLEY, A. E. M.   *The Life and Correspondence of H. J. Temple, Lord Palmerston*   (1879)

ASHWELL, A. R.   *Life of Bishop Wilberforce*   (1850)

ASPINALL, A.   *Lord Brougham and the Whig Party*   (1927)

BALFOUR, Lady Frances,   *Life of George, earl of Aberdeen*   2 vols. (1902)

BASSETT, A. T. (ed.)   *Gladstone to his wife*   (1936)

BATTISCOMBE, Georgina   *John Keble*   (1963)

BEALES, Derek   *From Castlereagh to Gladstone*   (1969)

BEATRICE, Princess (ed.)   *In Napoleonic Days: Extracts from the private diary of Augusta duchess of Saxe-Coburg-Saalfeld*   (1941)

BELL, H. C. F.   *Lord Palmerston*   (1936)

BENNETT, Daphne   *Vicky, Princess Royal of England and German Empress* (1971)

BENSON, A. C. and ESHER, Viscount   *The Letters of Queen Victoria*   First Series 3 vols.   (1908)

BENSON, E. F.   *As We Were*   (1930)

BENSON, E. F.   *Daughters of Queen Victoria*   (1939)

BENSON, E. F.   *Queen Victoria*   (1935)

BEST, G. F. A.   *Lord Shaftesbury*   (1964)

BLAKE, Robert, Lord   *Disraeli*   (1966)

BIBLIOGRAPHY

BLAKE, Robert, Lord *The Office of Prime Minister* (1975)
BLOOMFIELD, Georgiana, Lady *Reminiscences of Court and Diplomatic Life*
  2 vols. (1883)
BOLITHO, Hector *Albert the Good* (1932)
BOLITHO, Hector *Albert, Prince Consort* (1964)
BOLITHO, Hector *A Biographer's Note-Book* (1950)
BOLITHO, Hector (ed.) *Further letters from the archives of the House of*
  Brandenburg-Prussia (1938)
BOLITHO, Hector (ed.) *The Prince Consort and his Brother* (1933)
BOLITHO, Hector *The Reign of Queen Victoria* (1949)
BOLITHO, Hector *Victoria and Albert* (1938)
BRIGGS, Asa *The Age of Improvement* (1959)
BRIGGS, Asa *Victorian People, 1851–67* (1954)
BROCK, M. C. Politics at the Accession of Queen Victoria, in *History Today* 3
  (1953) 329–339
BROOKFIELD, C. and F. *Mrs Brookfield and her Circle* (1905)
BROUGHTON, Lord (J. C. Hobhouse) *Recollections of a long life* 6 vols.
  (1909–11)
BUNSEN, Frances, Baroness *A Memoir of Baron Bunsen* (1868)
BURY, J. P. T. (ed.) *Romilly's Cambridge Diary, 1832–42* (Cambridge 1967)
CARLYLE, Thomas *New Letters* (ed. A. Carlyle) 2 vols. (1904)
CECIL, Lord David *Lord M.* (1954)
CHADWICK, Owen *The Victorian Church* (1966)
CHANCELLOR, F. B. *The Prince Consort* (1931)
CLARENDON, George, Earl of *Life and Letters* (ed. H. Maxwell) (1913)
CLIFFORD SMITH, H. *Buckingham Palace* (1931)
COLE, Sir Henry *Fifty Years of Public Work* 2 vols. (1884)
CONACHER, J. B. *The Aberdeen Coalition* (Cambridge 1968)
CONACHER, J. B. *The Peelites and the Party System* (Newton Abbot 1972)
CONINGHAM, W. *Lord Palmerston and Prince Albert* (1954)
CONNELL, Brian *Portrait of a Whig Peer* (1957)
CONNELL, Brian *Regina v Palmerston* (1962)
COOKE, C. Kinloch *A memoir of H.R.H. Mary Adelaide, Duchess of Teck*
  2 vols. (1900)
COOKE, E. *Delane of The Times* (1915)
COOPER, C. H. *Annals of Cambridge* (Cambridge 1843)
CORTI, Egon Cesar, Count *Leopold I of Belgium* (1923)
COWLES, Virginia *Edward VII and his Circle* (1956)
COWLEY, Henry, Earl *The Paris Assembly during the Second Empire* (ed.
  F. A. Wellesley) (1928)
COWLEY, Henry, Earl *Diary and Correspondence, 1790–1846* (ed. F. A.
  Wellesley) (1930)
COWLING, M. J. *1867: Disraeli, Gladstone and Revolution* (1967)
CRABITÈS, P. *Victoria and her Guardian Angel* (1937)
CRAWFORD, Emily *Victoria, Queen and Ruler* (Bristol 1903)
CRESTON, Dormer *The youthful Queen Victoria* (1952)
CROKER, J. W. *Correspondence and Diaries* (ed. L. J. Jennings) 3 vols.
  (1885)
CRUSE, Amy *The Victorians and their Books* (1935)
CUST, Sir Lionel *King Edward VII and his Court* (1930)
CUST, Sir Lionel *Pictures in the Royal Collection* (1911)

BIBLIOGRAPHY

DALLAS, G. M.   *Letters from London 1856–60*   (1870)
DANGERFIELD, George   *Victoria's Heir*   (1941)
DASENT, A. I.   *John Thaddeus Delane: His Life and Correspondence*   2 vols.
   (1908)
D'AUVERGNE, E. B.   *The Coburgs*   (1911)
DOUGLAS, Mrs Stair   *Life of William Whewell*   (1881)
DUFF, David   *Victoria in the Highlands*   (1968)
DUNKLEY, H.   *The Crown and the Cabinet*   (1878)
EASTLAKE, Elizabeth, Lady   *Journals and Correspondence*   2 vols. (ed. C.E.
   Smith) (1895)
EMERTON, J. A.   *A Moral and Religious Guide to the Great Exhibition*   (1851)
ERNEST II, duke of Saxe-Coburg and Gotha   *Memoirs*   4 vols. (1888)
ERSKINE, Mrs Steuart (ed.)   *Twenty Years at Court, 1842–62: from the cor-
   respondence of the Hon Eleanor Stanley*   (1916)
ESHER, Reginald, Viscount (ed.)   *The Girlhood of Queen Victoria*   (1912)
ESHER, Reginald, Viscount   *The Influence of King Edward*   (1915)
EYCK, F.   Fresh light on the Constitutional Monarchy, in *The Listener* 20 June
   1957, 933–4
EYCK, F.   *The Prince Consort*   (1959)
FITZMAURICE, E.   *Life of Lord Granville*   2 vols. (1906)
FRITH, W. P.   *My Autobiography and Reminiscences*   (1888)
FULFORD, Roger   *The Prince Consort*   (1949)
GASH, Norman   *Politics in the Age of Peel*   (1952)
GASH, Norman   *Sir Robert Peel*   (1972)
GIBBS-SMITH, C. H.   *The Great Exhibition*   (1950)
GLADSTONE, W. E.   *Gleanings of Past Years*   (1899)
GREVILLE, L.   *The Greville Memoirs* (ed. Lytton Strachey and Roger Fulford)
   8 vols. (1938)
GREY, C.   *The Early Years of the Prince Consort*   (1867)
GRUNER, L.   *The Decoration of the Garden Pavilion in the grounds of Bucking-
   ham Palace*   (1846)
GUEDELLA, Philip   *The Duke*   (1931)
GUEDELLA, Philip   *Palmerston*   (1926)
GUEDELLA, Philip (ed.)   *The Queen and Mr Gladstone*   (1933)
GUIZOT, F. P. G.   *Memoirs of Sir Robert Peel*   (1857)
HAMLEY, E. B.   *Wellington's Career: a Military and Practical Summary*   (1860)
HARDIE, F. M.   *The Political Influence of Queen Victoria*   (1935)
HENDERSON, G. B.   The Influence of the Crown 1854–56, in *Juridical Review*
   48 (1936) 297–327
HIBBERT, Christopher   *The Court at Windsor*   (1964)
HIBBERT, Christopher   *The Destruction of Lord Raglan*   (1961)
HIRST, F. W. (ed.)   *Early Life and Letters of John Morley*   2 vols. (1927)
HOBHOUSE, Christopher   *1851 and the Crystal Palace*   (1937)
HODDER, Edwin   *Life and Work of the seventh Earl of Shaftesbury*   3 vols. (1886)
HOHENLOHE-SCHILLINGSFURST, Prince Alexander of   *Memoirs* (ed. G. W.
   Chrystal)   2 vols. (1906)
HOPE, N. M.   *The Alternative to German Unification*   (Wiesbaden 1973)
HOWARTH, T. E. B.   *Citizen King: the life of Louis Philippe*   (1961)
HYAM, Ronald   *Britain's Imperial Century*   (1976)
JAGOW, E.   *Letters of the Prince Consort*   (1938)
JARMAN, D. F.   *The Proposed Opening of the Crystal Palace on Sundays*   (1851)

BIBLIOGRAPHY

JENNINGS, W. I.   *Cabinet Government*   (1936)
JERROLD, W. N.   *Life of Napoleon III*   4 vols. (1874–82)
JERSEY, Margaret, Countess of   *Fifty-one years of Victorian life*   (1922)
KEITH, A. B.   *The Constitution of England from Queen Victoria to George VI*   2 vols. (1940)
KITSON CLARK, G. S. R.   *The Making of Victorian England*   (1962)
KITSON CLARK, G. S. R.   *Peel and the Conservative Party*   (1964)
KURTZ, H.   *The Empress Eugénie*   (1964)
LANG, Andrew   *Life of Lockhart*   (1897)
LAYARD, Sir Austen   *Autobiography and Letters* (ed. W. N. Bruce)   (1902)
LEE, A. G. (ed.)   *The Empress Frederick writes to Sophie*   (1955)
LEE, Sir Sidney   *Queen Victoria*   (1904)
LeMAY, G. H. L.   Prince Albert and the British Constitution, in *History Today* 3 (1953) 411–416
LESLIE, C. R.   *Autobiographical Recollections*   2 vols. (1860)
LIEVEN, Princess   *Unpublished Diary and Political Sketches* (ed. H. W. V. Temperley)   (1925)
LONGFORD, Elizabeth, Countess of   *Victoria R.I.*   (1964)
LONGFORD, Elizabeth, Countess of   *Wellington*   2 vols. (1969–72)
LYTTELTON, Sarah, Lady   *Correspondence* (ed. H. Wyndham)   (1912)
MacCARTHY, Desmond and RUSSELL, Agatha (eds.)   *A life of Lady John Russell*   (1910)
MacCARTHY, Justin   *A History of our own Times*   3 vols. (1905)
MacCARTHY, Justin   *Reminiscences*   2 vols. (1899)
MAGNUS, Sir Philip   *King Edward the Seventh*   (1964)
MALMESBURY, Earl of   *Memoirs of an ex-Minister*   2 vols. (1884)
MAREK, G. R.   *Gentle Genius: the story of Felix Mendelssohn*   (1973)
MARKHAM, V. R.   *Paxton and the Bachelor Duke*   (1935)
MARTIN, Kingsley   *The Triumph of Lord Palmerston*   (1924)
MARTIN, Sir Theodore   *Life of the Prince Consort*   5 vols. (1875–80)
MARTINEAU, Harriet   *Autobiography*   3 vols. (1877)
MAXWELL, Sir Herbert   *Life and Letters of George, earl of Clarendon*   2 vols. (1913)
MAXWELL, Sir Herbert   *Sixty Years a Queen*   (1897)
MELBOURNE, William, Viscount   *Papers* (ed. L. C. Sanders)   (1889)
MOORMAN, J. R. H.   *History of the Church in England*   (1953)
MORLEY, J.   *Life of William Ewart Gladstone*   3 vols. (1903)
MORSHEAD, Sir Owen   *Windsor Castle*   (1951)
MOSSE, W. E.   The Crown and Foreign Policy in *Cambridge Historical Journal* 10 (1951)   205–224
MUNDY, H. G. (ed.)   *The Journal of Mary Frampton, 1776–1846*   (1885)
MUSGRAVE, C. W.   *The Royal Pavilion, Brighton*   (1951)
NAMIER, Sir Lewis   *The Monarchy and the Party System*   (Oxford 1952)
NEWSOME, David   *Godliness and Good Learning*   (1961)
NEWSOME, David   *A History of Wellington College*   (1959)
NEWSOME, David   *The Parting of Friends*   (1966)
PARKER, C. S. (ed.)   *Sir Robert Peel from his Private Correspondence*   3 vols. (1891)
PARRY JONES, E. (ed.)   *Correspondence of Lord Aberdeen and Princess Lieven, 1832–54*   (1938)
PEEL, Sir Robert   *Memoirs* (ed. Stanhope and Cardwell)   2 vols. (1856–7)

PENDERED, M. L.   *John Martin, Painter*   (1923)

PICKEN, Hilda   *A Party of Pleasure*   (1961)

PONSONBY, Arthur, Lord   *Henry Ponsonby*   (1942)

PONSONBY, D. A.   *The Lost Duchess*   (1958)

PONSONBY, Magdalen   *Mary Ponsonby: A memoir, some letters and a journal*
   (1927)

POUND, Reginald   *Albert*   (1973)

PREST, J.   *Lord John Russell*   (1972)

PROTHERO, R. E.   *Life and Correspondence of Dean Stanley*   (1895)

READ, D. and GLASGOW, E.   *Feargus O'Connor, Irishman and Chartist*   (1961)

READ, Donald   *Cobden and Bright: A Victorian Partnership*   (1967)

RIDLEY, Jasper   *Lord Palmerston*   (1970)

RIMMER, A.   *The Early Homes of Prince Albert*   (Edinburgh 1883)

RYAN, P.   The Marquis of Salisbury, in *History Today*   1 (1951) 30–37

SANDWICH, Earl of   *Memoirs* (ed. S. Erskine)   (1919)

SAUNDERS, Edith   *A Distant Summer*   (1947)

SCOTT, Sir George Gilbert   *Personal and Professional Recollections*   (1879)

SETON WATSON, R. W.   *Britain in Europe*   (1937)

SMILES, Samuel   *Self-Help*   (1859)

STANLEY, Augusta, Lady   *Letters 1849–63* (ed. Baillie and Bolitho)   (1927)

STANMORE, Arthur, Lord   *The Earl of Aberdeen*   (1893)

STEEGMAN, John   *Consort of Taste*   (1950)

STEEGMAN, John   *The Rule of Taste from George I to George IV*   (1936)

STEEGMAN, John   *Victorian Taste*   (1971)

STOCKMAR, Christian, Baron von   *Memoirs* (ed. F. M. Müller)   2 vols. (1872)

STOCKMAR, E. von   *Denkwürdigkeiten aus den Papieren des Frh. C. F. von
   Stockmar*   (Brunswick 1872)

STRACHEY, Lytton   *Queen Victoria*   (1921)

STUART, C. H.   The formation of the Coalition Cabinet, 1852, in *Trans. Royal
   Hist. Soc.*   4 (1954) 45–68

STUART, C. H.   *The Prince Consort and Ministerial Politics*, in *Essays presented to Keith Feiling* ed. H. R. Trevor-Roper   (1965)

STUART, D. M.   *The Mother of Victoria*   (1941)

SURTEES, Virginia   *Charlotte Canning*   (1975)

SYKES, Christopher   Colonel Sibthorpe, in *History Today*   1 (1951) 14–21

SYKES, Christopher   The Emperor entertains: Napoleon at Compiègne, in
   History Today   3 (1953) 50–61

TAINE, H.   *Notes on England* (ed. E. Hyams)   (1957)

TAYLOR, A. J. P.   The Crimea, in *History Today*   1 (1951) 23–31

TAYLOR, A. J. P.   *The Trouble-Makers*   (1957)

TAYLOR, A. J. P.   *Rumours of Wars*   (1952)

TEMPERLEY, H.   *The Crimea*   (1936)

TISDALL, E. E. P.   *Restless Consort*   (1952)

TOOLEY, Sarah   *Personal Life of Queen Victoria*   (1890)

VITZTHUM von ECKSTAEDT, C. F.   *St Petersburg and London in the years 1852–64*
   2 vols. (1887)

VICTORIA, Queen   *Leaves from the Journal of our Life in the Highlands, 1848–61*
   (ed. A. Helps)   (1868)

VICTORIA, Queen   *More Leaves from the Journal of our Life in the Highlands*
   (1884)

VILLIERS, George   *A vanished Victorian: The life of Lord Clarendon*   (1938)

WARD, J. T. *Sir James Graham* (1967)
WATSON, Vera *A Queen at Home* (1952)
WELLINGTON, Duke of The Great Duke's Funeral Car, in *History Today* 2 (1952) 778–787
WEMYSS, Rosslyn *Memoirs of Sir Robert Morier* 2 vols. (1911)
WILLIAMS, N. *The Royal Residences of Great Britain* (1968)
WINSTANLEY, D. A. *Early Victorian Cambridge* (Cambridge 1955)
WOODHAM-SMITH, Cecil *Florence Nightingale* (1950)
WOODHAM-SMITH, Cecil *The Great Hunger* (1962)
WOODHAM-SMITH, Cecil *Queen Victoria, her Life and Times* (1972)
WOODWARD, Sir Llewelyn *The Age of Reform* (1962)
YOUNG, G. M. (ed.) *Early Victorian England* (1934)
YOUNG, G. M. and HANDCOCK, W. D. *English Historical Documents* vol. 12 (1956)
ZIEGLER, Philip *King William IV* (1971)
ZIEGLER, Philip *Melbourne* (1976)

Manuscript Sources

Bayerisches Staatsarchiv Coburg, Schloss Ehrenburg
1. Various papers and correspondence, the main bulk of which consists of a series of letters written by Albert to his brother Ernest between 1838 and 1861. (Some of these letters were imperfectly edited by Hector Bolitho as *The Prince Consort and his Brother*.) All are cited as *CA*, with date.
2. A collection of papers on loan from Freiherr Stockmar von Wangenheim. These are cited as *CAS* when they are from Stockmar's own hand, as *CAL* when they concern King Leopold.

British Library
The Aberdeen, Ellenborough and Peel papers.

Chatsworth
The Paxton papers and other corrrespondence.

Schloss Friedrichshof, Kronberg
Correspondence between Queen Victoria and Prince Albert and their daughter the Empress Frederick, and other papers. Cited as *KA*, with date.

Trinity College, Cambridge
The Affleck, Macaulay and Whewell papers.

University Library, Cambridge
The diary and other papers of Joseph Romilly.

Victoria and Albert Museum
The diary and other papers of Sir Henry Cole.

Wellington College
Letters and papers concerning the foundation.

Reference Notes

The following abbreviated titles of works frequently quoted are used in the notes which follow. Full titles are given in the Bibliography on p. 395.

Conacher	Conacher, *The Aberdeen Coalition*
Connell	Connell, *Regina v Palmerston*
Croker	Croker, *Correspondence and Diaries*
Eyck	Eyck, *The Prince Consort*
Gash	Gash, *Sir Robert Peel*
Girlhood	Esher, *The Girlhood of Queen Victoria*
Greville	Lytton Strachey and Fulford, *The Greville Memoirs*
Leaves	Queen Victoria, *Leaves from the Journal*
Letters	Benson and Esher, *The Letters of Queen Victoria*
Letters P.C.	Jagow, *Letters of the Prince Consort*
Letters to Sophie	Lee (ed.), *The Empress Frederick writes to Sophie*
Longford	Longford, *Victoria R.I.*
Martin	Martin, *Life of the Prince Consort*
Memoirs, duke Ernest II	Ernest II, *Memoirs*
Speeches	Albert, Prince Consort, *Principal Speeches and Addresses*
Woodham-Smith	Woodham-Smith, *Queen Victoria, her Life and Times*

page   1   'This paradise of our childhood'

4   'as if Coburg were a great empire': Grey, 372
7   For her part Luise: Ponsonby, *The Lost Duchess*, 19
7   'la belle Grecque': Ponsonby, *The Lost Duchess*, 32
8   instantly burst into wild sobs: Ponsonby, *The Lost Duchess*, 19
8   never wished to leave: Ponsonby, *The Lost Duchess*, 17
8   offspring of a liaison: Ponsonby, *The Lost Duchess*, 108
8   did not care for the marriage: Girlhood, i, 153
9   until conclusively disproved: Bolitho, *Albert the Good*, 18

page

9   the most painful thing: Ponsonby, *The Lost Duchess*, 151
9   'On the way I cried': Grey, 33
10 'Papa always said': *Letters to Sophie*, 200
10 'Children find a way': *CAS* April 1853
10 too frightened to complain: *Memoirs, duke Ernest II*, i, 25
11 Victoria and Albert remembered her walking: *Letters* I, i, 342
11 for instance, her Lutheran faith: *CA* undated
11 When the boys stayed with her: *CA* undated
12 'a species of second parent': *Letters* I, i, 342
12 too much feminine coddling: *CA* undated
12 'for a woman accustomed': Grey, 26
13 such studies might lead to anarchy: *CA* 15 April 1837
13 nothing could have been a better preparation: Grey, 98
13 the classified collection of rock specimens: *Memoirs, duke Ernest II*, i, 21
14 the best of friends: Grey, 35
14 Albert once told her: Grey, 213–14
14 'the pendant to his pretty cousin': Grey, 19
15 Victoire had to give way to Victoria: *CA* undated

2   'To sacrifice mere pleasure to real usefulness'

16 Leopold had maintained a regular correspondence: *Letters*, I i, 23
17 Albert was the kind of youth: *CAL* 3 April 1836
17 'He is said to be prudent': Stockmar, *Memoirs*, i, 365–7 *and* Martin i, 18–19
18 'The Prince bears a striking resemblance': Stockmar *Denkwürdigkeiten*, 311; *Memoirs*, ii, 5–6 *and* Fulford, 29
20 Albert's good looks and pleasant ways: Grey, 131
21 It made his hair stand on end: Grey, 129
21 a phase of hero-worshipping his uncle: Grey, 139
22 'reasoned and calm letter': *CA* 29 November 1836
22 preparing Albert for an important position: Stockmar, *Memoirs*, i, 160
22 Stockmar recommended Bonn: Stockmar, *Memoirs*, i, 369
22 'through work and effort': *Memoirs, duke Ernest II*, i, 78
22 first prize in a fencing competition: Grey, 143
23 Albert sent her a polite little note: *CAL* 25 July 1837
23 she did not think him sufficiently experienced: *Girlhood* i, 153
23 a possible marriage with Victoria: Stockmar, *Memoirs*, i, 200
23 there must be love as well: Stockmar, *Memoirs*, i, 367
23 'He looks at the question': Stockmar, *Memoirs*, i, 369
24 'Albert did not depend enough on himself': Stockmar, *Memoirs*, i, 391
24 a scrap of Voltaire's handwriting: Grey, 155
24 'I must now give up the custom': *CA* 29 November 1858 *and* Grey, 184
24 'bereft of everything': *CA* undated
25 'as a precaution': *CA* 20 December 1838 *and* 2 January 1839
25 'like a fish in water': *CA* 10 January 1839
25 one in particular attracted him: *CA* 25 January 1839
26 Albert learned more Italian: *CA* 4 February 1839
26 'But for some beautiful palaces': Grey, 199
26 'very kind and civil': Grey, 200
26 'on many subjects mature beyond his years': Stockmar, *Memoirs*, ii, 7

REFERENCE NOTES

page

27   Albert quickly found better accommodation: *CA* 4 February 1839

27   he had never been so happy: *CA* 21 May 1839

27   'you seem to think that changing one's character': *CA* 29 *and* 31 May 1839

27   'the virago queen': *CAS* undated

27   'yesterday I nearly hanged myself': *CA* 9 August 1839

28   'when I say the word "university" ': Grey, 206

28   'in many respects far behind': Grey, 206

28   'Art treasures are an unremitting source': *CA* 13 January, 19 February, 7 March 1839 *and* Grey, 197

28   'let her wait': *CA* 27 August 1839

28   'We really have no option': *CAS* 29 August 1839

29   'I can make no final promise': *Letters* I, i, 177

29   Albert's reaction was blunt: *CA* 5 September 1839

29   'The only excuse': Memorandum of the Queen, *in* Grey, 220

30   'The childish time of youth': *CA* 29 August 1839

30   'calmly and steadily in the right path': Grey, 261

30   'so much admired in certain eminent men': *CAS* 10 October 1839

31   everything was going to be all right: *CAL* 12 October 1839

32   The noise woke Albert's greyhound: *CAS* 14 October 1939

32   'He has no idea': *Girlhood*, i, 271

32   'riding like an old hand': *Girlhood*, i, 271

32   'giving England as good a recommendation': *CA* 14 October 1839

32   she had not slept well lately either: *Girlhood*, i, 268

32   'that it would make me too happy': *Girlhood*, i, 268

33   'longed to spend his life with her': *Girlhood* i, 268

33   'The eye beholds the heavens open wide': Grey, 226

33   how perfect Albert was: Grey, 227

33   'Albert is my second self': Grey, 260

34   'the radiant parts of my life': *Letters P.C.*, 33–4

34   'which alters his view of life altogether': *CA* 14 November 1839

34   'The song of the orange blossoms': *Letters P.C.*, 47

34   'I kiss you a thousand times': *Letters P.C.*, 31

34   'Now, though I know you never would': *Letters* I, i, 199

35   'there is no essential difference': Stockmar, *Memoirs*, i, 341

35   Melbourne bungled the question: *Girlhood* i, 280

35   the Queen could allow her Consort precedence everywhere: Greville ii, 232

36   'For God's sake, Ma'am': Cecil, 269

36   Albert would have to reside: Greville ii, 231

36   the expense of Albert's household: Greville ii, 231

36   Pride kept Albert silent: *Letters P.C.*, 49

36   'Shame, shame': *Letters* I, i, 213

36   the Tories had voted to a man: *CA* 5 January 1840

37   'As a German prince': *Letters* I, i, 213

37   'I would not have it otherwise': *Letters P.C.*, 54

39   'either the establishment is formed': *CA* 13 January 1840

39   'I declare calmly': *Letters P.C.*, 51–2

40   'only enough gentlemen': *CAS* 5 January 1840

41   'we must make this different': *Girlhood* i, 279

page
60   Instantly she was on her high horse: Fulford, 64
61   Later the same evening: *CA* 14 July 1840
62   'dry as dust'; *CA* 17 July 1840
62   Russia must be watched: *CA* 25 July 1840
62   Nemours shook his head: *CAS* 27 July 1840
63   'it is not convenient this year': *CA* 21 August 1840
63   he had no influence: *CAL* 21 August 1840
63   he did not believe that Palmerston would risk war: *CAL* 27 August 1840
63   she would be glad for him to see all the papers: *CAS* 25 August 1840
63   A talk with Palmerston: *CAS* 28 August 1840
63   Albert had written his first State paper: Connell, 27
63   'my birthday is over': *CA* 4 September 1840
64   'Such an affectionate surrender': *Memoirs, duke Ernest II*, i, 117
64   Two days later he was made a Fishmonger: *CA* 4 September 1840
64   'logical separation of what is great': Martin i, 90–2
65   an idea which originated with Lehzen: *Letters* I, i, 224
65   Stockmar's conclusions were blunter: Stockmar, *Memoirs*, 30 May 1840
66   he was ashamed to be reminded: *CA* 29 November 1840
66   'It is hardly to be believed': *CA* undated but probably written on 21 November 1840
66   she must be kept 'as calm as possible': *CAS* 29 November 1840
66   he had prohibited prayers: Lyttelton, 308
67   'dear festival time': *CA* 1 January 1841
67   'I feel as if in Paradise': *CA* 12 January 1841

4 'Everything I do is for the Queen'

68   She did not like Tories: Eyck, 24
69   the Queen's political education had been narrow: *CAL* 2 January 1841
69   'I do not think it necessary to belong to any party': Memo by Albert 15 April 1840 *in* Eyck, 24
69   'more havoc can be caused by offended feelings': *CA* 11 February 1841
70   to re-establish the proper role: *CA* 24 February 1841
70   He should assert himself more: *CA* 5 March 1841
70   Nothing had changed for the better: *CA* 16 March 1841
71   The real position was very different: Memo by Anson July 1841 *in Letters* I, i, 295
71   what a help Albert was being: *Letters* I, i, 275
71   'I have been carrying out all her duties': *CA* 8 December 1840
71   the Queen proposed he should see all foreign despatches: Lee, 127
72   but the Queen had overriden him: *CA* 12 March 1841
72   a woman who had once been all in all to the Queen: Fulford, 63
72   Albert should strike at once: *CAS* 24 March 1841
73   Lehzen was so ignorant: Fulford, 63
73   'Nothing will induce me'; Fulford, 67
73   attentions to her favourite pleased the Queen: *CA* 5 September 1841
73   he became little more than her lackey: Stockmar, *Memoirs*, i, 12 October 1840
73   it was really Lehzen who prevented Albert: *Letters* I, i, 219
73   he feared the Queen would not back him up: Stockmar, *Memoirs*, i, 20 September 1840

page

73 He longed to fight: Stockmar, *Memoirs*, i, 18 February 1839
73 This was the important occasion: *Letters* I, i, 81
73 Stockmar had declined the Queen's offer: *CA* undated
74 'I have managed to wall her out': *CA* 22 August 1840
75 'foreigners are inferior': *CA* 10 June 1840
75 'I have done it': *CA* 18 July 1840
75 'like a twaddling old woman': Greville, iv, 29
76 'started on a right course': Memo by Anson, *Letters*, I , 224
76 A servant-girl in Dresden: *CA* 30 May *and* 26 June 1840
77 Albert was left to pay: *CA* 8 June 1840
77 Ernest pleaded with crocodile tears: *CA* 22 August *and* 26 September 1840
77 'Always money, money, money': *CA* 12 November 1840
77 'exposed to all sorts of casualties': Stockmar, *Memoirs*, i, 359 *and* Martin, i, 105
77 If Melbourne fell: Stockmar, *Memoirs*, i, 310
78 'You must do it': *CAS* 15 March 1841
78 'a tendency to rest satisfied': Martin, i, 103–4
78 if he never saw State papers: *CAS* 6 April 1841
78 'A Ministry in Jeopardy': *Letters* I, i, 268
79 Peel's 'doggedness and pertinacity': *Letters* I, i, 271–4
79 'This is very true': *Letters* I, i, 276
79 'cool, calm and collected': *CAS* 12 May 1841
79 she must let the Prince assist her: *CAS* 12 May 1841, *cf Letters* I, i, 270
79 Albert decided that his household: *CAS* 16 May 1841
80 'it bears the stamp of her cunning': *CAS* 30 June 1841
80 he had made two conditions: Martin i, 111
80 'The moon is on the wane': *CA* 1 June 1841
80 'such Raphaels, Correggios': *CAS* 14 July 1841
81 'the annual exhibition of the sovereign': Hodder i, 337
81 'Stockmar is the only person': *CA* 25 July 1841

5 'Let us be better, and everything will be better'

82 the power that was to leave its mark: Morley i, 242
82 'He understands everything so well': Martin i, 117
83 this was the height of folly: Memo by Anson 29 August 1841 *in Letters* I, i, 303
83 Melbourne allowed himself an occasional indiscretion: *Letters* I, i, 375
83 'he considered it his first and greatest duty': Greville, iv, 408
83 Stockmar had cut uncomfortably near the bone: *Letters* I, i, 338–42
84 'two of the most irresponsible men in England': *CA* 5 April 1843
84 'determined either to stand or fall by his opinion': Martin i, 163
84 'what better man can be found': *CA* 10 March 1842
85 'a very long speech': *CA* 5 June 1840; *Letters P.C.*, 69 *and Speeches*, 81–2
86 'I hasten to fulfil my promise': *CA* 1 August 1841
86 'Someone ought to tell him to resign': *CAS* undated
87 'the fear that you might stir me up against her': *CA* 29 July 1841
88 'another door is open to me': *CA* 18 April 1841
88 'Mama would never have fallen': *CA* 18 June 1861
88 The furore over Conroy: *CAS* undated
89 'She was praising herself': *CA* 11 September 1841

page

89   Stockmar forbade study: *CA* 15 August 1841

89   her boxes were not delivered to Albert: Greville iv, 244

90   King Frederick William of Prussia had hinted: Aberdeen, *Correspondence*, 11 November 1841

90   criticism from the High Church party in England: Chadwick, 189–93

90   King Leopold took the opposite view: *Letters* I, i, 379, 4 February 1842 *and CA* 5 January 1842

91   Albert averted something like an international incident: Aberdeen, *Correspondence*, 14 January 1842

91   he always told the Queen what he knew she wanted to hear: Lyttelton, 323 *and* Stockmar, Memoirs, i, 329

92   Victoria flew to her defence: Longford, 160

92   'I went quietly down the stairs': *CA* 24 January 1842

92   Nothing would break the spell: *CAS* 17 January 1842

92   The Queen had evidently not weakened: *CAS* 18 January 1842

92   Further quarrels like this: *CAS* 23 January 1842

93   agreed with Lady Lyttelton: Lyttelton, 322

94   he was given a horse to ride: Grey, 334

95   the ice gave way: *Letters P.C.*, 72

95   'the skill of a diplomat': *CA* 24 March 1842

6   'The first link has been forged'

99   'I depended on him for everything': Cowley, *Paris Embassy*, 232

99   She complained that his shyness: *Letters* I, i, 337

99   'it would give me great satisfaction': *Letters* I, i, 382

100   Working closely with her: *Letters* I, i, 304

100   When the earl of Munster: *Letters* I, i, 387

100   As he explained to the duke of Wellington: Martin i, 74 *and* ii, 259–60

100   Mendelssohn, a regular visitor: Martin i, 489

101   'abominable stinking holes': *CA* 15 December 1843

101   'there must be some better way': *CA* 12 May 1842

101   fit only for formal tasks: *CA* 12 May 1849

102   'men who have done great deeds': *CAS* 11 March 1840

102   'crude and unnecessary insult': Hodder i, 387

103   closing the roads through the Home Park: Ames, 10

104   The chief sources of trouble: *CA* 5 April 1841

104   Peel warned Albert to have a care: *CA* 4 January 1843

104   The health aspect: Watson, 97

105   'beautiful beyond words': *CA* 12 September 1836

105   'the country is full of beauty': *Letters P.C.*, 87

105   'crammed in wretched dog-holes': Greville v, 128

106   secret courts of honour: Martin, i, 169

106   Wellington thought the mere question: Longford, *Wellington*, i, 242

106   'quiet perseverance': *CAS* 26 April 1845

106   'regarded as an idiot': Gash, 188

107   'was due to her own judicious conduct': Greville iv, 315

108   placed them in an awkward position: Gash, 388

108   He stirred up the old royal family again: *Letters* I, i, 497

108   for him to take her place: Martin, i, 165

108   This did not make Albert more popular: Greville iv, 129

page
108   more than he could manage: *CA* 29 August 1843
109   a sign that Albert had cast off: Stockmar, *Memoirs*, i, 243
109   'cut-throats and vandals': Aberdeen, *Correspondence*, 9 November 1841
109   England would come to her assistance: Aberdeen, *Correspondence*, 11 November 1841
109   Prussia had not yet recognised Belgium: Aberdeen, *Correspondence*, 1 January 1843
109   When Leopold's reply was evasive: Aberdeen, *Correspondence*, 23 *and* 25 January 1843
110   Victoria and Albert set out for Eu: *CA* 21 August 1843
110   Albert had already been fishing: Aberdeen, *Correspondence*, 17 August 1843
110   their conversation was entirely about philosophy: Guizot, *Memoirs* iii, 145
110   there was no truth in the rumours: Guizot, *Memoirs* iii, 146 *and* Martin iii, 145
110   the tone of the British Press: *The Times* 5 September 1843
111   the Master's wife was made quite ill: Douglas, 302
111   he had no intention of looking like a waiter: Romilly Papers, Cambridge University Library
112   to greet the Queen and Albert a second time: Douglas, 302
112   'for the crowd was overpowering': Stockmar, *Memoirs*, i, 198
112   'The mayor is a hosier': *Letters* I, i, 506
113   how a prince should behave: *CAL* 24 November 1860
113   Albert cheerfully assured the Cabinet: *CAS* 5 October 1860
113   'Now everyone can live like a king': Anon, *The Progresses*, 84
113   the visit had been a useful counter-balance: *Letters* I, i, 511
113   the monarchy was above party: *CAS* 29 December 1843
113   'indescribable mixture of dignity and deference': Mundy, 413–19

7   'To me, Prince Albert is King'

114   'rode like a demon': *CA* 19 December 1843
114   'If I proceeded like Papa': *CA* 14 January 1844
114   'Why isn't there more?': *CA* 24 May 1843
114   he was afraid to open letters from Coburg: *CAS* 10 November 1840
115   the ambitions of the house of Coburg: Aberdeen, *Correspondence*, 20 May 1842
115   his father approached Aberdeen direct: Aberdeen, *Correspondence*, 22 October 1843
115   'My darling stands so alone': Martin, i, 202
115   'bowed down by the loss': *Letters* I, ii, 6
115   'The trunk has fallen': *CA* 4 February 1844
116   'I will help Ernest': Martin i, 203
116   the two brothers exchanged mementoes: *CA* 13 February 1844
116   his care of her was like a mother's: *KA* 9 June 1858
116   'Bear up and do not give way'; *Letters P.C.*, 91
117   some of the palace servants did not recognise him: *Letters P.C.*, 93
117   'I have often to refuse myself': *CA* 14 January 1844
118   Albert was able to secure . . . a triptych: Agnew, 54
118   Albert sent Gruner to bid: Agnew, 54
119   he felt sure that he had written the pamphlet: *Letters* I, ii, 12

page

119   showing Peel a letter from Ellenborough: Ellenborough, *Correspondence*, 6 April 1843 *and* Gash, 487

120   all England required from France: Martin i, 217

120   Albert had to open her eyes: *CAS* 24 June 1844

120   Peel unbent enough: *CAS* 4 August 1844

121   Ernest was furious: *CA* 12 September 1844

121   When the invitation was accepted: *CA* 11 September 1844

121   he now played up to Albert: Bunsen i, 271

121   William listened attentively: *CAS* 25 September 1844

121   '*le prince Albert, c'est pour moi le roi*': Argyll, 105

121   'Ill-assorted and of no use': *CA* 14 October 1844

122   Louis was not impressed with Claremont: *CAS* 17 October 1844

122   'I have found a second paradise': *CA* 18 October 1844

122   Therein alone lay security: *CA* 30 October 1844

123   reminded him of the Rosenau: *CA* 12 August 1846

123   Some of his experiments were unsuccessful: Chatsworth archives, 12 April 1850

124   When the King of Prussia came to Windsor: Bloomfield, 34

124   Peel put on his 'wooden face': Fulford, 71

124   'short, crisp and explanatory': *CA* 10 March 1845

8   'I wish that he should be equal in rank to me'

126   Albert's careful management: Martin i, 153

127   'if the monarchy was to rise in popularity': *CAS* 28 November 1844

127   'superintending responsibility': Stockmar, *Memoirs*, i, 258

127   'He ought to be above me in everything really': Martin, i, 257

127   a personal appeal by the Queen: *Letters* I, ii, 34

127   'You have the substance': Martin, i, 256

128   'It is a very exaggerated story': *CA* 14 March 1845

128   building a house with wooden bricks: Fulford, 95

128   coachman of the gay little sledge: Fulford, 93

128   watching the first races for the Americas Cup: Lee, 24

128   never tired of watching his children at play: *Letters P.C.*, 16 February 1843

129   'Papa is my father': *KA* 8 May 1858

129   encouraged towards freedom of thought: Martin ii, 176–7 *and* 185

129   'It may be able to do much': *Letters* I, i, 365

130   'the danger inherent': *CAS* 3 February 1846

130   a 'perfect man'; Fulford, 254

130   'The only way to achieve this miracle': Magnus, 5

130   Baron Bunsen . . . was more practical: Fulford, 255

130   'treasure of political knowledge': *Letters P.C.*, 108

130   'to be accustomed early': Queen's Journal, *quoted in* Lee, 17

130   Macaulay agreed: Macaulay, *Letters*, March 1845, Trinity College Library, Cambridge

130   'longs for his poor country to rise again': *CAS* 23 February 1845 *and* Martin i, 256

131   Albert interpreted this: *CAS* 5 March 1845

131   'right to cut across prejudice': *CA* 13 April 1845 *and* Martin i, 261

131   'bigotry is more common than shame': *Letters* I, ii, 37

page
131 'assistance for popery by the state': Best, 61
131 'a giant among Prime Ministers': *CAS* 4 April 1845
131 'I do not covet honours': Martin i, 264
131 the dress he designed for Victoria: Broughton vi, 748
132 'Kowtowing to the king': *CA* May 1845
132 His heavy-handed speech: Bunsen ii, 89 *and* Martin i, 278
132 'I had such a lump in my throat': *CAS* 16 August 1845
133 'Here I stand': *CAS* 4 September 1845
133 Everything was as it always had been: Martin i, 285
134 Louis Philippe said that he would like his son to marry: *Letters* I, ii, 44–5
134 'fraught with the greatest political complications': *CA* 11 November 1845
135 Peel had been urging the Cabinet: Peel, *Memoirs* ii, 121
135 Albert's sarcastic comment: Stockmar, *Memoirs*, ii, 195
135 'Edinburgh letter': Prest, 202 *and* Gash 554–61
135 'one of the most painful moments of my life': Memo by Albert, *Letters* I, ii, 48–50
136 'must be made to understand': Greville v, 256
136 Palmerston would be sure to endanger: Memo by Albert, *Letters* I, ii, 59
136 he wanted Peel to remain Prime Minister: Peel *Memoirs* ii, 248 *and* Martin i, 311
136 'he is king to all intents and purposes': Greville vi, 257
136 'We are now standing . . . on our feet': *Letters P.C.*, 98
136 'there is one part': *Examiner*, 25 December 1845
137 'I begin to think that the *Spectator* is right': Eyck, 37
137 'a great Statesman': *CAS* 29 January 1846
137 On 27 January Albert was in the House: Gash, 570
137 He had thrown caution to the wind: Martin i, 321
137 the opportune moment never arises naturally: Peel, *Memoirs*, ii, 160
138 to untax the poor man's loaf: *CAS* 29 February 1840
138 Croker's malicious suggestion: Croker Papers ii, 66
138 Cobden's denunciation of the attacks on Peel: Gash, 579
138 nothing to do except sit it out: Gash, 588 *and* Memo by Albert *CAS* 25 April 1846
139 'I have every disposition to forgive': Peel, *Memoirs*, ii, 310
139 'behind the scenes': Memo by Albert, *CA* 4 July 1846 *and* Gash, 603
139 he even embarrassed Peel: Gash, 670

9 'There is no turning back the clock'

141 'the reply arrived with commendable speed: Gash, 672
141 the child quickly recovered: *CA* 30 May 1846
141 after the singing of a German anthem: Lyttelton, 364 *and* Martin i, 339
142 to provide the Prince of Wales with an income: Greville iv, 422
142 his own little steam yacht: *CA* 25 June 1846
143 Albert saw a welcome solution: *Letters* I, ii, 82
143 Most of Albert's misgivings: *CA* 4 September 1846
143 Palmerston as a man of no principle: *CAS* 22 May 1840
143 'Your Majesty may perhaps have heard': Connell, 34
143 Albert even accused *The Times*: *CA* 15 September 1846
144 'however hard the row': *CAS* 25 September 1846

page

145 Leopold's more equable temperament: Aberdeen, *Correspondence*, 15 December 1841

145 Albert tentatively renewed his proposal: Aberdeen, *Correspondence*, 15 December 1841

145 Ernest put the cat among the pigeons: *CA* 26 May *and* 2 June 1846

145 Peel had never seen him so distressed: *CAS* 29 September 1846

146 'What will Louis Philippe not have to answer for': *CA* 30 November 1846

146 he had indiscreetly passed on the information: Eyck, 33

147 'then she must give way to someone who has': *CAS* 12 March 1847

147 he was as resistant to reason: Greville v, 420

147 'not just royalty, but relations': *CAS* 18 March 1847

147 Ferdinand and Maria as obstinate as mules: *CA* 25 *and* 30 December 1846

147 Colonel Wylde went on the same mission: *CA* 27 April 1847

147 Greville abused the Palace openly: Greville v, 420

148 'they have not the least idea': *CAS* 2 August 1847

148 Cambridge would gain: *CAS* 23 February 1847

148 the Chancellor was only a figurehead: Winstanley, 98

148 the defence of the university's interests: Winstanley, 107

149 Albert's euphoria . . . vanished: *CAS* 20 February 1847

149 Albert was hinting to Colonel Phipps: Romilly Diary, 22 February 1847

149 'The Prince is an Englishman': Whewell Papers, February 1847

150 The interview was stilted and formal: Romilly Diary, 2 March 1847

151 'it is not a matter of the slightest consequence': Romilly Papers, 26 May 1847

151 'It is my first chance': *CA* 26 March 1847

151 a rumour soon spread that he was dying: Romilly Diary, 18 July 1847

151 'My Latin proved a success': Martin i, 399

151 there ought to be a bridge: Romilly Diary, 21 July 1847

152 'the humbug of Cambridge customs': Bunsen ii, 152

152 'use the knife for the first time': *CAS* 29 July 1847

152 entered into a kind of conspiracy with them: Winstanley, 203

152 'My plan for a reform of the studies': Martin ii, 114

152 the nation owed him a debt: Martin ii, 129

153 His dilemma was painful: Winstanley, 224 *and* 230

153 he urged the need for reform: Winstanley, 271 *and* 283–6

10   'Prince Albert has the right ideas'

154 'his natural vivacity': Stockmar, *Memoirs*, 12 April 1847

155 He founded and opened a sailors' home: *CAS* 14 July 1846

156 Albert devised a scheme: Chatsworth archives 11 October 1847

156 Macaulay was astonished at his enthusiasm: Macaulay letters, Trinity College Library, Cambridge

156 Music and the theatre were taken very seriously: Broughton, i, 240

156 'a kind of requiem': *CA* 11 December 1847

156 even the most innocent amusements: *CA* 2 January 1848

157 'I cannot imagine': *CA* 11 April 1847

158 houses like these would reduce the death-rate: Martin ii, 229

158 contacts with the lower classes: *CAS* 12 November 1849

159 Greville had hitherto written him off: Greville vi, 185

159 A day at the Braemar Games: Greville vi, 186

page
159 'Life in the Highlands': *CA* 12 November 1849
160 Albert was off to inspect the prison: *Leaves,* 109
161 No doubt he was much influenced by Peel: Hodder i, 451
161 'the bold stand you have taken up': *CAS* 30 March 1843
161 when Wriothesley Russell took communion: Bunsen ii, 112
162 His first sermon in the Chapel Royal: *CAS* 27 September 1841
162 'It is not thought proper': *CAS* 20 January 1843
162 why a game of chess was so much more wicked on a Sunday: *CA* 12 October 1844
163 'I have spoken as thoughts have struck me': Martin i, 132–4
163 the form of the letter: Bayerische Staatsarchiv Coburg, Stockmar-Archiv, II c.8
163 Wilberforce's appointment to Oxford: Newsome, *Parting,* 304; Chadwick, 229 *and* Fulford, 189
164 the connexion between private and public morality: Longford, 340
164 the Syriac scholar William Cureton: *Letters* I, ii, 121
164 Arnold's testimonial: Newsome, *Godliness,* 98
164 an undistinguished and unsuccessful bishop: Newsome, *Godliness,* 135–47
165 Stockmar warned Albert: *CAS* 12 December 1847
165 Albert's distress: *CAS* 13 December 1847
165 Greville believed that he bombarded Russell: Greville vi, i *and* Fulford, 199
165 'shown the cloven hoof': *CAS* 4 December 1847
165 'a lack of prudence': *CAS* 9 January 1848
165 'waging war upon a minister': Memo by Albert *CAS* undated
165 'perhaps the next suggestion': *CAS* 18 January 1848
165 'mummeries of superstition': Martin ii, 338
166 'well-marked emphasis': Martin ii, 339
166 the Queen and Albert signified their disapproval: *Letters* I, ii, 279
166 it was a poor reward: Prest, 300
166 an indication that loyalty had survived: *CAS* 8 August 1849
167 'stab in the back': *CAS* 4 April 1848
167 it would soon be too late: *CA* 11 April 1848
167 proposed several solutions of his own: *CAS* 23 August 1847 *and* Martin ii, 135–8
168 a scheme for joint employer/employee savings: *CAS* 10 April 1850
169 The only permanent remedy: *CAS* 12 January 1844
169 'interest and sympathy for the lower orders': Eyck, 163

11 'Like a series of dissolving views'

170 'it could rest on its new foundations' *CA* 20 February 1848
170 'The political horizon grows darker': *CAS* 8 October 1847
170 'Civilisation and liberal institutions': Martin i, 432–3
171 'given the people the cold shoulder': *CA* 9 March 1848
171 'She was an angel upon earth': *Letters P.C.,* 135
172 'What has happened is a terrible indictment': *CA* 21 March 1848
172 'If the Parisians are resolved': Broughton i, 203
172 'You see, I know how to play the part': *CAS* 12 July 1843
173 when the foreigners refused to adapt themselves: Lyttelton, 374
174 'hard and unfeeling': Ridley, 336 *and CA* 24 March 1848

page
174   'Vive la Republique': Prest, 284
174   'people who sympathise with the French': *CA* 14 March 1848
174   the great Chartist demonstration: *CAS* 5 April 1842
175   he had advised Ernest to give way: *CA* 17 February 1846
175   unless he made concessions at once: *CA* 17 March 1848
175   'it all depends': *CA* 13 April 1848
176   It was an impossible amalgam!: *CA* 21 March *and* 11 April 1848; *also* *Letters P.C.*, 136–8
176   'Germany cannot do without men like William': Martin ii, 111
177   Palmerston knew nothing about Germany: *CA* 3 September 1848
177   he was the target of innuendo or attack: Eyck, 104
177   'see Germany wiped off the face of the earth': *CAS* 3 May 1848
178   'I honour the reserve': *Letters P.C.*, 174

12   'The drop which made the cup overflow'

179   The duke of Bedford had assured Victoria and Albert: *CAS* 25 September 1846
182   Even Greville thought this was going too far: Greville v, 433
182   'yielded to a sudden impulse': *CAS* 21 August 1848
183   no reason why a north Italian state should be set up: Eyck, 111
183   'absurdly' pro-Sardinian: Martin ii, 79
183   His own solution would be quicker: *CAS* 27 July 1848
183   'She cannot conceal from Lord Palmerston': *Letters* I, ii, 182
183   'the establishment of an *entente cordiale*': *Letters* I, ii, 186
184   came up with the preposterous suggestion: Memo by Albert, *CAS* 19 September 1848
185   'which would be very disagreeable': Memo by the Queen, *Letters* I, ii, 195
185   'very bad terms': Eyck, 117
185   Palmerston brushed the rebuke aside: *CAS* 21 December 1848
185   'I consider Austria's *rancune*': *CAL* 20 December 1848 *and* Eyck, 118
186   it was only boredom: Memo by Albert 24 January 1849, *and* Eyck, 120
187   placing the country in a terrible predicament: *CA* 14 February 1850
187   Albert remarked bitterly: Memo by Albert, *Letters* I, ii, 235 *and* Eyck, 132
187   'As the Roman in the days of old': Ridley, 387
188   'It will be more difficult': *CA* 27 June 1850
188   although Albert was generous enough: Martin ii, 285
188   'no very high standard of honour': Albert to Russell, 2 April 1850 *and* Eyck, 134
189   'Palmerston is mad': *CAS* 25 August 1850 *and* Stockmar, *Memoirs*, 458 *and* 162
189   'The least the Queen has a right to require': *Letters* I, ii, 238
189   it demonstrated her right to dismiss a minister: *Letters* I, ii, 264
189   in future he would obey her commands: Connell, 123
190   'we can no longer see the picture clearly': *CAS* 25 August 1850
190   'Prussia is saved': *CAS* 5 September 1850
191   'he is a thoroughly bad character': *CAS* 14 October 1850
191   a rare letter from the Prince of Prussia: *Letters P.C.*, 180
191   After a moment of blustering defiance: Connell, 132
192   'the drop which made the cup overflow': *Letters* I, ii, 348
192   the agent of his own destruction: *CA* 29 December 1851

page
192 'We have known for some time': *Letters P.C.*, 179
192 'Lord Palmerston is not coming off well': *CAS* 24 December 1851
192 'self-willed lord': Stockmar, *Memoirs*, 458
192 'There *was* a Palmerston': Dasent, 57
193 Victoria's far more intransigent attitude: Eyck, 152
193 'ignorance of the British constitution': Jennings, 160
193 It was he, not Stockmar: Greville vi, 324

13 'A monarchy that was a myth has become a reality'
197 Albert would supply some modern farming equipment: *CAS* 12 April 1848
197 he received a glowing report: *CAS* 5 June 1848
197 an estate in Bohemia: *CA* 20 June, 3 September *and* 20 October 1851
197 an exhibition of farm equipment: *CAS* 12 April 1848
198 'Science discovers the laws of power': Martin ii, 248
199 Albert suggested Leicester Square: Cole i, 424
199 One instance of this: Cole i, 125
199 his mission had been highly successful: Martin ii, 226
200 'Nobody who has paid any attention': Martin ii, 247–8
200 'Albert is indeed looked up to: Martin ii, 249
200 'this will stir others': Cole i, 168–9
200 'exactly the kind of hideosity': Paxton Papers 10 June 1850
201 'the same length as Portland Place': Paxton Papers July 1850
201 after a meeting of the Commissioners: *CAS* 28 July 1850
202 Gladstone had already seen the effects: Morley i, 372
202 'Peel, the best of men': Martin ii, 290
203 Sir John Airey . . . wrote a pamphlet: Cole i, 187
203 'this den of vice': Sykes, Colonel Sibthorpe, 14
203 constant accusations of tale-bearing: Cole, Diary, 5 March 1851
203 he threatened Fox and Henderson: Cole, Diary, 17 March 1851
204 'peace, love and ready assistance': Martin ii, 248
205 Cole reckoned that each visit: Cole, Diary, 17 April 1851
205 'I hear that the Ministers': *Letters P.C.*, 175
205 'It is probably': *Letters P.C.*, 176–7
205 his brother and his family would come: *CAS* 14 April 1851
205 'firm as ever in his constitutional views': Martin ii, 362
206 'this storm-tossed world': Stockmar, *Memoirs* i, 299
206 'God bless my dearest Albert': Queen's Journal, *quoted by* Martin ii, 266
207 news of its success would spread: Martin ii, 404
207 severe warnings about Russian power: *CAS* 9 *and* 30 May 1851
208 'We regret for their own sakes': Martin ii, 346
209 'we have distinctly pledged ourselves': Martin ii, 569–70
209 he had gone carefully into every detail: *CAS* 22 October 1851
209 'considering the enormity of the job': Cole i, 319
210 without him there would have been no exhibition: Cole, Diary, 21 May 1851
210 'I always say that the Exhibition: Cole, Diary, 30 July 1851
211 'a slouching hesitant air': Greville, iv, 260

14 'The duke had to be content'
212 more beautiful than ever at Balmoral: *Letters* I, ii, 321
212 'retreat into my shell': Martin ii, 391

page
212 'I don't think the Queen thinks of reading': Stanley, 172
213 'an individuality about them': Martin ii, 334
213 'one of the least obtrusive': Dasent, i, 434
213 using the Press as a mouthpiece: Dasent i, 163
213 Clarendon's connexion with *The Times*: *Letters* I, ii, 289
213 the only minister to show the right attitude: *Letters* I, ii, 375
214 *The Times* in prematurely leaking the news: Croker Diaries ii, 52
214 'ruled by a rod of iron': *CAS* 12 October 1846
214 'not to believe everything as gospel': *CA* 5 June 1855
214 'I cannot complain of this last year': *Letters P.C.*, 180
215 if he offered the post to Granville: *CAS* 23 December 1851
216 'Civis Romanus NON sum': *CAS* 3 January 1852
216 Another dig of Granville's: Memo by Albert, *Letters* I, ii, 344
217 Even a child as placid as Alice: *Letters* I, ii, 321
217 'as though he were asleep': *CAS* 2 April 1845
217 in these moods he took in nothing: *CAS* 12 May 1845
218 almost no progress by the age of six: Stanley, 122
218 'The duke of Cornwall for ever': Bunsen ii, 121
219 Again, it has been asserted: Woodham-Smith, 334
219 'a semi-gypsy life': Lyttelton, 363
219 the separation of Affie and Bertie: Longford, 274
220 'This is not my idea of family fun': Fulford, 95
220 'an atmosphere of affection': Woodham-Smith, 403
220 'a young, good-looking, amiable man': *Letters P.C.*, 149
220 might frown on shooting and dancing: *CAS* 12 January 1849
221 unsafe without constant supervision: *CAS* 20 November 1849
221 giving Birch so many notes and parting presents: Woodham-Smith, 336
221 Dr Varsin, the exponent of freedom: Magnus, 26
221 Dr Combe, the fashionable phrenologist: Fulford, 256
221 'small and not well shaped': Gladstone, *Letters*, 55
221 'like a person half silly': Hibbert, *Court at Windsor*, 234 quoting Gibbs's
     diary
222 'a most kind, disinterested friend': *Letters* I, ii, 204
222 'A very hard and painful loss': *CA* 8 November 1849
223 'it is the letter of an angel': *CA* 25 October 1850
223 'mortality, eternity and the Creator': *CAS* 15 September 1852
223 as though a clock had slowed down: Memo by Albert, *Letters* I, ii, 329
223 the duke of Wellington's funeral: *CA* 18 September 1852
223 A sketch was prepared by Professor Gottfried Semper: Duke of Welling-
     ton: The Great Duke's Funeral, *History Today* 2 (1952), 778–84
224 Wellington had come to Windsor: Martin ii, 252–62
224 'I should not like to undertake': *CAS* 25 April 1850
224 'I must discard the tempting idea': Martin ii, 260–1
225 'This position is a most peculiar and delicate one': Martin ii, 259–60
226 Lord Hardinge was the best choice: *CA* 17 September 1852
226 George of Cambridge was briefly considered: *Letters* I, ii, 393

15 'Deaf to the calls of honour and duty'

227 Albert entirely shared Palmerston's view: *CA* 8 February 1852
228 Albert had to cover for her: Memo by Albert, *CAS* 22 February 1852

page

228 'fitted the Foreign Office like a glove'; *CA* 27 February 1852
228 whose moral character was not above reproach : *Letters* I, ii, 371
228 'sound and fixed principles' : *CAS* 16 March 1852
229 convinced free-traders during the last six years : Morley ii, 426
229 'the Derby militia' : *CA* 10 March 1852
229 'Lord John Russell has lost all power' : *CA* 16 May 1852
229 'What a lot' : *CAS* 17 May 1852
229 to raise an army of 100,000 men : Gash, 552
229 'Men, we need more men' : *CA* 20 September 1845
230 England must not seem so defenceless : Peel Papers ii, 197 *and* Gash, 520
230 comparing strong military forces to an umbrella : Ridley, 401
230 'The country is fully alive to its dangers' : *Letters* I, ii, 399
230 Disraeli wrote a soothing letter : *Letters* I, ii, 399
231 a man in bed with a snake : *Letters* I, ii, 377
231 a flock of sheep, not statesmen : *CAS* 25 October 1852
231 a sample of the new Prussian needle-gun : *CA* 2 November 1852
231 the shipbuilding programme must be speeded up : Martin ii, 499
232 'that antiquated imbecility' : *CAS* 4 July 1849
232 'these valuable suggestions' : Memo by Albert, *Letters* I, ii, 414–15
232 'could not help laughing heartily : *Letters* I, ii, 420
232 'he cannot do any mischief' : Aberdeen, *Correspondence*, 301–5
233 'splendid' : Martin i, 473
233 'from a miserable eagerness' : *Addressess*, 139
234 it was all for her : *CAS* 4 December 1853
234 the beautifully embossed hunting book : *CA* 28 August 1852
234 'You think I only need to wave a wand' : *CA* 4 August 1851
235 exciting possibilities for the theatre : *CAS* 5 March 1853
235 'How much better it sounds' : *CA* 12 May 1854
237 the baby was a constant source of anxiety : *CA* 8 April 1853
237 Stockmar noticed this : Stockmar *Memoirs*, i, 289
238 'in peace as well as in war' : *CAS* 4 January 1853
238 'All this talk of waste of money' : *CAS* 10 June 1853
238 'If Boney comes to Chobham camp' : Ridley, 401
239 How versatile were the men : *CAS* 29 June 1853
240 The Queen fancifully attributed his slow recovery : *CA* 20 July 1853
240 'I am often astonished at the effect' : *CAS* 12 November 1853
241 'embittered the life of the Queen and the Prince' : Woodham-Smith, 329
242 'weigh up both sides carefully' : *CAS* undated
242 'the idol of the people' : Martin ii, 469
243 'Your appeal to me to take the place of the duke' : *Letters P.C.*, 184–5
243 'If Mama is Queen, why is not Papa King?' : *Letters of Lady Augusta Stanley*, 46

16   'Killed by their own people'

244 with such a calm and judicious Prime Minister : Conacher, 48
244 'The realisation of our own most ardent wishes' : Memo by Albert, *Letters* I, ii, 427
245 settled a problem over Turkey : Aberdeen, *Correspondence*, 100 *and* 110–11
245 wanted to reserve her strength for a State visit : Aberdeen, *Correspondence*, 182–9

page

245 to give Palmerston a private grievance: Aberdeen, *Correspondence*, 219–22

245 Aberdeen advised against cancellation: Aberdeen, *Correspondence*, 28 July 1853

245 'every museum in England must know about it': Hone, J., Queen Victoria in Ireland, 1853, in *History Today*, 3 (1953) 500–8

246 he shot twenty-six stags . . . at Balmoral: *CA* 20 October 1853

246 a Cabinet divided against itself: Conacher, 154 *and* Eyck, 218

247 de Redcliffe's . . . many contributions towards the maintenance of peace: Temperley, 314 *and* Henderson in *History Today* 2 (1952), 729–37

247 encouragement England and France had already given to Turkey: Martin ii, 521

247 'exhibits clearly on his part a desire for war': *Letters* I, ii, 460

247 in the hope that Palmerston would resign: Aberdeen, *Correspondence*, 382–3

247 The Aberdeen correspondence: Aberdeen, *Correspondence*, 382–3, 393–4

247 'outwit himself, as clever men sometimes do': *CA* 12 December 1853

248 'Now Palmerston is again in his seat': Martin ii, 535

248 'The Emperor of Russia now reigns in England': *CA* 7 January 1854

249 'it is too bad that one man': *Morning Herald* 15 January 1854

249 'The country is as loyal as ever': Martin ii, 541 *and* 542

249 'We might fancy we were living in a madhouse': *Letters P.C.*, 203

250 'one of the greatest scamps in all France': *CAS* 9 November 1853

250 no more than a tool of the Prince: Stockmar, *Memoirs*, ii, 489

250 the quarrel between Hardinge and Sir George Brown: Ridley, 424

250 'cold and unfeeling': *CA* 15 January 1854

250 The Lord Chancellor . . . wisely discouraged him: Macaulay Papers, 17 January 1854

250 he wondered whether he were not being blackmailed: *Letters P.C.*, 204

251 'I cannot wish': Martin ii, 545

251 'A very considerable section of the nation': Martin ii, 599–60

251 'When the people of this country': Stockmar, *Memoirs*, ii, 504

252 'Nothing could have been more clear': *CAL* 3 February 1854

252 'From what I have been able to learn': *CA* 27 August 1840

253 Frederick William could not sleep at night: *CAS* 25 March 1854

253 'This is the consequence': *CA* 14 April 1854

254 'terrible cry to arms': *CAS* 24 March 1854

254 'as uninteresting as they are innocent': *CAS* 7 April 1854

254 Francis Joseph intended to keep his country out of the war: *Letters* I, iii, 24

254 'the "sick man" ': *Letters* I, iii, 27

254 Delane's arguments were the weightier: Dasent, i, 155

255 His despatches corroborated all that Albert had been saying: Dasent, i, 175

255 she willingly rose before dawn: *Letters* I, iii, 14

255 to watch the fleet set sail for the Baltic: *CAS* 14 March 1854

256 'in Kronstadt or in Hell': Dasent, i, 172

256 Albert was inclined to defend him to the Queen: Aberdeen, *Correspondence*, 205–6

257 'I feel for you': Martin iii, 61

257 Napoleon deliberately set out to change: Aberdeen, *Correspondence*, 205–6

page

257   'We discussed foreign and domestic affairs': *CA* 12 September 1854
258   Napoleon needed the prestige: Aberdeen, *Correspondence*, 6 September 1854
259   By far his largest scheme: *Letters P.C.*, 231
259   Albert steered the Foreign Enlistment Bill: Conacher, 513
259   'a strange bit of home': *CA* undated
260   Russians had no need of espionage: Dasent, i, 201–2
260   But he was immediate sceptical: Martin iii, 129
261   'Precious time has been wasted': *CAS* 4 February 1855
261   'the man of the day': Morley i, 532
262   'I concur in His Royal Highness's remarks': Hibbert, *Raglan*, 296
262   a system of regular returns from the front: Martin iii, 179
262   No doubt Raglan was largely to blame: *CAL* 20 January 1855
263   'In his extreme desire': Hamley, 107
263   his interference had nearly broken Canrobert's nerve: Hibbert, *Raglan*, 324
264   'a great deal of German': Martin iii, 108
264   the Emperor was easy, calm and dignified: Martin iii, 249
264   A Council of War was held: *CAS* 20 April 1855
264   Evidently unused to such plain speaking: *CAS* 23 April 1855
265   'not to risk his neck in the Crimea': *Letters* I, iii, 155–7
265   'all three irreplaceable': *CA* 24 May 1855
265   'I consider it my duty': *CA* 2 August 1855
266   'playing the game for England': *CAL* 27 August 1855
266   confiscated the Orleanist family's private property: Greville viii, 15
266   would be delighted if Amélie passed through France: Martin, iii, 395
266   'You may well imagine what a strange impression': *Letters P.C.*, 231 *and* Martin iii, 359
267   They talked of Spain: *CAS* 30 August 1855
268   'He quite admits that it is extraordinary': Martin iii, 351
268   Aberdeen was wrong: *Correspondence of Aberdeen and Princess Lieven* 16 October 1843
268   Lord Derby had deprecated the tone: Croker Diary iii, 250
268   it was 'a piece of extraordinarily good luck': *CA* 12 May 1855
269   'Our bonfire on Craig Gowan': *Letters P.C.*, 233–4
269   'He bore his many trials like a true hero': *CAS* 12 July 1855
269   'when the fog that envelops everything': *CA* undated
269   'no one who has not taken part': Martin iii, 450
270   'my sovereign and her husband': Martin iii, 450
270   Prussia was only admitted: Dasent i, 234
270   Disraeli who defended him best: Blake, 365
270   Lord Cowley said that England would have obtained better terms: Greville vii, 209

17   'Friendship cannot go much higher'

271   It was a poor reward for his efforts: *Letters* I, iv, 168
272   Albert was suddenly overcome with emotion: *CAS* 25 January 1856
272   he discovered and launched John Martin: Pendered, 134
272   'to raise the whole standard of art education': *Letters and Journals of Lady Eastlake* i, 324

page
273 he was worn out by Gladstone's discouragement: Ames, 120
273 his friends among the Manchester Art-Treasures Commissioners: Ames, 123
273 'the fetters are not easy to break': *CA* 5 April 1854
275 Prussia's 'deplorable politics': *CAS* 17 September 1855
275 'playing at soldiers': *CAS* 28 September 1855
276 'What joy it will be for Vicky': *KA* 15 October 1855
276 'From the moment you declared your love': *KA* 15 October 1855
276 'My precious, madly-loved Fritz': *KA* 15 October 1855
276 'The intended is more and more in love': *CA* 30 October 1855
276 'an appendage of Russia': *KA* 5 August 1856
276 Victoria did not beat about the bush: *KA* 14 August 1856
276 'and the lower classes look on the Czar': *KA* 4 September 1856
276 'with your sound and sensible Teutonic background': *KA* 9 September 1856
277 'the Russians are getting all the principal families': *CA* 21 September 1856
277 Arthur Dasent . . . made it plain: Dasent i, 219
277 Albert has been praised for his courage: Eyck, 239
278 'Distasteful articles': *CA* 19 January 1856
278 Albert saw nothing ominous: *CAS* 2 June 1856
279 'It is enough': *Letters P.C.*, 247
279 'whatever may be the usual practice of Prussian princes': *Letters* I, iii, 321
279 'renounced her position': *KA* 9 February 1857
280 he insisted that Stockmar's son: *KA* 12 October 1857 *and cf Vicky*, 39
280 'She will be reconciled in time': *KA* 1 November 1856
280 It delighted Albert to know: *CAS* 12 November 1857
281 'It is a great pity that the designs are only Raphaels': *Journal of Lady Eastlake*, ii, 85
281 'I had to read all the speeches': *CA* 23 April 1857

18 'To fit a gentleman with a gentleman's education'

282 'In appearance, arrangement and marching': *CA* 15 September 1856
282 Aldershot had not been created: *CAS* 21 January 1857
283 In a memo which he drew up in 1850: *CAS* 12 August 1850
284 A letter to Ernest in 1849: *CA* 20 March 1849
284 'only through education': *CAS* 22 September 1850
284 Derby put a proposal before the Cabinet: Wellington College Archives, Derby to Temple, 20 March 1860
284 the draft of a public appeal for funds: Newsome, *Wellington*, 8–9
285 'the education of orphan children': Newsome, *Wellington*, 8–9
285 thus Wellington was neither to be a military school: Newsome, *Wellington*, 70
285 'hardly worth while to establish another public school': Wellington College Archives, Phipps to Benson, 8 September 1860 *and* Newsome, *Wellington*, 118
285 'I want my boy to go into life': Newsome, *Wellington*, 80–1
285 'educational testament': Newsome, *Wellington*, 83
286 a 'system of fagging and flogging': Wellington College Archives, Phipps to Benson, 28 February 1860

page

286 'His Royal Highness has the strongest feeling': Wellington College Archives, Phipps to Benson, 1 February 1861 *and* Newsome, *Wellington*, 119

287 'the closing act of the war': Martin iii, 499 *and CAS* 12 July 1856

287 'believed that he needed nothing else': Martin iii, 500

287 he longed to be at the helm of the *Fairy*: Martin iii, 500

288 'What a head': *Letters* I, iii, 170 *and CAS* 20 September 1856

288 delighted when she confirmed his opinion: Ridley, 518

288 a building 'which should cut a dash': Ridley, 508–9 *and* Woodham-Smith, *Florence Nightingale*, 215–17

288 Albert wrote a diplomatically-phrased letter to Napoleon: Martin iv, 31

288 'a revival of communications': *Letters* I, iii, 232

289 he was now statesman enough to know: *Letters* I, iii, 233–4

289 'so as not to arouse Czar Alexander': *CA* 25 July 1857

289 'and I have to rub my eyes to be sure': *CA* 9 August 1857

290 Albert persuaded Napoleon to reaffirm his loyalty: Martin iv, 99–113

290 'The Prince can say many things that we cannot': Martin iv, 98–9

291 The Emperor did not make him and Victoria feel any better: *CAS* 18 August 1858

292 'the eyes of all Europe': Martin iv, 271

292 'unalterable devotion to the English alliance': *CAS* 18 August 1858

292 when Napoleon escorted his guests back: Martin iv, 273–4 *and* Malmesbury, *Memoirs*, ii, 129

292 'the war preparations in the French marine': Martin iv, 278

292 the peril presented by the Cherbourg defences: Broughton vi, 77

293 To bring the navy up to standard again: *Letters* I, ii, 241–2

293 'Of course it ought to have been done long ago': *CA* 27 June 1857

293 difficult to make up for an opportunity: *CA* 29 June 1857

293 'an English prince has rights as such': *CA* 29 June 1857

293 'mischief-makers could easily have stirred up the Prince of Wales': *CA* 29 June 1857

294 'the beginning of a new era': *CAS* 21 June 1857

295 The Prussians were eager to meet the new-made Prince Consort: Eyck, 238

19 'A future disappearing into the past'

297 the *Morning Chronicle* published a long and admiring article: *Morning Chronicle* 8 September 1854

297 'We agriculturalists of England': *Speeches*, 92

297 Charles of Leiningen . . . had died: *CA* 20 April 1847

297 'as in a line facing the enemy': *CA* 8 December 1857

298 Victoria's moans about Prussia: *Letters* I, iii, 263

299 'too severe with the children': *CAS* 2 December 1857

299 'Claremont has claimed another victim': *CA* 11 November 1857

299 Albert acted as he should have done: *CA* 11 November 1857

300 'Vicky's last Christmas at home': *CAS* 27 December 1857

300 'I do not let any hint of this be seen': Martin iv, 150

300 'the people to whom you belong': *KA* 24 February 1857

300 'do not reflect the mood of the people': *KA* 22 November 1857

301 'Mama's fluctuating moods': *KA* 3 December 1857

page
301   the Queen wrote to Fritz: *KA* 6 December 1857
301   'we will manage it somehow': *CA* 23 December 1857
302   'For Alexandrine one maid': *CA* 15 January 1858
302   Fritz showed up splendidly: *CAS* 30 January 1858
302   'I should be neglecting a duty': *Letters P.C.*, 285
302   in her correspondence with Augusta: *Further Letters of Queen Victoria*, 60
304   'My heart was very full': *Letters P.C.*, 288

20   'It is the government, and not the Commons,
        who hold back'

306   Palmerston was genuinely taken aback: Bell ii, 142 *and CAS* 15 April 1856
306   to present the Queen with the *Resolute*: *CAS* 27 December 1856
307   'It is impossible to speak of the horrors': *CA* 4 September 1857
307   Let the Government rather fall on its knees: *CAS* 6 September 1857
308   'the Cabinet must look the question boldly in the face': Martin iv, 91
308   'I trust that no undue leniency will be adopted': Ridley, 476
309   'undermining native religions': Martin iv, 285
309   'a direct mention of railways': Martin iv, 285
310   'Danger is our business': Martin iv, 155 *and CAS* 15 January 1858
310   Conspiracy to Murder Bill: *Letters P.C.*, 289
310   this would mean the fall of the government: *CA* 26 February 1858
311   Ellenborough was demanding: Memo by Albert *CAS* 22 February 1858
       and Martin iv, 192
311   'You have kept down and overcome': *Letters P.C.*, 290
311   'The whole family is delighted': *KA* 22 April 1858
312   'sacred trust': *Letters P.C.*, 291
312   'that outside of and in close proximity to': *Letters P.C.*, 299
312   'still I cannot wish': Martin ii, 545
313   Albert understood that it was of the utmost importance: *Letters P.C.*, 298
314   'Please keep my visit a secret': *CA* 22 April 1858
314   'Leopold Brabant has promised': *CA* 22 April 1858
316   'it would not go down well in London': Martin iv, 238–9
316   'The relationship between the young couple': *Letters P.C.*, 302 *and*
       Martin iv, 241
317   Kurt was 'invaluable': Queen's Journal *quoted by* Martin iv, 281
318   'Fear stands in the way of love': *Letters P.C.*, 296
318   'Everyone . . . in Europe is waiting': *Letters P.C.*, 309
318   Ernest . . . turned up unexpectedly: Martin iv, 298
319   He had failed to interest a single MP: *CAS* 4 May 1846
319   'A plan afoot to rehouse': *CAS* 11 May 1858
320   'dwelling on the many lives': *CAS* 11 May 1858
320   'he had . . . reached the position of prime minister': Blake, *Disraeli*, 369

21   'Sentimentality is a plant that cannot grow in England'

321   the Reverend Charles Tarver defended him: Magnus, 21
321   Bertie's attempts at letter-writing: *CAS* 12 August 1857
321   he had been made to accompany his selfish old father: *CA* 18 August 1836
322   Albert had to remind him: *CAS* 27 February 1858
322   'He is idle and weak': *KA* undated

414

page

322 'Yes, yes, yes': *KA* 27 April 1858
322 'Quiet and gentle': *KA* 1 April 1858
322 he was to be kept 'away from the world': Martin iv, 206
323 the softening influence of Lord Valletort: Martin iv, 207
323 proper behaviour by example: Picken, 49
323 'I am in despair': *KA* 8 March 1858
323 The argument lasted so long: *CA* undated
324 'a good man and a thorough gentleman': *KA* 9 November 1858
324 'Unfortunately he takes no interest in anything': *KA* 17 November 1858
324 'harnessed to a good wife': *KA* 1 December 1858
325 another complaining letter to Vicky: *KA* 1 December 1858
325 the Queen still found him 'very dull': *KA* 4 December 1858
325 'all head and no face': *KA* 2 December 1858
325 'To play such tricks on a servant': *KA* 12 December 1858
325 'a little less factual': *KA* 18 December 1858
326 'sombre Holyrood': *CA* 4 September 1857
326 He was to go to Oxford in the autumn: Romilly Papers, 1859
326 his mother scolded him for eating too much: *KA* 5 March 1859
326 'I must not censure him': *KA* 11 January 1859
327 'When one considers that he might be called upon': *KA* 4 January 1859
327 'The greatest improvement': *KA* 9 April 1859
327 'the improvement in your son': Martin v, 87
327 'that you see so many signs of improvement': Martin v, 87
328 'distant rising countries': Martin v, 88
328 'He has a strange nature': *CA* 27 April 1860
328 'Is that not remarkable': *KA* 31 October 1860
328 'As Ambassador Extraordinary': *CAS* 5 November 1860
329 'It is sad': *KA* 20 November 1860
329 the Poet Laureate having flatly refused: *Cambridge Daily News* 19 January 1860
329 the glowing accounts Lady Affleck gave: Affleck Papers, January–March 1861, Trinity College Library, Cambridge
330 'photographs show the Prince of Wales looking small': Woodham-Smith, 407
331 'the difference in their ages': *CA* 12 May 1856
331 'two other considerations': *CA* 1 March 1857
332 'Sentimentality is a plant': *CA* 23 May 1857

22 'He is king in all but name'

333 a statement 'as to the force of screw-ships': *Letters* iii, 242
334 Greville noted a conversation: Greville vii, 305
334 'King in all but name': Greville vii, 305
334 Albert had written some of the best papers: Greville vii, 306
334 outvoted at a meeting of the Trustees: *CAS* 27 May 1857
335 he got his way at once: Martin iv, 60–2 *and Speeches*, 183
335 that dreadful thing, democracy: *CAS* 25 May 1859
335 'the Prince Consort exhibits great discretion': Dallas, 45
337 'the true niceness and charm': Eastlake i, 263
337 he allowed a second exhibition to be planned: *CAS* 4 March 1859
338 Palmerston behaved most sensibly: *CAS* 12 June 1859

page

339   Napoleon was only a 'paper ogre': *KA* 12 January 1859
339   admitted that war was indeed likely: *KA* 30 January 1859
339   'cold, unfeeling and hard': *CA* 2 February 1859
339   he lacked his usual good judgement: Eyck, 245
339   'The boasting of the Austrians': *CA* 18 June 1859
340   Public imagination was 'captured by the sight': *CAS* 10 August 1859 *and* Martin iv, 437
340   'Fritz would have been surprised': *KA* 27 June 1860
340   Albert agreed about their appearance: *CA* 13 May 1860
340   'which in some papers': *KA* 20 March 1860
341   'the best spirit prevails among them': *KA* 27 June 1860 *and* Martin v, 127
341   'I read thick volumes': *KA* 10 August 1859
341   'They tumbled out of four wagonnettes': *KA* 19 September 1859
341   stalking deer with Grant: *CA* 19 September 1859
342   'violent cramp at the pit of the stomach': Martin iv, 500
342   'All around you there is a want of thoughtful care': Martin iv, 501
342   'muddled, contradictory and dangerous': *KA* 4 May 1860
343   letting off steam to Vicky about Napoleon III: *KA* 15 June 1860
343   'not caring what happens to our children': *KA* 13 June 1860
343   he sent Louis away: *KA* 12 August 1860
343   provision should now be made in advance: Connell, 303
343   Alfred wrote cheerful letters: *CA* 23 February 1860
344   His presence justified the salute: Stanley, 346
344   She thought his clothes 'quite frightful': *KA* 7 April 1860
344   Stockmar had been warning him: *CAS passim*; *cf CA* 4 May 1848
344   he urged on Ernest: *CA* 16 March 1848

23   'Like the hawk, I must not sleep, but be for ever
on the watch'

346   William was indeed ageing: *KA* 25 October 1860
346   deterioration in Albert's appearance: *KA* 2 November 1860
346   'surely he is meant for great things': *KA* 20 October 1860
347   he remarked to his old tutor Florschütz: *Memoirs*, duke Ernest II, iv, 55
348   he would never see Coburg again: *Memoirs*, duke Ernest II, iv, 55
349   'England's life-blood lies in the sea': *CAS* 16 November 1860
350   'smash the British navy to atoms': *CAS* 20 November 1860
350   'It is a perfect disgrace to our country': Martin v, 256–7
350   equality with France was not enough: Martin v, 256–7
350   Albert went down with another attack: *KA* 6 December 1860
350   'I was too miserable yesterday': Martin v, 255
351   'though I don't expect much good of it': *CA* 29 December 1860
352   a long lecture on European affairs: *KA* 27 February 1861
352   'a bad deed, but in a good cause': *KA* 16 July 1861
352   'Pray Heaven not to make us a present of Herr von Bismarck': *CA* 12 July 1861
352   Physical symptoms of ill health multiplied: *CAS* 15 July 1861
354   not for nearly another week: Martin v, 295–6
355   'gone out like a light': *CA* 1 March 1861
356   The duchess had thrown nothing away: *KA* 10 April 1861
356   deny the 'vile rumours': *CA* 18 June 1861

page

356 'I love to dwell on Mama': *KA* 13 April 1861
357 to the mausoleum at Frogmore: Lee, i, 117
357 'Unfortunately, princesses do not spring up like mushrooms': *KS* 20 April 1861
357 'You must marry the Prince of Wales off': *KA* 1 October 1861
357 goings-on at Hesse-Cassel: *KA* 29 April 1861
357 'how little he has to offer': *KA* 12 April 1861
358 'I don't think he is capable of enthusiasm': *KA* 25 April 1861
358 'a strange nature, real Brunswick': *CA* 27 April 1860
358 would wait because he was the best match: *KA* 7 May 1861
358 could not be made to fall in love to order: *KA* 8 May 1861
358 beginning to be attracted to Alexandra: *KA* 4 June 1861

24   'Everything but health'

359 His temperature rose again: *CA* 16 May 1861
359 attacks were becoming more frequent: *CAS* 26 May 1861
359 the success of Aldershot: *CAS* 28 May 1861
360 'Men have not the sympathy . . . of women': *KA* 31 May 1861
360 begged Leopold to persuade the Queen: *CAL* 19 June 1861
361 'used up physically and politically': Martin v, 407
362 He even upbraided Ernest: *KA* 11 May 1861
362 'If we are to found Bertie's future': *CA* 21 July 1861
362 The case of the Sandhurst cadets: Martin v, 367
363 'I know I dare not stop for a moment': *CA* 30 August 1861
363 a slighter companion of Hesse-Darmstadt: *KA* 2 January 1861
364 'nothing dries up creative talent like neglect': *CAS* 25 May 1859
364 'Tomorrow our marriage': *Letters P.C.*, 358
365 'sure to carry the day eventually': Martin v, 404
365 the Queen began to recover her spirits: *Leaves*, 216
365 Affie would be serving in American waters: *CA* 3 September 1861
365 a load off his mind to receive from Vicky: *KA* 26 September 1861
365 If only Louis' uncle: *KA* 1 October 1861
365 William's excuse, passed on by Vicky: *KA* 5 October 1861
366 the Queen was writing to Vicky: *KA* 1 November 1861
366 soon reduced to begging Phipps: Martin v, 413
366 hope that . . . no deaths in the Queen's family: *KA* 15 November 1861
367 'stricken to the core': *CAS* 20 November 1861
367 Albert to have been in an abnormal state of mind: Woodham-Smith, 416
367 'I never saw him so low': *KA* 27 November 1861
367 'without the basis of health': *Letters P.C.*, 369
367 'Much worry and great sorrow': 29 November 1861
368 'I do not cling to life': Martin v, 415
368 'which touched me to the heart': *KA* 25 November 1861
369 'felt as if cold water': Martin v, 427
370 'There is no cause for alarm': *KA* 7 December 1861
370 from room to room in search of repose: *KA* 6 December 1861
371 he and Clark suspected a low fever: Martin v, 431
372 'Were you asleep?': From an anonymous account published in a German periodical (unidentified) of the 1860s, Staatsarchiv, Coburg
372 asked for the 'King's Room': *KA* 8 December 1861

page

372 Albert insisted on seeing them: *KA* 9 December 1861 *and* Martin v, 428 who places this call a week earlier

373 his tendency to wander in the mind: Martin v, 434

373 presumably his last instructions: From an anonymous account published in a German periodical (unidentified) of the 1860s, Staatsarchiv, Coburg

373 'too awful to contemplate': Martin v, 437

374 'never can I forget'; Martin v, 439

Epilogue

376 'the wickedness of the world': *KA* 27 December 1861

376 'I understand even every wish of his': *KA* 27 December 1861

376 'If I should die before you': *CAL* 12 October 1851

376 'he always felt ready': *KA* 29 December 1861

376 'My best wishes for your fortieth birthday': *CA* 18 June 1858

377 although he knew he was getting old: *CA* 27 August 1858

377 'I cannot overcome my astonishment': *CA* 17 September 1851

378 in 1854 told Frederick William: *CA* 26 December 1854

Appendix I

380 really the Whigs, not her ladies: Gash, 220–6

380 'The Queen strongly feels that she made a mistake': *Letters* I, ii, 108

Index